THE ENCYCLOPEDIA OF RURAL CRIME

Edited by
Alistair Harkness
Jessica René Peterson
Matt Bowden
Cassie Pedersen
Joseph F. Donnermeyer

First published in Great Britain in 2024 by

Bristol University Press
University of Bristol
1-9 Old Park Hill
Bristol
BS2 8BB
UK
t: +44 (0)117 374 6645
e: bup-info@bristol.ac.uk

Details of international sales and distribution partners are available at bristoluniversitypress.co.uk

© Bristol University Press 2024

British Library Cataloguing in Publication Data
A catalogue record for this book is available from the British Library

ISBN 978-1-5292-2200-5 hardcover
ISBN 978-1-5292-2201-2 paperback
ISBN 978-1-5292-2202-9 ePub
ISBN 978-1-5292-2203-6 ePdf

The right of Alistair Harkness, Jessica René Peterson, Matt Bowden, Cassie Pedersen and Joseph F. Donnermeyer to be identified as editors of this work has been asserted by them in accordance with the Copyright, Designs and Patents Act 1988.

All rights reserved: no part of this publication may be reproduced, stored in a retrieval system, or transmitted in any form or by any means, electronic, mechanical, photocopying, recording, or otherwise without the prior permission of Bristol University Press.

Every reasonable effort has been made to obtain permission to reproduce copyrighted material. If, however, anyone knows of an oversight, please contact the publisher.

The statements and opinions contained within this publication are solely those of the editors and contributors and not of the University of Bristol or Bristol University Press. The University of Bristol and Bristol University Press disclaim responsibility for any injury to persons or property resulting from any material published in this publication.

Bristol University Press works to counter discrimination on grounds of gender, race, disability, age and sexuality.

Cover design: blu inc, Bristol
Front cover image: Getty/Norbert Kuklovsku/EyeEm

Contents

List of Figures		ix
About the Editors		x
Notes on Contributors		xii
Introduction		1
	Alistair Harkness, Jessica René Peterson, Matt Bowden,	
	Cassie Pedersen and Joseph F. Donnermeyer	

PART I	**Theories of Rural Crime**	
	Introduction to Part I	11
	Matt Bowden	
1	Civic Community Theory	13
	Joseph F. Donnermeyer and Matt Bowden	
2	Classical Theories and Contemporary Legacies	16
	Joseph F. Donnermeyer	
3	Crime and Place	20
	Joseph F. Donnermeyer	
4	Cultural Criminology and Representations of Rural Crime	23
	Karen Hayden	
5	Environmental and Green Criminology	26
	Rob White	
6	Feminist Theory	30
	Amanda Hall-Sanchez	
7	Late Modernity, Surveillance and Securitization	33
	Matt Bowden and Artur Pytlarz	
8	Left Realism	37
	James Windle	
9	Male Peer Support Theory	40
	Walter S. DeKeseredy	
10	Primary Socialization Theory	43
	Joseph F. Donnermeyer	

11	Rational Choice, Routine Activity and Situational Crime Prevention *Vania Ceccato*	46
12	Safety and Security Studies *Gorazd Meško and Andrej Sotlar*	50
13	The Anthropocene and Criminological Theory *Clifford Shearing, Emiline Smith and Jared Walters*	53

PART II Rural Crime Studies

	Introduction to Part II *Joseph F. Donnermeyer and Alistair Harkness*	59
	People and Crime	
14	Abuse against Children, the Elderly and within Families *Sarah Wendt*	63
15	Consumer Fraud *Cassandra Cross*	66
16	Corporate and State Crimes *Victoria E. Collins*	70
17	Cybercrime and Cybersecurity *Qingli Meng and Joseph F. Donnermeyer*	74
18	Dark Tourism *Jenny Wise*	78
19	Drugs and Public Health *Katinka van de Ven and Natalie Thomas*	81
20	Drug Use and Dependence *Anke Stallwitz*	84
21	Genocide *Hollie Nyseth Nzitatira and Brandon Moore*	88
22	Hate Crime *Rachel Hale and Melina Stewart-North*	91
23	Modern Slavery and Cross-border Transportation of People *Richard Byrne*	95
24	Resource Extraction: Crime Impacts *Callie D. Shaw and Rick Ruddell*	98
25	Rogue Farmers *Robert Smith*	101
26	Technology and Interpersonal Violence *Bridget Harris*	104
27	Tourism, Crime and Rurality *Joseph F. Donnermeyer and Alistair Harkness*	108
28	Violence against Farmers *Anni Hesselink and Cecili Doorewaard-Janse van Vuuren*	111

29	Violence against Women *Walter S. DeKeseredy*	114
30	Violent Extremism *Rachel Hale*	118
	Property and Other	
31	Acquisitive Farm Crime *Kyle Mulrooney and Alistair Harkness*	125
32	Animal Rights and Activism *Jarret S. Lovell*	129
33	Blood Sports *Angus Nurse*	133
34	Cross-border Livestock Theft *Willie Clack*	137
35	Drug Cultivation, Manufacture and Movement *Ralph A. Weisheit*	141
36	Food Crime *Allison Gray*	145
37	Heritage Crime *Louise Nicholas*	148
38	Illegal Hunting and Trespass *Alistair Harkness, Kyle Mulrooney and Matthew Box*	151
39	Organized Crime *Robert Smith*	155
40	Trophy and Big Game Hunting *Angus Nurse*	158
41	Water Crimes *Gorazd Meško and Katja Eman*	162
42	Wildfires: Causation and Prevention *Janet Stanley and Belinda Young*	166
43	Wildlife Crime, Trafficking and Poaching *Rob White*	170
PART III	**Rural Criminal Justice Studies**	
	Introduction to Part III *Jessica René Peterson*	177
	Law Enforcement	
44	Anti-social Behaviour: Police–Community Relationships *Andrew Wooff and Larissa Engelmann*	181
45	Law Enforcement Misconduct *John Liederbach, Chloe Ann Wentzlof and Philip Matthew Stinson*	184

46	Police Discretion and Informal Sanctions *Jessica René Peterson*	187
47	Police Engagement with Rural Farming Communities *Cameron Whiteside, Ann Brennan and Kyle Mulrooney*	191
48	Policing Rural Small Island Developing States *Danielle Watson and Casandra Harry*	195
49	Policing the Rural Global South *Tariro Mutongwizo*	198
50	Public Order Policing *David Baker*	201
51	Reassurance Policing in Rural Communities *Larissa Engelmann and Andrew Wooff*	205
52	Rurality, Cultures and Policing *Richard Yarwood*	208

Courts and Corrections

53	Community Corrections *Dawei Zhang, Jessica René Peterson, Alistair Harkness and Joseph F. Donnermeyer*	215
54	Court Reform Challenges in Rural Jurisdictions *Alyssa M. Clark*	218
55	Desistance from Crime *Rachel Hale*	221
56	Informal and Decolonized Alternative Criminal Justice *Zahidul Islam*	224
57	Jails and Prisons *Rick Ruddell*	228
58	Judicial Policies and Procedures *Alyssa M. Clark*	231
59	Populism and Punitiveness *Kyle Mulrooney and Jenny Wise*	234
60	Post-release, Rural Re-entry and Recidivism *Kyle C. Ward*	237
61	Punishment and Rurality *Rosemary Gido*	241
62	Restorative Justice and Therapeutic Jurisprudence *Ziwei Qi*	245

Access to Justice and Responses to Crime

63	Access to Justice *Rachel Hale*	251
64	Access to Legal Representation *Andrew L.B. Davies and Shelby Peck*	255

65	Closure of Law Enforcement Stations *Christian Mouhanna*	258
66	Rural Crime Prevention *Tarah Hodgkinson*	261
67	Technology in Rural Criminal Justice Systems *Jessica René Peterson*	265

PART IV Rural Peoples and Groups

	Introduction to Part IV *Cassie Pedersen*	271
68	Anti-government Groups and Militias *Joseph DeLeeuw*	273
69	Indigenous and First Nation Peoples *Juan Tauri*	276
70	LGBTIQA+ Identities *Cassie Pedersen*	280
71	Lifestyle and Amenity Migration *Nick Osbaldiston*	284
72	Outlaw Motorcycle Clubs *Mark Lauchs*	287
73	People with Disabilities *Marg Camilleri*	290
74	Rural Enclaves *Joseph F. Donnermeyer*	294
75	Rural Folk Crime *Rob White*	298
76	Tropes of Rural Offenders and Victims *Belinda Morrissey and Kristen Davis*	301
77	Working Tourists *Donna James*	305
78	Youth and Youth Sub-cultures *Matthew D. Moore*	308

PART V Geographic Status of Rural Criminological Research

	Introduction to Part V *Alistair Harkness and Joseph F. Donnermeyer*	313
79	Africa *Willie Clack and Emmanuel Bunei*	314
80	Antarctica *Rebecca Kaiser and Rob White*	319
81	Asia *Alistair Harkness, Joseph F. Donnermeyer and Qingli Meng*	324

82	Europe	329
	Gorazd Meško and Matt Bowden	
83	North America	333
	Denisse Román-Burgos, Joseph F. Donnermeyer and Rick Ruddell	
84	Oceania	338
	Alistair Harkness, Kyle Mulrooney and Danielle Watson	
85	South America	343
	Vania Ceccato and Monica Perez	
Notes		348
Index		349

List of Figures

1	Chronology of the developments in rural criminology, 2019 onwards	3
2	Political map of Africa	317
3	Political map of Antarctica	323
4	Political map of Asia	327
5	Political map of Europe	332
6	Political map of North America	336
7	Political map of Oceania	341
8	Political map of South America	346

About the Editors

Matt Bowden is a senior lecturer in sociology at Technological University Dublin, Ireland, and is an adjunct lecturer at the University of New England, Australia. He has taught social theory, criminological theory, policing and security governance and was programme leader in criminology from 2011 to 2016. His research interests are in the politics and everyday realities of security, plural policing and crime prevention and he is currently researching on rural security/safety, security consumption, police culture and police habitus.

Joseph F. Donnermeyer is a professor emeritus in the School of Environment and Natural Resources at The Ohio State University, United States, and an adjunct professor at the University of New England, Australia. He is co-editor of the *International Journal of Rural Criminology*. He is the first chair of the American Society of Criminology's Division of Rural Criminology, and is the inaugural president of the International Society for the Study of Rural Crime. He edited the *Routledge International Hand Book of Rural Criminology* (Routledge, 2016), and is authoring *The Criminology of Food and Agriculture* (Routledge, 2023).

Alistair Harkness is a senior lecturer in criminology at the University of New England, Australia. He is co-director of the Centre for Rural Criminology at the University, Treasurer of the International Society for the Study of Rural Crime and co-editor of the *International Journal of Rural Criminology*. His primary research interests are in acquisitive crime, with a particular emphasis on crime prevention, policing responses and community partnerships. He is co-editor of *Locating Crime in Context and Place* (The Federation Press, 2016), editor of *Rural Crime Prevention* (Routledge, 2020), co-editor of *Crossroads of Rural Crime* (Emerald, 2021) and co-editor of *Transformations of Rural Crime* (Bristol University Press, 2022).

Cassie Pedersen is a lecturer in criminology and criminal justice at Federation University Australia. She has published in the spaces of cultural and visual criminology in addition to undertaking research on farm trespassing by animal activists that examines the ideological and place-based tensions that arise between city-dwelling activists and farmers residing in rural locales. Her primary research interests include rural criminology, feminist criminology, queer criminology and justice responses to people from LGBTIQA+ communities.

Jessica René Peterson is an assistant professor in the Criminal Justice Department at Southern Oregon University in Ashland, Oregon, and is an adjunct lecturer at the University of New England, Australia. She is Secretary of the International Society for the Study of Rural Crime. Her primary research interests include police and community relations, police training, rural crime and communities and juvenile crime and policy. She enjoys using qualitative methods and working with practitioners to produce impactful research with practical application. She is a co-editor of *Research Methods for Rural Criminologists* (Routledge, 2022).

Notes on Contributors

David Baker is an adjunct associate professor in criminology at the University of New England, Australia.

Matt Bowden is a senior lecturer in sociology at the Technological University Dublin in Ireland, and an adjunct senior lecturer in criminology at the University of New England, Australia.

Matthew Box is a sessional academic and research associate at the University of New England, Australia, and a sessional academic and doctoral candidate at Federation University, Australia.

Ann Brennan is Policy and Project Officer for the New South Wales Police Force Rural Crime Prevention Team.

Emmanuel Bunei is a sessional researcher with the Centre for Rural Criminology at the University of New England, Australia.

Richard Byrne is a senior lecturer and Manager of the Rural Security Research Group at Harper Adams University, England.

Marg Camilleri is a senior lecturer in criminology and criminal justice at Federation University in Victoria, Australia.

Vania Ceccato is a professor at the Department of Urban Planning and Environment in the School of Architecture and the Built Environment at KTH Royal Institute of Technology, Sweden.

Willie Clack is a senior lecturer in the School of Criminal Justice at the University of South Africa.

Alyssa M. Clark is a senior research associate at the New York State Office of Indigent Legal Services, United States.

NOTES ON CONTRIBUTORS

Victoria E. Collins is a professor in the School of Justice Studies at Eastern Kentucky University, United States.

Cassandra Cross is an associate professor in the School of Justice at the Queensland University of Technology, Australia.

Andrew L.B. Davies is Director of Research at the Deason Criminal Justice Reform Center at Southern Methodist University, United States.

Kristen Davis is a lecturer in criminology in the School of Social Sciences at Monash University, Australia.

Walter S. DeKeseredy is Anna Deane Carlson Endowed Chair of Social Sciences, Director of the Research Center on Violence, and a professor of sociology at West Virginia University, United States.

Joseph DeLeeuw is an assistant professor of criminal justice at Ohio Northern University, United States.

Cecili Doorewaard-Janse van Vuuren is a lecturer and researcher at the Department of Criminology and Security Science, College of Law at the University of South Africa.

Joseph F. Donnermeyer is a professor emeritus in rural sociology at The Ohio State University, United States, and is an adjunct professor in criminology at the University of New England, Australia.

Katja Eman is an associate professor in the Faculty of Criminal Justice and Security at the University of Maribor, Slovenia.

Larissa Engelmann is a doctoral candidate at Edinburgh Napier University, Scotland.

Rosemary Gido is professor emerita in criminology and criminal justice at Indiana University of Pennsylvania, United States, and is Editor of *The Prison Journal*.

Allison Gray is a post-doctoral researcher at Western University, Canada.

Rachel Hale is an independent researcher based in Melbourne, Australia.

Amanda Hall-Sanchez is Programme Co-ordinator at Culture Reframed, United States.

Alistair Harkness is a senior lecturer in criminology and co-director of the Centre for Rural Criminology at the University of New England, Australia.

Bridget Harris is deputy director of the Monash Gender and Family Violence Prevention Centre and an associate professor in criminology at Monash University, Australia, and is an Australian Research Council 'Discovery Early Career Research Award' Fellow.

Casandra Harry is an assistant professor at the Institute for Criminology and Public Safety at the University of Trinidad and Tobago.

Karen Hayden is a professor in criminology and criminal justice at Merrimack College, United States.

Anni Hesselink is a professor and researcher at the Department of Criminology and Security Science, College of Law at the University of South Africa.

Tarah Hodgkinson is an assistant professor in the Department of Criminology at Wilfrid Laurier University, Canada.

Zahidul Islam is an assistant professor of law at the Independent University, Bangladesh.

Donna James is a doctoral candidate in the School of Social Sciences at Western Sydney University in New South Wales, Australia.

Rebecca Kaiser is a postgraduate student at the University of Tasmania, Australia.

Mark Lauchs is an associate professor in the Faculty of Creative Industries, Education and Social Justice at the Queensland University of Technology, Australia.

John Liederbach is a professor in criminal justice at Bowling Green State University, United States.

Jarret S. Lovell is a professor of criminal justice in the College of Humanities and Social Sciences at California State University Fullerton, United States.

Qingli Meng is an adjunct professor in the Department of Computer Information Sciences at the Niagara University, United States.

Gorazd Meško is a professor in the Faculty of Criminal Justice and Security at the University of Maribor, Slovenia.

Brandon Moore is a doctoral candidate in sociology at The Ohio State University, United States.

Matthew D. Moore is an associate professor of sociology and criminology at the University of Central Arkansas, United States.

Belinda Morrissey is a lecturer in literature at Federation University, Australia.

Christian Mouhanna is Permanent Researcher at the Centre de recherches sociologiques sur le droit et les institutions pénales [Centre for Sociological Research on Law and Criminal Justice Institutions], University of Paris Saclay, France.

Kyle Mulrooney is a senior lecturer in criminology and co-director of the Centre for Rural Criminology at the University of New England, Australia.

Tariro Mutongwizo is a lecturer in criminology at the University of New England, Australia.

Louise Nicholas is an independent researcher and education consultant based in Leicestershire, England.

Angus Nurse is Head of Criminology and Criminal Justice at Nottingham Trent University, England.

Hollie Nyseth Nzitatira is an associate professor of sociology at The Ohio State University, United States.

Nick Osbaldiston is a senior lecturer in sociology at James Cook University, Australia.

Shelby Peck is a research assistant with the Deason Criminal Justice Reform Center at Southern Methodist University, United States.

Cassie Pedersen is a lecturer in criminology and criminal justice at Federation University, Australia.

Monica Perez is an affiliate professor at the European School of Management and Technology (ESMT), Germany.

Jessica René Peterson is an assistant professor in criminal justice at Southern Oregon University, United States, and is an adjunct lecturer in criminology at the University of New England, Australia.

Artur Pytlarz is a doctoral candidate at the Technological University Dublin, Ireland.

Ziwei Qi is an assistant professor at Fort Hays State University, United States.

Denisse Román-Burgos is a post-doctoral researcher in the Centre for Citizenship, Civil Society and the Rule of Law at the University of Aberdeen, Scotland.

Rick Ruddell is a professor and Law Foundation of Saskatchewan Chair in Police Studies at the University of Regina, Canada.

Callie D. Shaw is an assistant professor at Texas A&M University Corpus Christi and an adjunct professor of law at Texas A&M University School of Law, United States.

Clifford Shearing is a professor emeritus at the universities of Toronto and Cape Town.

Emiline Smith is a lecturer in criminology at the University of Glasgow in Glasgow, Scotland.

Robert Smith is an independent scholar based in Aberdeen, Scotland.

Andrej Sotlar is an associate professor in the Faculty of Criminal Justice and Security at the University of University of Maribor, Slovenia.

Anke Stallwitz is a professor of social psychology at the Protestant University of Applied Sciences Freiburg, Germany.

Janet Stanley is an associate professor in the Faculty of Design at the University of Melbourne, Australia.

Melina Stewart-North is a doctoral candidate in criminology at Federation University, Australia.

Philip Matthew Stinson is a professor in the criminal justice programme at Bowling Green State University, United States.

Juan Tauri is a senior lecturer at the University of Waikato, New Zealand.

Natalie Thomas is a post-doctoral research fellow at the Institute for Social Science Research at the University of Queensland, Australia.

Katinka van de Ven is a senior lecturer in criminology at the University of New England, Australia.

Jared Walters is a research assistant at Griffith University, Australia.

Kyle C. Ward is an associate professor of criminology and criminal justice at the University of Northern Colorado, United States.

Danielle Watson is a senior lecturer in the School of Justice at the Queensland University of Technology, Australia.

Ralph A. Weisheit is a distinguished professor of criminal justice at Illinois State University, United States.

Sarah Wendt is a professor of social work at Flinders University, Australia.

Chloe Ann Wentzlof is a graduate student at Bowling Green State University, United States.

Rob White is a distinguished emeritus professor of criminology at the University of Tasmania, Australia and is an adjunct professor of criminology at the University of New England, Australia.

Cameron Whiteside is Detective Chief Inspector and the inaugural State Rural Crime Coordinator of the New South Wales Police Force Rural Crime Prevention Team.

James Windle is a lecturer in criminology at University College Cork, Ireland.

Jenny Wise is a senior lecturer in criminology and secretary of the Centre for Rural Criminology at the University of New England, Australia.

Andrew Wooff is an associate professor of criminology and the Head of Social Sciences at Edinburgh Napier University, Scotland.

Richard Yarwood is a professor of human geography at the University of Plymouth, England.

Belinda Young is a doctoral candidate in the Faculty of Design at the University of Melbourne, Australia.

Dawei Zhang is a professor in the Institute for China Rural Studies and Institute for Advanced Study in Political Science at Central China Normal University, China.

Introduction

*Alistair Harkness, Jessica René Peterson, Matt Bowden,
Cassie Pedersen and Joseph F. Donnermeyer*

'Rural', most crudely, is defined as 'non-urban', but this dichotomous delineation is grossly inadequate because it neglects the consideration of the nuances of geography, demography, attitudes, culture and issues of access both tangible and amorphous. These are vitally important considerations: there exists significant cultural and spatial separation between urban and rural because what is taken for granted in the city is not accessible or available outside of it.

There exists, most certainly, definitional difficulties about rural that will never go away. Should we just consider physical and demographic measures, such as population size and density, accessibility and remoteness? Such imprecision is typified by the existing definitions even within the same jurisdictions by different organizations and agencies of the same governmental units. Adopting a 'one size fits all' approach is unwise, though, as a universal measure will not account for the non-homogenous nature of geographic location, both within and across jurisdictions.

For instance, a coastal location in Australia dominated with former city dwellers cannot be easily compared to a rapidly populated boom town in Canada reliant on imported labour, to a primarily agricultural community in Ireland with multiple generations of the same families present, to the Yanomamo and Kayapo and other tribes in the rain forest regions of South America, nor to a remote settlement in the Siberian region of Russia or in the state of Alaska in the United States. Indeed, different places have different cultural origins – as scholars such as Hayden, Weisheit et al, Donnermeyer and DeKeseredy, Ceccato, Harkness (see suggested readings) and many other scholars already have observed. Hence, the rural can also be considered a state of mind as much as a particular place found on a map. There is just no way to define all the diversity of rural localities with a single word, sentence, paragraph and, perhaps, even in a single book.

Definitional contestation is a source for healthy and constructive debates amongst rural criminologists, but it also complicates comparisons of the incidence of crime across rural localities in different regions of the world, and of comparisons with urban crime. And the rural, howsoever defined, is changing. The proportion of the world's population considered rural is decreasing as cities and regional centres grow, yet actual population numbers are growing. It is simply that the population of urban centres is growing faster. Even many decades from now there will remain billions of people who live in millions of villages, small towns, farming communities and in environments as diverse as deserts, jungles, steppes and tundra.

Adding to the complexity is development, such as the social and economic dynamics between existing residents of a rural location with newcomers and outsiders. Effectively a culture clash, this change is exacerbated with the introduction of larger housing developments in once sleepy villages and townships, particularly when located on an expanding urban fringe of a big city or regional hub – the so-called rurban.

Growth of rural criminology

Rural criminology is a developing branch of study within the wider criminology discipline. During the decade 2011 to 2021, there was much expansion in this area. In his edited handbook, Donnermeyer (see suggested readings) created a chronology of the development of rural criminology, from the early, scattered theory-less works from which emerged rural criminology as we know it today. He updated this chronology in a 2019 article in the *International Journal of Rural Criminology* (Donnermeyer, 2019). Such is the pace and the enormous energies emerging particularly at the turn of the third decade of the twenty-first century, a further update is necessary (see Figure 1 below).

Purpose of this encyclopedia

The impetus for this encyclopedia emerged from a growing frustration that there is currently no ready reference guide in what is a significant and growing area of scholarship. Whilst there exists a number of dictionaries and encyclopedias of crime and criminology, no volume offers a consideration or rural criminology and there is no collection which specifically addresses rural criminology. *The Routledge Handbook of Rural Criminology* (Donnermeyer, 2016) offers consideration of an extensive number of rural crime related topics, but contributions are chapter length and are focused on specific geographies.

The central aim here, then, is to offer a collection of unique, concise outlines and discussions of topics central to both rurality and crime that

Figure 1: Chronology of the developments in rural criminology, 2019 onwards

2019	• Creation of the Routledge monograph series *Studies in Rural Criminology* (Donnermeyer, 2016)
	• February: Workshop – 'Understanding Crime and Rural Communities', at Federation University, Gippsland campus, Victoria, Australia, organized by A. Harkness, N. Smith, B. Strating and R. White
	• April: The International Society for the Study of Rural Crime (ISSRC) founded
	• May: M. Hollis and S. Hankhouse (eds) – special rural crime issue in the *Crime Prevention and Community Safety* journal
	• September: launch of the Centre for Rural Criminology, University of New England, K. Mulrooney (co-director)
	• September: session on rural crime at the European Society of Criminology annual meeting
	• October: special thematic issue on 'Security and safety in local communities: Rural and urban perspectives', in *Revija za Kriminalistiko in Kriminologijo* (eds G. Meško and T. Bobnar)
	• November: multiple paper sessions and roundtables presented at the American Society of Criminology annual meeting in San Francisco, including a co-sponsored roundtable by the Association of Chinese Criminology and Criminal Justice and the Division of Rural Criminology
	• December: special issue on rural crime from Harkness et al, workshop papers in the *International Journal of Rural Criminology* (Volume 5, Issue 1)
2020	• May: launch of the Bristol University Press *Research in Rural Crime* book series (Bowden and Harkness, eds)
	• May: creation of the European Society of Criminology's Rural Crime Working Group (facilitated by K. Smith and A. Pytlarz)
	• May: A. Harkness (ed) – publication of *Rural Crime Prevention: Theory, Tactics and Techniques* (Routledge)
	• August: launch of the Centre for Rural Criminology Podcast series (K. Mulrooney, ed)
	• September: Colloquium 'Safety, resilience and community: Challenges and opportunities beyond the city' (virtually from Stockholm, arranged by V. Ceccato)
	• November: K. Hayden – publication of *The Rural Primitive in American Popular Culture* (Lexington Books)
	• November: W. DeKeseredy – publication of *Violence Against Women in Rural Places* (Routledge)
	• ISSRC: two roundtables: Access to Justice (July) and Rural Policing (September)
2021	• July: Relaunch of the *International Journal of Rural Criminology* (IJRC) (J. Donnermeyer and A. Harkness, eds) with full advisory board
	• May: A. Harkness and R. White (eds) – publication of *Crossroads of Rural Crime* (Emerald)
	• ISSRC: two roundtables: Rural Policing in North America (September) and Crime Impacts of Resource Extraction (November)

(continued)

Figure 1: Chronology of the developments in rural criminology, 2019 onwards (continued)

	• September: Biennial Conference on Criminal Justice and Security in Central and Eastern Europe (virtual), organized by the Faculty of Criminal Justice and Security, University of Maribor, Slovenia – theme of the conference was 'Perspectives of rural safety, security and rural criminology' • September: launch of the Centre for Rural Criminology Researcher Snapshot series (A. Harkness, ed.) • November: American Society of Criminology annual meeting in Chicago, three roundtables: (i) The Division of Rural Criminology and its prospects for the decade of the 2020s; (ii) The future internationalization of rural criminology; and (iii) The future of rural criminology as a discipline • Series of rural-focused virtual workshops by the Center for Empowering Victims of Gender-based Violence at the Fort Hays State University in Kansas, United States, including Researching Gender in Rural Communities (September) • Special issue (focus section) in *Professional Geographer* (volume 73, number 4) on 'The geography of crime and policing in the global countryside', V. Ceccato and R. Yarwood (eds) • Special issue published in *International Criminology* (volume 1, number 3) on 'Crime, fear of crime and environmental. harm in rural areas', V. Ceccato and G. Meško (eds)
2022	• R. Weisheit, J. Peterson and A. Pytlarz (eds) – publication of *Research Methods for Rural Criminologists* (Routledge) • M. Bowden and A. Harkness (eds) – publication of *Rural Transformations and Rural Crime* (Bristol University Press) • A. Harkness, J. Peterson, M. Bowden, C. Pedersen and J. Donnermeyer (eds) – *Encyclopedia of Rural Criminology* (Bristol University Press) • Special issue on rural policing, *International Journal of Rural Criminology*
2023 and beyond	• J. Donnermeyer – expected publication of *The Criminology of Agriculture* (Routledge) • R. Hale and A. Harkness (eds) – expected publication of *Rural Victims of Crime* (Routledge) • Curated PDF library of rural criminological peer-reviewed research • Wikipedia entry – *Rural Criminology* • Sustained annual presence at the American Society of Criminology, the European Society of Criminology and other international conferences

are not offered in any other format. The editors have extensive interest and networks in this rapidly growing sub-discipline and, as teachers and researchers, recognize a gap in the reference text lists which presents a glaring omission in the canon of rural criminological works.

This encyclopedia brings together, in one volume, a precis of key issues pertaining to rural crime, criminology, offending and victimization, and both formal and informal responses to rural crime. Essentially, this volume offers short, sharp introductions allowing immediate familiarity with the key issues on the topic, specifically to:

- provide concise overviews of a wide array of criminological topics and issues as they relate to 'the rural';
- serve as a ready reference source – for scholars, students, practitioners and the lay persons alike – which will sit alongside other books and texts on desks and bookshelves the world over;
- coalesce a wide array of distinct yet related topics in a single compendium; and
- offer a key reference work which will be relied on for many years.

To ensure a high level of consistency in approach, contributors were asked to include the following when assembling entries:

- a definition of the topic;
- an outline of distinctive features which link the topic centrally to rurality and global themes;
- a discussion of the topic with an international focus;
- identification of issues and impacts on communities, people and places (such as, for example, issues around resourcing); and
- where appropriate, entries to consider aspects of both offending and victimization.

To guide the reader, up to five suggested readings follow each entry. Even though one or two might be older ('classic') references, in the main most are of recently published works of scholarship which will allow readers to more easily 'snowball' back to a larger set of salient sources on their own.

Structure of the encyclopedia

This encyclopedia is based on contemporary scholarship, but aimed at offering summaries rather than arguments. And it seeks to serve as a vehicle to engage others in rural criminological research. It includes 85 individual entries, offered from a wide diversity of scholars, and each providing an international lens to key issues.

Topics have been carefully chosen to encompass the broad landscape of issues relevant to rural people and places. Although some topics are clearly and obviously rural in focus (livestock theft for instance does not occur in highly urbanized settings), other types of offending are not geographically dependent (for example, violence offences). However, with the latter there are rural dimensions.

Topics have been grouped and themed in five parts, each provided alphabetically within each section:

- Part I: Theories of rural crime (13 entries)
- Part II: Rural crime studies (30 entries)

- Part III: Rural criminal justice studies (24 entries)
- Part IV: Rural people and groups (11 entries)
- Part V: Geographic status of rural criminological research (7 entries)

Beyond this encyclopedia: studying rural criminology

At the end of this introduction is a short list of suggested readings. In addition, for scholars, both established and emerging, we recommend examining the rural crime book series found at both Bristol University Press and Routledge, plus the *International Journal of Rural Criminology*. There is also a rural crime listserv where questions and advice can be posted to other scholars. The Centre for Rural Criminology at the University of New England (Armidale, New South Wales) coalesces significant relevant research and hosts a podcast/vodcast series. The International Society for the Study of Rural Crime is a membership based, not-for-profit association aimed at uniting scholars, students and practitioners around the world, so that rural criminology scholars with similar interests can engage in meaningful conversations about their interests (see suggested websites).

Acknowledgements

The editors are most grateful to all the contributors of entries for their work and assistance in allowing this collection to emerge. Particular thanks go to Rebecca Tomlinson, the most excellent commissioning editor for criminology at Bristol University Press, and her team.

Acknowledgement, too, is made to all the scholars with a wide array of disciplinary histories and interests who seek to produce research aimed at improving circumstances for rural peoples and places. Similarly, much appreciation is offered to those practitioners who strive day in and day out, whether involved in criminal justice or other service provision, to make rural communities safer and healthier.

Suggested readings

Ceccato, V. (2016) *Rural Crime and Community Safety*, London: Routledge.
DeKeseredy, W.S. (2021) *Woman Abuse in Rural Places*, London: Routledge.
Donnermeyer, J.F. (2019) 'The international emergence of rural criminology: Implications for the development and revision of criminological theory for rural contexts', *International Journal of Rural Criminology*, 5(1): 1–18.
Donnermeyer, J.F. (ed) (2016) *The Routledge International Handbook of Rural Criminology*, London: Routledge.
Donnermeyer, J.F. and DeKeseredy, W. (2014) *Rural Criminology*, London: Routledge.

Fulkerson, G.M. and Thomas, A.R. (eds) (2016) *Reimagining Rural: Urban-Normative Portrayals of Rural Life*, Lanham, MD: Lexington Books.

Harkness, A. (ed) (2020) *Rural Crime Prevention: Theory, Tactics and Techniques*, London: Routledge.

Harkness, A., Harris, B. and Baker, D. (eds) (2016) *Locating Crime in Context and Place: Perspectives on Regional, Rural and Remote Australia*, Sydney: The Federation Press.

Weisheit, R.A. (2016) 'Rural crime from a global perspective', *International Journal of Rural Criminology*, 3(1): 5–28.

Suggested websites

Bristol University Press *Research in Rural Crime* book series, https://bristoluniversitypress.co.uk/research-in-rural-crime

Centre for Rural Criminology at the University of New England, Australia, https://www.une.edu.au/about-une/faculty-of-humanities-arts-social-sciences-and-education/hass/humanities-arts-and-social-sciences-research/centre-for-rural-criminology

Centre for Rural Criminology at the University of New England, Australia (YouTube), https://www.youtube.com/channel/UCignCDlOjiHlUAqALMbjnIw

International Journal of Rural Criminology, https://ruralcriminology.org/

International Society for the Study of Rural Crime, www.issrc.net

International Society for the Study of Rural Crime (YouTube), https://www.youtube.com/channel/UC7siAfSEkwvkv6KW5_Wf7xg

Routledge *Studies in Rural Criminology* book series, www.routledge.com/Routledge-Studies-in-Rural-Criminology/book-series/RRC

Ruralcrime listserv ruralcrime@lists.osu.edu

PART I
Theories of Rural Crime

Introduction to Part I: Theories of Rural Crime

Matt Bowden

Theories of crime

Theorizing the rural is a critical rejoinder to the urban normative bias in criminology. Central to the entries in this section is a concern with meeting this challenge, but it is not only a restorative or indeed ameliorative pursuit. Rather, it is one that celebrates the diversity and richness, in terms of both the application of theory and the formation of theory in rural contexts. The criminological theories reviewed in this section are those previously used by rural crime scholars in their studies.

From the outset, criminological theorizing has centred around a number of paradigmatic divisions, and derives its origins from sociology. Critically here, we have grand narratives such as those of Durkheim who sought to frame a science of how a whole society integrates or disintegrates and the structuring power of morality in bringing together social functions with individual adjustment. Or, indeed, Marxist scholars who sought to capture the direction of history and to encapsulate crime as part of historical and dialectical materialism. The historical appeal of the Chicago School in their noble project to capture the major transformations of the early twentieth century can easily be dismissed for contributing to the normalization of the urban (and therefore generalizable to all spaces). Yet they have each left us a legacy of the qualitative tradition and the tools for theory-building that continues to enrich both sociological and criminological imaginations today.

The entries in this section bring together examples of theory-testing and theory-building in equal measure and provide readers with a short capture of some of the main points of note, along with suggested reading. With a project like this encyclopedia, we have sought to provide a broad scope of theoretical perspectives drawing from traditions across the globe, from a range of areas such as theories of modernity, feminist theory and civic community theory, but also extant challenges to criminology such as thinking about the implications of the Anthropocene as a new epoch capturing the existential challenges facing the future of human and non-human species. In addition, we include an entry on the place of theories of the middle range to underline the need for both testing the validity of theories but also how they might help to operationalize empirical research. Entries herein this section are from a range of disciplines – from sociology, geography, feminist theory and political science.

A major challenge ahead is to think of the rural as a rich living laboratory for theory building in criminology: in relation to crime, deviance, social control, policing, security, gender-based violence, hate crimes and so on. Critically, however, the challenge is an epistemological one and about how the rural speaks back to the urban.

1

Civic Community Theory

Joseph F. Donnermeyer and Matt Bowden

Civic community theory is one of several ecological approaches to understanding the associations of crime with various characteristics of places. It was developed by Matt Lee, an American rural sociologist, and his colleagues, who published extensively on the results of various statistical tests using the theory's framework in both criminological and other social science journals, mostly during the first decade of the twenty-first century.

It is similar to social disorganization theory, yet very distinctive from it. First, its approach begins from a non-criminological literature about the core elements of a civil society that define civility based on the strength of community groups and a culture whereby local citizens are involved in activities at the places where they live. Indicators for a strong local ecology includes such social characteristics as home ownership, locally-owned businesses and voter turnout, amongst others.

A second distinctive characteristic of civic community theory is that its origins are not based on an urban criminology, but on a body of previous scholarship in rural sociology. Rural sociologists have long examined how social change impacts the socio-cultural make-up of smaller places. Subsequently, some of these rural scholars turned their attention to examining how change influences the emergence of various social problems, such as crime. It is from this heritage of research and theory that civic community theory emerged.

It is similar to social disorganization and most other criminological theories of place because it views crime as a product of social change, assuming that change disrupts established forms of social control within a community. As civility declines, crime increases. In this sense, it resembles the systemic version of social disorganization theory which seeks to explain variations in crime rates based on the structure of localized networks of residents that, in turn, are presumed to control delinquent and criminal behaviours.

Historically, much of this thinking recalls Durkheim's ideas about social change and its impact on social solidarity that produces anomic conditions. Hence, patterns of crime are reflective of changes with major shifts in norms, values and social mores.

All of the research by Lee and colleagues relies on secondary data aggregated to the level of a United States county or other geographic entities, such as towns and cities. Counties are convenient for civic community theory because there are over 3,200 counties in the United States, and about two-thirds of them are non-metropolitan. Selecting a sample for a nationwide study of crime in non-metropolitan United States counties with less than 25,000 persons easily yields a large sample size.

As well, civic community theory is similar to modern-day applications of social disorganization theory because it relies on quantitative measures for both its dependent and independent variables. The dependent variables are mostly indicators of violent crime based on statistics from the annually issued *Uniform Crime Reports* of the United States Federal Bureau of Investigation. There is also a plethora of secondary data sources reporting on the demographic, economic and sociological characteristics of places, such as can be found from the United States Bureau of the Census.

Conceptually, civic community divides the independent variables into three major subsets. The first is residential stability which can be measured, for example, by the rate of out-migration and the proportion of housing units that are occupied by owners. A second subset of civic community measures are those normally associated with indicators of a strong middle class, including the percentage of all manufacturing businesses with 20 or fewer employees and the per capita number of family-owned farms. A third group is referred to as civic engagement. Measures of civic engagement can include voter turnout in national elections, the number of religious congregations per 1,000 persons, and the per capita number of civic and business associations. These and other independent variables are normally subjected to factor analysis to generate broader measures of civility, which in turn are analysed through multivariate statistical techniques, such as linear and log-linear analyses.

The statistical success of civic community theory, as indicated by the amount of variance explained, is similar to quantitative studies that examine crime variations through the lens of other place-based theories, such as the statistical comparison of civic community theory with social disorganization theory by Wells and Weisheit. It is perhaps for this reason that the adoption of civic community theory during the second decade of the twenty-first century by criminologists is low. Another reason is possibly that the larger criminological community views the theory as limited to rural places, and not relevant to larger, more urban localities. Third, its logic, its dependent and independent variables and its data analytic techniques resemble the published work of researchers who use social disorganization theory; hence, it is likely not viewed as a theoretical substitute or improvement. A fourth barrier to its wider use in criminology is that the logic itself and how it measures crimes and crime predictors is heavily reliant on a United States context.

Despite these limitations, civic community theory has proved important for the development of rural criminology. Its future, however, will depend on extending its conceptual reach beyond the United States, and of its complete reliance on quantitative data. One possible route is to think about what happens to disorganize or destructure social institutions in the work of the Polish sociologist Zygmunt Bauman and his concept of liquid modernity. Here the source of disorganization and the reduction of civility rests with the fluidity of capital – which is 'light' because it can travel globally and has no loyalty to community or place – and labour which is 'heavy' and fixed to place.

The old institutions associated with civility, such as paid work, strong community ties and family and kin structures, are undermined thus by the global fluidity of capital. This sets off a spiral of change resulting in the conversion of solid, local institutions into liquid. Without constant reflexivity and re-adaptation or re-organization, individuals and communities are trapped in a vortex of what Bauman calls the unholy trinity: uncertainty, insecurity and unsafety, undermining trust in civic institutions and fueling neo-conservatism and political populism.

Suggested readings

Bauman, Z. (2000) *Liquid modernity*, Cambridge Malden, MA: Polity Press.

Doucet, J.M. and Lee, M.R. (2014) 'Civic community theory and rates of violence: A review of literature on an emergent theoretical perspective', *International Journal of Rural Criminology*, 2(2): 151–65.

Lee, M.R. (2008) 'Civic community in the hinterland: Toward a theory of rural social structure and violence', *Criminology*, 46(2): 447–78.

Lee, M.R. (2004) 'Love thy neighbor? Moral communities, civic engagement, and juvenile homicide in rural areas?', *Social Forces*, 82(3): 1001–35.

Wells, L.E. and Weisheit, R.A. (2012) 'Explaining crime in metropolitan and non-metropolitan communities', *International Journal of Rural Criminology*, 1(2): 153–83.

2

Classical Theories and Contemporary Legacies

Joseph F. Donnermeyer

Theory in criminology is a socially constructed framework to explain why people commit crimes, what kinds of crimes they commit and why some people are more likely to be victims than others. One important point made in popular contemporary criminological theory books, such as by Lilly et al and Burke, is that theory is socially constructed because the main authors and proponents of a particular theory acquired their perspective by attending university classes in criminology or an allied scientific discipline, reading numerous books and articles, discussing their ideas with colleagues at professional meetings such as the European Society of Criminology, writing down their version of a criminological explanation, sharing it with colleagues, publishing it as a book or article and then revising it based on the suggestions and criticisms of peers. Hence, criminological theory is a living thing, not a static thing.

Criminology as a science began to develop in the nineteenth century, and matured into its present form during the twentieth century. Its development continues in the twenty-first century. The first fully articulated theories of crime were very much biased toward individualistic explanations of criminal behaviour. Early scholars associated with such names as Beccaria, Bentham and Lombroso, amongst others, sought to explain criminal behaviour and its deterrence by considering the traits that lead to illegal actions and how they could be deterred through punishment. They did consider macro-level factors in the context of juxtaposing concepts of human free will with constraints imposed by society.

As the field of criminology advanced, these theories become increasingly less salient. In the twenty-first century, however, biosocial theories of criminal behaviour have emerged. Instead of Lombroso's so-called bumps on the head, today's biosocial theories seek to understand how such individual traits as hyperactivity, susceptibility to alcoholism and other addictions and a slew of other physical, mental and psychological traits are correlated with criminal behaviour. A second contemporary variant on biosocial theories focuses on traits that reduce the chances of criminal behaviour, such as a more developed empathy for others.

Succeeding various nineteenth-century criminological theories came a much greater sociological focus on crime and society in the twentieth century. From Plato to Hobbes and Durkheim to Marx, social control theories are a large part of the criminological landscape. Social control theories, like all other genres of criminological theory, contain great variety in their formulations. Reiss examined criminal behaviour, especially delinquency, as a product of an individual's acceptance of societal rules and regulations, which in turn is dependent upon successful socialization through primary social institutions in society, including family and school. Hirschi emphasized the role of social bonds to explain criminal activities. Along with Gottfredson, Hirschi also formulated a theory of self-control and the repeated commission of deviant and criminal offenses, which was conditioned by the nature of the offense itself.

One important and distinctive variation on social control are various place-based theories, which are described in this encyclopedia in a separate entry. Theories such as social disorganization, associated with Shaw and McKay and others of the Chicago School of Sociology in the first half of the twentieth century, and the more recent theory of collective efficacy articulated by Sampson and colleagues, seek to understand how crime is associated with the cultural, economic and social characteristics of neighbourhoods and cities.

Durkheim pioneered the sociological concept of anomie – or normlessness – as he attempted to explain the transition of societies from agrarian and rural to urban and industrial. How individuals are integrated into society is arguably the biggest consideration in all criminological theories about crime, and the stability of the normative order plays an important role in that consideration. The theories of Merton and of Messner and Rosenfeld build from this theme to examine the relationship of a person's ability to achieve societally defined goals, and how obstacles to achievement and success create deviance and foster criminal sub-cultures. The most prominent version that harkens back to the legacy of anomie is strain theory developed by Agnew. Agnew attempted to expand the concept of strain by considering all types of obstacles to progress towards, and achieve, goals.

Related to social control theories are those whose basis is more firmly embedded in the concept of social learning. Nineteenth-century theorists tended to reduce learning to a type of stimulus-response logic whereby individuals seek to minimize pain and enhance pleasure. Hence, people steal to alleviate their poverty and to acquire resources, or to derive pleasure from hedonistic acts and brutality, with those motivations often and falsely associated with such things as race, ethnicity and even the climate where people lived. Two contemporary versions of social learning theory are Sutherland's differential association theory and Akers' social learning theory. Differential association theory emphasizes the ways people learn through their interactions with others; hence, it reinforces theories that also examine the development of deviant and criminal sub-cultures. Social learning theory adds into the mix by emphasizing the kinds of messages or definitions people learn through their interactions with others, including sources of mass media.

Critical criminology can be said to arise from conflict theory, at least to some extent. From Marx's view of conflict as arising from capitalism to Chambliss' view of criminal behaviour as a product of laws formed by the powerful and enforced against the less powerful, conflict theories take explanations of crime beyond individualistic and place-based perspectives. It should be noted that Chambliss' analysis of vagrancy laws can be seen as a pioneering example of theory that had a substantial rural focus.

Young, along with Taylor and Walton, was a pioneer in the development of critical criminology, which is a view that criminal behaviour and other dimensions of policing and the criminal justice system can only be understood when examined from the viewpoint of the ways social structure shapes power relationships within societies, promoting selective and discriminatory development of laws and their enforcement. One important variant of critical criminology theory is left realism, pioneered by Young and his colleagues and revised and advanced more recently by DeKeseredy and his scholarly friends. Left realism not only examines the causes of crime as expressions of power and inequality in society, but how to alleviate and solve crime problems.

The important roots of the large variety of contemporary feminist theories lies within the broad spectrum of conflict and critical criminological perspectives. Pioneered and advanced by Adler, Chesney-Lind, Daly and DeKeseredy, amongst others, all variants on feminist approaches emphasize the role of patriarchy as a key expression of power, social structure, male dominance and subordination of females. Hence, crimes such as violence against women often are ignored and dismissed in favour of utilizing the resources of the police and the criminal justice system against other crimes.

The final set of criminological theories focuses on the role of the state and corporations, that is, 'crimes of the powerful'. Within the broad umbrella of criminological theories of crime and the state is labelling theory. Pioneered by Vold, Quinney and others, labelling theory recognizes that crime is a socially constructed by-product of society and the relationships of power and inequality that shape criminal justice systems, schools and other social institutions. However, theories by Lynch, Collins and others take it a step further by recognizing governments and capitalist enterprizes as having agency, that is, they not only shape the structure of society, but are themselves capable of criminal actions. These may include genocide, egregious violations of environmental regulations, mistreatment of workers, consumer fraud and a long list of issues that continuously make headlines in the twenty-first century.

All theories are related and all theories have relevance to rural criminology; similarly, rural criminological studies have relevance to all theories by testing their validity for rural contexts and by critical revisions to their frameworks.

Suggested readings

Burke, R.H. (2014) *An Introduction to Criminological Theory* (4th edn), London: Routledge.

Dekeseredy, W.S. (2022) *Contemporary Critical Criminology* (2nd edn), London: Routledge.

Lilly, J.R., Cullen, F.T. and Ball, R.A. (2019) *Criminological Theory: Context and Consequences* (8th edn), Thousand Oaks, CA: SAGE Publications.

3

Crime and Place

Joseph F. Donnermeyer

It can be argued that theories of crime and place are the most prolific amongst all genres of criminological theory. As Wilcox and others demonstrate, the variety of place-based theories in criminology span nearly its whole history and include an incredible variety of perspectives. Often associated with the Chicago School of Sociology, the theory of social disorganization was one of the earliest attempts to examine the economic, normative and social milieu of neighbourhoods and variations in levels of crime, especially juvenile delinquency.

Subsequent generations of criminological theories about place arrived when the focus shifted away from a neighbourhood-level examination to smaller sub-units, such as 'hot spots', the situational nature of crime, routine activities and crime, the concept of broken windows and crime, crime prevention through environmental design and crime mapping. The shift from larger units of analysis to smaller ones was also accompanied by a significant transition from a focus on places as generators of criminal behaviour to localities with relative differences in risk to victimization.

Even though they are urban-based theories, considerations of crime and place were and continue to be instrumental in the development of rural criminology. The one exception to the urban-centric origins of crime and place theories is the one known as civic community theory.

Social disorganization theory was first developed by Shaw and McKay, both academics from the Chicago School of Sociology in the first half of the twentieth century. Their focus was on explaining why certain neighbourhoods of Chicago differ so greatly in rates of delinquency, describing these areas as possessing such characteristics as high levels of poverty and population turnover. Their essential argument was that those forms of social control as expressed through a strong, locally based social order – both through various social institutions such as schools and the willingness of neighbours to watch out for each other – displayed lower rates of delinquency because they were not disorganized.

The significance of this original formulation is three-fold. First, it shifted thinking about crime away from explanations that emphasized the pathologies of individuals to a more sociologically focused explanation. In doing so, it was part of the twentieth-century development of criminological theories that emphasized social control, social bonding, labelling, delinquent and criminal sub-cultures and even corporate and state crime. Almost all criminological theory today is sociological in nature, even though there are varieties of contemporary criminology which continue to emphasize individual traits, both biological and psychological.

Second, over approximately 100 years of its existence, social disorganization theory has stimulated a great volume of peer-reviewed research, both quantitative and qualitative, although various forms of statistical analyses have been more dominant over the past several decades. As well, it spawned the creation of variants on the basic theme that socially disorganized localities are breeding grounds for crime. For example, the structural antecedent version of the theory focuses on broad social structural forces that are presumed to influence the inner socio-cultural dynamics of places. The systemic version of social disorganization theory turns its attention to these inner dynamics or local social ecology, such as networks of friends and neighbours, schools and civic organizations, amongst others. More recently, the concept of collective efficacy was proposed as a way to understand what happens at specific places that function to reduce crime. The theory refers to the ways that groups within a community, especially people living in the same neighbourhood, influence control over individual behaviours associated with explaining variations in crime, such as the willingness to call the police.

Third, it is the most often tested criminological theory used by rural criminologists. Rural criminology is clearly a sub-discipline where considerations of place and crime dominate, given the millions of rural localities and their diversity found throughout the world. Hence, social disorganization became the most popular theory to select from the smorgasbord of theories available for selection by rural criminologists. However, the rural criminological literature began to cast doubts on its generalizability to smaller places, and also questioned the presumed direction of causality to crime ascribed to social disorganization and collective efficacy. Some rural scholars contend that the label 'social disorganization' is inaccurate and that what is really being described is 'organization'. Other rural scholars take the criticism even further, arguing that the logic is flawed, or at least only half right. Forms of social organization, or alternatively collective efficacy, not only constrain criminal behaviour, but can also facilitate it.

Beyond the theory of social disorganization, there is a variety of other place-based criminological theories of crime. Ceccato's research on security and safety in rural Sweden, for example, employs a variety of place-based theories. These include crime pattern theory to consider the relationship of 'opportunity space' to the intersection of the victim and offender. This theory has a great many similarities to routine activities theory, which also informs the work of Ceccato. It is a theory that began as a way to explain broad, long-term trends at an aggregate level, such as a society, but has since been adopted for more micro-level examinations of crime, including within localities. This theory examines variations in targets, guardians and motivated offenders. Clack also applied crime pattern theory and routine activities theory to the examination of farm crime in South Africa.

Criminological theories of crime and place either attempt to explain criminal behaviour or examine how victimizations occur. Yet both consider space important because it is within specific spaces that patterns of human interaction influence crime.

Suggested readings

Ceccato, V. (2016) *Rural Crime and Community Safety*, London: Routledge.

Clack, W.J. (2015) 'Environmental criminology theories: An analysis of livestock theft cases', *Acta Criminologica: Southern African Journal of Criminology*, 28(1): 92–106.

Donnermeyer, J.F. (2015) 'The social organization of the rural and crime in the United States: Conceptual considerations', *Journal of Rural Studies*, 39: 160–70.

Rogers, E. and Pridemore, W.A. (2016) 'Research on social disorganization theory and crime in rural environments', in J.F. Donnermeyer (ed) *The Routledge International Handbook of Rural Criminology*, London: Routledge, pp. 23–32.

Wilcox, P., Cullen, F.T. and Feldmeyer, B. (2018) *Communities and Crime: An Enduring American Challenge*, Philadelphia, PA: Temple University Press.

4

Cultural Criminology and Representations of Rural Crime

Karen Hayden

Cultural criminology explores the cultural context of deviance, law breaking and social control. Cultural criminologists study sub-cultures of resistance, constructions of crime and media representations of criminals by critically examining these phenomena within the social, cultural, political and economic contexts of late capitalism. Cultural criminology sheds light on images of crime, styles of crime, portrayals of crime and the interactions between crime and crime control.

Cultural criminology grew out of the British/Birmingham School of Cultural Studies and British 'new criminology' of the late 1970s. Theorists and researchers within these schools of thought turned criminological attention away from simply counting crime and measuring criminal behaviour to examining the cultural meanings of crime: for the criminals and criminal sub-groups who take part in crime, to the mass news media that selectively report on crime, to the creators and consumers of the 'crime as entertainment industry' and to the politicians and business owners who capitalize off the fear of crime.

The cultural criminological notion of the 'carnival of crime' asserts that post-modern, late capitalist cultures are steeped in violence, hate and senseless acts of harm. In *Cultural Criminology and the Carnival of Crime*, Presdee argues that the economics of late capitalism have provoked a popular cultural desire for extreme, oppositional forms of pleasure. This desire has caused some acts to be deemed criminal by those in power. Presdee (2000) applies this carnival of crime idea to joyriding, street crime and anti-social behaviour on the internet, as well as the preoccupation with hate, hurt and humiliation in various forms of popular culture.

Cultural criminologists focus on representations of crime in popular culture. Drawing on symbolic interactionist sociology as well as the framework of moral panics, cultural criminologists look critically at the social and cultural construction of criminals, criminal sub-cultures, crime waves and so-called drug epidemics. In the tradition of social constructionism, a cultural criminological approach examines how certain behaviours under certain circumstances are made illegal. Symbolic interactionism views society and social knowledge as actively and creatively produced through human interaction. Social norms and laws exist because people have made them real through language and interaction, social conventions, habits and etiquette.

Labelling theory is one approach to deviance and crime that grew out of the symbolic interactionist perspective and set the groundwork for cultural criminological approaches to crime. Emerging in the 1940s and 1950s, labelling theorists explored how and why some acts are defined as deviant whilst others are not; and further how and why some deviant acts are then labelled as not simply deviant, but criminal. For labelling theorists, the *act* itself is not as significant as the *social reactions* to the act. Instead of seeing deviance and crime as unambiguous categories of behaviour, labelling theorists pose questions about why particular rules and laws exist in the first place. 'Criminal' is not the quality of the act itself; it is a consequence of the application of rules and labels to the act and the actors.

Later social theorists, such as Stanley Cohen in his influential work *Folk Devils and Moral Panics*, developed the idea that labelling can cause an amplification of the labelled behaviour – an embracing of the label. Therefore, applying rules or laws to some individuals or groups may actually encourage the behaviour that the laws are attempting to prohibit. Indeed, Cohen argued that cultural criminology is a variation of labelling theory that includes social, structural and political contexts.

Following in this intellectual tradition, cultural criminology appeals to those interested in a critical approach to the study of society, culture, crime and law because it attempts to address the interconnections between and amongst power, social control, stratification, cultures of resistance, social movements, and the social organization of the law and criminal justice. Cultural criminologists critically examine portrayals of crime and the criminal in popular culture: in the traditional news media, in movies, in crime television – both true crime television and fictional crime shows – as well as in popular music and on new forms of social media.

The focus on these claims makers in constructing social problems, crimes and laws can be traced to the work of the American sociologist Howard Becker, who wrote the book *Outsiders* in which he examined the development of criminal laws against marijuana. In 1937, the Narcotics Bureau defined marijuana as a social danger; they used horror stories to build their case against marijuana. Becker noted that in 1930s United States

Congressional Hearings, the Commissioner of Narcotics reported multiple crimes that were committed under the influence of marijuana, including a Florida mass murder. These hearings led to the 1937 Marijuana Tax Act which was intended to stamp out the drug that had also been linked to Mexican immigrants who were constructed in the media as a dangerous class, as described in Becker's book.

Several cultural criminologists have turned their attention to representations of rural crime. Neil Websdale's study of battered women in rural Kentucky, *Rural Woman Battering and the Justice System: An Ethnography*, is considered a key text within both cultural criminology and rural criminology because it demonstrates how rural patriarchal traditions and the prevailing good old boys' law enforcement network and local power structures produce and reproduce the subordinate, vulnerable, isolated status of many rural women. Works by Dekeseredy and Donnermeyer have strengthened this cultural turn in rural criminology, broadening its scope to include representations of rural crime in popular media outlets such as movies and pornography.

Suggested readings

Becker, H. (1963) *Outsiders: Studies in the Sociology of Deviance*, New York: Free Press.

Cohen, S. (1988) *Against Criminology*, New Brunswick, NJ: Transaction.

Cohen, S. (1972) *Folk Devils and Moral Panics*, London: Macgibbon.

Donnermeyer, J.F. and DeKeseredy, W.S. (2014) *Rural Criminology*, London: Routledge.

Presdee, M. (2000) *Cultural Criminology and the Carnival of Crime*, London: Routledge.

Websdale, N. (1997) *Rural Woman Battering and the Justice System: An Ethnography*, Thousand Oaks, CA: Sage.

5

Environmental and Green Criminology

Rob White

Environmental crimes and harms are rife in rural and remote areas, partly because they avoid close government scrutiny owing to their location, and partly because of activities such as mining, forestry and agriculture, with which some crimes are associated, are intrinsic to areas outside of urban centres. Given that environmental crime generally involves some type of natural resource use (such as illegal harvesting of plants and animals), contamination and pollution (such as illegal waste disposal) and/or modification of natural environments (such as illegal land clearance), it is not unusual to find such crimes associated with the countryside rather than the metropole (see Barclay and Bartel, 2015).

A conventional approach to environmental criminology views environmental crime primarily through the lens of legality. This means that it is concerned with harmful activities that have been formally criminalized in international and domestic law as criminal offences. Typically, these crimes include the illegal taking of flora and fauna (which includes activities such as illegal, unregulated and unreported fishing; illegal logging and trade in timber; and illegal trade in wildlife), pollution offences (which relates to issues such as illegal dumping as well as water, air and land pollution associated with industry) and transportation of banned substances (which refers to the illegal transport of radioactive materials and illegal transfer of hazardous waste).

Relying solely on legal definitions of environmental crime has its limitations, however. This is acknowledged by writers who adopt ecological understandings of nature and who thereby have different conceptions of how crime and harm might be conceived.

An ecocentric approach to environmental harm, for example, starts from the premise that the environment has value for its own sake apart from any instrumental or utilitarian value to humans. Protection of the environment may be based on either one of or a combination of conceptions of the *rights of* nature (as subject with rights, or object worthy of protection) and *duties to* nature (its intrinsic worth which therefore imposes a moral obligation and duty of care). From this perspective, environmental harm in its various manifestations, whether legally allowed or not, is worthy of critical criminological attention. For instance, logging may in some circumstances be legal, but if it includes the logging of old growth forests, using methods such as clear-felling (which involves cutting down all trees within a designated logging coup), then this is seen as wrong and ecologically 'criminal' by critics.

Viewing the world from an ecological rather than anthropocentric (or human-centred) perspective also allows criminology to consider the plight of not only the human but the non-human. For example, whilst the central concern of most criminology is with human actors (as offenders and victims), it is also important to study the situation of both living and non-living features of the natural world. The term 'natural object' describes non-living entities such as rivers, mountains and oceans. Fauna is ordinarily described using the term 'animal' (which can be sub-divided into, amongst other categories, 'native wildlife' and 'threatened species'), whilst flora (plant life) ordinarily makes reference to the broad category 'vegetation'. Ecosystems have been defined as a dynamic complex of plant, animal and micro-organism communities and their non-living environment interacting as a functional unit. Together these entities comprise what can be described as non-human environmental entities (see White, 2022).

Green criminology combines an interest in the legal definitions of environmental crime (such as illegal fishing) with ecological definitions of environmental harm (such as unsustainable or damaging transformations of the landscape) in its analyses. As part of this, it incorporates the consideration of power and interests, with particular attention given to systemic global harms (such as carbon emissions based on the economic growth imperative), transgressions linked to transnational corporations (such as the spilling of mining tailings into nearby rivers), and harms stemming from state–corporate crime (such as support for mega-projects that cause widespread environmental degradation and destruction).

Key dimensions of green criminology include the nature and dynamics of *environmental crimes and harms* (that may incorporate wider definitions of crime than that provided in strictly legal definitions), *environmental laws* (including enforcement, prosecution and sentencing), *environmental regulation* (systems of administrative, civil and criminal law that are designed to manage, protect and preserve specified environments and species, and to manage the negative consequences of particular industrial processes) and *eco-justice* (the valuing of and respect for humans, ecosystems and non-human animals and plants).

Like traditional criminology, green criminology is oriented towards the study of offences (what crimes or harms are inflicted on the environment, and how), offenders (who commits crime against the environment, and why), victims (who/what suffers as a result of environmental damage, and how) and responses to environmental crimes (for example, policing, penalties and crime prevention) (see Brisman and South, 2021).

What distinguishes green criminology from other branches of criminology is the underlying concern with nature and its ecological components. This has important implications. For example, harm is established by virtue of factors intrinsic to the health and wellbeing of the non-human, rather than solely in reference to human needs or interests, and through reference to ecological concepts such as interconnectedness, totality, community, diversity, relationships and scale.

A green approach therefore centres justice around both human and non-human victims. This eco-justice framework is comprised of three interrelated elements (see White, 2022):

- *environment justice* – environmental rights are seen as an extension of human or social rights so as to enhance the quality of human life, now and into the future: the victim is human;
- *ecological justice* – humans are one component of complex ecosystems that should be preserved for their own sake: the victim is specific environments; and
- *species justice* – animals have an intrinsic right to not suffer abuse, and plants the degradation of habitat to the extent that threatens biodiversity loss: the victim is non-human animals and plants.

A fundamental premise of green criminology is that environmental crime needs to be defined and studied in relation to harm, and not solely on the basis of legal definitions, and that victims include the non-human. For rural criminology, there are several crimes of particular note. For example, freshwater is increasingly scarce worldwide. It is needed not only for human consumption but for agricultural and pastoral industries, mining, fracking and other uses. It is also essential to wildlife and plant survival. This can lead to conflicts between different stakeholders over water use (such as farmers versus miners). It is also associated with water-related crimes ranging from water theft to pollution of freshwater streams and rivers.

Depending upon the circumstances, the illegal taking of water may be perceived as significantly harmful and potentially criminal (for example, when linked to large companies and industries such as cotton growing) or it may be 'excused' as an act of subsistence (for example, the family farmer who needs water for livestock in a period of drought).

Disposal of hazardous waste and stockpiling of rubbish in non-urban areas is also problematic, as is use of pesticides and other chemicals that contaminate soils, kill bees and pollute ocean reefs through run-off.

Environmentally harmful economic activity in countries such as Australia, Brazil, Colombia, Mexico, Nigeria and Republic of the Congo tends to congeal around two key areas of concern: resource extraction (such as mining, forestry and fishing) and contamination (the pollution of land, air and water associated with production and consumption activities). Other crimes include biopiracy (the unethical taking of and claims to ownership of genetic material from forests) and illegal mining, matters of particular concern in Latin America and Africa (see, for example, Goyes et al, 2017; Arroyo-Quiroz and Wyatt, 2018).

Part of the green criminology critique of the exploitation of nature in rural and remote areas is that nature is viewed entirely through the prism of economic calculus, rather than intrinsic importance (see White, 2022). Resource extraction companies, such as oil, coal and gas companies as well as large agricultural (for example cotton) and pastoral (for example cows) businesses tend to receive privileged support from governments regardless of the damage they cause to specific environments or the contributions they make to global warming. This is evident, for example, in government policies in Canada (the Alberta Tar Sands project) and New Zealand (the dairy industry).

From a green criminology perspective, the destruction of the environment in ways that adversely affect humans, ecosystems and non-human species can be conceptualized, criminologically, as a specific type of crime – ecocide. This describes an attempt to criminalize human activities that reduce and destroy the wellbeing and health of ecosystems and species within these, including humans. Where this occurs as a result of human agency, then it can be said that a 'crime' has occurred. The diminishment through exploitation of the world's natural resources certainly fits this description of serious harm.

Suggested readings

Arroyo-Quiroz, A. and Wyatt, T. (eds) (2018) *Green Crime in Mexico: A Collection of Case Studies*, London: Palgrave Macmillan.

Barclay, E. and Bartel, R. (2015) 'Defining environmental crime: The perspective of farmers', *Journal of Rural Studies*, 39: 188–98.

Brisman, A. and South, N. (eds) (2021) *The Routledge Handbook of Green Criminology*, London: Routledge.

Goyes, D., Mol, H., Brisman, A. and South, N. (eds) (2017) *Environmental Crime in Latin America: The Theft of Nature and the Poisoning of the Land*, London: Palgrave.

White, R. (2022) *Theorising Green Criminology: Selected Essays*, London: Routledge.

6

Feminist Theory

Amanda Hall-Sanchez

Defining feminism and feminist theory is challenging, but most feminist criminologists agree that it is more than just adding women to pre-conceived notions of crime and social control. In its most confined sense, feminism is a collection of political ideologies focused on women's oppression to advance women's equality through strategies for social change. In a more comprehensive, multifaceted sense and in terms of feminist scholarship, feminism is an array of interconnected contextual frames utilized for the observation, analysis and interpretation of the intricate ways in which the social realities of gendered inequality are constructed, structured, imposed and demonstrated on a macro (societal and institutional) scale to the micro (individual lived realities) scale.

Feminist criminology is commonly recognized as a main division of critical criminology and, although much of early critical criminological theory was androcentric and gender-blind, the study of gender, sex and sexuality now features prominently in this discipline. Although there are at least 12 variants of feminist criminological theory – including liberal, radical, Marxist/socialist, postmodernist/poststructuralist, standpoint, multiracial, Indigenous, Black, queer and intersectional – most feminist theorists explicitly theorize gender, embrace diverse empirical epistemologies and contend that many countries are characterized by patriarchy: gendered structures in which women are dominated by men (see Renzetti, 2013).

Critical feminist criminologists maintain a theoretical, empirical and policy-driven commitment to a plethora of significant social and global harms, including women and girls' pathways to crime, drugs and the criminal–legal system; sexual harassment and intimate violence; moral panics about girls' violence; the positionality of women in male-dominated criminal–legal domains (such as policing and corrections); hyper-sexualized media culture and pornography; commodification and trafficking of girls and women; and the demonization of girls and women of colour.

Contemporary feminist criminologists prioritize women's experiences, attitudes and behaviours, whilst acknowledging that they differ by class, race, ethnicity, nationality and sexuality, and that the form of women's oppression varies. Although a critical examination of the role of gender/sex constructions of crime and crime control is paramount, not all feminist criminologists examine *women's* experiences, as highlighted in the study of masculinities.

Further, feminist theorists recognize that not all men benefit equally in patriarchal societies and some women have more privilege than others, which has perpetuated the need to examine intersectional realities. Intersectional analyses focus on how racism, patriarchy, class oppression and other discriminatory systems contribute to inequalities and the relative positions of women of different races, ethnicities, classes and so on. Intersectional theorists prioritize the impact of these interconnected identities and apply them to experiences of crime, the social control of crime and any crime-related issues (see Potter, 2013).

Rural critical criminology, primarily dominated by place-based (that is, social disorganization) theories, has also situated conceptualizations of sex/gender at the margins of scholarly theoretical work in the field. The 1990s marked the beginning of contemporary critical feminist research on rural crime and social control, with a focus on violence against women and their experiences in the social and criminal–legal systems in rural Appalachia in the United States. With an eye towards the broad roots of crime and social control in rural spaces, rural feminist criminologists since then have been deeply concerned with economic crises in rural areas, the patriarchal structure of rural communities and criminal–legal systems and the spatial dimension to the construction of rural masculinities that contribute to harms against rural girls and women (see Carrington et al, 2014).

North American and Australian researchers have long studied rural masculinities as a robust instrument of violence against women, as some rural men's masculine identity has become challenged owing to rural social and economic shifts. To date, much intersectional theorizing is urban-centric and those in rural spaces are seldom discussed as relevant to an intersectional analysis. Therefore, there is a tremendous need for research on rural violence against women to include the rural as social locations that intersect with women's experiences of intimate violence. Advancing feminist theory on rural violence against women may also be accomplished through empirical investigations. For instance, Hall-Sanchez (2014), one of the first rural feminist criminologists to employ a talk-back methodology in a rural woman abuse study, discovered two important themes in the relationship between rural hunting culture and woman abuse: male peer support and patriarchal dominance and control.

Rural feminist criminologists maintain that it is imperative to theorize place as it exists not only as a geographic entity with apparent obstacles for rural women but also as it stands as a social and cultural backdrop that houses imbedded ideologies of patriarchal domination and control. These theorists must continue to see place as it intersects within the context of women's lived rural realities and serves to structure their available options, as well as to theorize how men attempt to reconstruct masculinity in non-controlling and non-violent ways within the context of rural spaces.

Chesney-Lind and Morash (2013) make the case for a transformative critical feminist criminology that includes an explicit commitment to social justice through the theorizing of gender, masculinities and intersectionality that embraces feminist epistemologies and methods, and is increasingly global in scope. By remaining theoretically committed to understanding women's multiple oppressions and actively seeking real social change through consciousness raising and policy recommendations, rural critical feminist criminologists are paving the way for the development of this vision of a global, transformative critical feminist criminology.

Suggested readings

Carrington, K., Donnermeyer, J.F. and DeKeseredy, W.S. (2014) 'Intersectionality, rural criminology, and re-imaging the boundaries of critical criminology', *Critical Criminology*, 22: 463–77.

Chesney-Lind, M. and Morash, M. (2013) 'Transformative feminist criminology: A critical re-thinking of a discipline', *Critical Criminology*, 21: 287–304.

Hall-Sanchez, A.K. (2014) 'Male peer support, hunting, and separation/divorce sexual assault in rural Ohio', *Critical Criminology*, 22: 495–510.

Potter, H. (2013) 'Intersectional criminology: Interrogating identity and power in criminology research and theory', *Critical Criminology: An International Journal*, 21(3): 305–18.

Renzetti, C. (2013) *Feminist Criminology*, London: Routledge.

7

Late Modernity, Surveillance and Securitization

Matt Bowden and Artur Pytlarz

Modernity and tradition have long been presented as a dichotomy in sociology and the social sciences to distinguish social development based on industrialization from that based upon agriculture. The former represents an ideal-type for the process of transformation to urban society which we can date following the industrial revolution to the late twentieth century. The latter, by definition, is regarded as the stage from which most industrial societies have transitioned in this period. In sociology, and indeed introductory criminology, students are taught that the traditional society is based upon social institutions that are ascriptive, agrarian and have extended families; the modern is meritocratic, industrial and has nuclear families.

However, in the last quarter of the twentieth century, transformations in technology, politics and culture gave rise to the weakening of the established institutions of industrial modernity – the end of paid work for life, the introduction of lean production or flexible specialization, and the closing of heavy industries. The closure of mines in the valleys of Wales and in other industrialized countries such as Belgium undermined the industrial working-class communities that had been built around them. These were the crisis years accompanying the economic model of neo-liberalism ushered in by regimes in the United Kingdom and United States under Thatcherism and Reaganism. Skilled and semi-skilled industrial jobs were exported to lower cost countries in the developing world, public utilities were privatized and were met with considerable resistance.

Whilst the automation of production undermined 'good' manual jobs in trades and industry, computers aided design and manufacturing enabled products to be made with higher precision. In the countries that abandoned heavy industry for high-tech growth, labour markets polarized resulting in a predominance of high-paid jobs at the top of the occupational structure, the collapse of industrial and trade jobs and the rise of a substantial precariat at the bottom of the employment structure. Ultimately this led to a period of economic and, by default, social restructuring that fractured lives and communities. The demise of heavy industrialization also had costs in rural areas as it reduced the need for heavy extractive industries located in valleys, villages and small towns, and redistributed them to other parts of the world in search of minerals to produce in response to our demands for consumer goods.

The invention of the micro processer gave rise to a new technological mode of capitalist development – the information age – where information and data has become both the raw material and the output of advanced industrial production. Equally, the scale of that production is global, and the markets for software and smart phone apps are relatively free of national boundaries. The economic liberalization of the 1980s, too, gave capital greater freedom from territorial strictures and enabled the greater fluidity of capital. Once this occurred, capital could remove itself from the local and separate the relationship to local labour.

Considering the implications of this shift, Bauman (2007) argued that we had entered a new modernity in which the old solid institutions based upon the national territory were themselves liquifying and becoming more fluid. The state too, as a solid institution of modernity, was hollowing, reducing in size and capacity, as neo-liberal ideology was by its core principles, against a large, economically and social active state. The market was then proffered as the principal means of producing and distributing goods and providing services. This in turn elevated and gave centrality to the 'consumer' and downplayed the 'citizen'; hence, the late modern consumer society began.

Capturing these transformations, Giddens (1991) likened them to a fast-moving vehicle – a juggernaut – with tremendous opportunity and yet bearing unparalleled risks. We might view the global experience with the COVID-19 virus through this lens: a global phenomenon that the 'flows' of people around the world had helped to spread; with every opportunity it appears that there are new risks. Modernization, which was based upon industrialization in the nineteenth and twentieth centuries, has produced the greenhouse gases that are responsible for climate change: whilst modernity has found more advanced technologies to produce 'goods', it has also produced 'bads'.

Criminologists writing about this period have suggested that these are dizzying times and one in which the previous institutions that gave us security have all but vanished. Garland (2001) wrote of these times as reflecting a 'cultural turn', whereby a neo-liberalist ideology became the structuring logic of a switch from welfarist principles to a more highly politicized and popular punitiveness in criminal justice systems. A culture of control characterizes late modern times and is accompanied also by the message that one should not expect the state to provide for one's security. Garland suggested that part of this cultural turn was greater responsibilization of individuals and households to act in more prudential manners by protecting themselves.

In line with Foucault's 1977 ideas on governmentality and power (see suggested readings), Garland captured the culture of control as the state divesting its authority away from the core to the 'capillaries' – from the centre to the various islands within a dispersed carceral archipelago. The prison might remain as a strong central institution in late modern times, but it is argued that this decentring of state power is accompanied by even greater panoptic power through the extension of criminal justice apparatuses into prevention, penetrating civil society as it does and mobilizing new surveillance technologies such as closed-circuit television, and more latterly, big data. Rather than losing power by hollowing out the criminal justice state, the state in theory gains more power as it is dispersed over a wider space.

That said, in the context of the late modern era, we have witnessed somewhat of a preventive turn – which involves divesting responsibility for everyday security to individuals and households. This sparks off new expertize and specialisms and generates 'a security field'.

Whilst it might be easy to dismiss the late modern era as an urban, consumerist phenomenon, it has effects on rural areas too. The late modern scale of organization is global and localities are 'glocalized', when they are penetrated by global processes. The building of a new road across rural areas enables global flows of goods and labour to occur. Similarly, urban regeneration for globalized production puts pressure on urban land, scattering people to rural areas in search of lower rents and property prices and sparking off commuting as a late modern phenomenon. Equally, as late modern society rises on the back of informational capitalism, rural areas also become sites for large-scale data centres, thus integrating them within the late modern space of flows.

As a 'socio-spatiality', rural areas therefore experience and endure new processes, relationships and risks – an example of the latter in the context of rural crime is the rise of rural drug markets. A global supply chain, which is a flow process, penetrates rural areas previously unfettered by these issues. Similarly, illegal labour supply – the flow and even trafficking of humans – is typical of a late-modern process in which the labour of migrants is used away from the prying eyes of urban based control institutions and regulation.

In spite of the compelling arguments in this tradition, critical realist writers have questioned the nomothetical or 'grand narrative' nature of these theories, pointing to the role that time, space and practice traditions within a more dispersed apparatus play in determining how power is wielded and for what purpose. Thus, we need to be mindful to the specifics of practice in time and space and to conduct empirical studies, especially in rural contexts.

We specifically need to understand how security fields manifest themselves in rural areas. One such rural criminology case study by Bowden and Pytlarz (2022) points out that rural crime prevention, which formed the basis upon which the rationales for fortifying homesteads and protecting farms with hard, solid materials – locks, walls, alarms – were being utilized alongside a move towards informational forms of security practice.

These latter more 'liquid' forms see rural communities using combinations of official SMS text alert schemes, along with unofficial Facebook and WhatsApp groups, to arm themselves with informational capital. Rural community members, left out of the flow of information, felt excluded from the network. Hence, rural security moves from modern to the more fluid late-modern form and potentially divides those within security and safety networks from those without informational security capital.

Suggested readings

Bauman, Z. (2007) *Liquid Times: Living in an Age of Uncertainty*, Cambridge: Polity Press.

Bowden, M. and Pytlarz, A. (2022) 'Late modernity and the governance of rural security: from solid to liquid', in M. Bowden and A. Harkness (eds) *Rural Transformations and Rural Crime: International Critical Perspectives in Rural Criminology*, Bristol: Bristol University Press, pp. 49–65.

Foucault, M. (1977) *Discipline and Punish: The Birth of the Prison*, London: Penguin.

Garland, D. (2001) *The Culture of Control: Crime and Social Order in Contemporary Society*, Oxford: Oxford University Press.

Giddens, A. (1991) *The Consequences of Modernity*, Cambridge: Polity Press.

8

Left Realism

James Windle

Left Realism is an applied integrative theory. It is founded upon a social democratic position and draws from a range of sociological theories. It emerged during the late 1980s in response to the growing scholarly and policy influence of more conservative criminology.

Elliot Currie suggests that there are two variants of left realism. Original Left Realism (with capitals) was pioneered by Jock Young and colleagues. The second, which Currie calls 'plain left realism' (without capitals), shed some elements that were of its time and place (that is, in the United Kingdom in the late 1980s) and is a 'big tent' under which many criminologists meet, including those who may not identify with original Left Realism. Nonetheless, several common principles draw all left realists together: they take lived experiences seriously, acknowledge that crime affects some communities more than others and identify crime as an endemic product of inequality.

Traditionally associated with street crime in urban areas, Left Realism has been used by a small number of scholars to explore a range of rural issues. The theory has influenced, for example, James Windle's research on opium cultivation in Asia and farm theft in Ireland, and Walter DeKeseredy, Joseph Donnermeyer and Martin Schwartz's collaborative and individual work on sexual violence against women in rural areas, agricultural crime and rural drug markets. The latter's body of work advanced Left Realism by employing feminist and masculinity theories, areas original Left Realism failed to sufficiently engage.

The original Left Realists critiqued the critical criminology literature for: dismissing that crime disproportionally affects the economically disadvantaged and socially excluded; ignoring issues which most concerned working-class people; romanticizing crimes committed by the working class; ignoring that most crime was inter-class; and dismissing people's experiences of crime by suggesting that fear was more prominent than actual victimization. They also took critical criminologist's to task for refusing to work with the state.

Young summarized Left Realism as composed of five key principles. First, and most importantly, researchers, policymakers and practitioners must be 'faithful to the nature of crime'. That is, they must acknowledge the precise form that rural crime takes and where it takes place, grounded within political and economic context. This must involve all four dimensions of the 'Square of Crime'. As original Left Realism's core concept, the Square points to the need for all research, policy and practice to account for interactions between the state, offender, victim and community.

Second, much criminological theory focuses on one cause or two dimensions of the Square of Crime; however, most crimes have multiple causal factors operating at different levels and involving all dimensions of the Square. Consequentially, integration of existing theories can be fruitful, although the original Left Realists favoured anomie-based sub-cultural theories. They would, for example, reject the proposition that absolute poverty explains cannabis farming, suggesting instead that cultivation represents a sub-cultural response to the strain of relative deprivation.

Third, communities experience crime and preventitive measures differently. Consequently, blindly adopting theories developed in one context to explain phenomena in another will likely be unsuccessful. As Left Realism was originally developed in response to street crime in urban areas, applying it to rural crimes may appear contradictory. As an integrative theory it does, however, show much flexibility in its approach and calls for narrower geographical enquiries. For example, instead of administering generic national surveys of farmers' experience of fraud, Left Realists would focus on a smaller number of farming communities, whilst paying attention to the urban bias of existing theories used to explain the results.

Fourth, gauging lived realities requires that those most impacted by crime be consulted about policy and practice. Original Left Realism proposed that local victimization surveys measure community opinions and the realities of crime (although contemporary left realists use a variety of data sources). Once the local reality of crime is understood, the state can allocate resources to where they are most needed and communities can use the data to lobby for themselves. Essentially, rural communities know what has happened and what they want done about it, so they should be asked. Left Realism is the criminological theory which best embodies the popular slogan 'Nothing About Us without Us'.

Fifth, original Left Realists emphasized what Currie called social crime prevention over policing. This involves, for example, investing in social goods (health, housing, employment and so on) which can promote social control and have longer-term impacts than criminal justice approaches.

Police and other agents of formal control are seen as necessary but should be used minimally and democratically (that is, police and community priorities should align). The nuance of Left Realism is apparent here. For example, disrupting trafficking networks may prevent heroin use or opium farming in the short-term but longer-term policies require altering the structural factors and underlying reasons for using heroin use or cultivating opium (indeed, research shows that repressive interventions against drug crop farming can increase outputs and destabilize areas).

Herein lies an unresolved contradiction of Left Realism. It demands that communities are heard whilst its explicit social democratic position opposes strict law enforcement-based approaches. As many rural peoples support conservative policies over longer-term structural approaches, the principle of democratic policing may be untenable. Furthermore, communities often exhibit diverse views and the most vulnerable are often the least vocal, so gauging a community's position is itself difficult.

The greatest strength of both variants of left realism is the rejection of simple explanations coupled with the realist amalgamation of theories and practices which acknowledges both short- and long-term solutions. The original Left Realists acknowledged that urban communities do not need abstract empiricism or theorizing, they need to be heard and supported. The same is true for rural communities.

Suggested readings

Currie, E. (2010) 'Plain left realism: An appreciation, and some thoughts for the future', *Crime, Law and Social Change*, 54(2): 111–24.

DeKeseredy, W.S. and Schwartz M.D. (2010) 'Friedman economic policies, social exclusion, and crime: Toward a gendered left realist subcultural theory', *Crime, Law and Social Change*, 54(2): 159–70.

Donnermeyer, J.F. and DeKeseredy, W. (2014) *Rural Criminology*, London: Routledge.

Windle, J. (2022) 'A left realist approach to rural crime: The case of agricultural theft in Ireland', in A. Harkness and M. Bowden (eds) *Rural Transformations and Rural Crime: International Critical Perspectives in Rural Criminology*. Bristol: Bristol University Press, pp. 87–101.

Young, J. and Matthews, R. (1992) *Rethinking Criminology: The Realist Debate*, Thousand Oaks, CA: SAGE Publications.

9

Male Peer Support Theory

Walter S. DeKeseredy

Violence against women in rural and remote areas has many determinants and one of the most significant ones is 'male peer support'. The theory arose in Canada but has international applications, based on a review of the literature by DeKeseredy. It is attachments to male peers and the resources that these men provide that perpetuate and legitimate both the online and offline victimization of women. Nearly 35 years of rigorous quantitative and qualitative empirical work shows that male peer group dynamics that encourage and rationalize various types of abuse against women are also prevalent in metropolitan locales. Likewise, male peer support is multidimensional. Consider that research consistently identifies these four variants of male peer support:

- *routine activities with other men*, such as playing sports or going to bars, pubs or nightclubs;
- *informational support*, which refers to the guidance and advice that influence men to assault their current or former intimate female partners;
- attachments to male peers who have abused their current or former intimate female partners; and
- peer pressure to have sex.

As DeKeseredy and Schwartz note, in 1988 the very first male peer support model of woman abuse was developed and tested. It is heavily informed by 'social support theory'. Social support theory is generally used to explain the role of social support in health maintenance and disease prevention. However, it was reconceptualized to explain violence against women. This theory argues that many men experience various types of stress in university/college dating relationships, ranging from sexual problems to challenges to their perceived male authority. Some men try to deal with these problems themselves, whilst others turn to their male friends for advice, guidance and various other kinds of social support. The resources provided by these peers may incite and justify woman abuse under certain conditions. Furthermore, male peer support can influence men to victimize their dating partners regardless of stress.

Since 1988, seven more male peer support models have been developed (see DeKeseredy and colleagues in the suggested readings), with two of them constructed in an attempt to explain separation/divorce sexual assault in rural communities. The first of these two was published in 2004 and it is the 'feminist/male peer support model of separation/divorce sexual assault' and the second, published in 2007, is the 'rural masculinity/male peer support model of separation/divorce sexual assault'. They are middle-range perspectives and provide empirically informed answers to the question 'Why do rural men sexually assault female partners who want to leave or who have left them?'.

The first model situates separation/divorce within the larger context of societal patriarchy. Many examples of patriarchal practices and discourses could easily be provided here. Nevertheless, a constant such as societal patriarchy cannot be used to explain variations in the frequency and severity of male sexual assaults during and after separation/divorce. In other words, if we live in a patriarchal society that promotes 'male proprietariness' (another key variable in this model), why, then, do some men sexually assault during and after the exiting process, whereas most others do not? Also, there are variations in male proprietariness, which is the tendency of men to think of their intimate female partners as sexual and reproductive property that they can control and dominate.

Based on a wealth of data, this model contends that many women resist or eventually will resist their spouse/cohabiting partners' proprietariness in a variety of ways, such as arguing, protesting and fighting back if they have been abused. There are also numerous women who defy men's control by exiting or trying to exit a relationship and their attempts to leave or their successful departures challenge male proprietariness. Yet exiting alone cannot account for sexual assault. Thus, this theory also emphasizes that many abusive patriarchal men have male friends with similar beliefs and values and these peers reinforce the notion that women exiting a relationship is a threat to a man's masculinity. Not only do these men verbally and publicly state that sexual assault and other forms of abuse are legitimate means of maintaining patriarchal authority and control, they also serve as role models because many of them physically, sexually and psychologically harm their own intimate partners.

As reviewed by Donnermeyer and DeKeseredy, the key objective of the second theory of rural abuse against women is to make visible the realities of male-to-female violence and to understand its links to rural social and economic changes, not as sources of social disorganization or disruption, but as transformations that create and/or reinforce localized forms of social organization associated with male peer support for separation/divorce sexual assault.

This model incorporates parts of the first theory, but it also addresses key rural realities excluded from the first one such as the disappearance of work and the loss of family farms, factors expanded upon in the work of DeKeseredy and Rennison. It focuses on these and other factors that enhance a sociological understanding of separation/divorce sexual assault, masculinities and the United States rural gender order. Additionally, this model, like the one that preceded it, does not reduce gender to an afterthought or to a control variable in a regression equation. Certainly, if battered lesbians, women of colour and female members of other ethnic or racial groups have been delegated to the margins of mainstream criminology, the same can be said about socially and economically excluded rural women who endure male violence.

It is currently unclear whether elements of male peer support theory can explain other forms of abuse against women in rural places such as beatings in marital/cohabiting relationships and acquaintance rapes. This research gap needs to be filled and the way forward also involves testing theories of violence against rural women using quantitative data. In the meantime, though, rural women who are now being assaulted by men who belong to patriarchal sub-cultures of violence cannot afford to sit back and hope that researchers and theorists develop greater insight into how pro-abuse male social networks function. Research and changes to policy and practice must be undertaken now to effectively alleviate their pain and suffering.

Suggested readings

DeKeseredy, W.S. (2021) *Woman Abuse in Rural Places*, London: Routledge.

DeKeseredy, W.S. (2021) 'Male-to-female sexual violence in rural communities: A sociological review', *Dignity: A Journal of Analysis of Exploitation and Violence*, 6(2): 1–19.

DeKeseredy, W.S. and Rennison, C.M. (2020) 'Thinking theoretically about male violence in rural places: A review of the extant sociological literature and suggestions for future theorizing', *International Journal of Rural Criminology*, 5(2): 162–80.

DeKeseredy, W.S. and Schwartz, M.D. (2013) *Male Peer Support and Violence Against Women: The History and Verification of a Theory*, Boston, MA: Northeastern University Press.

Donnermeyer, J.F. and DeKeseredy, W.S. (2014) *Rural Criminology*, London: Routledge.

10

Primary Socialization Theory

Joseph F. Donnermeyer

Primary socialization theory attempts to explain involvement in substance use and misuse, especially amongst adolescents. It is one of three theories attempting to explain criminal behaviour that has substantial rural roots. The other two are civic community theory created by Matt Lee and colleagues, and male-peer support for violence against women led by Walter DeKeseredy and associates.

Primary socialization theory was developed during the 1990s by Eugene Oetting and colleagues who worked at the Tri-Ethnic Center for Prevention Research, Colorado State University in the United States. Their academic backgrounds were in psychology and social psychology, although their work was informed later by the sociological concept of community. The name 'Tri-Ethnic' derives from a focus on three important ethnic and cultural groups who live in areas outside of the cities and suburbs in the western region of the United States. These rural populations, especially in the Western United States, are Hispanic–American, Native American and White American. Even though primary socialization theory has its origins in the study of drug use amongst rural populations, it can also be applied to an urban context.

The predecessor theory to primary socialization theory developed by Oetting and associates at Colorado State University was called 'peer cluster theory'. This theory has a basis in social learning theory whereby it attempted to model factors that either constrain or enable adolescent substance use by positing that interaction with close friends, not merely a generic form of peer culture, is the key explanatory variable. Attitudes and behaviours must be learned, and those closest to adolescents, especially peers they know well, form a reference group for what they decide to do.

Accounting first for individual-level personality characteristics such as risk-taking, it sees the learning of attitudes and the modelling of behaviours associated with either drug use or abstinence as a product of friends with whom an adolescent may associate. However, these associations are in turn affected by the strength of the bonds which adolescents possess, both within their immediate family and in the schools they attend. It also accounted for the strength of support and involvement of an adolescent's family with the school attended by their offspring, and the extent to which close friends were known and approved by the adolescent's family. In this sense, peer cluster theory is a psycho-social model of adolescent substance use based on Bronfenbrenner's rendition of the ecology of human development.

The theory was subsequently revised to account for a wider milieu of factors associated with the community in which adolescents live. It was at this point that the name of the theory was revised to 'primary socialization theory'. These external or exogenous influences were referred to in the theory as secondary sources of socialization, operating indirectly by influencing the immediate social ecology in which an adolescent learns both attitudes and behaviours related to substance use. In this way, a community was conceived as a geographic mediator through which young people experience to an increasing extent the trends and events of society as they transition from childhood to adulthood.

It considered various community-level factors, particularly those that characterize rural localities, in terms of their influence on adolescent rates of substance use, based on the extant research literature in criminology about the relationship of crime and locality. These factors included population size and density, race and ethnic composition of the population, population growth and decline, net migration, occupational structure of the population at particular localities and levels of poverty. In this sense, it resembles the structural antecedent version of social disorganization theory, whilst its predecessor, peer cluster theory, is similar in its logic to the systemic version of social disorganization theory.

In regard to population size and density, primary socialization theory argues against the notion that smaller population size and assumed sociocultural homogeneity of rural areas uniformly provide a type of normative protection against influences that lead to deviant and criminal behaviours. Citing evidence from national-level self-report surveys of youth, such as the Monitoring the Future longitudinal study and the Tri-Ethnic Center's own survey, the American Drug and Alcohol Survey, primary socialization theory shows variability in rates of substance use when comparing results across the population size of communities (from rural to urban) in which young people live. Hence, for some kinds of substances, rates amongst rural youth when compared to urban youth are higher.

Over time, substance use rates have converged across the rural–urban divide in the United States. Plus, primary socialization theory argues that the variability of rural communities in the United States by population turnover, rates of poverty, race and ethnic composition, amongst other factors, means that blanket statements about the protective dimension of places with smaller populations is not correct. In fact, small, rural communities may display higher levels of deviance and crime than those of cities, such as the research on rural substance use by Garriott and Shukla demonstrates, but again it depends on the kinds of behaviours under consideration and the matrix of community-level factors that may be correlated with criminality.

A series of five articles on primary socialization theory were published in the journal *Substance Use and Misuse*, and the theory is both cited and occasionally tested by scholars, especially researchers in psychology and social psychology who focus on adolescent development. Its cross-over to criminology is largely through the work of rural scholars, whose focus is more squarely on rural community characteristics and crime. In this regard, primary socialization theory is similar to various theories of crime and place, including the systemic version of social disorganization theory and civic community theory of Lee and colleagues.

Suggested readings

Garriott, W. (2011) *Policing Methamphetamine: Narcopolitics in Rural America*, New York: New York University Press.

Oetting, E.R. and Beauvais, F. (1987) 'Peer cluster theory: Socialization characteristics and adolescent drug use – a path analysis', *Journal of Counseling Psychology*, 34(2): 205–13.

Oetting, E.R. and Donnermeyer, J.F. (1998) 'Primary socialization theory: The etiology of drug use and deviance', *Substance Use and Misuse*, 33(4): 995–1026.

Oetting, E.R., Donnermeyer, J.F. and Deffenbacher, J.L. (1998) 'Primary socialization theory: The influence of the community on drug use and deviance', *Substance Use and Misuse*, 33(8): 1629–65.

Shukla, R.K. (2016) *Methamphetamine: A Love Story*, Oakland, CA: University of California Press.

11

Rational Choice, Routine Activity and Situational Crime Prevention

Vania Ceccato

A growing number of researchers in rural criminology adopt a rational choice perspective to tackle problems relevant to people in rural areas. Rational choice provides a theoretical framework for other situational theoretical references used in rural criminology such as routine activity, situational crime prevention and other related approaches (such as crime pattern theory and crime prevention through environmental design). Rational choice assumes that crime is a result of individual decision-making processes.

As pointed out by Cornish and Clarke, a person's decision to commit a criminal act depends on the expected benefits that are weighed against the risk of being detected. The rational choice perspective assumes that individuals try to choose the best means available to achieve these goals even if they are risky. Such a decision is, according to Cornish and Clarke, a deliberate act, committed with the intention of benefiting the offender. This theoretical approach also suggests that criminal behaviour unfolds in a sequence of stages and decisions and that criminal decision-making is crime-specific because rewards and risks differ from case to case. Therefore, the factors that offenders consider before committing a crime differ with the nature of the offence, leading to the conclusion that crime prevention should also be crime-specific.

According to the rational choice perspective, criminal choices are expected to fall into two broad groups: 'involvement decisions' and 'event decisions'. Whereas involvement decisions concern an offender's criminal career as well as initiation, habituation and desistance, event decisions are crime-centered and concentrate on crime commission and concern choices and decisions made when preparing for, carrying out and concluding the commission of a specific type of crime.

Rational choice has been criticized because offenders may not always act rationally; they act within a bounded rationality. Critics postulate that rational choice fails to contextualize offending and its meanings within the background of individuals' lives and lifestyles. Cornish and Clarke note that the perspective has focused too much on opportunity structures, disregarding the interaction between types of individuals and types of environments for crime commission or that rational choice works better to explain the commission of instrumental crimes, such as theft or drinking and driving, rather than expressive crimes, such as assault or manslaughter. Yet, as Eck and Clarke argue, the current evidence for its effectiveness in urban areas is substantial.

The influence of the environment and situation on behaviour is central in the rational choice perspective. The focus on crime prevention based on this perspective is not on individuals but on criminogenic situations. A crime opportunity results from the interaction of elements: an individual willing to commit an act; an attractive and suitable target; the target and the willing individual in the same place at the same time; and the absence of any powerful protection at the target location. These are the essential elements of routine activity approach as originally formulated by the pioneering work of Cohen and Felson in 1979. Thus, situational factors can stimulate crime, and addressing these factors can reduce crime opportunities.

Offenders choose to commit crimes based on their perceptions of available opportunities. Thus, situational factors can stimulate crime, and addressing these factors can reduce crime. According to Eck and Clarke, situational crime prevention focuses on specific categories of crime or disorder and takes particular note of crime concentrations. Situational crime prevention is intended to affect routine activities in daily life, both by impacting the decisions taken by those individuals with a propensity to choose deviant behaviour as well as by changing the environment and physical design of situations to make them less attractive for potential offenders. As Aransiola and Ceccato note, in attempts to reduce crime opportunities and the rewards of committing a crime, locks, cameras, lighting sensors and remote aerial vehicles (drones) are examples of technologies that are finding a place in crime prevention in many rural landscapes around the world.

For instance, if potential offenders know that farmers in a region are present on their properties, they may look for regions where farms are equally attractive in terms of reward but which have been left unattended. However, if offenders find out that in this region farms differ in level of protection, they may direct their actions towards those farms that are less risky. Additionally, if some of these unattended farms are equipped with heavy crime prevention devices (such as guard dogs, good illumination, modern locks, CCTV cameras) and formal and informal social control is present (such as regular police patrols, neighbours keeping an eye on the property), motivated offenders may move their search for potential targets elsewhere, unless the reward is large enough to outweigh the risk of being caught.

Interestingly, physical elements such as the design of the barn and farm buildings and gates fulfill a protective function, whilst equipment features such as well-positioned windows, locks and video surveillance have a guarding function. Thus, the absence of capable guardians may be partly offset by the design and arrangement of the physical environment. However, capable guardians can vary greatly in behaviour and factors fundamental in defining a place as a crime attractor, though can also not vary.

Crime opportunities do not appear randomly over space, and especially not in rural areas. Brantingham and Brantingham argue that the key to obtaining a better understanding of the dynamics of crime is to consider that crime reflects an individual's activities during the day, week or different seasons. Primarily tested in urban rather than in rural environments, this theoretical approach utilizes components of the environment such as activity nodes, paths between nodes, areas and edges (such as neighbourhoods) and the socio-economic backdrop, in conjunction with the routine movements of the population, to explain crime distribution over space and time. In rural areas, crime may concentrate at farms close to urban centers (within the perpetrator's spatial awareness) and less so in remote rural areas (see Ceccato, 2016).

Past and current research, as Aransiola and Ceccato point out in their review of technology applied to crime prevention in rural settings, has shown that rural areas have endemic characteristics which nurture specific crime opportunities, offering particular opportunities for situational crime prevention that may differ from those found in urban areas. Although the current evidence for situational crime prevention effectiveness in urban areas is substantial, more evidence from research on rural areas is needed, especially in contexts other than those in the Global North.

Suggested readings

Aransiola, J.T. and Ceccato, V. (2020) 'The role of modern technology in situational crime prevention in rural areas: A review of literature', in A. Harkness (ed) *Rural Crime Prevention: Theories, Tactics and Techniques*, London: Routledge, pp. 58–72.

Brantingham, P. and Brantingham, P. (2021) 'Crime pattern theory', in H. Pontell (ed) *Oxford Research Encyclopedia of Criminology and Criminal Justice*. Available from: https://oxfordre.com/criminology.

Ceccato, V. (2016) *Rural Crime and Community Safety*, London: Routledge.

Cohen, L.E. and Felson, M. (1979) 'Social change and crime rate trends: A routine activity approach', *American Sociological Review*, 44: 588–608.

Cornish, D. and Clarke, R. (2016) 'The rational choice perspective', in R. Wortley and M. Townsley (eds) *Environmental Criminology and Crime Analysis: Situating the Theory, Analytic Approach and Application*, London: Routledge, pp. 48–80.

Eck, J.E. and Clarke R.V. (2019) 'Situational crime prevention: Theory, practice and evidence', in M. Krohn, N. Hendrix, G. Penly Hall and A. Lizotte (eds) *A Handbook on Crime and Deviance*, Cham: Springer, pp. 354–83.

12

Safety and Security Studies

Gorazd Meško and Andrej Sotlar

Safety is a perception on the part of individuals that places are not dangerous or that they are not at risk to injury or crime; security is the protection of a person, building, organization or country from crime or attacks by foreign countries or other outside entities. As a combination, safety and security are fields of study in criminology and criminal justice, and differ from and are not to be confused with security studies per se, with the latter part of political science and international relations. Security studies deal with security in international relations, whilst safety and security studies together predominantly address internal security matters of the state and of the peoples and communities within.

Safety and security studies can be found in many universities of Central and Eastern Europe, but also in Western Europe and in the United States. In this context, it is necessary to define safety and security with quite clear distinctions, even though sometimes the terms are used interchangeably. Many languages do not make a distinction between safety and security and consider both terms as one, but not so in English.

The term 'safety' refers to the condition of being protected from aspects of a situation that are likely to cause harm to individuals. Also, the term safety can be used to refer to the state at which one has control over things that might cause or increase harm; hence protecting oneself against unintended risks. 'Security' is broadly used to refer to the protection of individuals, organizations and assets against external threats and criminal activities that can be directed to such entities, hence rendering them inactive. It is important to note that security is highly focused on the deliberate actions that are geared towards inflicting harm on an individual, organization or even assets.

The study of safety and security is defined as the devotion of time and attention to gaining knowledge, especially by reading literature and conducting research, that increases understanding and knowledge about the dimensions of risks and harms from victimization. Universities, where safety and security studies are taught and researched, emphasize the role of the United Nations Sustainable Development Goals and other quality-of-life issues related to security and safety, especially concerning resilient communities and human and community security as well as social cohesion.

The International Classification of Education defines security services as an educational discipline from bachelor degrees to master's and doctoral studies. Another classification would define criminal justice and security studies as a convergence of two fields of studies – criminology and criminal justice, with security studies as a hybrid discipline focusing on the protection of people and property. Its focus is more on practical, professional perspectives of understanding safety and security threats (including crime) and legal and legitimate ways for the provision of safety and security (state, local or private).

Several academic institutions globally cover safety and security studies. For example, the Faculty of Criminal Justice and Security of the University of Maribor, Slovenia, aims at examining phenomena associated with safety and security, and with developing and studying mechanisms developed by society to ensure the safety and security of the state, local communities, companies and individuals against actions that can harm these entities. For example, the Institute of Criminal Justice and Security at Maribor has conducted a research project on local safety and security, emphasizing both urban and rural criminological perspectives. As well, it seeks to review and revise theories related to safety and security, including their application to the social, economic and cultural contexts of rural environments in Eastern Europe and around the world.

One research project by Meško (2019–24) deals with rural perspectives on local safety and security. The project includes the provision of security by various state agencies operating on a local level, and safety issues of individuals and groups of people, such as civil society initiatives and organizations (such as voluntary fire brigades, civil protection and health emergency services). On the one hand, the goals of the project are related to the understanding of the nature and extent of reported crime, misdemeanours and perceptions of crime and other security threats in rural settings. On the other hand, the police and other criminal justice institutions' capacity to maintain a civil society, including social cohesion and informal control, were also part of the research.

As pointed out by Meško, the field of local safety and security in rural communities includes a vast array of research topics. These include an analysis of reported security threats; crime and perceptions of the safety of residents; cooperation of security institutions and organizations; informal and formal social control; policing (especially community-oriented policing); the efficiency of state and local institutions; legal perspectives on safety and security; human and civil rights perspectives; security partnerships in local communities; prevailing methods of self-help; tactics for self-protection; crime prevention (physical, social and situational); quality-of-life perspectives related to perceptions of safety and the use of public spaces by citizens; and satisfaction with the quality and accessibility of services of local governments, local wardens and inspectorates, health and social services, non-governmental organizations in the field of safety and security (especially voluntary fire brigades) and issues associated with cybersecurity.

Suggested readings
Ceccato, V. (2016) *Rural Crime and Community Safety*, London: Routledge.
Harkness, A. (ed) (2020) *Rural Crime Prevention: Theory, Tactics and Techniques*, London: Routledge.
Meško, G. (ed) (2021) *Varnost v lokalnih skupnostih – primerjava med urbanimi in ruralnimi perspektivami* [Local Safety and Security – between Rural and Urban Perspectives], Maribor: Univerzitetna založba Univerze v Mariboru.
Meško, G. (2020) 'Rural criminology: A challenge for the future', *European Journal of Crime, Criminal Law and Criminal Justice*, 1(28): 3–13.
United Nations Development Programme (UNDP) (n.d.) *Community Security*, Available from: https://www.rolhr.undp.org/content/ruleoflaw/en/2019/Focus/Community-security.html.

13

The Anthropocene and Criminological Theory

Clifford Shearing, Emiline Smith and Jared Walters

Extensive resource extraction serving a fast-growing global human population has, on the one hand, brought about rapid economic growth and prosperity, whilst on the other hand has caused climate change, pollution, destruction of ecosystems and species extinction. As a result, a geological transition is underway in which the earth is shifting out of the Holocene epoch (that is, time since the last ice age) to a post-Holocene era. This new era is characterized by degraded environmental conditions that differ significantly from the 'safe operating space' (see Rockström et al, 2009) that humans, along with all other species, have depended upon for their wellbeing and survival. A proposed term to identify this new era, the Anthropocene, emphasizes how humans have impacted these developments as they transitioned from being 'insignificant animals' to being a significant 'geological force' (Holley and Shearing, 2018) over the past couple of centuries.

Ontological and epistemological developments that recognize the human/non-human entanglements that the Anthropocene foregrounds, have challenged conceptions that posit the existence of two *sui generis* realities, namely a social world studied by social science and a natural world studied by natural sciences, in favour of a single socio-material reality. In understanding the rapidly increasing impact of human activities on the natural world, considerable attention has been paid to urban-based industrialization – particularly the extraction and use of fossil fuels – and its effects on global climate change and rising sea levels.

Less front and centre have been the broadly conceived 'rural': countryside and ocean-based industrial developments such as extensive land and ocean-based harvesting of minerals (industrial-scale mining) and food production through industrial-scale fishing, as well as industrial-scale agriculture and aquiculture. This (over)harvesting of resources has been facilitated by the largely uncoordinated and poorly regulated use of a plethora of technological advancements, most recently artificial intelligence. Technological advancements have also been employed to mitigate or adapt to the effect of humanity's ever-increasing consumption of natural resources.

These planetary developments have profoundly changed rural terrains, and the non-human and human lives that exist within them. For example, lifestyles associated with agriculture and aquaculture have been fundamentally impacted as food production methods have become increasingly industrialized; a development that has negatively impacted biodiversity. At a human level, these developments have been associated with a massive migration to cities and dramatic shifts in the lifestyles of humans living within rural landscapes and seascapes. Terrains have been fundamentally altered by, amongst other things, mining, loss of topsoil, desertification, widespread toxins and a host of other developments (IPCC, 2019).

Recognizing the significance of this transition, criminological attention is increasingly shifting from criminal, unlawful behaviours to harmful, immoral behaviours. Environmentally focused criminologists, for example 'green criminologists', have focused attention on the regulatory arrangements that have sought to shape, and have shaped, geologically significant socio-economic developments that have resulted in local and global harms. This includes proposed arrangements to criminalize, as 'ecocide', the 'wilful destruction of natural environments' (Crook et al, 2018).

A central criminological concern that impacts both urban and rural terrains has been a concern with human and non-human rights, injustices and inequalities. A crucial area of concern has been the fact that those least responsible for these 'ecocidal' developments so often have borne the burden of Anthropocene impacts, in part because of exploitative systems of colonialism that continue to structure global inequalities. Similar concerns have been raised with respect to non-human entities, by thinkers who assign equal rights, roles and agency to humans and non-humans as part of one socio-material reality. A notable development here has been the incipient emergence of the idea that non-human entities can, and should, have legally recognized rights: for example, the recognition of rivers as rights-bearing entities in constitutional provisions.

The Anthropocene requires epistemological shifts that recognize human influences on ecological systems, with which they are entangled. This has implications for the new harms, risks and injustices that have emerged as a consequence of these socio-material entanglements. There is a pressing need to include more diverse perspectives if we are to successfully move beyond the conceptual framings, and associated practices, that have shifted ecological systems beyond the 'safe operating space' of the Holocene epoch. These developments, and the emerging responses to them, that may well include criminalization, are having, and will have, profound implications for rural practices and lifestyles and the possibilities for equality and justice that extends beyond humans.

Suggested readings
Crook, M., Short, D. and South, N. (2018) 'Ecocide, genocide, capitalism and colonialism: Consequences for Indigenous peoples and global ecosystems environments', *Theoretical Criminology*, 22(3): 298–317.
Holley, C. and Shearing, C. (2018) 'Thriving on a pale blue dot: Criminology and the Anthropocene', in C. Holley and C. Shearing (eds) *Criminology and the Anthropocene*, London: Routledge, pp. 1–24.
Holm, N. and Taffel, S. (2017) *Ecological Entanglements in the Anthropocene*, Lanham, MD: Lexington Books.
IPCC (Intergovernmental Panel on Climate Change) (2019) 'Summary for Policymakers', in P.R. Shukla, J. Skea, E. Calvo, Buendia, V. Masson-Delmotte, H.- O. Pörtner, D. C. Roberts, P. Zhai, R. Slade, S. Connors, R. van Diemen, M. Ferrat, E. Haughey, S. Luz, S. Neogi, M. Pathak, J. Petzold, J. Portugal Pereira, P. Vyas, E. Huntley, K. Kissick, M. Belkacemi and J. Malley (eds) *Climate Change and Land: An IPCC Special Report on Climate Change, Desertification, Land Degradation, Sustainable Land Management, Food Security, and Greenhouse Gas Fluxes in Terrestrial Ecosystems*. Available from: https://www.ipcc.ch/site/assets/uploads/2019/11/SRCCL-Full-Report-Compiled-191128.pdf.
Rockström, J., Steffen, W., Noone, K., Persson, A., Chapin, F., Lambin, E., Lenton, T., Scheffer, M., Folke, C., Schellnhuber, H., Nykvist, B., de Wit, C., Hughes, T., van der Leeuw, S. and Rodhe, H.J. (2009) 'Planetary boundaries: Exploring the safe operating space for humanity', *Ecology and Society*, 14(2). Available from: http://www.ecologyandsociety.org/vol14/iss2/art32/.

PART II
Rural Crime Studies

Introduction to Part II: Rural Crime Studies

Joseph F. Donnermeyer and Alistair Harkness

This section considers an array of specific types of crime; all entries are focused on studies of particular crime types which are rural-specific.

One of the challenges in assembling this section of the encyclopedia, though, was determining what to include and what to exclude. Stock theft is a quintessential rural crime, so of course was included without hesitation. There are many other topics in criminology which equally apply to rural and urban settings, though – one example is cybercrime – but yet there exist specific nuances about this when considering rural contextualization.

We have been quite conscious in limiting the entries to those things with a critical mass of rural work. Some entries in this section draw upon an established and burgeoning suite of theoretical and empirical scholarship; others are topics upon which scant rural-specific study has hitherto been attempted.

This section has been divided into two. The first canvasses 17 different topics for which 'people and crime' is the predominant focus. That is, the offending and victimization for which rural people are either perpetrators or victims of offending behaviours. The second attends to 13 topics for which property, animals, the environment and other targets are the primary focus.

The entries contained within this section is not exhaustive. There remains scope for other topics to be studied, and the editors of the encyclopedia hope that these entries will prompt scholars and practitioners – emerging and established, and regardless of geographic location – to engage in original research, data collection and publication to expand further collective understandings of crime in rural settings.

People and Crime

14

Abuse against Children, the Elderly and within Families

Sarah Wendt

To understand abuse against children, the elderly and within families in rural settings, a comprehension of family violence in general is needed. The World Health Organization recognizes that family violence occurs in all settings and amongst all socio-economic, religious, and cultural groups. Furthermore, the global burden of family violence is borne by women. Family violence can encompass child or elder abuse, or intimate partner violence (also known as domestic violence). Family violence refers to any behaviour within a family that causes physical, psychological, sexual, social or financial harm and it includes controlling and threatening behaviours.

Distinct rural features

It is difficult to ascertain accurate rates of family violence in any context, and this includes in rural settings. Research reviewed by DeKeseredy (2009) and Wendt (2021) indicates that women, children and the elderly living in rural places are more likely to have experienced family violence because of unique geographical and social structures. For example, reporting and seeking help can be difficult due to geographical isolation, lack of transportation options, not having access to income and lack of specialized services. Other factors that can influence the under-reporting of family violence in rural settings includes social values and norms that shape rural communities; for example, fear of stigma, shame and notions of family privacy.

The international rural context

Research has shown that there are common characteristics of family violence in rural settings across the globe.

First, geographical and social isolation compound secrecy and therefore deter families from seeking support, as found in research in the by Carrington et al (2013) on violence against women in rural communities.

Second, rural masculinity or male peer support have been identified as risk factors that shape family violence experiences in particular ways for women and family members, contributing to high levels of collective efficacy that promote abuse and discourage seeking help. Violent expressions of 'hypermasculinity' in rural settings shape the hidden nature of different forms of abuse (DeKeseredy, 2009; Carrington et al, 2013).

Third, by the nature of industries such as farming and agriculture in rural settings, families often have complex financial arrangements. Studies, including Wendt and colleagues (2021) on coping with violence, have found that financial dependency makes it difficult for women and their children to leave abusive relationships, and older parents often do not want to jeopardize inheritance, assets and property. Fourth, higher rates of gun ownership are seen in rural settings, and research has shown that victims of abuse often live in fear with the constant threat of harm by such weapons.

Despite this commonality, there is significant diversity in rural settings including social, cultural and economic characteristics. There are markedly different experiences of abuse for groups, including First Nations families and communities in colonized countries, culturally and linguistically diverse families, those with disabilities and those in same sex relationships. However, there is an absence in the family violence literature that explores such diversity of experiences in rural settings. Furthermore, little is known about rural immigrants and refugees, those who live in public housing or have transit and mobile lifestyles.

Experiences of abuse can also be shaped by the economic characteristics of the rural setting. For example, where generational family property, farms and businesses feature and reputations are highly valued, these contexts can discourage family members from disclosing or seeking help for family violence. Masculine constructions of 'mateship' that can dominate mining environments along with a drinking culture has also been shown to shape women's fear and impacts on women's decision to seek help or end a violent relationship. The influx of affluence to rural settings, it has been suggested, can cause socio-economic disadvantage and unemployment of local people and therefore make it harder for find alternative housing options. Finally, environmental disasters have been identified as impacting on rural settings in unique ways with research emerging showing that interpersonal violence and sexual assault can increase during or after a disaster.

Service provision

It has become well known that services for men living in rural settings who perpetrate family violence against their parents, partners and children are rare. Furthermore, men are often not held accountable for their abuse for two main reasons. First, the community may act to protect men, particularly if they are of high social standing or have visible roles in a community. Second, poor understandings of family violence by health, social and legal services in rural settings have been identified as a significant issue for children, women and the elderly who are survivors of family violence. Inadequate or unsympathetic police and criminal justice responses can be common and, hence, contribute to and reinforce male peer support networks and ideals of rural masculinity (see George and Harris, 2015).

For families living in rural settings, studies have established that there are challenges that affect both the provision of and access to services. These include service scarcity and distances that families must travel to reach appropriate services. Owing to distance and isolation, services in rural settings can then experience higher costs to operate, long waiting lists, lack of affordable legal services and delayed responses due to staff shortages and travel throughout geographical remoteness.

Suggested readings

Carrington, K., McIntosh, A., Hogg, R. and Scott, J. (2013) 'Rural masculinities and the internalisation of violence in agricultural communities', *International Journal of Rural Criminology*, 2(1): 1–22.

DeKeseredy, W. (2021) *Woman Abuse in Rural Places*, London: Routledge.

George, A. and Harris, B. (2015) *Landscapes of Violence: Women Surviving Family Violence in Regional and Rural Victoria*, Geelong: Deakin University, Centre for Rural and Regional Law and Justice.

Wendt, S. (2009) *Domestic Violence in Rural Australia*, Sydney: The Federation Press.

Wendt, S., Bryant, L., Chung, D. and Elder, A. (2015) *Exploring Rural Women's Coping Experiences: State of Knowledge Paper*, Sydney: Australia's National Research Organisation for Women's Safety.

15

Consumer Fraud

Cassandra Cross

Fraud is a global issue. Whilst not new, technology has driven an exponential increase in the ability of offenders to target victims universally, including those in a rural context. Smartphones and other internet-connected devices have driven many positive developments across our everyday lives. However, it also increases exposure to fraud, usually targeting victims from outside their own jurisdiction.

A background to fraud

As described by Button and Cross (2017), fraud can be defined as the use of deception to gain a financial advantage. Synonymous with the concepts of lying and cheating, it uses a variety of techniques to manipulate and exploit others into providing a financial benefit (usually through either direct money transfers or personal credentials) under false pretences. In most cases, victims are persuaded to take actions that they would otherwise not do, under different circumstances.

Whilst there are endless plotlines used by offenders to perpetrate fraud, there are commonalities to some approaches. Advance fee fraud uses the future promise of a large amount of money in return for a smaller up-front payment. This is often seen in investment schemes and inheritance notifications. Romance fraud uses the guise of a genuine relationship to gain financial reward from the victim. During the relationship, an offender will ask a victim to send money for a variety of circumstances (including medical emergencies, criminal justice matters or business transactions).

Phishing is one of the most common ways that offenders gain personal credentials. Phishing usually comes in the form of an email purporting to be from a legitimate organization, requesting users to click on a link or to reply to the email directly to provide/confirm personal details. Once a victim does this, they expose themselves to identity crime and the potential for fraud.

The cost of fraud

Fraud is a global issue with millions of victims losing billions of dollars. In 2020, the Internet Crime Complaint Centre (United States) recorded fraud losses totalling $USD 4.2 billion, up from $USD 3.5 billion in 2019. In the United Kingdom, ActionFraud reported losses of £2.35 billion for 2020–1. Similarly, in Australia, the Australian Competition and Consumer Commission (ACCC) reported losses of over $AUD 851 million in 2020, up from $AUD 632 million in 2019 (see suggested readings). Importantly, fraud is a problem across both the Global North and Global South. For example, Hong Kong police reported that over $HK 8 billion was laundered through bank accounts in their country from fraud victims during 2020.

Whilst the monetary losses from fraud are significant, there are corresponding non-financial harms which further exacerbate the harm and suffering experienced by victims. This includes a deterioration of physical health, depression, relationship breakdown, unemployment, homelessness and, in extreme cases, suicide. Attached to this is a strong victim blaming discourse that associates a high level of shame and stigma to fraud victimization. This has the effect of inhibiting victims from disclosing to family, friends and/or third parties, leaving them to suffer in silence and isolation.

These barriers impact reporting rates of fraud. Less than one third of all fraud offences are estimated as reported to authorities, with online fraud being even lower. For those who do report, the experience can be further traumatizing, with them not being believed, being humiliated and belittled, or unable to lodge a complaint with an agency.

Of those who do report, the evidence suggests that fraud cuts across all demographics. Whilst the stereotype is that only older persons are vulnerable to fraud, this is not reflected in known statistics. For example, the ACCC demonstrated how each age group was targeted by different categories of fraud. Fraud perpetrated across all communication platforms from the internet, text message, phone calls, facsimiles and face-to-face. It affects both men and women, with men recording higher financial losses from investment fraud, and women recording higher monetary losses to romance fraud. In this way, it is argued that all individuals are vulnerable to fraud, if targeted in the right way at the right time. Further, fraud vulnerability is not fixed, but can be viewed across a continuum which is contingent upon a range of static and dynamic circumstances.

Fraud in a rural context

The evolution of technology has revolutionized society. In particular, the internet has reduced the physical barriers between individuals across local and global contexts. Whilst the internet has not created fraud, it has significantly altered the ways it is perpetrated. Further, it has exponentially increased the potential victim pool at a global scale. This is especially relevant in a rural context, as noted by Cross (2020). Whilst previously those in regional and remote locations may not have been exposed to fraud in the same ways as those in metropolitan areas, this is no longer the case. Instead, increased connectivity and use of devices has opened up communication channels between victims and offenders.

This means that anyone with a smartphone or a device connected to the internet can be exposed to fraud, and is liable to being targeted. Despite the surge in internet connectivity and the embracing of online platforms to conduct daily activities, there has been limited exploration of how this affects those in rural contexts. Rather, most fraud research conceptualizes geography in terms of state or national jurisdiction. This posits all fraud victims as a homogenous group in relation to location, without accounting for any nuance or complexity arising from a rural context.

Based on existing fraud research and knowledge of rural contexts, those in regional and remote communities are likely to have a different vulnerability profile to those in urban centres. This will impact on the ways in which offenders can successfully target those in rural areas, and further impact the ability of victims to disclose victimization, report to authorities and seek help in the aftermath of any victimization (see Button et al, 2009; Cross et al, 2016). This is particularly relevant to approaches of investment fraud, affinity fraud (schemes which seek to exploit personal and community connections of victims) and romance fraud.

Overall, there is a critical need to better understand the ways in which fraud is experienced by those in rural contexts. Existing fraud research lacks any meaningful discernment of the urban–rural divide. Fraud devastates the lives of millions globally, including those in rural areas, and it is imperative to determine how to better prevent and support those individuals who are successfully targeted in an appropriate manner.

Suggested readings

Australian Competition and Consumer Commission (2019) *Targeting Scams: Report of the ACCC on Scam Activity 2018*. Available from: https://www.accc.gov.au/publications/targeting-scams-report-on-scam-activity/targeting-scams-report-of-the-accc-on-scam-activity-2018.

Button, M. and Cross, C. (2017) *Cyber Fraud, Scams and Their Victims*, London: Routledge.

Button, M., Lewis, C. and Tapley, J. (2009) *A Better Deal for Fraud Victims*, London: Centre for Counter Fraud Studies.

Cross, C. (2020) 'Preventing fraud victimisation in rural areas', in A. Harkness (ed) *Rural Crime Prevention: Theory, Tactics and Techniques*, London: Routledge, pp. 165–78.

Cross, C., Richards, K. and Smith, R.G. (2016) *Improving Responses to Online Fraud Victims: An Examination of Reporting and Support Final Report*, Canberra, ACT: Criminology Research Grants.

16

Corporate and State Crimes

Victoria E. Collins

Rural corporate and state crimes disproportionately impact people, communities and environments in rural areas. These crimes vary across localities, states, regions and continents, and involve a large array of actors – making them, and their study, complex. Examples include, although not limited to, atrocity crimes, toxic waste dumping, environmental harms such as corporate polluting and employment abuses such as the exploitation and violation of the rights of workers across many industries that depend on rural populations (such as fossil fuels, sweatshops, farming and so on). To understand the complexity of rural corporate and state crimes it is necessary to define the terms 'corporate crime' and 'state crime'.

Corporate crime

Corporate crimes are illegal behaviours or acts committed by corporations or those working for or on behalf of a corporation. The criminological study of corporate crime falls under the larger field of white-collar crime attributed to Edwin H. Sutherland (1940). In his seminal address to the American Sociological Society in 1939, Sutherland drew academic and public attention to crimes committed by those in the upper classes, including those in respected business.

In his later work, *White Collar Crime* published in 1949, Sutherland explored the different forms of harm committed by major corporations as well as those in the upper classes protecting their own interests. He included both the organizational deviance of corporations, but also heavily emphasized an individualistic framework. The variability in which Sutherland used the term created significant ambiguity about the 'proper' definition, leading to a decades-long definitional debate. Independent of the specifics of the debate, what is important here is that two core types of white-collar crime emerged: corporate (organizational) and occupational crime.

State crime

Like corporate crime, state crime can also be considered under the broader definition of white-collar crime. Introduced as a concept by William Chambliss' 1989 seminal address to the American Society of Criminology, state crime addresses the harms perpetrated by states, their governments, militaries and actors both historically and in modern times.

There is also a definitional quagmire surrounding the topic, with two dominating competing definitional frameworks having been advanced: the social harms or zemiological perspective and the legalistic perspective. The former perspective has its origins in the work of Herman and Julia Schwendinger (1970) who argued that 'crime' as a concept is too narrow in its definition. They argue that there exist basic human rights that ensure equality and any infringement on these rights should constitute a criminal act. In contrast, the legalistic perspective argues that state crimes are only those behaviours that violate criminal law. Through this lens, a state only commits a crime when their behaviour directly violates their own criminal laws. This argument has been built upon to include state violations of international laws such as human rights law, principles, agreements, principles established by international bodies, as well as varying composites of human rights law and international legal codes. These opposing approaches have led to disagreement over the types of behaviours that should be considered when studying state crime.

Direct and indirect rural influences

Independent of the definitional debate, the study of corporate and state crime has resulted in a wealth of academic literature that is rich and diverse. This includes analyses of crimes committed by states in conjunction with corporations, termed state–corporate crimes. Whilst there is considerable variability across type, harms caused, actors involved and global geographies, many of these corporate, state–corporate or state-perpetrated harms have a relationship with the rural, either directly or indirectly. Those that are direct are more easily identified, whereby the corporate or state actions or omissions lead to harm in the regions in which they are operating.

An example of a direct rural state–corporate crime is the environmental destruction and chronic illnesses due to corporate toxic waste dumping in rural regions where there is lax enforcement of state and local regulatory protections. Whether it is chemical, nuclear, toxic or electronic waste, poor rural communities are often targeted for their disposal, meaning already under-resourced vulnerable people are subjected to a multitude of harms that impact their environment, economies and health.

Indirect instances of rural corporate and state crimes are more complex. In many situations they are migratory, transregional and transnational in nature, especially as it relates to globalization. Rural corporate and state crimes are not only impacted or facilitated by global markets, but by what happens in urban settings. Likewise, urban situated corporate and state crimes are impacted by the rural.

Consider the example of sweatshops in Bangladesh's garment district. The harms perpetrated against sweatshop workers are often subsumed under the heading of everyday corporate capitalism, neglecting the responsibility of both the state to their citizens, and the employment rights owed by the corporation to their employees. Important to the rural are the push–pull factors that attract large numbers of workers to Dhaka from the surrounding rural provinces. A large percentage of the workforce migrate to the factory district from rural areas with little understanding of the lack of regulatory enforcement and conditions in which they will be employed, all of which pose significant risk to their health and safety.

This rural to urban migration that fuels the workforce also impacts migration households and rural community economies as workers send back monies to their families supporting their communities of origin. This push–pull economic relationship between the urban and the rural extends beyond the spatial demographics and the centralization of factories in the urban garment district, to the geopolitical and economic realities of globalization, global capital markets and the rural provinces that feed, depend and suffer the consequences of labour and the exploitative practices.

Studying rural corporate and state crime

Studying rural corporate and state crimes means being well-versed in local and regional policies, national and international laws, as well as geopolitical, historical and socio-economic happenings that inform not only their commission but the harms that result. The challenge to their study revolves around the enduring definitional debates both in the study of corporate and state crime, and rural criminology more broadly, as well as their complexity and variability. This may explain why in the field of criminology there is still little corporate and state crime scholarship focusing explicitly on the rural.

Suggested readings
Barak, G. (ed) (2015) *The Routledge International Handbook of the Crimes of the Powerful*, London: Routledge.

Chambliss, W.J. (1989) 'State-organized crime – The American Society of Criminology, 1988 Presidential Address', *Criminology*, 27(2): 183–207.

Rothe, D.L. and Kauzlarich, D. (2016) *Crimes of the Powerful: An Introduction*, London: Routledge.

Schwendinger, H. and Schwendinger, J. (1970) 'Defenders of order or guardians of human rights?', *Issues in Criminology*, 5: 123–57.

Sutherland, E.H. (1940) 'White-collar criminality', *American Sociological Review*, 5(1): 1–12.

17

Cybercrime and Cybersecurity

Qingli Meng and Joseph F. Donnermeyer

It was not that long ago that cybercrime and concerns about cybersecurity would be considered as an exotic type of crime, one that only happens in the high-tech world of computers and software, far removed from the everyday lives of people and businesses around the world. Those days are now long gone.

Cybercrime may be defined as an action that is considered illegal by governmental laws and regulations related to electronic forms of communication and communication networks. It involves the use of the internet, computers and related technologies in the commission of crime. Cybersecurity is the actions taken to protect computer systems and networks from attacks that steal information and disrupt the flow of information.

One primary reason why cybercrime has shifted from an exotic crime to an everyday crime is quite simple. The information environment is now hyper-connected, dynamic and evolving – and ownership of computers increases every year. For example, the World Bank estimated in 2019 that nearly half of all households worldwide have a computer in their homes, even though the presence of computers in private residences can vary widely. In countries with advanced market economies, the rates exceed 80 per cent, whilst in less developed and poor countries rates are as low as 30 per cent.

The adoption and ownership of computers has multiplied the amount of e-commerce, which is now a large part of the economies of many societies around the world. Over 2.4 billion people, it is estimated, now make online purchases, and that number rises steadily from year to year. Further, nearly two-thirds of shopping begins online, even though the actual purchase may be in-person or by telephone. Add in the number of people who rely on computers for personal and business communication, and the ubiquity of the cyber world is revolutionary when compared with the 1990s.

Also, the widespread use of tablet devices and smart phones now makes everyday lifestyles for most of the planet's population at least partially dependent on the maintenance of the internet. As documented by Koeze and Popper (2020), the COVID-19 pandemic accelerated this dependency, from countless Zoom meetings for businesses, schools and to replace face-to-face visits with distant family and friends, to shopping for everything, from food to prescriptions and clothes.

With new technological developments of any kind comes new opportunities for crime, but not necessarily new kinds of crime. It is like the proverbial phrase 'new wine in old bottles', meaning that the actual offenses of cybercrime are about the same as those committed before computer technology came along. However, the modus operandi have changed. In a recent survey of over 10,000 adults commissioned by Norton and conducted by The Harris poll in 10 countries, including Australia, Japan and the United States, two-thirds of adults are spending more time online but admit they do not know how to prevent a cybercrime (see Norton, 2021). Moreover, more than half of those surveyed experienced a cybercrime over within the 12 months prior to answering the survey. The most frequent crime included the detection of malicious software on their electronic devices, unauthorized access to email accounts and unauthorized access to social media accounts. The most common reaction was anger, followed by feelings of stress and vulnerability. The average time spent solving a cyber victimization by individuals, that is, fixing the software, was nearly seven hours, with an estimated 2.7 billion hours of lost time globally.

In general, cybercrimes include varieties of theft, fraud and violence (see Hill and Marion, 2016). There is phishing, which are attempts to collect personal and other forms of information from people by posting messages on social media sites or through email, pretending to be legitimate inquiries. Hacking bank accounts and other places where personal information is stored can lead to serious financial loss. Identity theft victimizes millions of people who frequently suffer financial loss when the hacker uses a victim's personal information to apply for credit cards and other assets, or to remove funds from banks and other accounts. Ransomware refers to hacking into the information of a person or business and holding that information for ransom before it is released. Electronic forms of property theft or piracy include posting copyrighted materials for free download. Not only does this steal from the authors and artists, but it is also a crime in which many people participate, taking advantage of the savings and thinking little of the consequences on victims. Then, there is consumer fraud through false advertisements: products are never delivered or the commodity sent is of much poorer quality or construction than what was advertised.

Cybercrime can also include online advertisements and social media for prostitution, drugs and the solicitation of minors to meet in person at which time the underaged child will be sexually abused, and online fraud associated with the internet is also used for locating and sharing pornography, including child pornography. Viewing pornography is associated with family abuse, especially violence against women.

Is there a rural dimension to cybercrime? It is common to think of lower adoption of computers and other electronic technologies by rural people, but that depends on the country. Furthermore, it might be assumed that rural people are more vulnerable because they are less aware of ways to protect themselves from cybercrimes. However, there is no real evidence to suggest that the rural–urban divide on these issues is large in most parts of the world.

One area where there may be a greater presence of cybercrime committed against rural people is cyber-bullying and cyber-stalking, especially actions directed against rural women. Technology facilitating forms of violence, as described by both Harris and Woodlock (2019) and Dragiewicz et al (2019) describes the dynamics for how these new technologies combine with older, patriarchal norms that are more frequently found in rural settings to promote violence against women. Moreover, racist and hate groups are more likely to be rurally located in many countries, but the internet provides them with ways to reach others around the world with messages promoting violence against minorities.

This jurisdiction-free dimension of cybercrime blurs the rural–urban divide. Increasingly, agriculture producers are increasingly becoming the new targets of cybercriminals. In June 2021, a Russian cybercrime cell carried out a ransomware attack on the world's largest meat producer until a ransom was paid. Similarly, in September 2021, Russian hackers levelled a ransomware attack on a farming co-operative in Iowa in the United States. Hackers demanded a large ransom which, unless paid, would result in the computer networks being locked and thus disrupting and paralysing the food supply chains for chickens, pigs and cattle.

Suggested readings

Dragiewicz, M., Burgess, J., Matamoros-Fernández, A., Salter, M., Suzor, N.P., Woodlock, D. and Harris, B. (2018) 'Technologies of coercive control: Domestic violence and the competing roles of social media platforms', *Feminist Media Studies*, 18(5): 609–25.

Harris, B.A. and Woodlock, D. (2019) 'Digital coercive control: Insights from two landmark domestic violence studies', *British Journal of Criminology*, 59(3): 530–50.

Hill, J.B. and Marion, N.E. (2016) *Introduction to Cybercrime: Computer Crimes, Laws, and Policing in the 21st Century*, Westport, CT: Praeger.

Koeze, E. and Popper, N. (2020) 'The virus changed the way we internet', *The New York Times*, 7 April. Available from: https://www.nytimes.com/interactive/2020/04/07/technology/coronavirus-internet-use.html.

Norton (2021) *Norton Cyber Safety Insights Report Global Results*, The Harris Poll, May. Available from: https://now.symassets.com/content/dam/norton/campaign/NortonReport/2021/2021_NortonLifeLock_Cyber_Safety_Insights_Report_Global_Results.pdf.

18

Dark Tourism

Jenny Wise

Defining dark tourism

According to Walby and Piche (2011), the term 'dark tourism' broadly refers to travel and tourist sites that provide representations of death, disasters, atrocities and other tragedies for either pedagogical and/or commercial purposes. Dark tourism offers many tourists a way to remember (and at times to celebrate), understand and confront a region or nation's darker aspects of history, heritage and culture. Further, dark tourist sites can play an important role in creating and building identities as well as sustaining economies (regional and national).

Dark tourism is usually considered to encompass travelling to sites of atrocity, such as Holocaust museums and sites; war sites or graves; cemeteries; convict and (usually) decommissioned penal institutions; courthouses and police museums; and sites of (or associated with) sensational crimes. However, it can also include travelling to sites of colonial violence, locations associated with bushrangers, crime and ghost tours – and there is even the potential for tourism of bushfire sites or 'deadly towns'.

Whilst there is substantial debate over what actually constitutes 'dark tourism' and what makes a destination 'dark', there is a consensus that travel to places of tragedy, death, destruction and atrocity has had a long history of being a leisure and/or pilgrimage activity. Additionally, it is important to recognize that there are many different types of dark tourist sites with varying aims and levels of 'darkness'. Stone (2006) has developed a 'darkest-lightest' spectrum which can be used to understand the type of experience a dark tourist site is offering, particularly in relation to the emphasis on educational resources versus sites more focused on entertainment.

Where dark tourism has been examined, it has largely focused on those sites located within urban settings. Whilst there has been some recognition and analysis of some rural dark tourism sites, this is still very much an under-researched area.

Rural dark tourism

There are many distinguishing aspects of rural and regional dark tourism travel. When we think of rural spaces, we often conjure an image of beautiful bushland or widespread, peaceful, idyllic countryside. This then becomes the rural idyll or rural utopia and can play a large role in marketing campaigns to attract local and international tourists. Within the rural idyll, communities are portrayed as having wholesome values; strong, close-knit communities and tight kinship systems that supposedly create a high level of social stability.

However, this rural idyll can quickly be challenged and subverted (often aided by growing popular culture references). The rural can become a place of conflict, hardship and violence (and also horror). Rofe (2013) refers to this as rural dystopia, which is described as the darker side of rural places, emphasizing inbreeding, an indifference to the hardships of others and the suspicion and even hostility of outsiders.

More recently, media reports have tended to label some rural areas as evil and rotting from the inside. Away from the urban, rural dystopia are spaces beyond the civilizing influences of cities where conflict and tragedy occur.

Within rural dark tourism, there is often a combination of the rural idyll and rural dystopia. The beauty of the landscape is juxtaposed with the site which inevitably becomes the rural dystopia. Take, for example, Trial Bay Gaol (New South Wales, Australia) and Port Arthur Heritage Site (Tasmania, Australia) – both sites represent 'dark' encounters which are starkly set within a beautiful and tranquil setting. Examining the landscape is vital to understanding the whole tourist experience and how rural and regional sites offer a different experience within dark tourism.

Whilst some communities have been stigmatized by the media with concepts of rural dystopia, others have openly embraced 'darker' tourism activities. As such, rural dystopias can offer communities the opportunity to invest in commercially viable dark tourism activities. Indeed, dark tourism within rural areas is a growing area with many towns choosing to adopt a 'dark tourism strategy' to encourage visitors to the area. According to Rofe (2013, p. 262), consumer-oriented economies are viewed by many government leaders and planners as a 'panacea for rural decline', with tourism as an important element of this economic renewal as rural places are 're-imagined, re-packaged and re-presented for a predominantly urban market'.

Tourism in rural areas can be seen as beneficial for many communities, improving the local economy through the provision of recreational facilities and cultural activities. Yet, in some areas, communities try to distance themselves from rural dystopias and unethical tourism practices. Further, as Kim and Butler (2015) state, dark tourism activities can be seen to foster negative stereotypes of an area and are therefore something to be discouraged, or avoided altogether, for some. There are several examples of rural and regional communities rejecting dark tourism activities within Australia and internationally.

In many cases, whether a community accepts such dark tourism activities often depends upon the length of time between the act of atrocity and the establishment of tourism activities. Yet, in many rural and regional areas, dark tourist activities occur regardless of the community's desires, particularly as sites of death and atrocity, as well as dark tourism itself, become more well known and prominent within popular culture.

Suggested readings

Kim, S. and Butler, G. (2015) 'Local community perspectives towards dark tourism development: The case of Snowtown, South Australia', *Journal of Tourism and Cultural Change*, 13(1): 78–89.

Rofe, M.W. (2013) 'Considering the limits of rural place making opportunities: Rural dystopias and dark tourism', *Landscape Research*, 38(2): 262–72.

Rosser, E. (2013) 'A place for monsters: *Wolf Creek* and the Australian outback', *Monsters and the Monstrous*, 3(2): 73–82.

Stone, P. (2006) 'A dark tourism spectrum: Towards a typology of death and macabre related tourist sites, attractions and exhibitions', *Tourism*, 54(2): 145–60.

Walby, K. and Piche, J. (2011) 'The polysemy of punishment memorialization: Dark tourism and Ontario's penal history museums', *Punishment and Society*, 13(4): 451–72.

19

Drugs and Public Health

Katinka van de Ven and Natalie Thomas

Defining rural drug use and public health

Research has shown that the burden of alcohol and other drug (AOD) use increases with remoteness. The majority of research on rural drug use and harm emanates from the United States, where there has been a clearly documented opioid overdose epidemic in recent times and previous research on other drugs that historically have affected rural populations (see Schalkoff et al, 2020; Thomas et al, 2020). There are distinctive features of rural environments that shape the risk of drug-related harms. Economic, physical, social and policy factors shape rural risk environments (a framework developed by Rhodes, cited in Thomas et al, 2020).

Economic risks

Economic conditions are an important factor in shaping risk in the lives of people using AOD. The decline of industries and loss of manufacturing lead to high unemployment rates and residents living below the poverty line. It also leads to changes in employment opportunities and a lack of opportunities to generate income, making healthcare or some harm reduction options cost-prohibitive.

This macro-environment of economic distress influences micro-environmental risk factors: for instance, job loss leads to the use of AOD to cope with stress or depression from the lack of economic prospects. Research has also shown that economic strains lead people to engage in riskier behaviours such as drug injecting as a means to cut costs associated with use. Owing to the lack of economic opportunities linked with economic restructuring or deterioration, informal economies have grown as alternative means of survival (such as drug dealing and prostitution), shaping the risk of drug-related harm in rural places.

Physical risks

There are several physical conditions that shape drug-related harm in rural areas. The dispersed nature of rural populations and the geographic distances between rural places and urban centres lead to several issues, such as less access to transportation (for example high expenses, limited public transport options) and greater travel to or an inability to access services. These spatial inequalities may lead to an increased risk of future AOD use, overdose and/or risky injection behaviours.

The lack of infrastructure and public transport is also linked with a lack of recreation opportunities in rural areas. AOD use is therefore sometimes seen as a way to alleviate boredom in rural areas. Adding to this is that services located in rural areas often have less qualified and experienced staff and experience difficulties in retaining (specialized) staff.

It is, however, important to note that rural services also have some advantages, particularly during the COVID-19 pandemic. For example, due to the greater availability of space, and often having standalone buildings, it is easier for rural services to comply with physical distancing requirements compared to services located in metropolitan areas (see van de Ven et al, 2021).

Social risks

Social conditions in rural areas are often quite different from those in urban areas, where rural areas often have much smaller populations and are more dispersed across a geographic area. The lack of anonymity afforded to people living in rural towns can discourage them from accessing treatment and/or other services for their drug use to avoid any kind of negative social consequences.

Stigma in rural areas can be more heavily felt where there are conservative attitudes amongst residents. People living in rural areas may also be more reluctant to seek treatment because of concerns about the confidentiality of their AOD treatment. Knowledge about drug use and related harms can also be poorer in rural areas, for example the knowledge about blood-borne virus risks from injecting practices such as sharing injecting equipment.

Some studies (see Paquette and Pollini, 2018; Schalkoff et al, 2020) have shown that 'people who inject drugs' (PWID) in rural settings are more likely to report the sharing of needles and other injection equipment than urban PWID. It is important to note that socio-cultural factors in rural areas can also provide protective factors against substance use and related harms, for example through networks that are disapproving of substance use.

Policy risks

These former conditions coalesce in the 'policy' conditions that have the potential to exacerbate drug-related harm in rural areas. Because of geographical issues, people in rural areas face limited coverage and availability of harm reduction and drug treatment services, which can lead to increased risk of blood-borne viruses, overdose and other drug-related harms.

The accessibility of services is also an issue in rural areas, where there is limited travel and an increased cost to service locations. Where services do exist, they are often under-resourced and providers are busy and constrained for time. Negative provider attitudes can also be an issue in rural areas, along with stigmatizing service provider practices.

Public health responses to drug-related harms in rural areas

There is a complex web of economic, social, geographic and policy factors which put people in rural areas at risk of AOD-related harms. Governments across the globe need to invest in public health care for people with substance issues, attending to economic, physical, social and policy conditions which are shaping the risk of alcohol and other drug-related harm in rural communities.

Suggested readings

Paquette, C.E. and Pollini, R.A. (2018) 'Injection drug use, HIV/HCV, and related services in nonurban areas of the United States: A systematic review', *Drug and Alcohol Dependence*, 188: 239–250.

Schalkoff, C.A., Lancaster, K.E., Gaynes, B.N., Wang, V., Pence, B.W., Miller, W.C. and Go, V.F. (2020) 'The opioid and related drug epidemics in rural Appalachia: A systematic review of populations affected, risk factors, and infectious diseases', *Substance Abuse*, 41: 35–69.

Thomas, N., van de Ven, K. and Mulrooney, K.J.D. (2020) 'The impact of rurality on opioid-related harms: A systematic review of qualitative research', *International Journal of Drug Policy*, 85: 102607.

UNODC. (2017) *Prevention of Drug Use and Treatment of Drug Use Disorders in Rural Settings*, Vienna: United Nations Office of Drugs and Crime.

Van de Ven, K., Ritter, A. and Stirling, R. (2021) *The Impact of the COVID-19 Pandemic on the Non-Government Alcohol and Other Drug Sector*, Sydney: UNSW Social Policy Research Centre.

20

Drug Use and Dependence

Anke Stallwitz

Drugs are psychoactive substances with the capacity to alter emotional, psychological and bodily functions. Per its definition, the term 'drugs' embraces substances of legal (for example alcohol and tobacco) and of illegal status (for example cannabis, heroin, cocaine, crack cocaine and amphetamines) alike. However, both in everyday and scientific language, the term primarily refers to illegal substances. Consumption patterns include a wide range from occasional controlled use employing harm-reduced routes of administration such as inhaling to dependent frequent injecting.

When trying to comprehend the nature of rural drug use and dependence, the literature does not provide a homogenous conception of 'rural'. With respect to social behaviours including drug use, its meaning very much depends on the specific context. Authors of scientific publications on rural substance use tend to employ descriptive, quantifiable criteria to identify rurality. These typically encompass population size and density, geographic location and accessibility, as well as sometimes economic and employment issues.

However, both legal and illegal substance use constitute highly complex social phenomena and their character and manifestation are fundamentally influenced by the respective cultural and geographic setting in which they occur. Hence, we need to complement the outer, descriptive appearance of a place by an analytic perspective of its inner social organization and ways of functioning including people's beliefs, values and norms. Only by considering quantitative, descriptive and qualitative analytic characteristics can substance use trends and patterns in different places can be grasped comprehensively.

Since places often encompass both rural and urban features, the term 'location-specific' might be more suitable when socio-geographically contextualizing substance use occurrences. For instance, an encompassing in-depth study of the heroin scene on Shetland, an island group located between Scotland and Norway in the North Atlantic, demonstrated that drug scenes of a substantial size exist in extremely remote, isolated locations. At such sites, a town of 9,000 inhabitants might be of a considerably more urban nature and greater significance for the local drugs market than in a more densely populated mainland region (see Stallwitz, 2012).

As opposed to the consumption of alcohol and tobacco, the general public as well as academic scholars have conventionally regarded illegal drug use as tied to urban areas. Hence, customarily, drugs research had been designed for and conducted in metropolitan contexts. However, since the turn of the twenty-first century, illicit drug use of non-urban character has gradually achieved a level of relative normalization in many parts of the world.

The results of international research suggest that drug-using trends first show in metropolitan districts and frequently reach rural areas with a certain delay. As indicated by the study on the Shetland heroin scene, drugs are consumed to partly enormous extents in extremely remote isolated regions including rural Alaska, Iceland and the Faroe Islands in the North Atlantic. The small fishing port of Fraserburgh by the Scottish North Sea counted the highest rate of heroin dependence in Great Britain and held the unofficial title of Scotland's heroin capital by the end of the 1990s. Globally speaking, scientific evidence indicates that drug consumption and trade occurs in non-urban locations of all five continents with, notably, the greatest part of research being carried out in the Western world.

Whereas the drug trade traditionally tended to centre on city districts, recent years show a notable expansion of rural supply networks. An example is the so-called County Lines which has been increasingly revealed in the United Kingdom in the 2010s Gangs and organized networks recruit youths and vulnerable individuals as dealers to transport drugs from metropolitan distribution hubs to small towns and country regions (see Robinson et al, 2019).

The term County Lines refers to the mobile and other telephone lines via which the drug deals are organized. In the media-driven public discourse, the often-young dealers tend to be constructed in polarized ways, either as victims of exploitation or as delinquent offenders. This paradox of the seemingly polarized conceptualization and handling of drugs issues is also reflected in the contemporary public discourse and media representation around drug usage and dealing amongst unaccompanied minor refugees. Similarly to the young persons involved in County Lines, unaccompanied youths engaging in drug-related behaviours tend to be viewed and pictured as vulnerable victims or criminal threats to society, depending on the respective context and perspective.

Prevention, intervention and policy

It becomes obvious that when designing drug prevention and intervention strategies for rural areas the location-specific socio-geographic particularities shaping the respective drug cultures and using behaviours need to be considered carefully. In developing location-sensitive, effective prevention and intervention concepts, policy, practice and interdisciplinary research need to collaborate in close exchange.

Effective methods can be community-based participatory approaches which consider the perspectives of all social groups affected by a drug scene, including people using (and possibly selling) drugs: residents; police; social services; authorities; and politicians. Such methods can benefit significantly from the conscious employment of peers, who can be engaged in not only prevention, intervention and research but also policy.

Depending on the context, 'peers' refers to, for instance, individuals currently or previously involved in the drug scene or youth moving in social or geographical areas where drugs are present. An interesting example is a culturally grounded programme aimed at the prevention of alcohol, nicotine, cannabis and 'hard' drug use and implemented in rural Hawaii. The video-enhanced, teacher-implemented curriculum was developed with the aid of culturally grounded and community-based participatory research (see Okamoto et al, 2020). Along similar lines, community-based participatory action has been applied in order to devise a framework for youth empowerment to prevent smoking in rural Indonesia (see Trisnowati et al, 2021).

The community-readiness model represents an approach in which community-oriented research, prevention, intervention and policy aspects can be integrated in a systematic and resourceful way. In an example from Nigeria (see Nwagu et al, 2020), the readiness for the prevention of drug use in two rural communities has been assessed and gaps have been identified in community readiness and capacity and informing strategies for community initiatives. Owing to rural places often possessing social structures of a close-knit nature, programmes utilizing community-minded concepts can be particularly efficient here.

Suggested readings

Nwagu, E.N., Dibia, S.I.C. and Odo, A.N. (2020) 'Community readiness for drug abuse prevention in two rural communities in Enugu State, Nigeria', *SAGE Open Nursing*, 6 (January): 1–10.

Okamoto, S.K., Helm, S., Chin, S.K., Hata, J., Hata, E. and Okamura, K.H. (2020) 'The implementation of a culturally grounded, school-based, drug prevention curriculum in rural Hawai'i', *Journal of Community Psychology*, 48(4): 1085–99.

Robinson, G., McLean, R. and Densley, J. (2019) 'Working county lines: Child criminal exploitation and illicit drug dealing in Glasgow and Merseyside', *International Journal of Offender Therapy and Comparative Criminology*, 63(5): 694–711.

Stallwitz, A. (2012) *The Role of Community-Mindedness in the Self-Regulation of Drug Cultures. A Case Study from the Shetland Islands*, New York: Springer.

Trisnowati, H., Ismail, D., Padmawati, R.S. and Utarini, A. (2021) 'Developing a framework for youth empowerment to prevent smoking behavior in a rural setting: Study protocol for a participatory action research', *Health Education*, 121(1): 30–47.

21

Genocide

Hollie Nyseth Nzitatira and Brandon Moore

Genocide is legally defined as the intent to destroy, in whole or in part, a national, ethnic, racial or religious group through targeted killings, forced displacement, sexualized violence and other forms of violence. Although the United Nations formally outlawed this crime in the wake of the Holocaust, genocides date back centuries. Genocides have also continued to occur, with upwards of 40 genocides eradicating millions of individuals since the 1940s.

Given the scope of this violence, this entry addresses the causes of genocide with an emphasis on national, subnational and individual-level risk factors. As many scholars study the crime of genocide, this entry emphasizes criminological findings but also incorporates interdisciplinary work on genocides across rural and urban settings.

National risk factors

Genocides are often, though not always, perpetrated by governments. Accordingly, much research has examined why genocide occurs by analysing the national-level conditions that have been associated with genocide during the twentieth and twenty-first centuries. These include, but are not limited to, political upheaval and threat; state structure and capacity; and ideology and social divisions.

Genocide typically occurs in contexts of political upheaval and threat. For instance, civil wars can lead to genocide. Rural, mountainous regions often foster civil wars because distance from centres of power aids rebellion. When rebellious factions in such regions (or others) initiate a civil war, genocide becomes more likely – either because political leaders attempt to remove insurgent threats or because civil wars can usher in repressive leaders via unconventional regime changes.

Successful coups and revolutions can similarly pave the way for repressive leaders, whilst unsuccessful ones threaten existing leaders, which can provoke harsh reactions. Assassinations, elections, riots and movements against the state also impact upheaval and/or threat, and countries that previously experienced upheaval, including prior wars and atrocities, are also at higher risk of genocide.

State structure and capacity have also been tied to genocide. Autocratic regimes with few checks and balances often harm their own people, though mixed regimes (that is, those that are not democracies or autocracies) are likewise associated with genocide. Strong state capacity has been linked to several prominent genocides (for example, the Holocaust during World War Two; Rwanda in 1994), as strong governments have the power to exert their will. However, new states, as well as any states with low income per capita, are also at risk of genocide, possibly because the governments cannot adequately respond to unrest.

Ideologies – or the distinctive political worldviews of individuals, groups and organizations – are associated with genocide as well. This is perhaps especially relevant for population projects tied to communist regimes' collective agricultural pursuits. For instance, during the genocide in Cambodia (1970s), the Khmer Rouge sought to create an agrarian, socialist society and idealized the rural, working peasants as the true national residents (an ideal that was mirrored in the Holocaust and the Armenian genocide). New research is also exploring how ideologies, divisions and discriminatory actions impact the relationship between genocide and climate change, especially in rural, land-stressed locations.

Sub-national risk factors

Once genocide begins, it unfolds within certain spaces. For instance, in the genocide that started in 2003 in Sudan, *all* violence occurred in the marginalized, rural region of Darfur. Similarly, the 1970s and 1980s genocide in Guatemala was particularly extreme in the northern rural provinces where Indigenous peoples lived and where the 'Guerilla Army of the Poor' operated. In other genocides, such as the 1994 genocide in Rwanda, violence took place throughout the country.

Sub-national factors shape where, how and when this violence occurs. In Rwanda, for instance, communities with lower integration of ethnic groups experienced earlier genocidal onset as it took time to break existing bonds and destroy social capital in cohesive communities. In one of many other examples, during China's Cultural Revolution, violence was particularly extreme in rural areas where local actors drew upon ethnic categorization and scapegoating – in the absence of local legal and moral constraints – to encourage violence.

Individual risk factors

Who commits this violence varies as well, such that there are also individual risk factors. Researchers assessing the people who perpetrate genocide have distinguished between those who plan genocide and those who carry it out. This distinction can be mapped on to positions of power, and leaders often orchestrate genocide when they are threatened or when their countries are in turmoil.

Those who enact the violence often wield comparatively less power and may be influenced by threat and fear, ideology and propaganda, group dynamics and coercion, social networks, age-graded and gendered expectations as well as other aspects of the social situation. In Rwanda, for example, roughly 97 per cent of the people found guilty of committing genocide were farmers, with factors such as farm size, access to land, social connections and ties to elites shaping participation.

Taken together, research has identified the national, sub-national and individual-level risk factors that coalesce to impact genocide. Whilst this entry considered these levels separately, it is important to remember that they interact, and factors at other conceptual levels (for example, the family level) also impact situations in which genocide ultimately occurs.

Suggested readings

Karstedt, S., Nyseth Brehm, H. and Frizzell, L.C. (2021) 'Genocide, mass atrocity, and theories of crime: Unlocking criminology's potential', *Annual Review of Criminology*, 4: 75–97.

McDoom, O. (2021) *The Path to Genocide in Rwanda*, Cambridge: Cambridge University Press.

Nyseth Brehm, H. (2017) 'Re-examining risk factors of genocide', *Journal of Genocide Research*, 19(1): 61–87.

Su, Y. (2011) *Collective Killings in Rural China During the Cultural Revolution*, New York: Cambridge University Press.

Woolford A., June, W. and Um, S. (2021) '"We planted rice and killed people": Symbiogenetic destruction in the Cambodian genocide', *Genocide Studies and Prevention: An International Journal*, 15(1): 44–67.

22

Hate Crime

Rachel Hale and Melina Stewart-North

A hate crime is any type of crime committed with a motivation of bias against a member of a specific group because of their involvement (actual or perceived) in that group. This prejudice can be based on race, ethnicity, gender, religion, ability, sexual orientation or membership of an alternative sub-culture. Essentially, a hate crime is targeting people because of who they are or who they are perceived to be. When this occurs in rural, remote or regional locations, the drivers, experiences and consequences can be unique compared to urban contexts.

Research on hate crime has traditionally adopted an urban-centric focus, neglecting victimization which is impacted by place. Further concealing the victimization of rural minorities is the idea of the rural idyll, often romanticizing rural and remote communities as crime-free, rendering the hostile and violent processes which underpin hate-based offending invisible (see Chakraborti and Garland, 2004). The burgeoning field of contemporary critical rural criminology challenges this myth, revealing the stark realities of rural crime and victimization.

Furthermore, there is a tendency for researchers and responders to categorize victims of hate crime into broad identity groups, a one-size-fits-all approach which fails to engage with and ignores the intersectionality of victim experiences and the disparities experienced *within* groups. As Hardy and Chakraborti (2020) point out, the intersectional and nuanced nature of hate-based victimization must be acknowledged, whereby rurality adds another dimension to the web of interrelated factors that exacerbate victim experiences.

Realities of rural hate-based victimization

Rural hate crime occurs as a process, not as an isolated event (see Garland and Chakraborti, 2006), and ranges from 'low-level' every-day acts (such as verbal abuse, micro-aggressions, symbolic violence and discrimination) to 'high-level', novel and horrific offences (such as extreme acts of violence and brutality). Hate crimes are generally under-reported and under-researched, and with so little research specifically focused on *rural* hate crime, its precise nature and prevalence remains unknown. However, rural hate crime is purported to be far more pervasive and omnipresent than is officially recorded.

The impact of hate crime on victims, in rural or urban settings, is significant. Victims of hate crime can experience post-traumatic stress, anxiety and pervasive feelings of unsafety within the community, disrupting their use of public space and inhibiting community involvement (see Perry, 2015). For example, victims may develop strategies based on avoidance to lessen the risk of victimization, such as avoiding certain venues, routes and spaces. Access to specialized, intensive support for victims of hate crime is therefore critical.

Services in rural areas are relatively limited in comparison with metropolitan locations, impacting the capability of victims of hate crime to access victim advocacy and support. Access to objective law enforcement can be compromised in rural areas by high levels of acquaintance density, where community members have pre-existing relationships with the police, creating a conflict of interest which may bias police responses to victims. Rural victims of homophobic hate crime, for example, may be reluctant to report to police in a rural community where there is an increased risk of being disregarded by police or 'outed' to fellow community members, including their family, which would place the victim at risk of further exclusion and isolation.

The harms of rural hate crime extend beyond the direct target or victim to the broader community, having a distal effect (see Perry, 2015). This suggests that the victim of the crime is not restricted to the individual(s), but rather the *message* of hate can extend to the victims' community. As members of 'the rural' are often perceived to be intimately intertwined with one another, including from one generation to the next, these distal effects of hate crime can ripple across both space and time.

Explanations for rural hate

Hate crimes perpetrated against persons in rural locations based on their personal characteristics may be traced to the more conservative values held by rural communities. For example, in rural communities there may be uncompromising opinions regarding sexual orientation and gender identity, reflected in heteronormative and cisnormative values (that is, gender identity matches biological sex), with those who identify outside of these normative boundaries at increased risk of harm.

Rural communities are, generally, more homogenous relative to metropolitan settings, and rural citizens may be highly established in their ways, those of which may be described as traditional or conservative. This homogeneity can manifest in resistance to difference and, potentially, hate crime. In Western nations, for example, rural communities have historically been predominantly 'White', 'Anglo-Saxon' and 'Christian'. However, the growing diversification of these communities has led to increased intercultural encounters. A lack of familiarity with diverse cultures in rural areas can lead to feelings of uncertainty and apprehension, and the resultant *fear* can motivate hate-based offending when communities diversify.

The visibility of 'outsiders' in rural areas is amplified by this homogeneity. The process of 'othering' is pertinent here. Othering refers to the labelling of groups (and individuals within them) as fundamentally different, potentially leading to the perception that they are inferior, undeserving and even sub-human. It occurs when community members are organized into an 'in-group' (if ideals match) versus the 'out-group' (if their values or beliefs do not align with the dominant majority). In the case of the latter, individuals belonging to the out-group are considered 'the other' – not belonging to the mainstream – which can lead to exclusion, isolation and hate-based offending.

In rural areas, there can be a perception that the 'others', or outsiders, who do not fit the traditional norms, should make every effort to embrace the mainstream ideals of the rural lifestyle or risk social exclusion. This exclusion, at its most devastating, can be in the form of a hate crime. Individuals who do not conform may be constructed as a threat to the dominant group or the status quo in a rural community. This perceived threat may be utilized as a rationale for hate, making it seemingly easier for offenders to justify their behaviour as an act of protection.

Community dynamics evidently impact on hate crime. As Nolan and colleagues (2020) found, in communities where residents are well connected and able to provide informal social control, hate crime is less likely. Conversely, when residents are dependent on formal mechanisms of crime prevention (such as police), the more likely hate crimes are. Targeting rural community dynamics is therefore a potential method of preventing hate crime.

Suggested readings

Chakraborti, N. and Garland, J. (2004) *Rural Racism*, Cullompton: Willan Publishing.

Garland, J. and Chakraborti, N. (2006) 'Recognising and responding to victims of rural racism', *International Review of Victimology*, 13(1): 49–69.

Hardy, S-J. and Chakraborti, N. (2020) *Blood, Threats and Fears: The Hidden Worlds of Hate Crime Victims*, New York: Springer.

Nolan, J., Nicewarner, R. and Momen, R. (2020) 'Preventing rural hate crime', in A. Harkness (ed) *Rural Crime Prevention: Theory, Tactics and Techniques*, London: Routledge, pp. 113–27.

Perry, B. (2015) 'Exploring the community impacts of hate crime', in N. Hall, A. Corb, P. Giannasi and J.G.D. Grieve (eds) *The Routledge International Handbook on Hate Crime*, London: Routledge, pp. 47–58.

23

Modern Slavery and Cross-border Transportation of People

Richard Byrne

The term 'modern slavery' is used to describe people who are exploited by others for personal or commercial gain. It was first adopted in the 1970s. It is, however, a phrase not used in international law, and as such as a legal term it is mostly confined to the United States and the United Kingdom. The term modern slavery is the basis of the United Kingdom's 2015 Modern Slavery Act (see Haynes, 2016) which combined previous legislation under one law and compels certain sized companies in England and Wales to examine their labour supply and set out steps to prevent labour exploitation.

Modern slavery as a term often lacks meaning outside of the spheres of the United States and the United Kingdom, and as a term may be locally misinterpreted or perceived as dismissing the horrors of historical transatlantic slavery in light of contemporary criminal exploitation activities. Furthermore, there is often an assumption that, when looking at issues in the Global South, modern slavery is a continuation of historical slavery or is somehow rooted in some cultural practice.

Internationally, many countries and organizations refer to the exploitation of humans by others for profit by the term of human trafficking, which is defined by the United Nations under the Palermo protocols as the recruitment, transportation, transfer, harbouring or receipt of people through force, fraud or deception, to exploit them for profit (see Allain, 2013). As a result of these issues, the term 'Modern Slavery Human Trafficking' (MSHT) is gaining traction in the United Kingdom as a way of bridging linguistic barriers. The key element of the human trafficking definition is to recognize that persons who are trafficked may not be initially forced but deceived into compliance with fake employment or education offers.

Facilitation of human trafficking

Human trafficking is facilitated by a range of organized crime groups (OCGs), who in some parts of the world work alongside terrorist organizations such as the Islamic State or co-operate with other OCGs to enable the efficient distribution of exploited labour and hence profit. The nexus of OCG–terrorist groups is a globally emerging area of concern. Possibly the most infamous example dates from 2014, when the Islamic State group sexually exploited thousands of Yazidi women and forced them into domestic servitude across a wide swath of Syria and Iraq, and possibly beyond (El-Masri, 2018 usefully expands on this). Subsequently, many displaced persons from the region fleeing conflict have succumbed to human trafficking and exploitation as they sought sanctuary.

Whilst violence and the threat of violence may be used against trafficked people, coercion and deception are powerful tools employed by traffickers to manipulate victims. Contrary to media portrayals of human trafficking, few people are snatched off the street, with most being lured into trafficking situations either because they desire to migrate and lack the appropriate documentation or because they seek work.

Migrants have many reasons to move, including economic, security, conflict and increasingly climate change: OCGs recognize this and tailor their 'offering' to each grouping. Whilst transnational trafficking is well known, by far the biggest activity is internal trafficking whereby persons are trafficked within a nation. Sexual exploitation of women and minors is a key example of internal trafficking, as is using young people to move drugs between urban centres. In the United Kingdom, the internal trafficking of youth to move drugs between cities and minor, often rural towns is dubbed 'County Lines'.

In the Global South, OCGs often work through networks of recruiters targeting communities and individuals, in person and through social media, promoting fake employment or education opportunities to attract victims. These range from jobs in information technology to hairdressing and football academies. They persuade families to pay the traffickers to initially smuggle their family members across international borders, only for them to be enslaved or held for ransom.

Indeed, a trafficked person may go through several changes of status from informal migrant, trafficked, ransomed and enslaved in a single journey. This is particularly common for those embarking on journeys in West Africa hoping to reach Europe, with the majority ending up working in mines, agriculture or industry in West Africa or pushed into the sex trade in these environments.

In Europe, in addition to externally trafficked peoples, OCGs exploit illegal migrants, refugees, the homeless and those with mental health or addiction issues. These people are often desperate for work or shelter and may not speak the language of their enslavers or the local language, making them easy prey. Additionally, people may be enslaved through debt bondage or bonded labour, being forcibly conscripted into an armed force such as child soldiers or being forced to marry. In whatever manner people are trafficked and enslaved, they are all subjected to degrading and dehumanizing acts by OCGs and their exploiters.

Forms of exploitation

Several scholars have suggested typologies of slavery and exploitation (for example, see Cooper et al, 2017). The main forms of exploitation include:

Sexual exploitation – the forcing of individuals into commercial sex acts which can involve the victim being trapped into the repayment of unlawful debts. Such exploitation can involve many environments from street prostitution to being made to work on webcams and video.

Forced labour – where trafficked people work for little or no pay often in primary industries, including agriculture. Increasingly in Western Europe and North America trafficked persons fill labour gaps left by legal migrant workers.

Domestic servitude – whereby a person is forced to provide services within a household or property with no ability to change the terms of their circumstances. Commonly, these victims are legally recruited then deprived of their travel documentation.

Organ harvesting – an increasingly common trade where a person is trafficked with the sole aim of taking their organs without their consent. This often leads to death or disability.

Suggested readings

Allain, J. (2013) '2000 protocol to prevent, suppress and punish trafficking in persons, especially women and children: Supplementing the United Nations Convention against transnational organized crime', in J. Allain (ed) *Slavery in International Law*, Leiden, The Netherlands: Brill Nijhoff, pp. 410–21.

Cooper, C., Hesketh, O., Ellis, N. and Fair, A. (2017) *A Typology of Modern Slavery Offences in the UK*, London: Home Office.

El-Masri, S. (2018) 'Prosecuting ISIS for the sexual slavery of the Yazidi women and girls', *The International Journal of Human Rights*, 22(8): 1047–66.

Haynes, J. (2016) 'The Modern Slavery Act (2015): A legislative commentary', *Statute Law Review*, 37(1): 33–56.

UNODC (2021) 'Global report on trafficking in persons', United Nations, Available from: https://www.unodc.org/documents/data-and-analysis/tip/2021/GLOTiP_2020_15jan_web.pdf [Accessed 30 October 2021].

24

Resource Extraction: Crime Impacts

Callie D. Shaw and Rick Ruddell

Crime and disorder in resource-based boom communities has captured the public's interest for over a century. One of the first widely reported examples was the violence and disorder occurring after the 1849 boom in the California goldfields. Since that time, there has been increasing awareness of the adverse impacts of resource extraction on the quality of life in rural communities throughout the world. This is a significant issue as the exploration and extraction of commodities is increasing in response to a growing demand for cheap energy and the changing needs of the green economy. Although the magnitude and duration of every boom differs, the criminogenic impacts of rapid population growth and industrialization in sparsely populated rural communities has gained considerable scholarly attention.

Life course of resource-based booms

Ruddell and Ray (2018) describe how resource-based booms have a life course. As local populations grow, there is a corresponding reduction in informal social control and a rise in social disorder as the population swells with newcomers who are predominately young men with little stake in these communities. A lack of safe and affordable housing is often the first social problem to emerge, although local health, education and social services are also overwhelmed with demands for service. Local justice systems are often stretched thin by the rising demands on their services, and the thresholds for arrest and detention increase, reducing their deterrent effects. Substance abuse, the exodus of older established residents and homelessness all increase, as do environmental impacts such as air, light, noise and water pollution. Along with those environmental and social problems comes an increase in crime, although the forms and volume of crime differ for each boom location.

Over 40 different studies published between 1976 and 2020 clearly establish that crimes increase after a boom beyond what can be expected with the rise in population. The social impacts and types of crimes increasing after a boom depend on the characteristics of a boom and the stage of the extractive activities. Some oil and gas booms, for instance, are spread about a large geographical area whilst others, such as a mine or energy development project, are confined to a single epicenter. In addition, the volume of crime in the early stages of the boom is often higher as more workers are required to construct the infrastructure, and crime rates usually contract after these projects make the transition into production. Some North American locales experience a series of booms and busts that have persisted for decades.

Crime impacts

Although the impact of crime on each location differs, most communities experience a significant rise in minor crimes associated with the influx of many young males, including common assaults, driving under the influence, drug possession, disorderly conduct, theft and other offences associated with substance abuse. There are, however, mixed findings as to whether increases in serious assaults or homicides and serious property crimes such as burglary and vehicle theft also occur. Some places experience increases in these serious and violent offences whilst others do not. Furthermore, nearly every boom community experiences a rise in aggressive and dangerous driving and a corresponding increase in collisions and traffic fatalities. These negative social impacts can be magnified in remote or isolated communities. In some locales the crime prevention efforts of the local justice system and community partners have successfully ameliorated crime rates in some jurisdictions.

There is increasing attention on the vulnerability of some rural populations after the onset of a boom, including women. Communities experiencing oil booms report elevated numbers of sexual assaults, domestic and dating violence and incidents of stalking towards women. Indigenous women in particular report increased rates of violence, including sexual assaults. Finn et al (2017) report that sexual assaults increased by 75 per cent on Indigenous women on a North Dakota reservation since the start of the region's latest oil boom after 2000. Violence perpetrated against women, however, is also closely connected to decreases in oil production. These economic busts result in layoffs and community stakeholders report increased numbers of domestic violence towards women. Martin and colleagues (2019) contend that violence towards women is a theme that is present throughout the boom's life course.

Gaps in knowledge

Despite the increased scholarship about the impact of booms on rural and remote communities, we still lack knowledge about the extent of these crimes in some jurisdictions due to a lack of accurate crime statistics. Furthermore, we do not have a clear understanding of who is engaging in these offences. Whilst residents attribute the increased crime to outsiders, they seldom acknowledge that crime was occurring in their communities before these booms started. We also lack an accounting of the impact of resource-based booms on Indigenous peoples, including their displacement and victimization by governments and corporations. Last, our lack of awareness of these crime-related and social problems is magnified in Africa, Asia, Eastern Europe and South America, as most research published prior to 2022 has had an Australian and North American focus.

Suggested readings

Finn, K., Gajda, E., Perin, T. and Fredericks, C. (2017) 'Responsible resource development and prevention of sex trafficking: Safeguarding native women and children on the Fort Berthold Reservation', *Harvard Journal of Law and Gender*, 40(1): 1–51.

Jacquet, J.B. (2014) 'Review of risks to communities from shale energy development', *Environmental Science and Technology*, 48(15): 8321–33.

Martin, K., Barrick, K.L., Richardson, N.J., Liao, D. and Heller, D.C. (2019) 'Violent victimization known to law enforcement in the Bakken oil-producing region of Montana and North Dakota, 2006–2012', Available from: https://www.ojp.gov/pdffiles1/bjs/grants/252619.pdf [Accessed 14 September 2021].

O'Connor, C.D. and Ruddell, R. (2021) 'After the downturn: Perceptions of crime and policing in the southeastern Saskatchewan oil patch', *The Canadian Geographer*, 65(3): 281–91.

Ruddell, R. and Ray, H. (2018) 'Profiling the life course of resource-based boomtowns: A key step in crime prevention', *Journal of Community Safety and Well-Being*, 3(2): 38–42.

25

Rogue Farmers

Robert Smith

Defining rogue farmers in a rural context

The concept of the 'rogue farmer' was first coined in 2004 by Robert Smith (see suggested readings) in a United Kingdom context in his study into the illegal halal trade/smokies to refer to farmers who knowingly and willingly engaged in criminal entrepreneurship in its many forms, including immoral, amoral and illegal for financial and reputational gain.

The genesis of the concept was in turn influenced by William Baumol's notion and theory of 'productive, unproductive and destructive entrepreneurship' (1990) which posited that not all forms of entrepreneurship are productive and legal and that some are in fact unproductive (in that they may be illicit, immoral or amoral and sit in the grey zone) and destructive (and are palpably criminal). The rogue farmers in the study knowingly participated in criminal acts from the theft of sheep to illegal slaughter of the sheep for human consumption despite it being patently illegal. The rogue farmers acted in a parasitical manner by generating a parallel income stream which lay outside of the official taxation system. The term rogue was applied because the farmers were believed to be acting as 'rogues' whilst still maintaining their identity as farmers. The clear inference was that they were not criminals in the true sense of the word.

In a number of follow up studies the concept was developed and expanded by Smith and McElwee (2014) and Sommerville into the theory of 'illegal rural enterprise' (IRE) to differentiate it from ordinary criminality carried out by farmers. In these studies, the type of crimes considered and investigated were split into ordinary crimes and IRE crimes. The former included the theft of livestock, theft of farm plant and equipment, renting out sheds for criminal purposes such as storing stolen property or drug cultivation. The latter included crimes such as hosting dog-fighting events, puppy farming, various food fraud offences and the illegal slaughter of animals as a service. This list is not exhaustive.

The twin theories of the rogue farmer and IRE were developed to include the notion of 'insider crime' because it was apparent that many of the crimes committed by so-called rogue farmers required a modicum of rural social capital and farming knowledge and skills in their perpetration. For example, in order to steal sheep, it is essential to use a sheep dog or quad bike to round them up. Indeed, loading sheep on to a trailer takes skill and practice and therefore not every urban criminal could commit the crime. Moreover, it is essential to have knowledge of how to launder hundreds of stolen sheep before arranging the slaughter and disposal of the animals into the food supply chain.

As in the case of defining organized crime in a rural context, there is no such crime as IRE. Accused are dealt with by a variety of common law crimes and offences which usually have low penalties, making their commission lucrative financially. In addition, the rogue farmers are seldom considered to be 'real criminals' and therefore they do not face the same censure from their peers or society.

Defining criminal farmers in a rural context

As the number of studies into the phenomenon expanded, it became apparent that there was a core group of so-called rogue farmers who were engaged in serial acts of criminality and could only be described as 'criminals' who flouted the ideology and practices of the stereotypical 'good farmer'. In 2016, Smith and McElwee (2016) posited the term of 'criminal farmer' to refer to such individuals. Although there are only a few such individuals who have been identified to date, it does suggest the existence of a rural criminal class or classes who utilize rural social capital, knowledge and skills in the perpetuation of their crimes. Like the Baumolian unproductive and destructive entrepreneur, the criminal farmer may also operate as a legitimate farmer.

The theories of the rogue and criminal farmer are still very much in their infancy and examples are still very much located in the United Kingdom and European contexts. However, the study of Goodall (2021) examined the case of badger and deer hunting in the United Kingdom and found that many of the culprits are from farming stock and poach the deer for financial gain as an additional income generating strategy. In the *Routledge International Handbook of Rural Criminology*, other examples of insider crimes in a United States context are highlighted (Donnermeyer, 2016). This is clear evidence of veracity of the theories and the need for further studies in other countries.

Identification of issues and impacts globally

Much of the emerging literature on rural rogues, criminal farmers and illegal rural enterprise is based upon the United Kingdom and European contexts and are from the developed world. There is a pressing need to encourage studies from a North American context and from South America, Africa and Asia too. In the United States, there is also a cattle 'rustling' industry, and there is now an expanding semi-legitimate industry in cultivating cannabis – but there are still many grey areas with criminal opportunities in rural spaces. This call for further research into rural crime and criminality is necessary because many farmers are trapped in poverty and are preyed upon by criminal cartels and warlords who force them to cultivate illegal drugs or tax them as a source of income. In Africa, the bushmeat problem is also of concern. In the Caribbean, farm theft is used to finance arms smuggling from Colombia and other unstable nations. Understanding the organized crime–rural nexus is an exciting area of criminology which remains underresearched. Context and culture are of vital importance in researching insider crimes in any rural setting.

Suggested readings

Baumol, W.J. (1990) 'Entrepreneurship: Productive, unproductive, and destructive', *Journal of Political Economy*, 98(5): 893–921.

Donnermeyer, J.F. (ed) (2016) *The Routledge International Handbook of Rural Criminology*, London: Routledge.

Goodall, O. (2021) 'The reality of rural crime: The unintended consequences of rural policy in the co-production of badger persecution and the illegal taking of deer', *The British Journal of Criminology*, 61(4): 1005–25.

Smith, R. (2004) 'Rural rogues: A case story on the smokies trade', *The International Journal of Entrepreneurial Behaviour and Research*, 10(4): 277–94.

Smith, R. and McElwee, G. (2016) 'Criminal farmers and organized rural crime groups', in J.F. Donnermeyer (ed) *The Routledge International Handbook of Rural Criminology*, London: Routledge, pp. 127–36.

Smith, R. and McElwee, G. (2014) 'Illegal rural enterprise', in A. Fayolle (ed) *Handbook of Research in Entrepreneurship: What We Know and What We Need to Know*, Cheltenham: Edward Elgar, pp. 367–88.

26

Technology and Interpersonal Violence

Bridget Harris

Interpersonal violence persists across all landscapes, yet research and efforts to prevent and regulate such harms have been focused primarily on non-urban locations. As technology infiltrates all spheres of our lives, it is increasingly used to enact interpersonal violence: this lethal and non-lethal violence occurs in both familial and care settings (including child abuse, intimate partner abuse, elder abuse) and community settings (such as bullying, harassment and assault by acquaintances, strangers or persons who may be known, in social environments, schools and workplaces).

To advance our understanding of and responses to these dangers, a spatial approach is key – this means recognizing how rurality shapes victimization and perpetration (see Harris, 2018; DeKeseredy, 2021). Additionally, it requires considering how the spacelessness of technology can be weaponized but can also offer opportunities for rural people to seek assistance and support.

Intersectionality and vulnerability

Anyone can perpetrate or be subjected to technology-facilitated violence. However, research suggests that harms are more likely to be experienced by cisgender women and gender and sexuality diverse people than cisgender men, and Black, Indigenous, people of colour more than White people.

Those who practice a religion (especially a religion other than Christianity) and people with cognitive, intellectual or physical disabilities and mental illness have also reported high rates of harm. Thus, an intersectional approach to studying technology-facilitated violence captures the interrelationship between discrimination, disadvantage, social categorization and victimization. Rurality, whilst not an intersecting oppression, adds a degree of vulnerabiliy and warrants attention, including in relation to technology-facilitated violence.

Technology-facilitated violence

'Technology' is useful as an all-encompassing term (although somewhat vague) and is often used to refer to telecommunication devices (phones, tablets, computers), trackers, digital media and the Internet of Things. However, thinking more holistically about technology helps us think more holistically about harm. Assistive technologies (such as hearing aids, screen readers, transfer devices and wheelchairs) are key for persons with physical, intellectual or cognitive disabilities.

Medication (for example contraceptives, hormone therapy, antidepressants) can arguably be viewed as technologies, and are essential for managing physical, sexual and mental health and lifestyle (see Fileborn and Ball, 2018). Denying access to or damaging such items or software can jeopardize a person's well being and safety.

Technology can be used to enact or extend other forms of harm, for instance to aid in real-world stalking or in-person bullying, as well as to:

- send harassing, denigrating, defamatory, abusive or threatening communications (this could include trolling and flaming practices);
- isolate or exclude;
- create or share audio and/or visual recordings (such as intimate images) without the consent of a party featured or recipient;
- dox (release private or identifying information) of a party, publicly;
- stalk (monitoring or surveilling movements, activities or communications); and
- engage in impersonation or identity theft.

It can also involve the destruction or manipulation of technology, such as by enabling an unauthorized function of a device or digital media or impairing an authorized function.

Identifying forms of technology-facilitated violence can aid in education and prevention efforts, but this is by no means a prescriptive list. We should expect that new technologies and behaviours will emerge and evolve over time. Some of these acts may constitute violations of law in some jurisdictions; in others these might instead be violations of what communities or individuals feel is acceptable.

Motivations for committing technology-facilitated violence vary; an offender might seek to bully, harass, coerce, control, humiliate, defraud and isolate. It is key to examine context, because readings of actions can vary depending on the setting in which it takes place, a target's experiences and history and their relationship with an offender. Social media stalking, for instance, can be problematized, romanticized or normalized by different actors. What is important to recognize is the effect of an incident or incidents on a target.

Spacelessness and rurality

Technology-facilitated abuse is often connected to other forms of abuse, but it is unique in how it moves beyond physical and temporal borders. Someone can be exposed to this harm anywhere and anytime they use devices or digital media, and so perpetrators can seem omnipresent and omnipotent. An experience and response to this spaceless violence, though, is shaped by the resources, values, structures and ideologies in a particular location.

Barriers to help-seeking in rural areas are greater than in urban areas. Those subjected to harm may be geographically and/or socially isolated, which can make accessing cybersafety agencies, the police and support services challenging. Cultural values and belief systems can be a hindrance to help-seeking too; self-sufficiency is embedded in some communities, particularly where residents have battled natural disasters (such as floods, fires, droughts, tornadoes) which are more common in rural than urban areas.

Privacy may be prized, but is not assured when responding to violence in smaller communities, which can be a deterrent to disclosing victimization. It can be hard to leave a place that feels unsafe, if perpetrators are in the community, as accommodation can be limited as can financial, education and employment opportunities that aid relocation.

Fortunately, technology can be harnessed to overcome some of these barriers. Experts, advocates and practitioners who can assist victims can be contacted using information communication technologies. Support groups can be accessed anonymously and remotely. This is particularly helpful for people who feel marginalized in their physical community as they can use technology to connect with virtual communities with shared experiences.

Such initiatives can require minimal resources and so be attractive to non-government and government agencies too, seeking to capacity build and bolster prevention and regulation of violence in rural zones. Yet connectivity can be restricted by the digital divide, which plagues many rural areas and marginalized groups.

In the future, there is a need to address both how technology is used to enact interpersonal violence and also its potential to transform, protect and empower individuals who have been victimized in rural communities.

Suggested readings

DeKeseredy, W. (2021) 'Male-to-female sexual violence in rural communities: A sociological review', *Dignity: A Journal of Analysis of Exploitation and Violence*, 6(2): e7–e7.

Fileborn, B. and Ball, M. (2018) 'Queer experiences of technology and violence' [Paper presentation], 1–2 August, Technology and Domestic Violence: Experiences, Perpetration and Responses, Brisbane, Australia.

George, A. and Harris, B. (2014) *Landscapes of Violence: Women Surviving Family Violence in Regional and Rural Victoria*, Geelong: Deakin University.

Harris, B. (2018) 'Spacelessness, spatiality and intimate partner violence: Technology-facilitated abuse, stalking and justice administration', in J. Maher, S. Walklate, J. McCulloch and K. Fitz-Gibbon (eds) *Intimate Partner Violence, Risk and Security: Securing Women's Lives in a Global World*, London: Routledge, pp. 52–70.

Kowalski, R., Giumetti, G.W. and Limber, S.P. (2017) 'Bullying and cyberbullying among rural youth', in K.D. Michael and J.P. Jameson (eds) *Handbook of Rural School Mental Health*, Cham: Springer, pp. 231–45.

27

Tourism, Crime and Rurality

Joseph F. Donnermeyer and Alistair Harkness

The dominant images of tourism are romanticized visions of majestic mountains, azure oceans, white sand beaches, historic monuments, grand examples of architecture, exotic cultural settings and, of course, a happy, smiling tourist couple or parents with children in-hand, enthralled by the wonders before them. Nowhere in a brochure is there an image of a tourist frantically searching for his attaché case which housed his laptop, stolen whilst he waited in line to register at a hotel, or the panicked visage of a woman whose wallet is missing from a purse slung over her shoulders whilst she stood with a group of her friends about to board an excursion boat – both were the victims of well-trained and experienced thieves, individuals whose presence is as ubiquitous as the attractions themselves.

As Jones, Barclay and Mawby point out (2012), where there is tourism there will be crime. There should be nothing unusual about that observation, because all human endeavours display examples of deviance and crime. Further, as noted by many scholars interested in the criminological dimensions of tourism (see Sharpley and Stone, 2009), a great deal of tourism itself makes money off of heinous crimes, such as tours of the streets of London where Jack the Ripper stalked his victims in the late 1880s, or the house where Lizzie Borden allegedly killed her parents with an axe in the town of Fall River, Massachusetts (there is even a children's rhyme about that case).

One distinction to be made is the difference between leisure and tourism (see Botterill and Jones, 2010). A leisure activity, such as sitting at a table in one's backyard reading a book on a warm sunny day, or building a snow fort with one's children in the bright whiteness of newly fallen snow, is not tourism, but is certainly leisure. Tourism requires travels away from one's abode or usual surroundings to new places where new things can be seen and new experiences can be gained – and where new risks can be encountered.

As White points out (see Raymen and Smith, 2019, chapter 13), although crimes related to tourism can happen anywhere, a great amount of the crime–tourism relationship is within the context of a rural environment, from small, quaint, historic towns to remote, rugged regions of the world. Hence, it is a topic of interest to rural criminologists. However, warnings about safety and security issues at these places will rarely, if ever, be found in advertisements of any kind that seek to attract the money of tourists. Simply, it would belie the idyllic images of destination points and reduce tourist-based revenues.

Crimes committed against tourists at rural locations are not really any different from the similar fates awaiting tourists in urban places, except perhaps for the issue of guardianship. According to the criminological theory known as routine activities, motivated offenders and attractive targets are only two out of three dimensions by which to understand victimization. There is the dimension of guardianship, that is, the presence of people (alert persons, the police and so on) or objects (such as warning signs, cameras) who deter crimes. In many rural and remote locations, guardianship can be much lower. Hence, crimes such as pocket-picking, purse-snatching, theft of items from unlocked vehicles or vandalism of these vehicles all may be more easily and readily committed at rural-located tourist sites. Further, as the research on tourism and crime often notes, attention to even simple security, such as locking doors to a rental cabin or to an automobile or van, may be less often practiced by tourists at their destinations than when they are at home (see Jones et al, 2014, chapter 14).

In some rural areas, particularly those in coastal or mountainous locations, or regions with lakes or other natural amenities, there is a propensity for urban dwellers to invest in holiday or seasonal homes: that is, a second rather than a primary place of residence which people will use during holidays or occasional weekends throughout the year. An issue here is again the lack of capable guardianship since they are unoccupied a great deal of the time, as well as the limited resources of police in the area to be actively present. By way of example, along a 90-mile stretch of beach in eastern Victoria, Australia, many of the dwellings in the small hamlets have a permanent occupation of approximately one third of the population. This makes the remaining dwellings, which are vacant for most of the year, vulnerable to residential burglary.

Also, tourists can be the victims of fraud; that is, false or exaggerated advertising about the attractive attributes of rural localities and of facilities there meant to service tourists. Companies may tout the benefits of a wildlife tour with pictures of exotic animals that are either difficult to see or rarely seen.

Sometimes, victimizations are examples of tourist-on-tourist crimes, especially when there is a conflict in the use of outdoor space and recreational areas. The same river or ocean space may be used by kite-boarders, windsurfers or wing-surfers, with conflicting uses that can result in arguments that escalate into interpersonal conflict. The same came be said of the mix of off-road vehicles, all-terrain vehicles and hikers, or of snowboarders and skiers.

Tourists themselves can also be the offenders in other ways. Drunken and drug-induced behaviours, littering, violation of campfire restrictions, destruction or vandalism of heritage sites and natural attractions, trespassing on private property or public properties with restricted access by humans, hunting out of season and many other offenses harm and degrade rural-located tourist sites and may even create perceptions that certain places are no longer safe. Finally, research indicates that the drunkenness that comes with hunting by men is associated with an increased risk of domestic violence, especially against the wife or partner when the trip is over and the male returns home, according to Hall-Sanchez (2018).

Suggested readings

Botterill, D. and Jones, T. (eds) (2010) *Tourism and Crime: Key Themes*, Oxford: Goodfellow Publishers.

Hall-Sanchez, A.K. (2018) 'Male hunting subcultures and violence against women', in W.S. DeKeseredy, C.M. Rennison and A.K. Hall-Sanchez (eds) *The Routledge International Handbook of Violence Studies*, London: Routledge, pp. 329–38.

Jones, C., Barclay, E. and Mawby, R. (2012) *The Problem of Pleasure: Leisure, Tourism and Crime*, London: Routledge.

Raymen, T. and Smith, O. (eds) (2019) *Deviant Leisure: Criminological Perspectives on Leisure and Harm*, London: Palgrave.

Sharpley, R. and Stone, P.R. (2009) *The Darker Side of Travel: The Theory and Practice of Dark Tourism*, Bristol: Channel View Publications.

28

Violence against Farmers

Anni Hesselink and Cecili Doorewaard-Janse van Vuuren

Violence and the threat of violence against farmers is an age-old phenomenon. In 1831, widespread riots occurred as angry, distressed and poor agricultural workers in eastern and southern England attacked threshing machines, burned barns, destroyed farmhouses and maimed cows. The protests were aimed against farmers who lowered workers' wages and against the workers' harsh working conditions. Many farmers claimed that they could not afford to pay the workers' daily wages, but out of fear for their and their families' safety, fires and damage to their properties, they paid 40 per cent more wages than what they could afford to avoid losing their property and to secure their safety. Contemporaneously, violence against farmers has become a common occurrence in countries such as India, Israel, the Philippines and South Africa.

Violence against farmers as an axiom

According to De Villiers (2020), violence against farmers and attacks on farmers include any act of violence, such as assault, armed robbery, attempted murder, murder, rape and/or any other act aimed at inflicting bodily harm against any individual living, working on or visiting a farm or smallholding.

Violence against farmers is associated with political agendas, government control, poverty, unemployment, racial issues and decreasing economies. In this regard, in India farmers protested against agriculture laws which escalated to the death of several farmers. In Israel, settler violence occurred against Palestinian farmers during harvest time, whilst in the Philippines farmers were beaten with truncheons, shot at and killed whilst protesting over government relief, emergency government funds and sacks of rice during the drought period. Doorewaard (2020) reports that the use of violence or threat of violence to gain livestock is a common occurrence in African countries, such as in Lesotho, Kenya and South Sudan. In turn, South Africa has become infamous for the brutality of farm murders and attackers using excessive violence and torture to murder farmers (see Clack and Minnaar, 2018; News24, 2020).

Distinctive features

Although not the norm with all violence directed at farmers on a global scale, many farm attacks are politically and racially motivated and driven by economic gain, the acquisition of firearms, money, weapons and tradable goods such as computers and cellular phones. With rising unemployment rates, waning economies and increased poverty rates, farmers remain vulnerable targets for violent crime. The brutality of farm murders on South African farmers, though, makes no sense. The increased levels of violence and torture against South African farmers are linked by some political parties to racial hatred. On this point, and during a discussion on farm murders, it was asked why a farmer was dragged by the ankles whilst tied-up by barbed wire, if only jewellery was stolen. The isolated setting of the farms, supported by telephone lines and electricity lines that are cut off, provide the offenders with adequate time and the opportunity to abuse farmers compared with urban areas where there might be a quicker response to the victimization and a higher risk of being apprehended.

Farmers as victims of violence and perpetrators of violence against farmers

Desperate, angry and opportunistic offenders use the isolated setting of the farms and the extended timeframe (linked to a successful get away as opposed to crimes in urban areas) to their advantage, whilst politically driven violence against farmers is characterized by a misuse of power. Often, poor farmers, living on the breadline, are targeted for their land, whereas other farmers are targeted because of their race or political affiliation.

Doorewaard found that offenders of livestock theft are able and willing to use violence to secure livestock and are motivated by money or items that they can sell in return for money. Hence, for some offenders, calculated decisions, farmers that are perceived as easy targets, inside or other available information and the remote risk of being caught on the crime scene play a prominent role in offenders' motivation to commit their crimes.

The impact of violence against farmers

Some farmers take up to five years to recover from the anxiety, trauma, loss they suffered and to be productive again. The economic impact on the farming community is immense, with farmers that survived facing the ongoing fear of re-victimization, implementing increasing security measures and revising personal movement and freedom, where other farmers vacate their farms and move to more secure environments (nearby towns and becoming day-farmers). Farmers' support structure (such as other family members and friends) and access to policing resources are more remote than persons living in urban areas. Lastly, violence against famers might deter future young farmers from entering the industry as farming might be perceived as a risky career (see Hornschuh, 2007).

Violence against farmers is an increasing global problem characterized by many different causes (such as poverty) and motives (such as racial hatred). Offenders are from all strata of life – from influential and powerful entities (governments/political parties) to unemployed, angry and opportunistic perpetrators. Acts of violence against farmers have devastating (such as loss of life) and long-lasting effects (such as trauma) for the victims, their families, workers and for society as a whole, impacting the economy and food supply for society.

Suggested readings

Clack, W. and Minnaar, A. (2018) 'Rural crime in South Africa: An exploratory review of "farm attacks" and stock theft as the primary crimes in rural areas', *Acta Criminologica: Southern Africa Journal of Criminology*, 31(1): 103–35.

De Villiers, J. (2020) 'INSIGHT / Farm murders and rural crime: Unpacking violence, race and statistics', 20 July, Available from: https://www.news24.com/news24/analysis/insight-farm-murders-and-rural-crime-unpacking-violence-race-and-statistics-20200719 [Accessed 17 September 2021].

Doorewaard, C. (2020) 'Livestock theft: A criminological assessment and sample-specific profile of the perpetrators', Unpublished MA in Criminology, University of South Africa, Pretoria.

Hornschuh, N. (2007) 'A victimological investigation of farm attacks with specific reference to farmers' perceptions of their susceptibility, the consequences of attacks for farmers and the coping strategies applied by them after victimisation', Unpublished MA dissertation, University of Pretoria, South Africa.

News24 (2020) 'Farm murders and rural crime: Unpacking violence, race and statistics – South Africa', 21 July, Available from: https://farmingportal.co.za/index.php/component/content/article?id=4696:farm-murders-and-rural-crime-unpacking-violence-race-and-statistics-south-africa [Accessed 10 October 2021].

29

Violence against Women

Walter S. DeKeseredy

Patriarchy and its hurtful symptoms endure around the world. Hence, it is not surprising that multi-country research consistently shows that one in three women globally will be physically or sexually assaulted in their lifetime. Undoubtedly, violence against women is one of this planet's most compelling social problems, but some groups of women are at much more likely to be targeted than others.

Rates of victimization

Rural women are especially vulnerable, and their high rates of victimization add further empirical support to the claim that rural rates of crime, in general, may be higher than urban rates in particular types of rural places and for specific types of crime. Consider United States National Crime Victimization Survey data showing that the rates of all types of intimate violence in non-metropolitan districts are higher than those of their urban and suburban counterparts. Furthermore, the national Australian Longitudinal Study on Women's Health found that rates of violence against young women are the highest for those living in remote/very remote areas and the lowest for those living in major cities. There is also ample evidence from smaller-scale investigations done around the world that rural women experience higher and more severe rates of sexual and physical violence than those who live in more densely populated locales. A few studies, too, reveal that rural women experience the highest rates of police-reported intimate violence victimization.

Types of violence

Violence against rural women, however, is not limited to acts of interpersonal violence such as forced penetration and beatings. It also consists of non-physical behaviours such as online stalking, as well as corporate and state–corporate violence against women. Corporate violence is any behaviour undertaken in the name of the corporation by decision makers or other persons of authority within the corporation that endangers the health and safety of employees or other persons who are affected by that behaviour.

Even acts of omission, in which various decision makers refuse to take action to reduce or eliminate known health and safety risks, must be considered corporate violence. State–corporate violence involves violent behaviours resulting from political institutions pursuing a goal in direct cooperation with corporations. The sexual harassment of female farmworkers in the United States is a prime example of state–corporate violence against rural women. It is estimated that eight out of every ten of them have experienced this harm, and the victims are not protected by United States federal anti-discrimination law.

Scholarship

Empirical and theoretical work on violent crimes of the powerful committed against rural women is slowly growing, but most rural criminologists who examine violence against women have so far focused on acts of interpersonal violence occurring in private places. Moreover, the bulk of the extant literature on beatings, sexual assaults and other types of face-to-face assaults that rural women experience is currently dominated by United States and Australian feminist offerings. This is not a major pitfall, but the field needs to become more internationalized, and research done in non-English speaking countries should be a top priority.

Risk factors

The primary risk factors associated with male-to-female interpersonal violence in rural and remote communities are:

- high rates of gun ownership;
- membership in sexist, all-male peer groups;
- male pornography consumption;
- separation/divorce;
- natural disasters;
- male hunting sub-cultures;
- an 'ol' boy network' that includes criminal justice officials;

- substance abuse;
- natural resource extraction booms;
- community norms prohibiting women from seeking social support;
- geographic and social isolation; and
- the absence of social support agencies and public transportation.

Theoretical frameworks

Unlike mainstream criminological research on a myriad of topics, conceptual and theoretical developments in the study of violence against rural women draw heavily from radical feminism and male peer support theory. Radical feminists view patriarchy as the 'root cause' of all social relations, inequality and crime. Moreover, they see patriarchy as the chief source of oppression in any society. Male peer support theorists agree with radical feminists, but they also assert that key sources of woman abuse are attachments to male peers and the resources that these men provide that incite and legitimate abuse against women.

There are currently only explanations of separation/divorce sexual assault in rural places that are informed by these two schools of thought, and it is unclear whether these theoretical contributions can also effectively explain other types of woman abuse in non-metropolitan districts. Still, these sociological theories are unique because feminist sociological thought in the area of violence against women has become marginalized since 2008. In fact, sociological insights are being pushed out of criminological studies in general.

Policy and practice

New ways of thinking theoretically about violence against rural women are much needed. So are innovative and effective policies and practices. Rural survivors of woman abuse face many barriers to service due in large part to the lower levels of funding in rural communities compared with urban communities and to the greater efficiency required of rural service providers in using the limited government funds they receive. Linked to these hurdles is that rural areas have far fewer shelter services and fewer shelter beds than do more densely populated places. Additionally, rural women must travel long distances to obtain services. This is one main reason why they are more likely to delay or refrain from seeking medical and other types of help. Even if they have a car, the time to travel to and from a service takes up much of the day, and it is difficult to hide a long trip from an abusive partner. There are, of course, other barriers to service identified in the violence against rural women literature, and they are not likely to be eliminated soon.

Since the COVID-19 pandemic depleted government resources around the world, improved services provided by government agencies may seem like 'pipe dreams'. Yet the fact remains that policy changes such as building more shelters and hiring more social service providers will require a major increase in government funding to support rural abused women. In a United States context, opponents to tapping the public sector will say that doing so costs too much money that should be used to lower the deficit. If money is not too tight for military spending, bailing out large corporations and building new prisons, then money can be found for state-supported solutions too – if that is what people want. What is needed now is a major reformation in thinking about funding prevention and protection services for rural women.

Suggested readings

DeKeseredy, W.S. (2021) 'Male-to-female sexual violence in rural communities: A sociological review', *Dignity: A Journal of Analysis of Exploitation and Violence*, 6(2): 1–19.

DeKeseredy, W.S. (2021) *Woman Abuse in Rural Places*, London: Routledge.

DeKeseredy, W.S. and Rennison, C.M. (2020) 'Thinking theoretically about male violence in rural places: A review of the extant sociological literature and suggestions for future theorizing', *International Journal of Rural Criminology*, 5(2): 162–80.

Saunders, S. (2015) *Whispers from the bush: The Workplace Sexual Harassment of Australian Rural Women*, Sydney: The Federation Press.

Websdale, N. (1998) *Rural Woman Battering and the Justice System: An Ethnography*, Thousand Oaks, CA: SAGE Publications.

30

Violent Extremism

Rachel Hale

There is considerable definitional ambiguity surrounding extremism, with terms such as violent political extremism, hateful extremism, terrorism and radicalization used, sometimes interchangeably, even though differences exist. A *universal* definition of extremism is unlikely – what is considered 'extreme' is relative and subjective, dependent on individual attitudes and beliefs.

Despite the complexity and subsequent blurriness in this space, extremist views and actions have generally been characterized as those which sit at the periphery of society and are divisive, intolerant, fanatical, supremacist, anti-democratic and authoritarian in nature. More specifically, 'violent extremism' refers to support for or use of violence to achieve a political, religious or ideological goal.

The vulnerability of rural communities to violent extremism

The impact of place upon personal identity and social relations is widely accepted, with its impact on crime and victimization at the core of rural criminology. The unique, place-based socio-cultural and socio-historical contexts of rural communities are of relevance to violent extremism. Location-specific circumstances can impact the viability of a community as a target for extremist recruitment or activity, as well as the degree to which violent extremist activity is supported or rejected by a community (see Puecker et al, 2020 for an example of disparate local responses). For example, if extremist messaging targets an existing grievance within a community, support is more likely, making mobilization easier to achieve.

The economic climate of a given place can impact levels of support for extremism, albeit indirectly. In rural and remote areas there is generally a higher concentration of disadvantage, which can make rural citizens vulnerable to violent extremism. For example, in the African Sahel, unemployment is high, food supply is low and there is poor governance of land and natural resources, which has enabled violent extremism to take hold (see Freudenberger et al, 2019).

Widespread corruption creates high levels of distrust and hostility against the state, which violent extremist groups leverage, particularly targeting disenfranchised youth. Violent extremist groups promise to fulfill the needs of the vulnerable citizen if they will join their cause, which may be an enticing offer for those living in dire circumstances in remote, isolated areas of the globe.

Violent extremist militant groups have also been seen to exploit the *isolation* of places across the Sahara Desert, which are difficult to access. Remote locations, by their very geographic placement, can therefore create vulnerabilities to violent extremist activity. The abundant open space of remote locations may present an opportune environment in which extremist groups can establish a base and undertake practical training, spaces which are geographically distant and sparsely populated and hence lacking in oversight from police or other citizens. The dense bushland of some rural areas can assist in concealing and camouflaging extremist activities.

Conversely, the fallacy of the 'rural idyll' (a peaceful, crime-free space) may provide an ideal backdrop against which to contrast the stark aggression and violence of extremist groups. This was evident when over 30 balaclava-clad men from an Australian neo-Nazi group organized in the picturesque Grampians National Park in rural Victoria in January 2021, chanting White-supremacist sentiments and performing Nazi salutes, disrupting the serene image of the iconic regional location. This attracted much media coverage and attention from both the public and law enforcement, a central aim of extremist exhibitions.

The homogenous nature of rural communities may produce opposition to diversity and plurality, which can cultivate violent extremist ideology, particularly of the far-right. In Switzerland, for example, those locations with a higher prevalence of right-wing extremist activity are rural and comprised of very few foreigners, leading to dominant conservative and xenophobic views. Similarly, in Germany, far-right groups are believed to have a relatively stronger presence in rural areas where there are fewer immigrants, higher migration out of the area and an older population. In these settings, far right-wing extremists may be viewed as a means of protection against the threat of outsiders, thus attaining community support (see both Schellenberg, 2013 and Davolio et al, 2006 for the European context).

Addressing rural violent extremism

The unique characteristics of rural areas call for different responses to violent extremism from those utilized in urban locations.

Whilst the isolation and intimacy of rural locations can act as an incentive for violent extremists, it also presents an opportunity for intervention owing to the relative transparency of rural and remote communities in comparison to densely populated urban settings. Violent extremist activity in rural locations may be more easily identified by rural citizens and local law enforcement, presenting an increased opportunity for intervention. However, this relies on the willingness to report, as well as attitudes which denounce violent extremism which motivate people to act.

The mobilization of civic society to counter violent extremist efforts is paramount. Where the public become more accepting of diversity and difference, extremist ideology is more likely to be viewed negatively and, therefore, resisted (see Carlsson, 2006). High levels of civic pride held by rural communities can also counter violent extremist efforts, wherein rural citizens do not want their community reputation to be tainted by violent extremism (see Peucker et al, 2020).

Strong ties to community, family and work may also deter engagement in extremist activity, wherein there is more to lose for the rural citizen if extremism is strongly denounced by their community and involvement would therefore lead to exclusion and shame. In the case of young people in rural areas, who may be particularly vulnerable to recruitment, strengthening their bonds to community and reducing levels of disadvantage and disenfranchisement may serve to thwart violent extremist recruitment efforts.

Whilst social control can assist in reducing the likelihood of violent extremists mobilizing rural citizens, it is not a panacea, and there are numerous macro influences – economic and political – which must be addressed. This includes the relative disadvantage experienced in rural communities, lack of investment in social services and justice resources and political messaging which paints diversity as a threat to be feared – each permeating all communities but resonating particularly with homogenous rural communities.

Suggested readings

Carlsson, Y. (2006) 'Violent right-wing extremism in Norway: Community based prevention and intervention', in P. Rieker, M. Glaser and S. Schuster (eds) *Prevention of Right-Wing Extremism, Xenophobia and Racism in European Perspective*, Halle: Deutsches Jugendinstitut e.V., pp. 12–29. Available from: https://www.dji.de/fileadmin/user_upload/bibs/96_6736_Prevention_of_Right_Wing_Extremism.pdf [Accessed 19 November 2021].

Davolio, M.E, Gerber, B, Eckmann, M. and Drilling, M. (2006) 'The special case of Switzerland: Research findings and thoughts from a context-oriented perspective', in P. Rieker, M. Glaser and S. Schuster (eds) *Prevention of Right-Wing Extremism, Xenophobia and Racism in European Perspective*, Halle: Deutsches Jugendinstitut e.V., pp. 30–47. Available from: https://www.dji.de/fileadmin/user_upload/bibs/96_6736_Prevention_of_Right_Wing_Extremism.pdf [Accessed 19 November 2021].

Freudenberger, M., Sanjak, J., Tagliarino, N. and Thomson, N. (2019) 'Climate change, land and resource governance, and violent extremism: Spotlight on the African sahel', 1 May, Climate Change, Land and Resource Governance, and Violent Extremism Issue Brief. Available from: https://www.tetratech.com/en/documents/climate-change-land-and-resource-governance-and-violent-extremism-spotlight-on-the-african-sahel [Accessed 19 November 2021].

Peucker, M., Spaaij, R., Smith, D. and Patton, S. (2020) 'Dissenting citizenship? Understanding vulnerabilities to right-wing extremism on the local level: A multilevel analysis of far-right manifestations, risk and protective factors in three local municipalities in Victoria', Melbourne: Victoria University.

Schellenberg, B. (2013) 'Right-wing extremism and terrorism in Germany: Developments and enabling structures', in R. Melzer and S. Serafi (eds) *Right-Wing Extremism in Europe: Country Analyses, Counter-Strategies and Labor-Market Oriented Exit Strategies*, Berlin: Friedrich Ebert Foundation, pp. 35–74. Available from: http://dx.doi.org/10.15496/publikation-5604 [Accessed 19 November 2021].

Property and Other

31

Acquisitive Farm Crime

Kyle Mulrooney and Alistair Harkness

Farm crime refers to criminal offending which impacts upon the function of the pastoral, agricultural and aquaculture industries. Common forms of victimization include trespassing, illegal shooting and hunting, breaking and entering, the theft of equipment and tools, with livestock theft being the 'quintessential rural crime', as well as the theft of farm supplies and inputs (such as fencing supplies, chemicals and fuel), firearms, water, fruit crops and personal items.

Farm crime devastates lives and communities in rural settings, provincial towns, smaller urbanized regional areas and at the urban fringe. Offending on farming sites has been largely forgotten historically in the canon of scholarly literature, although it is now receiving far greater attention, not least because of the financial implications for farming communities but also for its psychological and sociological impacts.

Aspects of locational context and cultural geography have deeply shaped incidents and responses to crime in rural spaces. This is especially true of farms where the tyranny of distance, lack of access to public services, dense acquaintanceship networks and ideals of self-sufficiency are salient. Evidence also suggests a significant 'dark figure of crime' in rural spaces (where crime occurs but is not reported and recorded), and sometimes strained relationships between the police and the policed.

Victimization

The impact of crime on farmers, workers and other rural property owners is significant. Victims of farm crime not only sustain physical losses as a consequence of theft, but also lost work time and impact on annual income, higher insurance premiums and the loss of breeding stock and the intellectual property in developing a blood line.

Productive farmers may leave the sector owing to the personal stress and anxiety associated with victimization. Farm crime can have additional flow-on effects, impacting pricing, distribution and the availability of produce. Additionally, high levels of victimization contribute to a loss of community cohesiveness, decreasing the capacity of communities to prevent and respond to crime more generally. In regional areas, perceptions of a community, its safety, people and culture can affect tourism, impacting on its attraction of high-quality health professionals or teachers and retention of other essential service providers.

Farms can be targeted by motivated offenders who are well-organized, well-equipped and highly skilled – with cultural and industry knowledge and ready markets to dispose of stolen items. Offenders can also be opportunistic. Research indicates that victimization and repeat victimization against farmers is high. For example, a 2020 survey of farmers in New South Wales, Australia by Mulrooney indicated that 80.8 per cent of farmers reported having been a victim of some type of farm crime, and that there were high levels of repeat victimization.

Explanations for such victimization is multifactorial, complex and relate to locational context and the role cultural geography plays in offending behaviour and crime control. Distances between settlements and properties are much greater than in urbanized environments, and population densities are significantly lower. Local policing presences are much sparser. Consequently, the risk–reward calculation made by a potential offender is skewed to them favourably as there are a myriad of valuable assets on farms, yet 'eyes' in the paddock are sparse.

Reporting of farm crime

Culturally, there are historically more relaxed attitudes to security in the rural. Reticence to report crime exists, in large part, because of three categories of factors:

- institutional (a belief that police are not able to do anything; a perception that police do not have sufficient agricultural knowledge; a worry that police will not take a report seriously; hassles of the legal process);
- evidence-based (no evidence or too much time has passed; unable to prove ownership of stolen property; not sure a crime has occurred; feeling that the crime is not serious enough to report); and
- community-based (the offender was known or living in the community; fear of revenge; the farmer solved it themselves).

These factors lead to a disparity between crime committed and reported, and subsequently an impact on policing resourcing and operational practices based on an incomplete picture of the true extent of offending and victimization.

Crime prevention

The successful prevention of farm crime requires awareness, education, resilience, engagement and the creation of 'active citizens' providing capable guardianship. A shared responsibility and partnerships – between individuals, communities, police and government – is vital. Use of technology is also useful, including motion-activated cameras deployed strategically, smart animal ear tags, transferable liquid property marking and alert apps.

Livestock theft prevention is a particular challenge; one which warrants both specific and situational approaches. Livestock thefts may be more problematic near state and national boundaries because it is more difficult to police border areas. Adopting generalized, urban-derived approaches are not likely to be successful because of the uniqueness of rural areas (geography, demography, farm size, terrain and vegetation and proximity to public roads).

Policing

Four key challenges are present for the policing of farm crime: (i) physical geography and the tyranny of distance between properties and from formal elements of the criminal justice system, notably police; (ii) rural stoicism and significant under-reporting of crime, which limits police ability to apprehend offenders and results in an incomplete picture of actual offending rates for policy and decision makers; (iii) familiarity between police and rural residents, and the strain that this places on rural-based police who must maintain a dual identify as law enforcer and local resident; and (iv) resource provision to rural-based police and rural-specific training for officers sent to work in rural locations and dealing with agricultural crimes.

Future responses to rural crime prevention look promising in terms of intervention with technological and environmental innovations, but farmers also desire informed and engaged rural police who are well-resourced and who can be relied upon to be both proactive and reactive. Specialized rural policing teams – such as the New South Wales Rural Crime Prevention Team – can play a vital role in not only enforcing the law but also in preventing offending from occurring by bridging police and rural communities.

Suggested readings

Barclay, E. (2016) 'Farm victimisation: The quintessential rural crime', in J.F. Donnermeyer (ed) *The Routledge International Handbook of Rural Criminology*, London: Routledge, pp. 107–15.

Clack, W. (2020) 'Livestock theft prevention', in A. Harkness (ed) *Rural Crime Prevention: Theory, Tactics and Techniques*, London: Routledge, pp. 205–19.

Harkness, A. and Larkins, J. (2019) 'Farmer satisfaction with policing in rural Victoria, Australia', *International Journal of Rural Criminology*, 5(1): 47–68.

Harkness, A. and Mulrooney, K. (2020) 'Conclusion: The future of rural crime prevention', in A. Harkness (ed) *Rural Crime Prevention: Theory, Tactics and Techniques*, London: Routledge, pp. 319–29.

Mulrooney, K.J.D. (2021) 'The NSW Farm Crime Survey 2020', The Centre for Rural Criminology, University of New England. Available from: https://spark.adobe.com/page/zsV05pknxXl7N/ [Accessed 24 September 2021].

32

Animal Rights and Activism

Jarret S. Lovell

Do the animals we rely on for food, clothing and medicine deserve legal protections from human action? Conversely, are animals simply property whose sole purpose is to serve humans? These questions are ones that philosophers, spiritual leaders, legal scholars and legislators struggle to answer, and they represent the core issue at the heart of the debate over animal rights.

The animal rights debate

How humans view and socially construct animals has been a centuries-old debate. In the seventeenth century, philosopher René Descartes argued that animals are machine-like *things* operating solely on instinct: they have no capacity to suffer. It was therefore preposterous to suggest that animals deserved protections from harm. Today, most people recognize that animals are not mere machines but instead have consciousness, self-awareness and the capacity to experience pleasure and pain. Given that humans now recognize animals can experience suffering, philosophers and activists alike insist that humans have a moral obligation to treat animals in a manner that respects their interests not to suffer (see Singer, 2002; Taylor, 2009).

More specifically, they argue that animals are deserving of protections from unnecessary harm via *rights*. Rights are legal provisions that acknowledge and protect the interests of others. The precise extent to which humans ought to protect animals is hotly debated, even within the animal rights movement.

The 'animal *welfare* movement' believes humans have an obligation to minimize animal suffering whenever possible; however, humans are free to use animals for food, clothing and entertainment. The 'animal *liberation* movement' argues that any unnecessary infliction of pain or suffering on animals is immoral, and that animals are not for humans to eat, wear or use for entertainment purposes since these uses are wants, not necessities. Clearly, how we choose to conceptualize and legally construct animals has far reaching implications, especially for the world's rural and farming communities where the use of animals is a way of life. In some cases, the recognition of animal rights can even criminalize previously legal and culturally accepted behaviours, such as certain farming practices or the hunting of legally protected species.

Animal rights activism

Historically, animals have had the legal status of property and were not granted many (if any) protections. Sentiment towards animals began to change during the eighteenth and nineteenth centuries. During the debate over slavery in the United States, abolitionists drew attention to similarities between the status of slaves and animals, and found that the arguments for legal protections applied to humans and animals alike. The publication of Charles Darwin's work on evolution explained that humans *are* animals and share ancestry with other species.

During the twentieth century, industrialization changed animal husbandry. Small farms gave way to massive and mechanized factory farms. In the twenty-first century, such farms process tens of thousands of animals each day in an assembly line fashion, extracting 'products' such as milk and eggs, or turning animals into meat. Activists argue that these factories cause immense suffering as animals are cramped, denied access to sunlight and must undergo painful farming procedures such as castration, dehorning and amputation without anesthetic. Climate scientists, meanwhile, explain that factory farms are harmful to the environment as animal waste run-off pollutes water supplies, and the mass production of animal products contributes to climate change.

Every day, approximately 70 billion animals are raised globally for future human consumption. Animal rights activists largely channel their efforts into exposing the harms of factory farms, as farming animals for food represents the single largest use of animals by humans. Primarily located in rural communities, these farms benefit from their remoteness. Therefore, organizations such as People for the Ethical Treatment of Animals (PETA) rely on undercover investigators to bring images of factory farming to public light. Investigators travel to rural communities to gain employment as factory farmhands. Whilst on the job, they secretly photograph the conditions of animals and disseminate the images to news organizations and, contemporaneously, through social media. This strategy has proven immensely effective. For example, after the Humane Farming Association ran a media campaign in 1986 featuring images of veal calves on factory farms, sales of the meat plummeted by more than 66 per cent, and the numbers remain low today.

Beginning in the 1990s, legislators in the United States, the United Kingdom, Australia and elsewhere responded to activists' investigations by enacting legislation criminalizing the taking of pictures *at* animal enterprises without the owner's consent. These animal enterprise interference statutes (dubbed 'Ag-Gag' laws by opponents, see Fiber-Ostrow and Lovell, 2016) continue to meet legal challenges from many sides, as news organizations contend that they pose a challenge to a free press, whilst labour organizations fear the impact such laws will have on whistleblower protections for workers from the meat, dairy and other industries. Meanwhile, activists are now circumventing these laws by using aerial drones to capture images from above, rather than *from* or *at* animal enterprises directly. It remains to be seen whether these laws or the efforts around them will withstand legal challenges.

Animal rights and rural criminology

The debate over animal rights is a debate that questions the social construction of animals, the meaning of humanity, morality and criminality. The debate over whether to acknowledge animals as potential victims in a criminal court, and their human counterparts as potential defendants, places the animal rights debate at the heart of rural criminology. So too does the geographical component of the debate which pits the values and customs of rural communities against those of urban and suburban regions.

The contribution of factory farms to crimes against the environment places the debate within the scope of green criminology, whilst the disproportionate impact that run off from these enterprises has in farming communities (which are often populated by lower income and minority households) should be of interest not only to rural criminologists, but to those occupying the mainstream as well. In short, the study of animal rights and the potential criminalization of farmers or activists is essential to a comprehensive understanding of rural criminology.

Suggested readings

Beers, D.L. (2006) *For the Prevention of Cruelty: The History and Legacy of Animal Rights in the United States*, Athens, OH: Swallow Press.

Beirne, P. (2007) 'Animal rights, animal abuse and green criminology', in P. Beirne and N. South (eds) *Issues in Green Criminology: Confronting Harms Against Environments, Humanity and Other Animals*, Portland, OR: Willan Publishing, pp. 55–83.

Fiber-Ostrow, P. and Lovell, J.S. (2016) 'Behind a veil of secrecy: Animal abuse, factory farms, and Ag-Gag legislation', *Contemporary Justice Review*, 19(2): 230–49.

Singer, P. (2002) *Animal Liberation*, New York: Ecco.
Taylor, A. (2009) *Animals and Ethics: An Overview of the Philosophical Debate* (3rd edn), Peterborough, ON: Broadview Press.

33

Blood Sports

Angus Nurse

Traditional 'field sports' such as hunting, shooting and fishing are predominantly lawful, albeit subject to regulation in the form of hunting licences and associated permits which authorize the killing and taking of wildlife subject to conditions. By contrast, the term 'blood sports' is associated with activities such as the hunting of wild mammals with dogs or underground 'sports' such as dog fighting and cockfighting.

Accordingly, blood sports can be defined as those activities involving combat either of humans versus animals or animals versus animals in which an element of pain and suffering is integral to the activity. This includes activities such as animal fighting (dog fighting and cockfighting), the baiting of animals or human inflicted harm for 'sport' (such as badger baiting or bullfighting) or the hunting of animals for entertainment that is invariably linked to the killing or harm of the animal (such as fox hunting and hare coursing).

Blood sports in context

A core factor in blood sports is an element of animal harm, where participants and supporters will distinguish between the suffering of animals for no purpose and the bravery and competitive values of animals who are participants in sports that are considered to have value to both humans and animals. As Lawson (2017) explains in respect of dog fighting, dogs will fight ferociously until one gives up, is seriously injured and cannot continue or dies. If a losing dog is not kept for breeding purposes because of its bloodline or because it frequently won in previous fights, it can be beaten or put to death by drowning, strangulation or with a gun. Often the beating or execution is a form of entertainment for the audience.

Thus, in the illegal blood sports world it is precisely the ability of certain animals to withstand suffering and to continue fighting (for example bulls, fighting dogs, game cocks and badgers) that identifies them as 'game' animals and worthy participants in the 'sport'. Blood sports may also be linked to associated illegal activity such as gambling (in the case of dog fighting, cock fighting and hare coursing) as well as elements of organized crime. The nature of blood sports – derived from field sports or tradition – is that they frequently take place in rural areas and thus are of interest to rural criminologists.

Green criminology's consideration of animal rights and species justice is arguably concerned with animal abuse and suffering (which includes crimes impacting on animals in the wild or living predominantly away from urban areas), but also with the notion of environmental and ecological crimes that relate to the exploitation of natural resources and are defined as environmental or ecological crimes. Thus, those blood sports that exploit animals in rural areas as a natural resource for human entertainment (such as hare coursing and fox hunting) are distinctly and simultaneously rural and green crimes.

International perspectives

At present there is no binding international treaty for the protection of animals and thus no clear international legal standard in respect of animal protection and anti-cruelty. Instead, it is broadly the responsibility of individual states to determine how best to provide for animal protection and anti-cruelty through domestic law. Yet most jurisdictions now have laws that make deliberate animal abuse an offence; albeit some variation exists in how offences are framed.

Animal law generally criminalizes deliberate individual acts of gratuitous cruelty towards most animals, whilst at the same time allowing the continued use of animals in food and other industries that arguably amounts to institutional cruelty. Attempts to enshrine protection against animal cruelty into animal law have been attempted via a Universal Declaration of Animal Rights which was presented to the United Nations Educational, Scientific and Cultural Organization (UNESCO) in 1978, but failed to gain necessary support.

Subsequently the World Society for the Protection of Animals supported by other non-government organizations pursued a proposal for a Universal Declaration of Animal Welfare to be adopted by the United Nations. To date this also has not been successful.

Key elements of both the Universal Declaration of Animal Rights and Universal Declaration of Animal Welfare are arguably incorporated into the Five Freedoms for Animal Welfare which originated with the 1965 Brambell Report (the report of the Technical Committee to Enquire into the Welfare of Animals kept under Intensive Livestock Husbandry

Systems) and has subsequently gained currency as an international standard for appropriate animal welfare standards. The five freedoms articulate welfare concerns in the form of: (i) freedom from hunger and thirst; (ii) freedom from discomfort; (iii) freedom from pain, injury or disease; (iv) freedom to express normal behaviour; and (v) freedom from fear and distress.

These five freedoms are primarily concerned with promoting general standards of animal welfare and ensuring good conditions and treatment which avoid animal suffering. However, they are also clearly applicable to preventing the deliberate infliction of pain that occurs in blood sports. An international consensus on the need for good animal welfare means that further criminalization of blood sports is a factor of contemporary environmental and animal law (see for example the United Kingdom's Hunting Act 2004).

Blood sports and communities

Masculinities are an integral part of blood sports and a significant factor in the animal harm caused by blood sports. Men are arguably attracted to cockfighting for prestige and to reinforce masculinity whilst also being attracted to activities such as bullfighting for both masculine and cultural reasons. In Spanish culture, for example, the bull is considered to represent nature and the matador represents human culture (see Iliopoulou and Rosenbaum, 2013). Thus, bullfighting can be said to represent the triumph of human culture over that of nature (or the animal).

Blood sports also illustrate complex attitudes towards crime and what is perceived as crime within rural communities where resistance to legislation to control or criminalize blood sports and hunting activities continues. Field sports are inextricably linked to a rural identity, and sports such as cockfighting and dog fighting identified with community acceptance and support for blood sports in rural settings, which illustrates the existence of a distinctly rural type of masculine offender engaged in crime and criminality directed towards animals.

Suggested readings
Forsyth, C.J. and Evans, R.D. (1998) 'Dogmen: The rationalisation of deviance', *Society and Animals*, 6(3): 203–18.
Iliopoulou, M. and Rosenbaum, R. (2013) 'Understanding blood sports', *Journal of Animal and Natural Resource Law*, 9: 125–40.
Lawson, C. (2017) 'Animal fighting', in J. Maher, H. Pierpoint and P. Beirne (eds) *The Palgrave Handbook of Animal Abuse Studies*, Basingstoke: Palgrave Macmillan, pp. 337–62.

Nurse, A. (2021) 'Green criminological perspectives on dog-fighting as organised masculinities-based animal harm', *Trends in Organized Crime*, Available from: https://doi.org/10.1007/s12117-021-09432-z [Accessed 30 October 2021].

von Essen, E. and Allen, M.P. (2017) 'Reconsidering illegal hunting as a crime of dissent: Implication for justice and deliberative uptake', *Criminal Law, Philosophy*, 11: 213–28.

34

Cross-border Livestock Theft

Willie Clack

Cross-border livestock theft occurs within the context of influences such as religion and wars and across rivers, mountains and oceans. Any attempt to discuss cross-border livestock theft is futile without conceptualizing the context of a border. A border can have an unprecedented number of meanings: the border between two farms; the boundary between police precincts; different policing counties; between states or provinces internally within a country; and between countries. No matter what determines country borders or boundaries between whom and whatever, borders do influence criminal activities.

Consideration as to how countries are formed and utilize borderlines is essential. Historically, treaties after a war, marriages between people of different kingdoms, colonialism, culture, religion and so on have determined country borders. In most cases, country borderlines have been determined by geographic features such as mountain ranges and rivers, or politically as lines drawn on a map such as the 'Scramble for Africa' in the late twentieth century.

The enforcement of borderlines is another factor that needs to be kept in mind when referring to livestock theft. Notorious borderlines are the security fence between North and South Korea, and the United States and Mexico borderline. The primary purpose of borders between countries is to protect the sovereignty of a nation, and – as a secondary purpose – countries regulate the movement of people and trade commodities. The factors which have determined country borders impact on crime in rural areas and livestock theft.

Religious challenges in cross border livestock theft

In 1947, Sir Cyril Radcliffe divided the old India using religion to separate Muslim and Hindu areas: the result was the creation of contemporary Pakistan, Bangladesh and India. The boundaries between these countries are artificial as there are no or limited natural borders. Hinduism (India) allots cows ethical treatment and respect: cows and their by-products are considered sacred. Muslims (Bangladesh), alternatively, do not prescribe special treatment for cows. The difference in religious attitudes towards cows provides a trade relationship but also increases livestock theft. Rustlers have been smuggling the animals from India to neighbouring Bangladesh for many years. There is a trend of cattle theft throughout India and their transporting for trade at the cattle corridors along the border between India's West Bengal and Bangladesh.

Organized groups and cross-border livestock theft

Livestock farming generates income for many people across the globe. In the Chad Basin, for example, thousands of cows were traditionally exported weekly to northeast Nigeria from Cameroon and Chad and sold in many markets near the border. Organized criminal groups, though, can present a disruptive influence. This particular export trade was common until the insurgency caused by Boko Haram, a designated terrorist organization operating in North Africa and especially in Nigeria. Boko Haram use the proceeds of crime to finance their terrorist activities. One of their main income lines is livestock theft, where cattle are stolen in one country and then taken to a neighbouring country for later sale. The modus operandi of the criminals, such as illegal armed groups and organized crime, also affect cross-border cattle theft in places such as Colombia. Here, livestock theft is just one of several illegal activities that transnational criminal organizations have taken to maintain revenue streams when profits from other trans-border crimes decrease.

Cross-border livestock theft amongst different demographic groupings

The Karimojong are members of a group of specialized pastoralist societies, including the Jiye and Toposa in South Sudan; the Nyangatom in Southern Sudan and Ethiopia; the Turkana in north-western Kenya; and the Iteso, Karimojong, Jie and Dodoth in northwest Uganda. The establishment of colonial authority in East Africa in the early twentieth century interrupted a long-standing tradition of inter-ethnic cattle raiding amongst the Karimojong. Presently, the raiding of cattle continues fiercely in this region with the distinction that, in most raids, AK-47 automatic rifles are used, leading to mortalities amongst people.

Mountainous borders and livestock theft

There are only three countries enclosed by one other country: San Marino, Vatican City and Lesotho. The former two do not have any agricultural activities, with only Lesotho (surrounded by South Africa) dependent on agriculture and migrant labour. Geographically, Lesotho is known as the 'mountain kingdom', and the borders with South Africa are the Drakensberg and Maluti Mountain ranges. Livestock theft is endemic along Lesotho's borders, with particularly those bordering the Eastern Cape suffering severely. Ironically, very little attention is provided to the Eastern Cape area and more attention is given to the Free State region. The reason for the Free State receiving more attention is the economic development of the areas and having political and judicial access. Livestock theft and related violence have reduced the living standards of an already impoverished populace, exacerbated social divisions and resulted in widespread violence both within Lesotho and across the border in South Africa.

Rivers, oceans and cross-border livestock theft

A surge in cattle and horse rustling plagues farmers along the Uruguay–Brazil border, and suggestions are that it is organized in nature. Rivers, mainly, constitute the border between these two countries. The increase in cattle theft in both countries has resulted in specialized units in the criminal justice systems to deal with livestock theft. Madagascar is a country situated in the Indian Ocean surrounded by water. Like Lesotho, it is an impoverished country, but when viewing media reports of the numbers of stolen cattle, it is excessive.

Suggested readings

Gray, S., Sundal, M., Wiebusch, B., Little, M.A., Leslie, P.W. and Pike, I.L. (2003) 'Cattle raiding, cultural survival, and adaptability of East African pastoralists', *Current Anthropology*, 44(s5): S3–S30.

Kynoch, G., Ulicki, T., Cekwane, T., Mohapi, B., Mohapi, M., Phakisi, N., and Seithleko, P. (2001) 'Cross-border raiding and community conflict in the Lesotho-South African Border Zone', SAMP Migration Policy Series No. 21, Waterloo, ON: Southern African Migration Programme.

Malnekoff, E. (2013) 'Cattle smuggling from India to Bangladesh', Honours Thesis, Western Michigan University. Available from: https://scholarworks.wmich.edu/honors_theses/2378 [Accessed 30 October 2021].

Nagle, L.E. (2013) 'Cattle rustling and ranching by illegal armed groups and organized crime', *International Enforcement Law Reporter*, 29(6): 1–3.

Okoli, A.C. (2021) 'Cows, cash and terror: How cattle rustling proceeds fuel Boko Haram insurgency in Nigeria', *Africa Development*, 44(2): 57–76.

35

Drug Cultivation, Manufacture and Movement

Ralph A. Weisheit

There is a large body of research on drug use and drug treatment. Less studied is the geographical dispersion of drug cultivation, manufacture and movement. These activities are skewed towards rural areas for a variety of reasons. Some activities require considerable space to operate at scale. The cultivation of marijuana, coca and poppies require physical space and is most cost effective when done outdoors. Methamphetamine production also depends on a precursor chemical derived from the ephedra plant, widely grown for thousands of years in the Middle East and China. Remote areas provide a level of physical privacy not possible in cities.

Rural areas also facilitate the dispersion of noxious odours from drug laboratories, as is the case with methamphetamine, cocaine and heroin production. Cultivated marijuana plants can also emit a strong odour. Production away from urban areas reduces the chances that citizens or authorities will detect these operations.

A rural and remote location presents another advantage to those making or trafficking in illicit drugs. Compared with urban areas, many rural areas are under-policed. Rural officers may cover large geographic areas, have fewer resources, frequently work alone and are often without backup nearby. In many countries, rural areas are also the poorest parts of the country, making underpaid and understaffed local officials easy targets for corruption. In some countries rural areas serve as a refuge for militant groups whose activities are funded by the illicit drug trade.

Drug cultivation, manufacture and trafficking hotspots

Reflecting the global extent of the problem, the United States Department of State (2021) has identified 22 countries involved in major illicit drug producing and/or drug-transit activities, including Afghanistan, The Bahamas, Belize, Bolivia, Burma, Colombia, Costa Rica, Dominican Republic, Ecuador, El Salvador, Guatemala, Haiti, Honduras, India, Jamaica, Laos, Mexico, Nicaragua, Pakistan, Panama, Peru and Venezuela.

Through its annual reports, the United Nations Office on Drugs and Crime (2021) identifies patterns and trends in drug production and drug trafficking. Following their lead, this discussion is organized by drug type.

Opiates

Afghanistan leads the world in opium production, accounting for an estimated 83 per cent of the opium produced worldwide. Regarding *seizures*, more than half of the opiates seized worldwide were seized in Iran (see United Nations, 2021). Where drugs are produced or transported, drug use generally follows. Iran has more Narcotics Anonymous meetings per capita than any other country. This might be unexpected given that Iran is an Islamic nation and Islam rejects the use of alcohol and mind-altering drugs, but the Islamic nations of Afghanistan and Pakistan also rank high on the list. Ultimately, economic, environmental, geographical and political conditions create market forces that matter more than the influence of religion.

Regarding the trafficking of opiates, the United Nations report (2021) identifies three main sources of supplies: (i) Afghanistan is a major supplier to neighbouring countries, including Iran, and to markets in Central Asia, Europe, South Asia, Africa and the Middle East; (ii) Myanmar and Laos supply markets in East and South-East Asia and Oceana; and (iii) Mexico (with some supply from Colombia and Guatemala) is the primary supplier to North America and to a lesser extent to South America.

Cocaine

Cocaine is the processed product of the leaves of the coca plant, a bush that has grown for centuries in the remote mountains in Colombia, Peru and Bolivia. The plants grow in rugged rural areas where the large-scale production of other crops is not economically practical. The leaves are processed in laboratories far from urban areas, utilizing chemicals with strong odours, including alcohol and sulfuric acid. Efforts to eradicate cocaine laboratories have pushed them farther east into Brazil's remote Amazon basin.

Trafficking patterns for cocaine have shifted over the years. At one point most of the cocaine produced in South America was destined for the

United States. More recently, South American producers have supplied cocaine to Western and Central Europe, moving shipments through Brazil and West Africa (see United Nations, 2021). The drug often enters European markets hidden in shipping containers through large urban ports. Colombian cocaine is also trafficked into Asia and Australia, often through Brazil.

Methamphetamine

Methamphetamine laboratories account for as many as 95 per cent of all amphetamine-type stimulant laboratories worldwide (see United Nations, 2021). The drug is easy to manufacture, and for this reason as many as 52 countries may be involved in methamphetamine production. Afghanistan has seen an increase in methamphetamine production as a way for rural farmers to survive, and revenue from methamphetamine may now exceed that from opiates (see European Union, 2020; Alcis et al, 2021). The odour from methamphetamine laboratories is noxious, making rural areas appealing as laboratory sites. The number of seized methamphetamine laboratories has gone down over time but the volume of methamphetamine produced by laboratories has gone up. The largest laboratories are found in Mexico, East Asia and South-East Asia. Both purity and potency have increased over time. The demand for methamphetamine has also triggered a growing illicit trade in precursor chemicals.

Marijuana

Marijuana production is global, as observed in the United Nations (2021) report, and can be grown in almost every country of the world. Of the ten countries with the highest amounts of seized cannabis, seven were in the Americas. The remaining three countries were India, Nigeria and Morocco. Most of the trafficking in cannabis is consumed within the same region in which it is grown, most often transported by land.

Conclusion

Across the globe, as Wainwright (2016) argues, the production and transport of illicit drugs can best be understood by taking a market perspective – what would a successful business do in the face of legal and social obstacles? From this perspective, using rural areas for the production and trafficking of illicit drugs makes good business sense. By providing physical privacy, more limited resources for law enforcement and a source of income in economically impoverished areas, the rural solves or reduces problems linked to the detection of illicit operations.

Suggested readings

Alcis, Mansfield, D. and Smith, G. (2021) 'War gains: How the economic benefits of the conflict are distributed in Afghanistan and the implications for peace', London: ODI, Available from: https://l4p.odi.org/assets/images/L4P-Nimroz-study_main-report-13.08.21.pdf [Accessed 25 August 2021].

European Union (2020) 'Emerging evidence of Afghanistan's role as a producer and supplier of ephedrine and methamphetamine', Available from: https://www.emcdda.europa.eu/system/files/publications/13410/emcdda-methamphetamine-in-Afghanistan-report.pdf [Accessed 28 August 2021].

United Nations Office on Drugs and Crime (2021) 'World drug report 2021', Available from: https://www.unodc.org/unodc/data-and-analysis/wdr2021.html [Accessed 7 September 2021].

United States Department of State Bureau of International Narcotics and Law Enforcement Affairs (2021) 'International narcotics control strategy report, Volume 1: Drug and chemical control', Available from: https://www.state.gov/wp-content/uploads/2021/02/International-Narcotics-Control-Strategy-Report-Volume-I-FINAL-1.pdf [Accessed 16 August 2021].

Wainwright, T. (2016) *Narco-nomics: How to Run a Drug Cartel*, New York: Public Affairs.

36

Food Crime

Allison Gray

Food crime involves the various, and often overlapping, patterns of deviance, harm, crime and injustice concerning the structures and institutional arrangements surrounding the production, processing, marketing, distribution, selling, consumption and disposal of food products.

The concept of food crime uses legal definitions of what is wrong or criminal as well as the problematizations of such classification, including (in)actions that are lawful but immoral or otherwise harmful. Many descriptions of food crime tend to focus on types of fraud within food chains, but these are insufficient in acknowledging the diversity of problems that arise involving food systems and all the elements involved.

There are often contradictions between definitions of food crime, where single practices or behaviours can be considered both legal as well as unjust, criminal or deviant whether in terms of means or ends. For example, the world's most successful chocolate company sells products comprised of cocoa beans harvested using child or forced labour. Similarly, vast amounts of pesticides are used on monoculture fields which leak into groundwater through runoff and contaminate the drinking reservoir of local communities.

Further, there are cases of pluriactivity – or when individuals are involved in both legitimate and criminal or harmful behaviour within or beyond food systems. This may include things such as dairy farmers who ensure the milk produced for food supply does not contain antibiotics because they refuse to treat ill cows and let them suffer, or wheat farmers who produce quality grain but keep seeds to plant in future seasons despite this being a breech of contract with the seed supplier, or the rancher who treats their cattle well but sells illegal firearms from their barn.

Rationale for food crime

Whilst there are cases of individuals in food production roles who commit food crimes for personal rational reasons, many food crimes result from socio-economic and cultural forces and are facilitated by unequal power relations.

The foundation of food production labour is comprised of vulnerable groups – the majority of the world's working poor are employed in the agricultural sector, including a large proportion of women in lower income countries – which facilitates victimization by the output- and profit-focused industrial agricultural industry (where one per cent of corporations control two-thirds of the world's agricultural land). For instance, employers requiring agricultural workers to spread liquid waste on fields causes direct environmental harm and indirect harm to the surrounding communities, and also puts those workers at high risk for personal victimization (such as physical injury and threat of disease) alongside threatening the wellbeing of the environment and the safety of food.

As such, food crimes often contain blurred boundaries between offending and victimization, including expanding conceptualizations of victims beyond humans to also include non-human animals and the natural environment.

These three general categories of victims often co-experience victimization across food production processes, whilst the offender is exclusively human. To be clear, food production necessarily entails a certain level of environmental harm, and often harm to animals as well. Growing food, particularly using intensive and industrial processes, uses a lot of the soil's nutrients and requires significant application of fertilizers to replenish those lost nutrients, along with vast amounts of water use and pesticide and herbicide dependence.

Whilst food crime spans across spaces, its experience is largely rural as much of the most resource- and labour-intensive stages of the food chain occur outside urban centres. The geographical space needed for food production is largely comprised of rural areas – fields for growing crops and pasturing livestock animals, large facilities for processing and storing grains and legumes, expansive operations for feeding, slaughtering and butchering livestock animals and everything in between.

The placement of agricultural on-goings is structured and regulated by spatial and zoning requirements, but sometimes placement is (also) due to pragmatic or business-based decisions. For example, abattoirs are often situated well outside urban centres to maintain a physical distance between livestock slaughter and human eyes – a distance which works to maintain ideological rifts of human consumers not 'meeting their meat' and facilitate the continuation of high rates of meat consumption. Alternatively, sprawling fields of monoculture crops are kept far from cities' edges so run-off from excess fertilizer and pesticide use will not impact larger-scale public health outcomes or comprise urban freshwater sources.

Owing to this physical proximity, rural communities and persons are disproportionately victims of food crimes and harms. Human and animal residents near agricultural operations suffer through things such as contaminated groundwater (including wells) from leaching pesticides or poor air quality from spreading manure onto crop fields which are linked to an array of health concerns – all of which also harm local environments and natural ecosystems. Animals residing in rural areas, including both livestock animals and wildlife, are also highly susceptible to victimization by food crimes, including the loss of habitat from deforestation strategies for field crop expansion or the emotional toll dairy cows experience every time her calf is stolen from her so her milk can be prioritized for human consumption.

Agriculture is the primary industry in the majority of rural communities around the world, and farming and food production is part of the very fabric of the rural experience. As such, how rural-residing individuals define food crimes and harms is often different from how urban-residing individuals may define them. Rural-residing individuals can be more often concerned with production-level crimes or harms that threaten their 'way of life' associated with food production, whilst urban-residing individuals can be more often concerned with consumption-level crimes or harms that threaten their experience with accessing, purchasing and eating foodstuffs.

Whilst food crime impacts everyone and everything, it is necessarily rural. Locating food crime, and ultimately understand its complexities, requires looking beyond the supermarket shelves of urban centres and contextualizing the behaviour of agricultural workers within the output-focused and corporate-driven food industry.

Suggested readings

Croall, H. (2012) 'Food, crime, harm and regulation', *Criminal Justice Matters*, 90(1): 16–17.

Gray, A. and Hinch, R. (eds) (2018) *A Handbook of Food Crime: Immoral and Illegal Practices in the Food Industry and What to Do about Them*, Bristol: Policy Press.

Rizzuti, A. (2021) 'Organised food crime: An analysis of the involvements of organised crime groups in the food sector in England and Italy', *Crime, Law, and Social Change*, doi:10.1007/s10611-021-09975-w.

Tourangeau, W. and Fitzgerald, A. (2020) 'Food crime and green criminology', in A. Brisman, A. and South, N. (eds) *Routledge International Handbook of Green Criminology* (2nd edn), London: Routledge, pp. 213–28.

37

Heritage Crime

Louise Nicholas

On the most basic level, rural heritage crime is any event that breaks the law and has a detrimental effect on protected heritage and historic assets within a rural context. The reality is more complex than this, both in definition of rural heritage and of what may be considered criminal.

Rural heritage is not just the physical heritage that we see in our rural societies. It is also the intangible, cultural heritage such as farming practices, language and storytelling and craft techniques. It can also include natural heritage such as protected hedgerows, coral reefs and Indigenous lands. The crime against these settings can be broad ranging.

Legality or illegality

It is important to consider that an action that is against the law in one jurisdiction may not be against the law in another jurisdiction: for example, the various protections (or lack thereof) offered to valuable forest lands. Governments may also grant themselves and others – usually powerful corporations – exceptions to commit acts which in any other circumstance would be illegal: for example, licensing polluting behaviours which damage waterways and consequentially traditional activities reliant on those resources. The granting of permits does not lessen the harm caused to rural heritage settings, nor make the outcome any less devastating for the people, natural environment and wildlife involved.

For these reasons, when we consider rural heritage crime we must take a more pragmatic zemiological (that is, social harms) approach. That is, we are less concerned with the letter of the law and more concerned with the spirit of the law. We look at the harms caused to rural heritage rather than whether a particular jurisdiction legislates for or against an action. In this way, we can see that governments and state actions can be equally guilty of rural heritage crime as individuals and organizations.

Rural heritage crime offences

There are a broad range of rural heritage crime offences. These can broadly be categorized as follows:

Targeted rural heritage crime. This is crime that is targeted specifically at rural heritage assets because of something intrinsic about the asset itself. This may be, for example, illicit metal detecting where individuals go to isolated locations and attempt to steal small valuable heritage items from the ground.

Incidental rural heritage crime. This is where a crime occurs that as a side effect also impacts upon rural heritage. For example, where thieves have broken in to steal farm equipment and, as they enter or exit the property, they have also caused damage to a protected heritage asset.

Rural heritage-specific offences. This is a crime that exists in law only because of the protected status of the rural heritage asset. For example, the destruction of Iron Age hillforts that are recognized and safeguarded by law. Various planning and development offences are also covered by this category, such as the demolition of a farm building that is recognized in law as historically worthy of protection.

State rural heritage crime. This is a harmful act carried out by authorities. For instance, state-sponsored archaeology which damages Indigenous lands during excavations and research activity – particularly, although not exclusively, lands that would otherwise be under legal protection. Arguably in the context of state rural heritage crime, inaction may also be considered as criminal or harmful. An example is the lack of management of the climate crisis which, as well as the well-documented harms to the environment and society, results in rural coastal heritage being eroded and lost to the sea.

Rural heritage harms. These are incidents, events and actions that are not generally able to be legislated against but nonetheless cause great harm to rural heritage assets and especially to intangible heritage. This may include land clearance or development which removes locally important features or makes the maintenance of heritage practices more difficult. Other actions that may be legal yet harmful to rural heritage could include the removal of funding for traditional methods of farming or crafts.

Study of rural heritage crime

Rural heritage crime is a relatively recent addition to the rural crime lexicon. Heritage crime research often focuses instead on the trafficking of cultural artefacts, or the impact of heritage damage in urban settings. There are difficulties researching rural heritage crime, most distinctly in that there is the compound problem of not only monitoring rural locations for evidence of disruption to heritage assets, but also that not all heritage assets are known to exist (outside of local communities, or at all), or (inter)nationally recognized as such when they are known. This makes identification of harm caused an incredibly difficult task, which is reflected in relatively scant academic literature.

The lack of knowledge and understanding around rural heritage crime, combined with the low priority it is generally given by authorities, set alongside common difficulties associated with effectively policing remote rural areas, means there is a significant risk of harm and loss for rural heritage. Prosecutions globally for rural heritage crime are rare. The impact of rural heritage crime is arguably greater for under-represented groups, whose cultural and tangible heritage are at risk of loss both because of the aforementioned issues and the lack of understanding and recognition of their heritage by those in power. These groups are at particular high risk of state-sanctioned rural heritage crime, and of rural heritage harms. There is a great deal of further work needed on rural heritage crimes and harms before we fully understand the nature and extent of loss for present and future generations around the world.

Suggested readings

Grove, L. and Thomas, S. (eds) (2014) *Heritage Crime: Progress, Prospects and Prevention*, Basingstoke: Palgrave Macmillan.

Hutchings, R.M. and La Salle, M. (2017) 'Archaeology as state heritage crime', *Archaeologies*, 13(1): 66–87.

LaPan, C. and Barbieri, C. (2014) 'The role of agritourism in heritage preservation', *Current Issues in Tourism*, 17(8): 666–73.

Maury, S.P. (1999) 'Surviving in the rainforest: The realities of looting in the rural villages of El Petén, Guatemala', 56. Available from: http://www.famsi.org/reports/95096/95096ParedesMaury01.pdf [Accessed 22 October 2021].

38

Illegal Hunting and Trespass

Alistair Harkness, Kyle Mulrooney and Matthew Box

There exists scant contemporary empirical consideration of the impacts of illegal hunting or shooting, such as damage to environments; harm to animals (native and livestock); risks of self-harm; harms to people and property; or the role of organized criminal elements. There is, though, a large volume of research related to illegal poaching, particularly poaching of endangered fauna in Africa and East Asia which has attracted transnational criminal elements. A differentiation between poaching and illegal hunting needs to be acknowledged: the former addresses notions of theft for profit; the latter often involves non-economic motivations and, in various instances, can be considered a 'folk crime', a form of political dissent, or resistance to conservation measures (see Pohja-Mykrä, 2016).

Trespass

Associated with illegal hunting is trespass. Unauthorized access to public (such as forests and parks) and private (such as farms) rural property can create social, psychological and economic harms to individual residents and rural communities – and to the rural sector by way of biosecurity threats. Such illegal access can result in confrontations, and in several countries has led to instances of farmers and hunters engaging in armed confrontation resulting in fatal injuries. In an Australian context, illegal hunting is a significant cultural phenomenon with a history dating back to the beginnings of colonization, with access to land and resources – for those who have none – being a long running issue. Such access has been an important part of the social history of many rural communities in economic, cultural and social terms.

Behaviours and impacts

Although recreational hunters contribute to local economies, there is serious concern regarding the activities of *illegal* hunting and shooting on both public and private land. The 2020 NSW Farm Crime Survey found that 46 per cent of farmers had experienced illegal hunting, the second most common offense after trespass (Mulrooney, 2021). Barclay's 2015 research found that whilst livestock theft was relatively stable there was growing concern regarding trespassing and illegal hunting associated with what has been referred to as the 'pig hunting craze' in these two states. Offenders often go equipped with off-road vehicles, night vision goggles, GPS systems and high-powered rifles.

Illegal hunting practices can result in disturbances to vegetation; the spreading of disease whilst trespassing which can impact on food safety and security; and the consequences of un-extinguished campfires. Other behaviours include illegal spotlighting on private property; trophy hunters killing stags for the head and leaving the carcass; safety and anti-social issues around shooting in towns, front yards and elsewhere on public and private land; and animal cruelty issues such as the use of under calibre ammunition.

The 'social contract'

Legitimate hunters and hunting organizations point to the negative impact which illegal hunting has on them: that is, illegal hunters put in jeopardy the social license which society grants to law-abiding hunters, giving all hunters a bad name. There are three competing social licences: (i) landowners and occupiers' rights regarding their land; (ii) the ability to exercise longstanding traditional hunting practices, especially of rural communities; (iii) cultural practices of first nation's communities.

Access to and control of natural resources for the purposes of hunting has been a significant issue, and is very much in competition with other developing political sensibilities around conservation and animal welfare. Internationally, this has led to conflicts and increasing contests, particularly between those who view hunting as a 'right' and those who prioritize animal welfare, often emphasizing the importance of sentience and the capacity of animals to experience suffering.

In countries where hunting is seen as a 'privilege', increasing restrictions have often emphasized this divide. In Sweden, illegal hunters have attempted to normalize and legitimize their actions by claiming illegal hunting is a result of their social license being infringed. In Australia, illegal hunting is justified by some perpetrators as they see conservation rules as politically based and driven rather than conservation-based. Property often comes into play as some landowners believe they hold 'sovereign rights' over their land and should be free to hunt threatened species on their land if they wish. Hunting by first nations people, whilst originally seen as illegal in many instances and subject to conflict, has progressively been understood as an important part of their cultural life, though tensions between cultural practices and government limits and restrictions remain.

Approaches to illegal hunting prevention
Policing

Plural and third-party policing is built around partnerships, and beneficial to policing are crime prevention programmes facilitated either by police with industry groups, farming organizations and other community groups such as rural fire services. Indeed, community groups are important partners given their own social license, penetration into the community and ability to overcome the perception of metropolitan measures being imposed upon a rural community.

Legislation and regulation

Often the distribution of legislative responsibility (i.e. state and territory) means that statutes are not uniform across jurisdictions, and this can create a conflict between laws. Even within a jurisdiction, there can be a split between 'game' and 'environment' responsibilities, as well as law enforcement and regulatory enforcement. Where there exists cross jurisdictional responsibility, cooperation amongst agencies is an essential element to effective responses. Differences between jurisdictions are not only due to their respective histories, but also the activities of lobby groups and official inquiries.

Technology

Some jurisdictions have opted for technological crime prevention and partnership approaches, such as the use of smart phone apps whereby landowners and legitimate shooters can share information, thus ensuring a degree of oversight as to who might be present on a property. An example of this is the 'Hunt NSW' app in New South Wales, Australia, which is based upon similar programmes that have been developed in the United States since the mid-2010s. In the United States, North Dakota declares all land is open unless it has been posted on a state database; in South Dakota, there was an attempt to negate the need for consent until the law was struck down by the State Circuit Court.

Suggested readings
Barclay, E. (2015) 'Survey finds crime on farms is increasing', 31 August, *Australian Cane Grower*, 15–17. Available from: https://issuu.com/canegrowers0/docs/2015-08-31_web_issuu [Accessed 28 October 2021].

Bradshaw, S. (2016) 'NSW stock theft and trespass review: Final report', June, Available from: https://apo.org.au/sites/default/files/resource-files/2017-07/apo-nid103371.pdf [Accessed 28 October 2021].

Mulrooney, K.J.D. (2021) 'The NSW Farm Crime Survey 2020', Armidale, NSW: The Centre for Rural Criminology, University of New England, Available from: https://spark.adobe.com/page/zsV05pknxXl7N/ [Accessed 28 October 2021].

Pohja-Mykrä, M. (2016) 'Illegal hunting as rural defiance', in J.F. Donnermeyer (ed) *The Routledge International Handbook of Rural Criminology*, London: Routledge, pp. 329–38.

Von Essen, E. and Allen, M.P. (2015) 'Reconsidering illegal hunting as a crime of dissent: Implication for justice and deliberative uptake', *Crime, Law and Philosophy*, 11: 213–28.

39

Organized Crime

Robert Smith

Defining organized crime in a rural context

The consideration of the influence of 'rural organized crime' and, indeed, 'organized crime in the rural' within the rubric of criminology is polarized and in its infancy. This is not a case of mere semantics but lies at the core of the issue one of the main issues underpinning organized crime in a rural context.

Apart from the dearth of literature, there is no clear definition of what constitutes rural organized crime. There are numerous definitions of what constitutes organized crime per se which link the concept to our understanding of organized criminality to mainly urban-based 'mafias' and 'organized crime groups' (OCGs). Additionally, there is at present no working definition because it is a conflation of two related phenomenon of 'organized crime' and 'rural crime' (see relevant chapters in Donnermeyer, 2016). Again, this is not mere semantics but underpins the topic.

As well as being located in the criminological and policing literatures, contemporary research on the topic has been conducted by geographers, sociologists, supply chain theorists and business school scholars. The literatures on food fraud and food crime are also related to organized crime in the rural.

When considering organized crime, there is an inclination to think of mafia-like organizations and shadowy 'Mr Big' figures connected to traditional OCGs. Indeed, the established and traditional view of organized crime in rural settings is guided by the 'urban marauder thesis' whereby OCGs from urban settings target rural homes and businesses. Although statistically these marauders do commit the majority of acquisitive crime in rural settings, they are only one side of the problem of organized rural criminality.

However, little consideration is given to either the existence of a rural criminal class or the involvement of rural criminals and industry insiders.

The sociologist Ferdinand Tönnies in defining the difference between urban and rural living (*Gemeinschaft* and *Gesellschaft*) stressed that urban areas are portrayed as visibly criminal and the rural as less criminal posited the existence of a smaller rural criminal class. This fits in well with a 'rural idyll' thesis and with the criminological 'alien conspiracy' thesis, whereby it is easier to blame outsiders for our problems than consider that our neighbours may be involved in criminality.

Over time, this 'outsider' bias became the established position in criminology. However, in the last decade research by business school scholars into rural criminality, food fraud and supply chain criminality have challenged this established viewpoint by arguing that so-called 'rogue farmers', 'criminal farmers' and 'industry insiders' are also part of the problem of organized rural crime because often the commission of acquisitive crimes (such as the theft of livestock and plant equipment) requires those involved to possess a modicum of rural social capital and skills, as suggested by the work of Smith and colleagues. Indeed, they went as far as to consider the existence of 'rural organized crime groups' who are composed of outsiders and insiders who prey on their neighbours and peer groups. This is corroborated by the work of the criminologist Goodall (2021) who argues that, in a European context, organized crime within the food industry is generally committed by 'food people' and by 'collaborators' within the farming industry.

Identification of issues and impacts on communities, people and places

Much of the rural organized crime literature, although expanding, deals mainly with developing offender typologies. There is very little written about rural organized crime, farmers and rural inhabitants as victims, albeit in the popular press the farmer is very much portrayed as a victim of marauding urban organized criminals. From a methodological perspective most of the literature is based on ethnographic or documentary research methodologies from media reports and official documents. As a result, there is ample scope for further empirical studies using other methodologies, in particular interviews with so-called 'insiders' and 'urban marauders'.

The literature is overly focused on urban marauders as the perpetrators of rural organized crime, and with farmers and rural inhabitants being the victims. Although mafia involvement is alluded to in the media, a holistic model of rural organized crime has yet to be fully articulated and developed in which the involvement of mafias and their infiltration of the legitimate economies is documented and theorized.

A central problem is that the literature is very Western centric, with separate literature evolving for the United States, Australia, the United Kingdom and the European Union, but little has been written about rural organized crime in African and South American contexts. For example, there is a big difference between the Italian Mafia involvement in European Union food subsidy fraud, marijuana cultivation in the United States and bushmeat hunting in Africa.

Rural and farm crime is a global phenomenon as evidenced by the international nature of the 2013 Horsemeat Scandal and the global nature of tractor and plant theft (see Smith and McElwee, 2019). This dictates that context and culture are of vital importance in researching organized crime in any rural setting because they both influence social constructions of rural criminality. Therefore, any over-arching theories of organized rural crime must take cognisance of both the insiders and outsiders.

Suggested readings

Donnermeyer, J.F. (ed) (2016) *The Routledge International Handbook of Rural Criminology*, London: Routledge.

Goodall, O. (2021) 'The reality of rural crime: The unintended consequences of rural policy in the co-production of badger persecution and the illegal taking of deer', *The British Journal of Criminology*, 61(4): 1005–25.

Smith, R. and McElwee, G. (2019) 'The "horse-meat" scandal: Illegal activity in the food supply chain', *Supply Chain Management: An International Journal*, 26(5): 565–78.

Smith, R. and McElwee, G. (2015) 'Stolen to order! Tractor theft as an emerging international criminal enterprise', in G. McElwee and R. Smith (eds) *Exploring Criminal and Illegal Enterprise: New Perspectives on Research, Policy and Practice*, Bingley: Emerald, pp. 121–54.

Somerville, P., Smith, R. and McElwee, G. (2015) 'The dark side of the rural idyll: Stories of illegal/illicit economic activity in the UK countryside', *Journal of Rural Studies*, 39: 219–28.

40

Trophy and Big Game Hunting

Angus Nurse

Trophy hunting and game hunting involve the killing, abduction and sometimes trade in dead wildlife. Trophy hunting generally involves a hunter paying a fee to kill an animal and claim its body or body parts as a trophy of conquest. In contrast to subsistence, hunting which involves killing of animals for survival (such as for food consumption or clothing) and providing for others, trophy hunting and game hunting consist of killing animals primarily for recreational purposes.

Game and trophy hunting are concerned with the pursuit of live quarry and consist of tracking and killing animals for pleasure or to display body parts such as horns, antlers, skulls, tusks or teeth (see Nurse, 2013). Trophy hunting is frequently sold via hunting safaris which, particularly in Africa, are based on the key 'Big 5' species: rhinoceros, elephant, leopard, lion and Cape buffalo.

From a criminological perspective, trophy hunting and game hunting engage with issues concerning the exploitation of wildlife as a natural resource and anthropocentric perspectives of animals and non-human nature as existing primarily to satisfy human interests. Trophy hunting also attracts the attention of green criminologists in respect of critical analysis of conservation and monetization of the rural environment and non-human nature. Green and rural criminologists also consider the extent to which the legal and illegal exist in a seemingly symbiotic relationship in legalized animal killing.

Trophy hunting, rurality and recreation

Trophy hunting's reliance on species which offer trophy opportunities represents an incursion into wild areas not entirely controlled by man. Accordingly, trophy hunting is arguably direct predation against animals of a type that goes beyond simple killing and that extends into encroaching on any rights that wildlife might be said to have where they exist away from man.

In this respect, trophy and game hunting typify how humans exercise control over animal habitats, not only through the encroachment of human developments on areas where animals have historically held sovereignty in respect of having control over a territory (including a right to kill other animals where necessary for survival) but also in respect of actively managing many areas where animals live freely. Thus, trophy hunting represents interference in the lives of (mostly) free, living wild animals and illustrates that wildlife's autonomy is limited to the extent that it is allowed by man and may be periodically (temporarily) revoked.

Trophy hunting directly engages with rural policy given that, in practice, game reserves, national parks, nature reserves and other wilderness areas often fall within the remit of the relevant government environment department. This raises a question concerning the extent to which wildlife and wild areas are legally considered to be *res nullius*. This is where resources such as the ocean, outer space or biodiversity have been considered to belong to no one and so arguably can be subject to unchecked private exploitation in the Lockean tradition, whilst simultaneously such resources might be considered part of the 'global commons' that belong to everyone and are considered *res communes*.

In practice, states exercise control and ownership of natural resources such as wildlife and regulate the use of game resources for the public good and in the national interest. Big game hunting is largely associated with African states with particular trophy hunting industries concentrated in Namibia, South Africa, Kenya, Tanzania, Zimbabwe, Botswana and the Democratic Republic of the Congo. Kenya is considered to be the birthplace of African trophy hunting, whilst Lindsay and colleagues (2006) identified 23 African countries as having hunting industries – with the largest in South Africa generating revenues of $USD100 million a year (revenues paid to operators and taxidermists). The United States also has an established trophy hunting industry.

Trophy hunting in an international context

Hunting is generally regulated through state legislation, although international law also applies in respect of rare and threatened species that may nonetheless be hunted in accordance with state legislation. The Convention on International Trade in Endangered Species of Flora and Fauna 1973 (CITES) provides a framework for the protection of endangered species that may be threatened by trade. However, CITES facilitates the use and exploitation of animals by allowing trade in wildlife under certain conditions through a permit system whilst also containing provisions that prohibit the use of endangered species and in principle providing for criminal enforcement of any breach of its provisions.

The 184 member countries of CITES are each required to establish an authority to supervise the permit process and an advisory group of scientists to comment on the status of species commercially traded (see Wyatt, 2013). Thus, CITES is arguably conservation, management and trade legislation combined, providing for regulation of trade in animals rather than an outright prohibition on the use and exploitation of wildlife. CITES primarily provides protection for the most vulnerable wildlife whose trade it prohibits.

Trophy hunting and communities

Contemporary debates about trophy hunting include the contextualization of trophy hunting as a form of conservation and consideration of the extent to which money paid by hunters benefits game animal populations and the local economy. African states with a limited industrial base and limited manufacturing or export industries may nevertheless be abundant in wildlife and thus have incentive to exploit natural resources and to develop a rural-based economy.

Trophy hunting can be linked to issues of masculinity as well as the drive to collect wildlife. Although African hunting is not exclusively carried out by White male hunters, this group makes up a significant proportion of hunters, in part because of the socio-economic factors existing as determining factors in hunting. The price of hunting packages, for example, is determined by market rules where the perceived value of the trophy is a significant factor. Thus, the rarer and more 'challenging' species will attract hunters from more affluent backgrounds willing and able to pay the premium for killing the rarer species and who may prize trophies that are far removed from their everyday experiences (see Palazy et al, 2012).

By contrast, local residents may be unable to afford trophy hunting opportunities except where concessions or exemptions from regulations are provided. In principle, rural communities and the rural environment benefit from trophy hunting where the proceeds of hunting are an important factor in endangered species conservation and the rehabilitation of wildlife by providing income for conservation without impacting on population growth. Trophy hunting is generally considered to be sustainable in respect of the limited extent to which the removal of males for hunting impacts on breeding populations. But the extent to which rural communities benefit from hunting is questionable given that, in several African states, trophies are government property and raise revenues primarily for the state. Whilst there may be employment opportunities for local communities in trophy hunting (for example as game wardens and guides), local communities may not otherwise directly benefit from trophy hunting revenues.

Thus, from a criminological perspective, trophy hunting raises questions concerning the extent to which its exploitation of wildlife identifies racialized power relationships where mostly White hunters from the Global North are able to exploit wildlife in the Global South and African states.

Suggested readings

Lindsey, P.A., Alexander, R., Frank, L.G., Mathieson, A. and Romanach, S.S. (2006) 'Potential of trophy hunting to create incentives for wildlife conservation in Africa where alternative wildlife-based land uses may not be viable', *Animal Conservation*, 9(3): 283–91.

Nurse, A. (2013) *Animal Harm: Perspectives on Why People Harm and Kill Animals*, Basingstoke: Palgrave Macmillan.

Palazy, L., Bonenfant, C., Gaillard, J.M. and Courchamp, F. (2012) 'Rarity, trophy hunting and ungulates', *Animal Conservation*, 15(1): 4–11.

Wyatt, T. (2013) *Wildlife Trafficking: A Deconstruction of the Crime, the Victims and the Offenders*, Basingstoke: Palgrave Macmillan.

41

Water Crimes

Gorazd Meško and Katja Eman

Water can be found almost everywhere on planet Earth and is the world's greatest renewable resource, crucial for human survival. Water appears in the form of oceans, seas, lakes, rivers and streams, canals and ponds, waterfalls and underground water caves, thermal springs, icy Arctic and Antarctic areas as well as lesser-known underground reservoirs.

Water is the second most important natural element, besides air, for the survival of the human (and other) species (note that approximately 75 per cent of the human body is composed of water). Water can be defined as a natural transparent liquid that is also colourless, odourless and tasteless. Water is an environmental resource damaged by crime, the object of a crime or the means to commit a crime.

Crime is an intentional act or omission (negligence) that constitutes an offence and is punishable by law. Clifford and Edwards (1998) note that an environmental crime is any act that violates the law or an environmental regulation. Environmental crime is an environmental intervention, which is every permanent or temporary act or resigning process which negatively influences the environment, people's health and the exploitation and use of natural goods.

Water is a natural good. Therefore, crimes against water present one form of environmental crime. Water crime can be defined as any punishable contravention or violation of the limits on human behaviour imposed by national criminal legislation, which uses surface and groundwater or water services as a means for committing other crimes.

Water and 'rural green criminology'

Water is precious, with no substitute. Therefore, water resources and systems are attractive targets for criminals. The harm and risk to the water supply are associated with multiple causes ranging from industrial pollution and water theft to global warming. Its importance to the personal, social and economic health and wellbeing has generated increasing criminological interest since the turn of the twenty-first century. Besides green criminology, rural criminology is increasingly interested in water crimes, as most water sources are located in rural areas and, consequently, most water crime occurs there. There is an urgent need to consider the nature, dynamics and impacts of water crimes from an environmental drivers' perspective (for example, land use, climate change and infrastructure). Rural green criminology is well aware that new typologies of crime have to be developed, new methodologies for research employed and new modes of social control devised to address present and future water issues adequately.

Types of water crime

Water crimes include any intentional act that poses potential harm or damage to water. Water-related crimes are often recorded under other offences, such as fraud, corruption, trafficking, falsification of documents and so on. Water crimes belong to the group of environmental criminality. A wide range of types of crime against water have emerged historically. Many countries and institutions have made lists of different crimes against water, which include these eight:

1. *water contamination/pollution* – the intentional, often industrial, contamination of water, contamination due to depletion of underground and surface water sources, contamination of surface and groundwater by fertilizer/chemical or effluent runoff from farmland;
2. *water fraud* – such as the alteration of sampling techniques or results to avoid treatment costs, thus causing negative health implications or fiscal artifices aimed at adulterating registered water consumption, thus generating an illicit gain;
3. *violation of water compliance and enforcement* – violation of water quality regulations and forced water privatization;
4. *water theft* – the unauthorized use and consumption of water before it reaches the intended end user, including the pumping, impoundment or diversion of water from irrigation channels, river systems, dams or groundwater bores without a licence or in contravention of licence conditions that cause changes to flows and reduce water access to neighbouring farms, livestock and riparian zone management;
5. *water-related corruption* – includes acts involving political decision makers, the (illegal) exploitation of natural resources, large-scale investments and procurement contracts or daily actions of small payments to gain access to water services or to avoid controls and fines;

6. *water-related organized crime* – the activity of criminal organizations that have taken control over the management of water or water services within a particular territory;
7. *water-related terrorism* – activities, such as the threat of terrorist attacks on the water sector, targeting the quality (such as poisoning) or availability (such as an attack on critical infrastructure) of water or taking control of water services to finance terrorist activities illicitly; and
8. *water-related cyberattacks* – intrusion into an information communication technology system, manipulation of information or networks, data destruction and so on of water management companies, including ransomware and malware attacks.

The present and the future

A survey of water crime in European countries revealed that criminal groups have found an ideal business to make an easy profit, mainly owing to loopholes in national environmental protection legislation and the considerable differences in this field between countries. As long as climate change, conflict and poverty continue to aggravate the Earth's dwindling water supply, crimes against water will remain a reoccurring and ever more intense global problem. Another problem is that water crimes are still viewed as petty offences or minor crimes within a national context rather than transnational organized crime issues. Therefore, they do not get enough attention from law enforcement authorities and will probably never be effectively resolved.

A scarcity of clean drinking water has become one of the crucial problems of the twenty-first century. For this very reason, rural (green) criminology must go in the direction of expanding the field of water protection and water crime prevention. According to Johnson and colleagues (2016), environmental protection should focus on legal and governmental actions that give priority to the human right to water and to the sustainability of natural resources instead of private interests. The task of rural green criminology is to produce a detailed study and analysis of the nature of water harms and water management (including enforcement, prosecution and sentencing practices) and the systems of criminal, civil and administrative law designed to manage, protect and preserve water. At the present moment, various crimes against water are emerging and present the core issues of social and environmental justice.

Suggested readings

Clifford, M. and Edwards, T.D. (1998) 'Defining "environmental crime"', in M. Clifford (ed) *Environmental Crime: Enforcement, Policy, and Social Responsibility*, Gaithersburg, MD: Aspen Publishers, pp. 121–45.

Eman, K., Meško, G., Segato, L. and Migliorini, M. (eds) (2020) *Water, Governance, and Crime Issues*, Cham: Springer.

Johnson, H., South, N. and Walters, R. (2016) 'The commodification and exploitation of fresh water: Property, human rights and green criminology', *International Journal of Law, Crime and Justice*, 44: 146–62.

42

Wildfires: Causation and Prevention

Janet Stanley and Belinda Young

In 2009, climate scientists reported that, without drastic action, human-induced global warming would soon reach a point of irreversibility. Despite this dire warning, and the hundreds of other scientific papers on climate change, even before 2009, the emission of greenhouse gasses continued to accelerate due to a failure to put in place sufficient preventative actions. One of the consequences of greenhouse gasses and thus higher temperatures is that megafires that are happening with increasing regularity around the world.

In Australia, the ongoing acceptance of wildfires, regardless of the ignition, has led to a dearth of understanding and leadership in wildfire prevention. Recognizing that wildfires are a mix of human-caused climate change as well as, often, human ignition, is vital to reducing the number and severity of wildfires.

An example of the need for prevention can be seen with the Dixie fire in California, which started on 13 July 2021, burnt 963,309 acres and was 94 per cent contained four months later. This outcome needed 6,579 fire fighters at the height of the fire and 1,792 miles of fire breaks created, the cost of firefighting reaching $USD610 million. Much of the burnt forest will not recover and will transition into a flammable shrubland.

The Californian fire agency reports that eight of the 20 largest fires recorded in that state were started by lightning, five were 'human-related', two were caused by powerlines and, for five of the fires, the cause was unknown. Determining the cause of wildfires such as the Dixie fire should involve a comprehensive evidence-based approach. Unfortunately, the current recording approaches (internationally) are not designed to assist future preventative action. They display variable recordings of the same type of ignition, at times based on little evidence or hearsay. Most fires are not recorded and many not officially investigated as to the cause, with few maliciously lit fires resulting in a conviction. All this results in large data gaps and often wide inconsistencies between data sets, even if they are covering the same geographical area.

Wildfire causation

A broad categorization of ignition causes may better assist fire prevention, thus avoiding the current tendency to explain many fires as 'an accident'. Human-caused ignition can be categorized as:

- *accidental* – for example, a vehicle accident that inadvertently creates sparks, flames or an explosion that ignites adjacent vegetation;
- *accidental plus poor decision-making* – for example, burning off too close to flammable material that ignites, or powerlines causing an ignition;
- *recklessness* – for example, burning off on a day when no fires are permitted; and
- *maliciousness* – for example, intentional lighting of a wildfire.

Romps et al (2014) have shown that the growing occurrence of lightening is linked with climate change, with a 12 per cent increase in frequency associated with each degree centigrade rise in the global average temperature, thus linking the prevention approaches with climate change mitigation.

Many causes of wildfire ignitions are overlooked in 'official' wildfire records (see Stanley and Young, 2021; Balch et al, 2021). Examples include burning off crop rubble, as still practiced in many countries, and burning for land clearing purposes. The latter problem is currently of significant concern in Indonesian and Brazilian rainforests, causing loss of ecological services and carbon storage, loss of land by First Nations and air pollution. Fire is used as a weapon of conflict, such as against the Rohingya villages in Myanmar, or as a terrorist's weapon (see Joose, 2020). In this sense, in terms of culpability and neglect in policing purposive fire-setting, some wildfires represent forms of state and corporate crime.

In addition, gathering information about the fire lighter is also very important to facilitate useful prevention responses, as not enough is known about motivations. Nonetheless, intentional fire-setting is better understood through an analysis of motivations, much in the same way that any other crime can be understood as a mix of motivations on the part of the offender. Children may light a fire, arising from curious play. Troubled youth may engage in anti-social activity that leads to a fire, behaviour frequently undertaken in groups. In the United States, 26 per cent of all juvenile crimes relate to arson, with youth under 15 years of age contributing to 58 per cent of that figure. Some people with an intellectual disability may also cause a fire. Campfires lit by travellers, campers, hunters or illegal timber collectors can ignite a wildfire. Unfortunately, some firefighters light wildfires, although little information is released about this. Fires may be purposely lit due to psychopathology or unresolved trauma, financial gain by a corporation or to achieve other goals such as revenge or to destroy evidence of a crime, or perhaps as a cry for help.

Ideology, lack of disclosure, poor record keeping and lack of research resources has confounded understanding around the cause of wildfires. In a rare examination of causes, one researcher found that, in six of every ten fires, where the cause was recorded in an Australian sample, half of these were said to be malicious or suspicious, and 35 per cent accidental (see Stanley et al, 2020). More recently, United States researchers reviewed data sets and satellite pictures for over 1.6 million wildfire events in California from 1992 to 2015 (see Balch et al, 2021). They classified 63 per cent of these fires as accidental and 21 per cent as malicious. They also found that the frequency of human-lit fires varied according to location: 97 per cent occurring on the interface between urban and rural; 85 per cent in low-density housing areas; and 59 per cent in forested areas. Human-lit wildfires were found to be larger and more intense than wildfires caused by lightning.

Discussion on wildfire prevention is stymied by the bygone belief that wildfires are a 'naturally' occurring event (see Stanley et al, 2020). However, there is a great risk that the failure to adequately prevent the risk of wildfires will mimic the failures to prevent climate change. Like climate change, whilst there is a lot to learn, enough is known to guide action to reduce both fire lighting and greenhouse gas emissions. The options are many, ranging from education and information; treatment and care of troubled youth; situational change, such as preventing access to high danger fire areas on fire danger days; patrolling of preferred arson sites; and more resources to apprehend malicious firelighters. Until leadership is taken on preventing wildfire ignitions and improvements are made in recording fire ignitions, countries such as Australia and the United States are likely to experience more megafires such as the Dixie fire.

Suggested readings

Balch, J., Iglesias, V. and Braswell, A., Rossi, M., Joseph, M. and Mahood, A. (2020) 'Social environmental extremes: Rethinking extraordinary events as outcomes of interacting biophysical and social systems', *Earth's Future*, Available from: https://agupubs.onlinelibrary.wiley.com/doi/10.1029/2019EF001319 [Accessed 10 November 2021].

Beale, J. and Jones, W. (2011) 'Preventing and reducing bushfire arson in Australia: A review of what is known', *Fire Technology*, 47(2): 507–18.

Joose, T. (2020) 'Human-sparked wildfires are more destructive than those caused by nature', 8 December, *Science*, Available from: https://www.sciencemag.org/news/2020/12/human-sparked-wildfires-are-more-destructive-those-caused-nature [Accessed 10 November 2021].

Romps, D., Seeley, J., Vollaro, D. and Molinari, J. (2014) 'Projected increase in lightning strikes in the United States due to global warming', *Science*, 346(6211): 851–4.

Stanley, J.R., March, A. Ogloff, J. and Thompson, J. (2020) *Feeling the Heat: International Perspectives on the Prevention of Wildfire*, Wilmington, DE: Vernon Press.

Stanley, J. and Young, B. (2021) 'Improved data will reduce the number of wildfires', *Australian and New Zealand Society of Evidence Based Policing Conference*, 17–20 August 2021.

43

Wildlife Crime, Trafficking and Poaching

Rob White

The term 'wildlife' generally refers to animals that live in a wild state outside of human control. In some circumstances it also includes flora as well as fauna. For example, the Convention on International Trade in Endangered Species of Wild Fauna and Flora (CITES) includes plants as well as non-human animals in its definition. For present purposes, the main focus will be on non-human animals. For crimes and harms pertaining to plants, refer to literature on threats to biodiversity, the United Nations Convention on Biodiversity and the work of the Intergovernmental Science-Policy Platform on Biodiversity and Ecosystem Services (IPBES).

Wildlife crimes include the illegal killing and cruel treatment of non-human animals, the illegal transport and trade in animals and the illegal taking of animals from their habitat for human uses (see Nurse and Wyatt, 2020). Put simply, wildlife crimes consist of illegal hunting, trafficking and using of non-human animals. Why and how this occurs varies according to the status of the animals and the social context within which transgression occurs.

Speciesism describes the treatment of non-human animal species in discriminatory and/or exploitive ways by humans, based upon an assumption of human superiority. Most wildlife crimes tend to privilege human interests (for example, facilitating the ongoing use of animals as a resource), rather than acknowledging the intrinsic worth or value of non-human animals (for example, through granting of legal personhood).

The status of animals can be distinguished according to two main criteria – *wildlife* or *domesticated* – and within each of these categories according to how the animal is perceived relative to human needs – *service to* or *service for*. These are inherently anthropocentric categorizations in the sense that the ways in which animals are classified reflect human interventions over time, and human notions of usefulness. Such descriptions are nonetheless essential in assessing matters pertaining to non-human animals as these are presently constituted in law and social practices (see Wyatt, 2013).

For instance, what is defined and what is valued when it comes to non-human animals is highly variable and subject to ongoing contestation at the level of philosophy as well as legislative practice and law enforcement. The ideas of 'pest' and 'invasive species', for example, reduces the life, energy, activity and wellbeing of creatures to that of threat, worthlessness and nuisance relative to human objectives. It tends to portray targeted species in ways that foster eradication and fear of species rather than understanding or appreciation of broader ecological and zoological processes and imperatives. The language used reinforces human categorizations of species that present them as somehow inherently evil rather than as *bona fide* sentient creatures in their own right. This, in turn, can lead to the diminishment of 'normal' standards of treatment in the rush to get rid of them. It can thus lead to and/or reinforce the inhumane treatment of animals.

Status is also conferred on the basis of prevalence or number of animals. For example, the notions of 'endangered' and 'threatened' species essentially speak to the survival status of particular species. Some are extinct (as with the thylacine, the dodo and the passenger pigeon), whilst others hover on the brink of extinction (orangutan, polar bear). Human intervention, including through CITES, reflects varying conceptions of animal rights and welfare, including differing perspectives on which animals ought to be saved, the urgency of the action needed and which species are prioritized over others when it comes to activist campaigns. Saving big cats such as tigers is publicly popular, stopping the killing of sharks or protecting bees, less so.

The laws that humans design to protect certain species may, however, also put them most at jeopardy. For example, measures designed to prevent the illegal trade in endangered species (for example, CITES) can make that species even more attractive to criminal syndicates or private collectors since it confirms their scarcity (and thus increases the commercial and collectible 'value') of the species in question. The damage that is manifest in phenomena, such as over-fishing and destruction of habitat (both of which may be legally undertaken), also affects the subsequent market prices for the commodity in question. Scarcity is a major motivator for illegal as well as legal forays into particular kinds of harvesting and production activity. The losers are animals and their environments.

The social processes associated with offending and the characteristics of offenders vary. For instance, categories of offenders include traditional criminals seeking to gain personal benefit from crimes such as wildlife trafficking, hobby criminals seeking to add to their collections, through to those who engage in illegal hunting since it reflects stereotypical traits of masculinity. There are also stages in some forms of offending, such as trafficking, that involve the harvesting of animals, an intermediary role connecting buyers and sellers, and consumption (these categories are not mutually exclusive).

Wildlife crime is broader than simply illegal trade in wildlife and can include, for example, a wide range of types of criminal activity, from unlawful gambling through to illegal poisoning. Specific countries and specific regions will be characterized by different types of wildlife crime (see United Nations Office for Drugs and Crime, 2021). For example, in Australia, commonly smuggled species include reptiles, birds, insects and spiders, as well as sugar gliders. Species taken in Southern Africa, India, Russia and Indonesia will vary according to local conditions and animal prevalence. Similarly, the parrot trade is linked to South American locations such as Bolivia, Colombia and Peru, whilst wildlife poaching in the United States and Canada include deer, moose, bears, turkeys and lobsters.

An animal welfare approach is probably the perspective most reflected in the protections surrounding animals. Closely associated with animal welfarism is the notion of protection of endangered species, and efforts to maintain the sustainability of animals in certain industries. For example, the poaching of abalone or lobster is prohibited insofar as it impinges upon the property rights of licensed fishers and taxation powers of the state, whilst simultaneously depleting species numbers. Legislation that prohibits the illegal trade of wildlife, particularly endangered wildlife, is meant to protect species from criminal exploitation, although why and how species become endangered is less frequently addressed (for example, the degradation of habitats generally and destruction of local ecology through, for instance, clear-fell forestry). Intervention is mainly pitched at the species level, with efforts being put into conserving and maintaining viable numbers of particular species.

People engage in poaching for a variety of reasons, and these reasons are partly related to immediate social context (for example, exotic consumer products for the new middle classes in China; traditional hunting practices in Greece; community and commercial collusion in the taking of lobster in the Canadian Maritime provinces; income supplementation in Bolivia). In some instances, poaching is perceived as a sort of 'folk crime' with widespread community support in some locales and under some conditions. What criminological research demonstrates is that, like the abuse of animals generally, there are a variety of motivations and offenders who engage in poaching and the illegal animal trade. Many aspects of the human–wildlife interaction are deeply embedded culturally, as well as reflecting the human need for sustenance and income.

Yet trafficking, poaching and illegal hunting can cause great harm. They can endanger species, involve animal cruelty, threaten other species, deplete resources and reduce biodiversity. They are also frequently tied up with cross-over crimes such as corruption, money laundering, violence, slavery and organized criminal networks.

There are also larger issues pertaining to wildlife crime that relate to the position of humans and non-human animals within nature. This engagement involves both *intrinsic value* and *instrumental use*. For instance, the use of animals for food and clothing does not necessarily have to occur within a relationship of exploitation per se. Indigenous communities around the world have for millennia had spiritually grounded respect and value for the creatures around them, including those which they harvest and utilize to meet their human needs. There is a context, historical pattern and interactive dimension here which precludes the separation of human from non-human animals, as each in its own way is consequential for the other.

Nonetheless, the victimization of non-human animals is of ongoing and growing concern, especially for those who place great emphasis on care and empathy for the animal 'other' (see Sollund, 2019). How humans treat animals – whether in a legal framework or not – is essentially a statement about the human condition and the broader state of the natural world. This is relevant to every aspect of wildlife crime.

Suggested readings

Flynn, M. and Hall, M. (2017) 'The case for a victimology of nonhuman animal harms', *Contemporary Justice Review*, 20(3): 299–318.

Nurse, A. and Wyatt, T. (2020) *Wildlife Criminology*, Bristol: Bristol University Press.

Sollund, R. (2019) *The Crimes of Wildlife Trafficking*, London: Routledge.

United Nations Office for Drugs and Crime (2021) Education for Justice (E4J) University Series, *Wildlife, Forest and Fisheries Crime*: Learning Module 1: Illicit Markets for Wildlife Products; Learning Module 2: International Frameworks; Learning Module 3: Criminal Justices Responses to Wildlife and Forest Crime. Available from: https://www.unodc.org/e4j/ [Accessed 27 November 2021].

Wyatt, T. (2013) *Wildlife Trafficking: A Deconstruction of the Crime, the Victims, and the Offenders*, Basingstoke: Palgrave Macmillan.

PART III

Rural Criminal Justice Studies

Introduction to Part III: Rural Criminal Justice Studies

Jessica René Peterson

The study of criminal justice systems, components and responses to crime problems is significant to policy formation that prevents, treats and reduces crime. Research on these topics predominantly focuses on and takes place in urban metropolitan locations where agencies tend to be large and clustered.

In rural settings, the systems tasked with addressing issues of crime and justice face distinctive challenges and may even operate under different philosophies. Crime problems in rural locations might include those that are uniquely rural, such as livestock theft or other farm-related crime, as well as 'ruralized' traditional criminal behaviour. Furthermore, everything from the quantity and quality of staff, training, equipment and technologies can differ in rural justice-related agencies – such variations affect rural systems' ability to address crime and residents' ability to access justice.

Approaches and reforms used in an urban context are not always applicable to the rural. Informal operations and responses by justice system actors are common, particularly in remote locations where social density is high and population density is simultaneously low. Common themes in rural criminal justice studies include issues with resource availability and lack of staff, geographic isolation and accessibility, density of acquaintanceship amongst residents and criminal justice actors, the connectivity gap, conflicts between the people and the state and more.

The entries in this section examine – comparing and contrasting with urban areas – the availability, function and access to law enforcement, courts and corrections in rural communities. Both the advantages and disadvantages that the rural context provides will be discussed from an international lens that addresses rural communities across the Global North and South. It is important to explore the global commonalities amongst rural justice systems, as well as the ways in which physical and socio-cultural contexts affect these studies. The authors in this section bring a much-needed voice to those who respond to crime in rural communities and are involved in rural criminal justice systems.

Law Enforcement

44

Anti-social Behaviour: Police–Community Relationships

Andrew Wooff and Larissa Engelmann

The oft remote or 'abstract' nature of service provision in rural communities means that there is an ever-present requirement to capitalize on and utilize existing community networks. This is particularly true with low-level 'nuisance behaviour', often termed 'anti-social behaviour' (ASB).

ASB in the United Kingdom is generally defined as harassment or action that can cause distress to someone not in the perpetrator's household (see Brown, 2013). A recent shift in the culture of crime control is evident through legislation criminalizing 'nuisance behaviour' and other policy around ASB, particularly in the United Kingdom. The devolving of crime control – from the 'police' to the third sector, community groups and other individuals responsible for control – means that criminal justice actors are no longer the only individuals in the crime control field.

The adaptive strategies of individual communities vary across space and time, leading to an uneven situation of crime control, with some communities engaging wholeheartedly in informal policing methods and others not having the apparent 'community capacity' to cope (see Garland, 2001).

ASB has most commonly been associated with urban environments, in part because there is statistically less ASB recorded in rural environments. Additionally, ASB is often associated as being less serious, intense and frequent in rural locations than that which exists in urban environments. The distinctive characteristics of rural environments, though, are central to understanding the nature, meaning and impact of ASB in this environment.

That is not to say that ASB in rural communities has less of an impact on people's lives. The police are required to respond to ASB in rural communities and often do so with a complex mix of 'soft policing' and urban style policing strategies, including the use of discretion and other tactics. In particular, owing to the large police beat areas in rural communities, police officers are often required to negotiate and work with communities to find solutions to low-level incivilities.

There are numerous examples internationally where the police have worked with different groups of people to prevent ASB in rural communities. This includes: 'Farmwatch' in rural Australia, where the police have teamed up with farmers to mitigate the risks of farm crime; policing Indigenous populations in Canada; and the use of storytelling amongst rural Dutch police officers to understand rural police–community interactions (see Harkness, 2020).

Thus, there is a developing international literature around rural policing and police interaction with communities that is relevant to these discussions and which emphasizes the need to consider different interactions in different contexts between the police and community. This is especially true with ASB, where a 'democratic deficit' often exists between those community members who the police predominantly engage with (often White, middle-class retirees) and those participating in perceived ASB (often young people). Community participation in local governance needs critical and considered attention, particularly when community groups can pejoratively make decisions which may impact on the rest of the community in relation to ASB.

Different communities and community members interact with the police to a greater or lesser extent in terms of negotiating order and therefore supporting the police informally in responding to ASB in rural locations.

Carr (2012) has devised a useful way of conceptualizing citizen–police interactions that helps underline the level of the citizen's role in negotiating order and identifies the extent to which communities may be engaged in supporting the police to overcome ASB in rural locations:

Citizen type	Role
Citizen partner	Takes active role in negotiating order
Citizen associate	Consulted about crime and safety but has no real means of making inputs
Citizen bystander	Takes no role beyond being a passive observer of law enforcement
Opponent	Completely alienated from police

The process of citizen–police interaction also operates unevenly at the community scale; it tends to be the powerful members of the community who determine who is considered 'in the community', including what behaviours should be acceptable or not.

As Wooff (2015) points out, many of the young people accused of committing ASB are in fact defined as anti-social by people who do not have an understanding of young people. Thus, many young citizens may feel like they are at odds with their community, even though the police would describe their relationships with young people as broadly positive. Police–community interactions are shaped by the nature of communities, including issues such as social deprivation and suspicion of the police. The context in which these relationships are developed, therefore, becomes important.

The police do have an important role in facilitating community resolutions to ASB in rural communities. Thus, understanding the way(s) that law enforcement polices rural communities is important for understanding how relationships between law enforcement and community members develop (see Herbert, 2006).

The burgeoning rural policing literature provides insights into what is important for positive police–community relationships to be fruitful. In some countries with more extensive rural locales (such as Australia and Canada), schemes such as 'Farmwatch' have proved to be successful in reducing farm crime and ASB. By the police linking with a wide variety of different community members, the democratic deficit described above can be minimized.

Importantly, there is no one-size-fits-all approach to how the police support rural communities in reducing ASB – it is important to remember the rural is nuanced, complex and varied – but, by beginning to think through Carr's schema and approaching policing in a context-dependent way, rural communities can be supported in tackling and reducing the ASB experienced.

Suggested readings

Brown, D.M. (2013) 'Young people, anti-social behaviour and public space: The role of community wardens in policing the "ASBO generation"', *Urban Studies*, 50(3): 538–55.

Carr, P.J. (2012) 'Citizens, community, and crime control: The problems and prospects for negotiated order', *Criminology and Criminal Justice*, 12(4): 397–412.

Garland, D. (2001) *The Culture of Control: Crime and Social Order in Contemporary Society*, Oxford: Oxford University Press.

Harkness, A. (ed) (2020) *Rural Crime Prevention: Theory, Tactics and Techniques*, London: Routledge.

Herbert, S. (2006) *Citizens, Cops and Power: Recognizing the Limits of Community*, Chicago: University of Chicago Press.

Wooff, A. (2015) 'Relationships and responses: Policing anti-social behaviour in rural Scotland', *Journal of Rural Studies*, 39: 287–95.

45

Law Enforcement Misconduct

John Liederbach, Chloe Ann Wentzlof and Philip Matthew Stinson

Law enforcement misconduct and crime includes a wide range of behaviours committed by sworn law enforcement officers who are given the general powers of arrest at the time these offenses are committed. Anecdotes, journalistic accounts, government-sponsored commissions and scholarship demonstrate that police officers commit various forms of misconduct and crime including murder, assault, larceny/theft, drug trafficking, predatory sex offenses and driving whilst intoxicated.

Other forms of law enforcement misconduct more specifically involve corruption, whereby police use their power and position to facilitate the operation of organized crime networks involved in the distribution of illegal goods and/or services (see Stinson et al, 2016).

The major problem in the study of law enforcement misconduct and police crime has been the lack of official data on these phenomena: governments generally do not collect or disseminate statistics concerning the prevalence or character of cases of law enforcement misconduct and crime. Furthermore, most of what is known describes the criminal and/or corrupt conduct of police who work in large urban places rather than rural jurisdictions.

Very little is known about the issue of rural law enforcement misconduct and crime. However, policing scholars have long recognized that police officers behave differently across community types, and some literature identifies factors that distinguish the work of rural police: (i) small police agencies are more concerned with crime prevention and service than large agencies; (ii) rural police are expected to perform a wider variety of tasks because these communities lack other social services resources; and (iii) police–community relations in rural jurisdictions are more personal and informal, mainly owing to dense relationship networks wherein citizens are more likely to know police on a personal level (see Liederbach and Frank, 2003; Weisheit et al, 2006).

Law enforcement misconduct occurring within rural jurisdictions is likely a function of the same place characteristics and culture that promote a unique style of rural policing as well as a unique opportunity structure for the perpetration of police misconduct and crime. Scholarship has identified some problems that seem to be more prevalent amongst officers working within rural jurisdictions that may contribute to law enforcement misconduct in rural places. Police working in rural jurisdictions are typically paid less than those working in urban jurisdictions. Low pay and other factors including boredom, inactivity and role strain associated with a lack of opportunities to engage in meaningful law enforcement may also be a source of police misconduct and crime within rural places.

Police corruption in rural places may also be a function of dense networks of relationships, wherein police develop long-standing personal relationships with local law breakers and criminal organizations. 'Community-condoned' policing refers to socially dense rural communities that value their privacy and which may be less likely to raise concern over corrupt police behaviour, particularly if the victims of corruption are 'othered' or outsiders. Rural police corruption may be less likely to be discovered or recorded, and issues with definitions of 'rural' could contribute to the lack of adequate data on the subject. Indeed, a very limited number of published studies provide empirical data specific to law enforcement misconduct in rural places.

Lopez and Thomas (2004) used data on police misconduct trials provided by the Civil Rights Division of the United States Department of Justice to study variations in the national distribution of cases of police misconduct. They found that 30 per cent of these cases involved officers employed by departments outside urban areas. Potter and Gaines (1992) used qualitative methods to identify and describe organized crime and police corruption in rural settings. They found that the operation of rural organized crime networks is often facilitated by police themselves, who maintain close personal ties to organized criminals operating within their jurisdiction and focused mainly on the production and delivery of illegal goods and services including the sale of black-market liquor, drugs, prostitution and gambling. Organized criminals in rural jurisdictions depend on police corruption and some type of accommodation with local police that either participate in the crime network themselves and/or neglect to enforce these crimes. Corrupt police were found to overlook illegal activity, 'lose' evidence, provide inadequate court testimony or make improper arrests to facilitate crime networks.

Additional data on rural law enforcement misconduct in the United States is contained within the Henry A. Wallace Police Crime Database. The database provides summary information that is not otherwise aggregated or publicly available for approximately 13,000 criminal arrest cases of sworn law enforcement officers from 2005 to 2016. All of the cases in this database refer to police officers who have been arrested for one or more criminal offenses.

Most of the criminal arrest cases in the database involved an officer employed by a law enforcement agency within a metropolitan area. However, rural police crime is still present and widespread throughout the United States. The United States Department of Agriculture's classification for non-metropolitan counties was used to identify rurality. It defines non-metropolitan counties by population density, geographic isolation and population thresholds.

By this definition, rural police crime in the United States accounts for roughly 15 per cent of all criminal arrest cases of sworn non-Federal law enforcement officers. There were 1,639 arrested sworn law enforcement officers employed by agencies in non-metropolitan counties accounting for 1,993 criminal arrest cases in the years 2005–16. These criminal arrest cases ranged in severity from misdemeanor assaults and petty theft to forcible rape and murder. The most common offense charged against arrested officers was official misconduct, followed by simple assault and driving under the influence. These offenses are consistent with the charges associated with officers employed by agencies in metropolitan counties. Nearly half of all rural police crime was violence-related (n = 954). Again, this is consistent with trends of violence-related police crime amongst metropolitan counties.

Suggested readings

Liederbach, J. and Frank, J. (2003) 'Policing Mayberry: The work routines of small-town and rural officers', *American Journal of Criminal Justice*, 28(1): 53–72.

Lopez, J.J. and Thomas, P.M. (2004) 'The geography of law enforcement malpractice: National patterns of official misconduct in the United States, 1989–1999', *Journal of American Studies*, 38(3): 371–90.

Potter, G.W. and Gaines, L.K. (1992) 'Country comfort: Vice and corruption in rural settings', *Journal of Contemporary Criminal Justice*, 8(1): 36–61.

Stinson, P.M., Liederbach, J., Lab, S.P. and Brewer, S.L. (2016) 'Police integrity lost: A study of law enforcement officers arrested', United States Department of Justice, Office of Justice Programs, National Institute of Justice, Available from: https://www.ojp.gov/pdffiles1/nij/grants/249850.pdf [Accessed 16 November 2011].

Weisheit, R.A., Falcone, D.N. and Wells, L.E. (2006) *Crime and Policing in Rural and Small-Town America* (3rd edn), Long Grove, IL: Waveland Press.

46

Police Discretion and Informal Sanctions

Jessica René Peterson

Discretion in the context of law enforcement is not easily operationalized, but the concept essentially refers to a law enforcement officer's agency and ability to choose how they will (or will not) respond to law violations and encounters with community members. The amount of discretion available to officers can be expanded or restricted based on the structural, cultural and situational context of their setting; these contexts also influence the *way* officers make decisions and utilize their available discretion.

Characteristics of the law enforcement agency, the officer, the community and the situation or involved persons are significant in the use of discretion (see Carrington and Schulenberg, 2003; Shukla et al, 2019). Urban-centric research finds that offense severity, prior record, offender attitude, presence of a victim, race or ethnicity, gender and officer philosophy are key common factors that influence the decision to arrest. Taking an individual into custody through arrest is the most formal method of social control that can be exerted by officers. However, officers also employ informal sanctions to exert social control in their communities. Such practices may include verbal warnings or threats, releasing a suspect, driving an offender home and more.

Effects of the rural on discretion, decision making and informal sanctions

In rural areas, police discretion is expanded owing to geographic isolation, lack of supervision or strict departmental policy dictating action, and density of acquaintanceship with residents and other actors in local justice-related agencies. Density of acquaintanceship refers to the personal knowledge, shared values and intimacy amongst community members who 'all know each other'.

Officers who are included in such thick social networks rely on them for constant streams of information and are influenced by them when addressing crime and deviance. Shared knowledge and trust with residents in the community can expand officers' ability to allow or facilitate informal methods of control. For example, tight relationships between an officer and the victim, offender and other justice-related actors can enable informal arrangements for restitution or restoration – such as an agreement that a vandalizer will fix the fence that they vandalized – in lieu of formal justice system processing. In situations such as these, the officer's presence symbolizes the formal action that *could* be enacted by the state and encourages a restorative justice approach and informal solution to the problem.

Street-level law enforcement officers in rural areas are both generalists and specialists, owing to the fact that agencies are less likely to have separate specialized units and patrol officers are responsible for responding to non-police problems such as calls for livestock on the road or conducting highly technical investigations involving serious violent crime.

Several researchers studying police discretion and decision-making have considered police and youth offender interactions. Some differences can be seen when comparing studies that report what officers 'say they would do' and studies including officer self-report narratives on what they actually performed. Skaggs (2017) provided surveys with vignettes to officers across five departments in rural Kentucky in the United States and found that officers indicated they would make an arrest in 56 per cent of the cases, with smaller agencies being more likely to make an arrest. Alternatively, research that evaluates officers' self-report narratives about what officers 'actually did' when encountering youth offenders finds that rural officers seldom make arrests (see Liederbach, 2007).

Factors related to the decision to arrest in rural communities include offense severity, attitude or demeanour of the offender, victim's wishes to proceed, age and other legal and extra-legal circumstances. Some of these do not differ greatly from the factors urban officers consider in arrest decisions. However, rural officers are more responsive to community needs and officers tend to rely more heavily on relational factors when addressing crime problems in their communities. They consider uniquely rural factors such as staffing availability, resource availability and location, the offender's social background and family life and more when deciding to respond informally.

Although the seriousness and severity of an offense is often one of the most important factors in decision making in both rural and urban settings, as Weisheit et al (2006) point out, *how* officers define severity is influenced by the structural, cultural and situational context of their setting. For example, a rural officer may deem the act of a juvenile driving without a license on public roads non-serious, as the structural and cultural context of a rural community demand or encourage driving from an early age to herd livestock or drive farming equipment, whereas an urban officer might perceive the violation as more severe.

Community-condoned policing

Informal handling of crime is so common in rural communities that these strategies along with the lack of formal records have been described as indicators of good policing in some rural agencies. Classic and recent research finds that rural law enforcement strategies most closely resemble an integrated community policing approach. Officers' decisions are guided by community norms and informal sanctions are used to maintain order.

The high density of acquaintanceship in many rural areas facilitates informal responses to crime problems and officers may use their discretion to refrain from action altogether (see Peterson, 2022). Failure to act sends a message about the behaviours and types of residents that are considered acceptable in a community. For example, an officer may choose to overlook an incident of assault so not to disrupt the social dynamics of a local organization. If the victim of said abuse is a woman in a community that historically and presently holds more conservative ideologies, patriarchal beliefs and traditional values, residents may accept or even celebrate the officer 'respecting matters of the home' and refraining from making an arrest. Thus, an officer may respond informally and act in accordance with community norms but fail to promote true justice. As a result, informal sanctions that benefit perpetrators may make it difficult for victims to seek justice when victim and advocacy resources are limited and transportation alternatives are scarce.

The reliance on relationships enables community–policing practices that can both promote or hinder justice for rural victims and offenders. The failure to recognize the significance of the rural setting in police discretion and decision making not only stifles proper representation of non-urban communities and agencies, but robs the field's literature of thorough comparative understandings, especially when police practice, reform and existence are widely scrutinized.

Suggested readings

Carrington, P.J. and Schulenberg, J.L. (2003) 'Police discretion with young offenders', *Report to the Department of Justice Canada*, Available from: https://www.justice.gc.ca/eng/rp-pr/cj-jp/yj-jj/discre/pdf/rep-rap.pdf [Accessed 9 November 2021].

Liederbach, J. (2007) 'Controlling suburban and small-town hoods: An examination of police encounters with juveniles', *Youth Violence and Juvenile Justice*, 5(2): 107–24.

Peterson, J.R. (2022) '"We handle it, I guess you'd say, the East Texas way": Place-based effects on the police decision-making process and non-arrest outcomes', *Police Practice and Research: An International Journal*, 1–19.

Shukla, R.K., Stoneberg, D., Lockwood, K., Copple, P., Dorman, A. and Jones, F.M. (2019) 'The interaction of crime and place: An exploratory study of crime and policing in non-metropolitan areas', *Crime Prevention and Community Safety*, 21: 200–14.

Skaggs, S.L. (2017) 'Understanding arrest in rural police-juvenile interactions: A factorial designed survey approach', *Policing and Society*, 29(7): 802–19.

Weisheit, R.A., Falcone, D. and Wells, L. (2006) *Crime and Policing in Rural and Small-Town America* (3rd edn), Long Grove, IL: Waveland Press.

47

Police Engagement with Rural Farming Communities

Cameron Whiteside, Ann Brennan and Kyle Mulrooney

Farm crime surveys consistently indicate very high rates of victimization amongst farmers, yet low rates of reporting (see Harkness, 2016; Department of Justice NSW, 2017). Explanations for this include perceptions of leniency on behalf of the courts, issues related to social density, a desire not to be seen as snitching on another in the community and concerns of revenge and retaliation. Another factor is a hesitance amongst farmers to report crime owing to perceptions that the police lack both the interest in responding to farm crime as well as the capacity to solve these crimes. Over time, geographic and cultural barriers have led to a disjunct between police and rural farming communities, thus limiting collaborative crime prevention efforts (see Barclay, 2016).

Surveys of farmers indicate a strong desire for an informed and engaged rural police force, which is well-resourced and can be relied upon to be both reactive (such as with clearance rates) and proactive (for example, public engagement; crime prevention) (refer to Mulrooney, 2021). In an Australian context, there exists strong support amongst farmers for a dedicated team of expert police officers trained to deal with rural crime specifically.

Past research indicates that a lack of subject matter expertize and cultural barriers have hindered engagement: general duty police may not grasp the nuances of rural crime – for example, the type of stock stolen or its market value, and its impacts on the victims both psychologically and economically. By contrast, specialized rural crime officers are better placed to address these issues, as they come armed with the knowledge of locational context and cultural geography, and are trained to deal with farm crime.

Rural policing teams around the world typically attend numerous and various in-person rural-related events throughout the year, such as agricultural shows, community meetings, stakeholder workshops and industry conferences. Such teams also maintain social media engagement through Twitter, Facebook and other bespoke online engagement platforms. This enables teams to highlight outcomes of operations, provide target hardening options, promote events, share relevant information from other stakeholders, seek assistance from the community and ensure the topic of rural crime remains a 'hot topic' in rural social media.

The geography of the rural emphasizes that addressing rural crime is a shared responsibility, and that farmers must participate and engage for crime prevention to be successful. Police cannot simply 'go it alone', particularly given the pressures on police resourcing in rural spaces where an instantaneous first response is highly unlikely. The importance of police engagement and interaction cannot be understated, especially in environments where relationships have historical fault lines or cracks. If public satisfaction and confidence in the police is low, it is unlikely that communities will report crime or engage in collaborative prevention efforts. In turn, this lack of engagement limits police ability to apprehend offenders and results in an incomplete picture of actual offending rates for policy and decision makers, undermining the capacity to combat rural crime.

The New South Wales Police Force Rural Crime Prevention Team

Specialized rural policing teams can play a vital role in not only enforcing the law but also in preventing offending from occurring by bridging the gap between police, farmers and rural communities more generally. Greater levels of satisfaction and higher rates of reporting may result from farmers feeling seen, heard and understood by the police and indicate greater confidence in these police to be able to respond to farm crime. Lessons from New South Wales, with a resourced and dedicated specialized police team, provide clear evidence of the importance of community outreach and engagement on making in-roads into rural communities and progress in combatting farm crime (see McKechnie, 2019).

Spurred on by rising concerns around farm crime and calls for more sustained police action, the New South Wales Police Force Rural Crime Prevention Team (RCPT) was formed in 2018. Operational officers are subject-matter experts specifically trained to investigate rural crime, manage livestock, maintain a high level of knowledge regarding legislation pertinent to crimes committed against rural industries and safeguard these industries. In addition to investigating rural crime and enhancing the capability and knowledge of general duties officers, a primary aim of the team is to raise the awareness and promote rural crime prevention strategies. The RCPT has also increased their focus on community engagement with relevant stakeholders in rural communities and industries.

The RCPT have undertaken a number of specific initiatives to connect and engage with rural communities. First, in addition to 'talking the part' through their Nationally Accredited Rural Crime Investigation Course, the RCPT also look the part with attire consisting of an 'office' (moleskin and light blue shirt) and 'work' (royal blue shirt and blue jeans) uniform. This has aided in landholders being able to readily identify investigators, resulting in increased awareness, contact and, subsequently, a growth in the flow of information and intelligence.

In conjunction with the NSW Farmers' Association, the RCPT have conducted 'Tackling Rural Crime' events which aim to connect and liaise with farming communities, enrich the understanding of their needs and desires and impart practical crime prevention knowledge and skills such as that focused on firearm security, target hardening and the preservation of evidence and crime scenes.

The RCPT have also utilized proactive enforcement measures to prevent livestock theft by confirming the origin of stock being transported. Importantly, whilst such efforts are undertaken to enforce the law, they also communicate to rural communities that the police are dedicating resources and energy to rural crime issues which matter to them. In essence, the 'bush telegraph' operates positively without having to detect stolen stock as farmers see such efforts as supporting and protecting them.

Suggested readings

Barclay, E. (2016) 'Farm victimisation: The quintessential rural crime', in J.F. Donnermeyer (ed) *The Routledge International Handbook of Rural Criminology*, London: Routledge, pp. 107–16.

Department of Justice NSW (2017) 'New stock theft and trespass review: Final report (the Bradshaw Review)', Available from: https://www.justice.nsw.gov.au/Documents/Media%20Releases/2017/final-report-NSW-stock-theft-and-trespass-review.pdf [Accessed 15 November 2021].

Harkness, A. (2016) 'Farm crime: The forgotten frontier', in A. Harkness, B. Harris and D. Baker (eds) *Locating Crime in Context and Place: Perspectives on Regional, Rural and Remote Australia*, Sydney: The Federation Press, pp. 96–107.

McKechnie, G. (2019) 'NSW Police Force and rural crime', *International Journal of Rural Law and Policy*, 2 (special issue on rural crime), Available from: http://www.austlii.edu.au/au/journals/IntJlRuralLawP/2019/7.pdf [Accessed 15 November 2021].

Mulrooney, K.J.D. (2021) 'The NSW Farm Crime Survey 2020', Armidale, NSW: The Centre for Rural Criminology, University of New England, Available from: https://spark.adobe.com/page/zsV05pknxXl7N/ [Accessed 15 November 2021].

48
Policing Rural Small Island Developing States

Danielle Watson and Casandra Harry

In most countries across the globe, police serve as the most visible arm of governance and have primary responsibility for the maintenance of law and order. For many countries, state police operate parallel to non-state regulatory bodies. However, the legitimacy of actors in varied policing contexts differs and is at times acknowledged, challenged or disregarded.

In rural contexts, where there is usually a lesser presence of state-appointed police, the responsibility for the maintenance of law and order is usually shared with non-state actors (see Mawby and Yarwood, 2016). The acknowledgement of contextual differences and the recognition of spatial distribution as impacting factors on policing primarily underscores rural policing scholarship.

Despite an initial primary focus on mining, fishing and agriculture-related crimes in sparsely settled areas on the distant outskirts of urban metropoles in developed countries, rural policing scholarship has shifted towards a broader focus. Recent scholarship on rural policing now explores societal manifestations of dysfunction in sparsely inhabited areas across the globe, contextually considered the inverse of the urban. These shifts have also resulted in further acknowledgement of the variations in understandings of rurality and the recognition of additional categories of spaces identified as 'rural', specifically rural areas in small island developing states (SIDS).

A total of 58 SIDS with a combined population of 65 million people have been identified by the United Nations. These SIDS tend to be characterized by geographic location and topography, population size and climatic and economic vulnerabilities. Many SIDS have rural economies and are further characterized as multi-island microstates dispersed across the Atlantic, Caribbean, the Indian and Pacific Oceans and the South China Sea.

For microstates, explanations of rurality are expanded to account for remote or outer islands (usually only accessible by irregularly scheduled petrol patrol boats) away from capital cities, towns or central business districts; as well as areas more densely populated than urban city centres that bare all the other characteristics of rural areas. The location, limited resource availability, remoteness, high transportation costs and high reliance on external support contribute to SIDS development and economic diversification challenges (see Newton, 1998).

Police presence in rural spaces in SIDS varies significantly. Postings may include small units with two or more sworn officers working alongside community police or liaison officers, solo officer postings with the officer operating from a temporary outpost or private residence or no police post within close proximity that can be accessed via land or sea. Some SIDS lack proper infrastructure to connect urban and rural areas, making land access difficult. Inhabited areas with no police postings within close proximity experience significantly delayed responses to calls for services.

In contexts where remote outer islands are serviced by patrol boats, a call for service may take between two to four weeks to be logged and an even lengthier period to be investigated or concluded depending on the severity of the incident or crime category. Resources required for basic day-to-day operations are often not readily available at remote postings (not to suggest availability at police headquarters or police stations located in capital cities) and have to be sourced by the officer.

Policing rural spaces in SIDS requires a multi-layered approach that considers available resources, policing capacity, high social capital (but often low economic capital) and the existence of parallel regulatory systems (see Newton, 1998). The police are often the only visible arm of state governance in rural areas in SIDS, with other justice stakeholders located in capital cities.

The singularity of representation does not impact positively on resource allocation from the state; this results in significant reliance on non-state stakeholders such as traditional, cultural or community led bodies, and contextual discretionary improvizations by poorly resourced state service providers. Arrangements may include partnerships with councils of elders, village councils, religious groups, formalized community policing arrangements or reliance on community members for support with formal duties as required. Police are usually seen as a secondary option in such community contexts as the legitimacy of non-state actors is recognized as the primary point of contact for crime and security related matters.

Unlike densely inhabited spaces with larger populations and low social capital, serious crimes (though known to occur) are seen as less relevant in rural SIDS contexts. Crimes of interpersonal violence are, perhaps, more of an issue (see Donnermeyer et al, 2013). The scholarship on the policing of interpersonal violence in rural SIDS contexts presents mixed views on preferred first responders and the legitimacy of state police to attend to such crimes. The fact that police are likely to come from the communities they serve and have strong community ties – unlike many rural places in more developed settler societies – presents another layer of complexity because of social positioning and embeddedness in communities (see Howes et al, 2021).

Whilst the bounded nature of SIDS is believed to contribute to crime prevention at the community level, the porous marine borders presents a major challenge for police. Policing of rural borders or SIDS Exclusive Economic Zones is a task beyond the capacity of the states. Collaborative agreements and formal regional and international policing partnerships exist as a strategy to address the capacity shortfalls of SIDS.

As Turvey (2007) points out, whilst similarities exist amongst rural spaces in SIDS, it is important to note that contextual variances (socio-economic, cultural, historical, political, police–community relations, police–state relations, police tradition and organizational resources) are likely to impact on policing in different ways. These variances should be acknowledged in the framing of rural policing narratives and further scholarship.

Suggested readings

Donnermeyer, J., Scott, J. and Barclay, E. (2013) 'How rural criminology informs critical thinking in criminology', *International Journal for Crime, Justice and Social Democracy*, 2(3): 69–91.

Howes, L.M., Watson, D. and Newett, L. (2021) 'Police as knowledge brokers and keepers of the peace: Perceptions of community policing in Tuvalu', *Police Practice and Research*, 22(1): 745–62.

Mawby, R.I. and Yarwood, R. (2016) *Rural Policing and Policing the Rural: A Constable Countryside?*, London: Routledge.

Newton, T. (1998) 'Policing in the South Pacific Islands', *The Police Journal*, 71(4): 349–52.

Turvey, R. (2007) 'Vulnerability assessment of developing countries: The case of small-island developing states', *Development Policy Review*, 25(2): 243–64.

49

Policing the Rural Global South

Tariro Mutongwizo

Since the turn of the twenty-first century, there has been acknowledgement that the realities of crime and criminal justice in the smaller, more remote places of the world are not sufficiently reflected in criminological theory and research agendas (see Donnermeyer, 2017). Additionally, the aftermath of colonization further confounds our understanding of crime and justice, particularly in the rural Global South where the colonial past still influences criminal justice and policing systems in rural communities. Moreover, the economic, social, political and cultural exploitation of rural communities and the disadvantaged endures.

Perhaps the most important contribution of rural crime studies to the development of a criminology of the Global South is that it encourages scholars interested in advancing criminology beyond its Western, urban biases and aids in the development of categories of knowledge that create new forms of thinking (see Carrington et al, 2016). The Global South and the rural are both commonly forgotten or ignored spheres in criminological scholarship. This has led to discussions on policing the rural Global South to be a victim of urban and Western normativity, whereby all aspects of crime and justice are measured against the West and the urban (see de Sousa Santos, 2015).

Whilst crime in the rural Global South, in most instances, is akin to crime in the Global North, other aspects differ. Through pointing out extensive examples of rural crime and criminalized actions in Africa such as farm theft and rural violence, witchcraft, same-sex relationships and cultural theft and environmental crime, Agozino (2017) demonstrates that the rural–urban dichotomy poses challenges for criminology. This is because crime that occurs in rural areas also occurs in urban areas, and this leads us to be hesitant about declaring that rural crime is in some way unique.

Other crimes seen globally and at a large scale in the Global South include land theft with the procurement of land for large plantation operations – such as palm oil developments in parts of Africa, Indonesia and South America – and their environmental and social impacts on local rural communities (see Butler and Laurance, 2009). Land theft itself ranges from governmental expropriation of the land of local rural peoples to the invasion of ranchers and logging companies on the traditional lands of Indigenous peoples, and of the physical violence and disruption or destructions of traditional ways of living inflicted on rural dwellers.

Additionally, the resources sector continues to push for access to natural resources such as coal, iron ore and oil. This has led to corruption, violence, the expropriation of landowners and environmental degradation in rural spaces in the Global South. Policing these spaces is not solely about maintaining social cohesion and respecting norms, but about responding to problems that are widespread because of the rural setting, such as domestic and family violence, the exploitation of land and labour and crimes against the environment.

Exploring these crimes from a rural and Global South informed perspective requires shifts in our criminological thinking. Adopting policing structures and practices, as suggested by Agozino through examples from Africa, may prove worthwhile for the Global South. Evidently, rural dwellers do not completely lack agency in the area of social control. It is therefore important that the technologies traditionally relied upon to maintain order be studied further, refined and harnessed to eliminate any oppressive aspects whilst the positive strengths should be conceptualized and applied to the organization of communities towards policing outcomes.

Another challenge that complicates our engagement with crime and policing in the rural Global South is the tendency to view the rural as a homogenous and cohesive space, whilst forgetting the strong role of patriarchy and hierarchical social relations that exist in rural spaces (particularly in the Global South). There is an urge amongst Western scholars to idealize the rural as cohesive and this leads to overlooking violence, especially sexual violence and domestic violence. Agozino advocates for the election of ruling councils with term limits rather than continuing to solely rely on colonial chiefs and the religious elite. He adds that state budgets should also include agricultural subsidies and enterprize start-up grants for rural dwellers, as this would work to reduce the inequalities that sometimes lead to power struggles over limited resources.

What is key is challenging urban normativity and developing policing structures that cater for the context, rather than applying urban forms of policing to rural areas in the Global South. The preoccupation with the urban and the Global North has led to a gap in research on what policing in the rural Global South looks like. It is also necessary for criminology and cognate disciplines to have a deeper engagement with the rural policing landscape of the Global South. Scholars such as Donnermeyer have pointed to the disadvantage seen in rural areas, particularly so in the Global South.

Suggested readings

Agozino, B. (2017) 'Critical perspectives on deviance and social control in rural Africa', *African Journal of Criminology and Justice Studies*, 10(1): 1+. Available from: https://link.gale.com/apps/doc/A509163569/AONE?u=anon~6cbad04&sid=googleScholar&xid=079d1d1d [Accessed 25 October 2021].

Butler, R.A. and Laurance, W.F. (2009) 'Is oil palm the next emerging threat to the Amazon?', *Tropical Conservation Science*, 2(1): 1–10.

Carrington, K., Hogg, R. and Sozzo, M. (2016) 'Southern criminology', *The British Journal of Criminology*, 56(1): 1–20.

de Sousa Santos, B. (2015) *Epistemologies of the South: Justice against Epistemicide*, London: Routledge.

Donnermeyer, J. (2017) 'The place of rural in a southern criminology', *International Journal for Crime, Justice and Social Democracy*, 6(1): 118–32.

50

Public Order Policing

David Baker

Public order policing covers a vast array of routine policing of public spaces (downtown central business districts; shopping malls) and public offences (drunk and disorderly; street violence; assaults; anti-social tourist behaviour). The public order policing of collective unrest in regional and remote locations includes the policing of protest events, rallies, marches, strikes and lockouts. Protests in rural locations are less frequent and of smaller numbers than urban occurrences, but nevertheless impact participants, communities and police.

The highly visible policing of public order represents special operational, logistical and political challenges for police strategies and tactics. Failure to prevent violence through police inaction, or escalating violence through police intervention, are constant dilemmas faced by police as they respond to conflicts. Public order policing comprises the state's law enforcement in establishing social control and maintaining order; unruly and riotous behaviour raises questions about police legitimacy and capability. The policing of public dissent in rural areas is influenced by many factors, including global events, but also the dynamics of the localized interaction of police and activist.

The myth of bucolic bliss – the mystical crime-free rurality, devoid of conflict – has been shown to be misleading, inaccurate and even dangerous. Regional and remote conflicts between colonial state police and Indigenous groups all too often occasioned bloody encounters. Rural policing is a specialized activity in itself. It is traditionally embodied within a community policing ethos with the local police station symbolic of stability and emergency assistance. Police remain the primary agency for identifying and interdicting rural crime and potentially violent conflict situations. Paradoxically, rural police are both the protectors and the prosecutors; a dichotomy of providing assistance and enforcing arrests.

As Baker (2014) points out, the coercive arm and guardian of the state, police – historically supported by governmental authority and the ruling power elites – have often assailed and quelled advocates of radical social change in a repressive and even brutal manner (peasant revolts; suffragettes; civil rights campaigners; anti-apartheid demonstrators; environmental activists; anti-globalization protesters) (see Baker et al, 2017). Public order policing is not confined to urban boundaries; for instance, in Australia, many vexatious, bitter and violent industrial disputes occurred in remote areas and resulted in pitched battles at shearing sheds, coal mines and regional wharves.

From about the 1990s onwards, many police departments the world over have employed dialogue, consultation and compromise with aggrieved groups. Dialogue initiatives create opportunities for negotiated arrangements that set parameters and expectations for crowd behaviour, limit surprises and establish some rapport. The dialogue that occurs in rural policing has much in common with urban protests, although on a more personalized level.

Although dialogue is not a panacea for all police–protester encounters as limitations are apparent and although some suspicion is inevitable, it remains in the self-interest of both police and protesters to facilitate peaceful protest through dialogue, whenever feasible. Superior police numbers once heralded police victories in public order fracas, but today negotiation, information gathering, intelligence, surveillance and ultimately psychological threat of force and riot technology are tools of police dominance of public disorders. By contrast, rural police often rely heavily on the cooperation of the local people, especially in times of conflict or emergency.

Dissent is becoming more fractured with many single-issue and geographically specific protests attracting a diverse array of participants in rural localities; we have farmers at anti-fracking protests alongside environmentalists challenging coal seam gas exploration. The local single-issue protest has become a more expansive concept in recent decades (for instance, opposition to fracking; uranium mining; steeple-jump racing; live animal exports; logging). The local policing of environmental protests challenges police to facilitate such protests but also maintain control and order. As climate change activists confront government and powerful energy corporations, it is inevitable that threatened direct action will precipitate police intervention. As environmental protests are regional, national and global, police realize that liaising and accommodating such protesters is a long-term challenge.

Rural police often lack the public order training and experience of city counterparts, but possess community insight and nous; that is, a sense of 'we-ness'. Police encounter special demands in rural communities due to large geographical distances, isolation and limited resources, although people generally have a higher level of confidence in local police. In handling protests, police are expected to intervene and act legally and decisively, but fairly and proportionately. Ironically, police determination to win all public order battles, especially those with protesters, can lead to a loss of public sympathy and support (see Scott and Jobes, 2007).

Police plan 'on-the-spot' for protests and usually initiate contact with potential activists. Rural police, providing a generalist service compared to the more specialist urban crowd controllers, often live within the local community and adopt a community-based model of policing through which they become immersed and embedded into rural values. Such community closeness and reliance poses a dilemma for police if protest erupts: the rural police officer may be sympathetic to the cause and personnel, but police are employed to enforce the law and they belong to the central police authority. The identity and standing of the local police leader in charge, the limitations of rural police numbers and resources, the difficulty in attaining reinforcements and a remote community's propensity to support its aggrieved people are crucial considerations of the police response to control public spaces.

As emphasized in several chapters of Harkness et al (2016), rural police encounter broad geographical expanses and dispersed populations, fewer resources, limited back-up and equipment and more distant communication with senior officers at centralized police headquarters. Regional centres do not possess specialist crowd-control police units, but must rely on assistance from police headquarters during emergencies. Protests in remote areas can attract an amalgam of disparate social, class and political groupings, and thus local sympathies are more problematic, diversified and sometimes divided (for example, anti-logging and pro-logging sympathies can divide a small community).

A key determinant of public order policing personnel is whether the conflict is handled by local police or whether there is a need for decisive specialist intervention. The local constable or law enforcement officer may live in the region, but the central police authority formulates operational guidelines and demands allegiance.

Suggested readings

Baker, D. (2014) 'Police and protester dialog: Safeguarding the peace or ritualistic sham?', *International Journal of Comparative and Applied Criminal Justice*, 38(1): 83–104.

Baker, D., Stenning, P. and Bronitt, S. (2017) 'Policing protest, security and freedom: The 2014 G20 experience', *Police Practice and Research: An International Journal*, 18(5): 425–48.

Harkness, A., Harris, B. and Baker, D. (eds) (2016) *Locating Crime in Context and Place: Perspectives on Regional, Rural and Remote Australia*, Sydney: The Federation Press.

Scott, J. and Jobes, P. (2007) 'Policing in rural Australia', in E. Barclay, J. Donnermeyer, J. Scott and R. Hogg (eds) *Crime in Rural Australia*, Sydney: The Federation Press, pp. 127–37.

51

Reassurance Policing in Rural Communities

Larissa Engelmann and Andrew Wooff

Reassurance policing remains an important visible policing strategy that can address the increasing disconnect between police and community created by more abstract forms of 'high' policing. Reassurance policing was conceptualized by Bahn (1974) who argued that increased visibility of police officers in the community can increase public feelings of security and safety. Early conceptualizations of reassurance policing described the importance of the police being visible, familiar and accessible.

The driver of this strategy was the identification of the 'reassurance gap', which describes the objective increase of safety through decreasing crime rates whilst fear of crime increases or stays the same due to an increased distance between police and the public (refer to Innes in the suggested readings). Identifying the reassurance gap has been key to realizing the limits of the crime management approach to policing which had, prior to reassurance policing, developed as the gold standard of professional policing.

Innes expands on earlier conceptualizations and argues that reassurance policing consists of three elements: (i) recognizing the performative act of policing by offering a visible presence in the community; (ii) using the signal crimes perspective to address the crimes and acts of disorder that are linked to feelings of insecurity in the community; and (iii) promoting the co-production of security by recognizing the role of the public in providing informal social control and the support from partner agencies, coordinated and guided by the police.

The focus on identifying and addressing crimes with 'signal values' attached to them is called the 'signal crimes perspective' and has been a crucial part in the development of reassurance policing. Some crimes (and here Innes and Fielding, 2002 is informative) have more 'signal value' attached to them than others and these can have a disproportionate impact on feelings of security.

These could be both serious acts of violence or, as is often the case in rural communities, smaller acts of disorder that disrupt daily routines.

So far, little attention has been paid to the impact and value of reassurance policing for rural communities. This is despite the fact that reassurance policing is ideally placed as a policing strategy for rural communities due to its appreciation of informal policing mechanisms and the traditionally closer relationships between the police and rural communities.

A policing style such as reassurance policing, that focuses on community engagement and partnership working, is both desirable and essential. Rural officers are often 'in and of' the community, applying discretion and negotiating order with the community. Thus, the relationship dynamics between rural police officers and rural communities may be different to that of urban areas and therefore a 'softer' approach to policing may be more beneficial to secure community engagement, compliance and support.

Nevertheless, the 'rural' is not simply an idyllic homogenous entity but also has various differences within and between communities that need a variety of enforcement and reassurance-based policing responses. Therefore, although reassurance policing can be effective in decreasing the fear of crime and increasing police legitimacy, other 'harder' forms of policing and crime management approaches are still necessary. However, compared to urban areas, these approaches are generally required less because of the cohesion, density and moral consensus in rural communities, making them more likely to be conducive to and in need of reassurance policing approaches.

Research from the Scottish islands (see Souhami, 2020) illustrates the complexity of rural environments: there is often a lack of training which can lead to negative experiences for victims of crime and thus lead to a decline in legitimacy for police officers working in these areas. Further, Souhami found that island communities' strong informal control mechanisms mean that police officers are under a lot of scrutiny. Reassurance policing approaches therefore help to promote effective partnership working, thus reducing any anxieties towards police that can arise through 'harder' crime management approaches.

These findings were supported by a Dutch study (see Terpstra, 2017) examining police officer identity construction in rural communities, which found that police officers often feel pressured to commit to urban policing styles in rural communities. This pressure and a perceived lack of understanding of rural policing needs translates into a greater distance between rural communities and their police officers. They coined this disconnect between police and community as 'abstract policing'. Abstract policing can be a significant barrier to reassurance policing as it can lead to less reporting and a lack of understanding about what the perceived key problems in rural communities are.

However, as long as the direct impact of reassurance policing on crime rates is difficult to measure and hierarchies in urban and rural perceptions of police effectiveness (general versus specialist crime response) persist, it is difficult to justify reassurance policing strategies and their implementation. Reassurance policing is often considered a 'nice to have' rather than a 'must have'; ideology driven by the current urban-centric neoliberal ideals of crime management and efficiency (see Millie, 2010).

Policing styles are as complex and diverse as the communities they are applied to. Research has shown that reassurance policing is deeply rooted in notions of the rural idyll. Yet there are tensions between urban-centric 'hard' policing approaches focused on enforcement and 'softer' community focused policing, as Wooff (2017) has observed. Thus, there are significant barriers to the use of reassurance policing in rural areas in particular. Perhaps, as Souhami suggests, the 'taken-for-grantedness' of urban policing should be called into question and the ordinariness of much rural policing in relation to reassurance work and community engagement should be celebrated and weaved through police forces across urban and rural areas. As Millie has argued, providing reassurance should be the 'golden thread' running through all of policing rather than an after thought or outcome of other strategies.

Suggested readings

Bahn, C. (1974) 'The reassurance factor in patrol policing', *Criminology*, 12(3): 328–45.

Innes, M. (2004) 'Reinventing tradition? Reassurance, neighbourhood security and policing', *Criminal Justice*, 4(2): 151–71.

Innes, M. and Fielding, N. (2002) 'From community to communicative policing: "Signal crimes" and the problem of public reassurance', *Sociological Research Online*, 7(2): 56–67.

Millie, A. (2010) 'Whatever happened to reassurance policing?', *Policing*, 4(3): 225–32.

Souhami, A. (2020) 'Understanding police work in the remote Northern isles of Scotland: The extraordinary ordinariness of island policing', *Edinburgh School of Law Research Paper*.

Terpstra, J. (2017) 'Storytelling about rural policing-the social construction of a professional identity', *European Journal of Policing Studies*, 5(1): 17–33.

Wooff, A. (2017) '"Soft" policing in rural Scotland', *Journal of Policy and Practice*, 11(2): 123–31.

52

Rurality, Cultures and Policing

Richard Yarwood

It is crucial to distinguish between 'rural policing' and 'policing the rural'. Rural policing refers to offences that are unique to rural environments, such as poaching, rustling, theft of agricultural machinery or certain environmental crimes. Policing the rural draws attention to the idea that rurality is socially constructed. Although meanings of rurality are contested, the hegemonic view is that the countryside is peaceful, idyllic and problem-free. This rural myth contributes to a widely held ideal that the countryside is, or should be, crime-free. This has three important consequences.

First, the rural idyll has hidden the scale, nature and reality of crime to such an extent that it has become invisible or, at best, regarded as much less of a problem than in urban areas (see Halfacree, 1994). Such views have contributed to a withdrawal of state policing that, in turn, has contributed to a sense that rural areas and their residents have been neglected by policy makers (see Woods, 2006, 2007). The rural idyll also hides some serious crimes. Of late, there has been a realization that slavery, people trafficking, domestic violence, agricultural thefts and illegal drugs can originate from, and impact upon, rural areas. These issues reveal the growing significance of organized crime in rural places and, in particular, how the processes, flows and impacts of international criminal networks reflect the increasingly interconnected, globalized nature of the countryside. Rural crime stretches beyond rural communities and cannot, therefore, be policed solely at the local level.

Second, what is considered 'criminal' is also culturally constructed, and very often bound up with ideas of rurality (see Yarwood, 2007). Thus, certain activities or people are regarded as 'out of place' in the countryside. These include, but are not limited to, young people 'hanging around', travellers, migrant workers or even ramblers – all of whom have been subject to surveillance and policing. This reflects a blurring of cultural threat with criminal threat: the rural idyll is being threatened rather than a crime taking place. At the same time, some illegal or contentious activities have formed part of rural imagination and identity. Thus, poaching, hunting or culls of animals are controversial yet central to some rural identities. Some farmers may also generate income through, for example, engaging in the illegal meat trade. These kinds of activities may go unnoticed, underreported or tacitly accepted due to social norms and community pressures to conform and keep the peace.

In both of these cases, criminality and policing reflects a dominant or hegemonic view of what the countryside should be. These ideas can be bound into the policing of the countryside in a variety of ways. Thus, legislation to prevent nomadic lifestyles or hunting directly outlaws some activities in rural places to reflect a particular vision of country life.

Equally, other forms of legislation or policing may impact directly on some groups. For example, laws banning the public consumption of alcohol, perhaps as an attempt to commodify a town for tourists, may impact on young people or Indigenous groups. It is worth noting at this point that policing refers to more than just the enforcement of laws by state forces but, more widely, the enforcement of codes, standards and ideals held by society. Thus, daily practices that include or exclude people from rural places, such as welcoming a stranger or forcing young people to play elsewhere, contribute to the policing of the rural. It is, therefore, also important to note that the ideas and practices of rural policing reflects a cultural politics and the interests of particular powerful groups.

Finally, and related to this, the rural myth has contributed to the neoliberal rolling back of state policing and their replacement with voluntary or private services. The idea of active citizenship has been widely used to persuade members of the public to provide services for themselves. This supports a convenient but uncritical shorthand that rural communities are the cause and solution of problems in their own localities. Recent years have witnessed many attempts to develop forms of plural policing that draw on local social capital, including rural or farm watch schemes, local crime partnerships, residents' patrols or recruiting unsworn officers from local communities (see Yarwood, 2015).

These initiatives are commendable for their innovation and have improved public–police relations and feelings of security for some. Whilst there are some benefits in involving citizens in local decision making, community policing is problematic for three reasons. First, by definition, communities exclude as well as include some people. There is also evidence that elite groups are more likely to participate in community policing and, second, use it to target minority groups such as young people, travellers or, simply, outsiders. Finally, communities are often considered as bounded space and, indeed, situational crime prevention relies on defining and protecting a 'defensible space'. Given the globalized nature of the countryside and the threat of organized crime, policing needs to move well beyond local communities.

It is clear, therefore, that rurality and policing are socially constructed and, as such, contested. These are intersectional and, together, have contributed to a hegemonic view that highlights some crimes, neglects others and, significantly, blurs criminality and cultural threat. In response, rural geographers and criminologists have been seeking ways to challenge these views using three significant perspectives.

Challenging traditional perspectives

First, 'Southern Criminology' (refer to Carrington et al, 2015) is contesting many of the orthodoxies associated with rural policing. In an effort to overcome a 'metropolitan criminology' of the Global North, Southern Criminology has sought to place a greater attention on the Global South and overcome the colonial vestiges that enslaved millions, exploited vast tracts of land and marginalized ingenious people through poverty, domestic violence and aggressive policing.

The Southern Criminology paradigm seeks to recognize and overcome these inequalities by drawing on diverse perspectives, Indigenous knowledge and the experiences of the Global South to decolonize the production of knowledge, destabilize established binaries and empower those who are seldom given voice.

As a result, work is starting to reveal how rurality is experienced and policed from a much wider range of perspectives. Positively, some work is examining how Indigenous practices can contribute to forms of restorative justice, both locally and at a global scale, as the impacts of colonization are recognized. Yet other work has challenged the assumption of a stable nation–state and the significance of formal policing to reveal the significance of informal policing for many. This might include the repression of women through cultural practices as well as the significance of organized criminal gangs in controlling people and places through extension and violence.

These perspectives point to the significance of a globalized countryside that is linked through flows of people, good, ideas, media and mobilities (see Woods, 2006, 2007). As perspectives from Southern Criminology reveal, these networks can be illicit and connect the Global North and South through illegal activities such as drug dealing or people trafficking (see Donnermeyer, 2016).

By examining connections and flows, these perspectives question the significance of rural communities as local, bounded places and call for forms of policing that are international, rather than local, in their perspective. This does not mean the end of community policing but, rather, encouraging people to look beyond the familiar to take a wider perspective on community. Thus, rather than regarding an immigrant worker as a threat to a hegemonic rural order, communities should question whether he or she is being exploited or is able to access justice. It calls on academics, the public and the police to rethink rurality in global terms and to reconsider how it can be policed as such.

Second, feminists have also argued that rural policing and, more widely, the study of rurality, has largely been focused on public space. Although the ideal of a home, and particularly a farmhouse, is closely embedded in many idyllic visions of rurality (together with associated gendered roles of domesticity), it is rare that research, or policing, intrudes on domestic space. This has had the impact of over-emphasizing crimes that occur in public space, contributing to women's fear of crime and excluding them from full participation in rural society by, for example, avoiding being out at night or travelling alone (see both Little et al, 2005 and Yarwood and Gardner, 2000). At the same time, domestic crime and violence are hidden as they occur in private spaces. Additionally, a lack of support services, as well as a police presence, may contribute to trapping women, children and some men in abusive relationships.

Finally, some geographers have drawn attention to the significance of more-than-human relationships in rural places. Whilst rural criminology has largely focused on people, green or environmental criminology has drawn attention to crimes against non-humans. These are particularly pertinent in the Global South and have largely been ignored by an orthodoxy that focuses on people or ignores the impacts of colonial and post-colonial practices.

Other crimes against non-humans include poaching and hunting, often regarded as part of rural life, as well as wider crimes against the environment that contribute to habitat loss, the destruction of species and climate change. Farmers may also engage in illegal culls of animals that they regard as pests, although wide acceptance of these practices in some localities makes them difficult to police. As an aside, it should also be noted that animals can play a role in the policing of rural localities: for example, dogs can be trained to search for missing people or illicit drugs. These collaborations between people and animals emphasize the hybrid nature of rural policing. Radical, less anthropocentric perspectives reflect the contested relationship between rurality, nature and policing.

To conclude, it is essential to understand how rurality and criminality are socially constructed and, crucially, contested through different forms of policing (see Yarwood, 2017). Rural criminology should be based on a critical appraisal of what rurality means and to whom. These foundations allow us to understand rural policing and policing the rural in inclusionary ways to the benefits of all rural society.

Suggested readings

Carrington, K., Hogg, R. and Sozzo, M. (2015) 'Southern criminology', *The British Journal of Criminology*, 56: 1–20.

Donnermeyer, J. (2017) 'The place of rural in southern criminology', *International Journal for Crime, Justice and Social Democracy*, 6: 118–32.

Halfacree, K.H. (1994) 'The importance of the rural in the constitution of counterurbanization – evidence from England in the 1980s', *Sociologia Ruralis*, 34: 164–89.

Little, J., Panelli, R. and Kraack, A. (2005) 'Women's fear of crime: A rural perspective', *Journal of Rural Studies*, 21: 151–63.

Woods, M. (2007) 'Engaging the global countryside: globalization, hybridity and the reconstitution of rural place', *Progress in Human Geography*, 31: 485–507.

Woods, M. (2006) 'Redefining the 'rural question': The new "politics of the rural" and social policy', *Social Policy and Administration*, 40: 579–95.

Yarwood, R. (2022) 'Policing the global countryside: Towards a research agenda', *Professional Geographer*, 74(2): 343–9.

Yarwood, R. (2015) 'Lost and hound: The more-than-human networks of rural policing', *Journal of Rural Studies*, 39: 278–86.

Yarwood, R. and Gardner, G. (2000) 'Fear of crime, cultural threat and the countryside, *Area*, 32: 403–11.

Courts and Corrections

53

Community Corrections

Dawei Zhang, Jessica René Peterson, Alistair Harkness and Joseph F. Donnermeyer

Community corrections are non-custodial criminal sanctions that have been adopted by courts and other criminal justice agencies, with a basic philosophy that, rather than relying on incarceration, the preferred approach is community-based alternatives to supervise, manage, rehabilitate and educate offenders. Alternatives to imprisonment include diversionary schemes for defendants, probation or suspended sentences for convicted offenders and parole or early release for prisoners. They are relatively low-cost sanctions and measures that do not consume prison space (see Groves, 2017).

Community corrections consist of two basic types of programmes: (i) sanctions that serve as alternatives to incarceration and (ii) programmes that assist prisoners in community re-entry after prison (see Cromwell et al, 2002). Community sanctions combine the purposes of controlling and reforming the offender. These diversionary schemes attempt to redirect certain offenders from the formal criminal justice system to various services that improve their chances for rehabilitation and improve re-entry back into the community, thereby reducing recidivism.

As Klingele (2021) points out, offenders may face many challenges in the communities where they live, including adequate housing, access to healthy and affordable food, addressing chronic physical and mental health issues, the need for vocational training and employment, transportation to various human services, childcare and so on. By meeting these needs, there is a greater chance that the supervision, management and rehabilitation of offenders who are on probation or have suspended sentences will be improved and thereby reduce re-entry back into a criminal lifestyle, potentially leading to additional arrests and jail time.

Rural community corrections

From a global perspective, and compared with urban areas, rural community correction work faces more challenges. First, there is an overall shortage of corrections workers in rural communities. In urban areas, there may be three or more staff per judicial institute, whilst in rural areas there are relatively few full-time staff. Coupled with the fact that in many instances rural residents live scattered across the jurisdiction and in relatively distant locations with inconvenient transportation options, correctional work in the community is more difficult.

Second, in some jurisdictions, the quality of corrections staff can be relatively low. The educational level of rural community correctional staff might be lacking in general and many might not have backgrounds in the field. Social workers, psychological counselors and other professionals are scarce and volunteer staff may receive relatively little pre- and post-job training. To undertake community corrections work, inadequate professional literacy and work ability have much room for improvement.

Third, compared with urban areas, rural areas often embrace punitive traditions which may deviate from the principles of community corrections, leading to resistance in implementation by correctional workers. The rehabilitation attitude of rural community correction workers towards community-based objectives may be lower than that of a punitive attitude, which may affect the original purpose of educational support of community correction.

Additionally, rural community corrections can be greatly influenced by folk culture and local knowledge. Even though community corrections originated in the West, it was rapidly adopted in China and many other non-Western countries. In a Chinese context – owing to uneven economic and social development across the country – local people are often more familiar with and agree with 'local knowledge' about crime and corrections (including traditional folk solutions). Such knowledge may inform civil law and vary the implementation of community corrections from one community to the next (see both Jiang et al, 2016 and Irwin et al, 2016).

Fourth, and again with a Chinese context, rural community corrections are greatly influenced by local customs and relationship ties. The customs, etiquette, values and concept of honour and disgrace in traditional rural Chinese society have fluctuated owing to the impact of the market economy, but the relationship between local social and familial networks remains strong and influences how justice is administered in general, including community corrections. Cultural bonds and density of acquaintanceship can be either advantageous or obstructive to the re-entry process for those under supervision.

Internationally, there is a relative shortage of social support and services for those living in rural communities who are serving community-based sentences, as funding for rural community corrections is often insufficient. This impedes the implementation of both emotional and social support for those who might benefit from a community-corrections approach to re-entry and rehabilitation.

Conclusions and countermeasures

Differences in funding and resources, culture and tradition and physical constraints of rural settings (such as isolation, residential dispersion and lack of transportation) leads to distinct challenges for community corrections in rural communities. There needs to be increased investment in rural community corrections – in terms of people, finances, services and so on. The disparity between urban and rural areas in terms of access to justice also needs to be addressed: this includes promoting the institutionalization and specialization of rural community corrections, improving the number and quality of community correction workers, and enhancing the legal awareness of community corrections for rural residents, so as to truly realize the integrated development of urban and rural community corrections.

Suggested readings

Cromwell, P., Del Carmen, R. and Alarid, L. (2002) *Community-Based Corrections*, Belmont, CA: Wadsworth (Chapters 1, 9 and 13 in particular).

Groves, A. (2017) 'Community-based corrections/justice', in D. Palmer, W. De Lint, W. and D. Dalton (eds) *Crime and Justice: A Guide to Criminology* (5th edn), Sydney: Lawbook Co., pp. 466–88.

Irwin, D., Zhang, D. and Wang, S. (2016) 'China's social transformation and the development of rural community corrections', in J.F. Donnermeyer (ed) *The Routledge International Handbook of Rural Criminology*, London: Routledge, pp. 419–28.

Jiang, S., Jin, X., Xiang, D., Goodlin-Fahncke, W., Yang, S., Xu, N. and Zhang, D. (2016) 'Punitive and rehabilitative orientations toward offenders among community correctional officers in China', *The Prison Journal*, 96: 771–92.

Klingele, C. (2021) *The Role of Human Service Providers during Community Supervision*, Washington, DC: National Institute of Justice, United States Department of Justice.

54

Court Reform Challenges in Rural Jurisdictions

Alyssa M. Clark

In his seminal work, Feeley argued that most solutions to reforming criminal courts would fail due to the fragmentation of courts, the adversarialism of United States case processing and the fallacy of formalism (the reliance of formal description of the criminal justice process for diagnosing and remedying problems) (refer to Feeley, 2013). Although rural courts do face these obstacles to reforming their courtrooms, they face additional obstacles based on the rural context in which they operate.

United States court reformers, such as the twentieth-century legal scholar Roscoe Pound (1870–1964), have advocated for a highly centralized hierarchical court system that is administered by some form of state supreme court, with most funding coming from the state. However, this kind of formal model assumes that all rural courts are included in one unified court system and would be funded directly by the state. For example, in New York, as in other states in the United States, there is a fragmented patchwork of approximately 1,200 rural courts that do not fall under the purview of the 'Unified Court System'. Rather, they are technically overseen by a different agency. Therefore, any reform measure that the Unified Court System instituted would not reach the rural courts, in part because of this fragmentation.

Even if there was state funding for rural courts, there would still be competition with urban courts for resources. Given that funding has traditionally followed a formula that takes a court's caseload into account, rural courts would receive limited funding. This is a result of rural courts having fewer cases than urban courts. In addition, there would still need to be some form of local funds (county, town, city and so on) dedicated to implementing reforms because no state court system is completely funded by the state. In rural areas in the United States, this is particularly daunting because rural communities traditionally have lower tax bases owing to smaller populations. Consequentially, rural communities are required to do more with less. In other words, mandates and reforms put further financial stress on rural areas with fewer resources.

Reformers often also fail to consider the issues and obstacles that plague a rural court (see Worden et al, 2017). In a United States context, in many rural jurisdictions, judges are locally elected, not appointed. Therefore, the local communities that elect these judges can retain significant influence in the courthouse. In essence, any form of unification or reform could only loosen judicial ties to the community, in contrast to completely severing those ties. As a representative from the community, judges may be more attentive to the criminal issues their community faces and deems a problem, not the issues that outsiders have determined need reform. Outsiders who determine the trajectory of reforms might well be out of touch with the people who implement the reforms. As applied here, urban policymakers do not fully understand the obstacles and barriers court actors in rural court face when trying to implement these reforms, nor do they understand the communities in which these court actors operate.

This is a particularly United States phenomenon, but elected judges then face the overwhelming obstacles of social and professional isolation and large geographic barriers that is characteristic of rurality. As a result, these judges are largely autonomous; some have even characterized these courts as fiefdoms. Reforms would thereby be implemented differently in each rural courtroom based on the judge presiding in the community.

Although it appears that most scholars such as Edmondson (1996) would hypothesize that rural courts would essentially 'fail' at implementing any court reform due to fragmentation, rural context obstacles and the lack of understanding in how rural courts function, there has been some research that shows a more positive outlook.

Programmes in rural communities could overcome these obstacles when three factors are in play. First, rural courts can successfully implement initiatives when they are able to tailor reforms to the specific problems and obstacles in their jurisdiction (a problem-solving approach); second, rural leaders can rely on their leadership skills, legitimacy and standing in their communities to get programmes off the ground and collaborate with other criminal justice agencies; and third, court actors must support the same goal (refer to Worden et al, 2017).

Other court scholars have noted that rural courts cannot be evaluated using the same metrics as in urban courts. Pound would have evaluated courts based on their organization and structure, as has been done in urban courts. In rural courts, there needs to be an emphasis on performance, recognizing the strengths of rural courts.

It would also be beneficial for evaluators to study the actual implementation (the process) of mandates in rural areas, including the overcoming of barriers and obstacles. For example, evaluators need not look simply at a cost–benefit analysis of rural courts or use national criteria to measure efficiency. These metrics fail to take into account the notion that providing justice in rural areas might simply cost more or that court appearances in rural areas are not as frequent as in urban areas due to low case volume. Although a model of this kind has not yet been proposed, there have been research agendas that will hopefully lead to the production of a model.

This entry has focused on the tenets of court reform and the addition of obstacles posed by a rural context using sources and information that pertain to United States courts. However, this does not mean that courts in other countries are exempt from these obstacles. Rural courts across the world battle large geographic distances, fewer resources and community influence. Courts with a similar legal system are also subject to Feeley's tenets. More research is needed to determine if rural courts positioned in a different legal system face the same obstacles as described earlier.

Suggested readings

Edmondson, C. (1996) 'Rural courts, the rural community, and the challenge of change', in T.D. McDonald, R.A. Wood and M.A. Pflug (eds) *Rural Criminal Justice: Conditions, Constraints and Challenges*, Salem, WI: Sheffield Publishing Company, pp. 93–110.

Feeley, M. (2013) *Court Reform on Trial: Why Simple Solutions Fail*, New Orleans, LA: Quid Pro Books.

Worden, A.P., Davies, A.L.B., Shteynberg, R.V. and Morgan, K.A. (2017) 'Court reform: Why simple solutions might not fail?: A case study of implementation of counsel at first appearance', *Ohio State Journal of Criminal Law*, 14(2): 521–51.

55

Desistance from Crime

Rachel Hale

The process of desistance from crime

Theories of offending have dominated criminological theorizing, with a plethora of different explanations having evolved over time. Contrariwise, the study of how and why individuals *stop* offending (desistance from crime) is relatively new. Adopting a strength-based approach to flip the age-old question of why crime occurs on its head is beneficial – it can inform responses that encourage and support the cessation of offending, potentially reducing reoffending.

Desisting from crime is widely accepted to be a process, rather than an event. It is non-linear and can involve periods of engagement and disengagement in law breaking. There has been much debate about how best to define and measure desistance. The scope of desistance research has extended beyond studies of the complete absence of offending to include reductions in law breaking, as well as intentions and efforts to stop offending.

Desistance from crime is impacted by an interplay of micro (individual), meso (community) and macro (structural) level factors. Whilst at the individual-level internal changes in identity, as well as readiness and willingness to desist, have been deemed critical, these factors have been found to interact with broader, structural conditions (see Hale, 2020). For example, though the individual may wish to desist, structural disadvantages can impede the ability to action these intentions. It is therefore important to acknowledge the relationship between individual agency and structure when considering the process of desisting.

Several factors have been identified as protective against offending and thus supportive of desistance from crime, including stable employment, secure housing, prosocial relationships and access to support. In rural areas, where disadvantages across these domains of social need tend to be amplified, increased barriers to desistance are likely.

Rural barriers to desistance

Whilst many of the typical barriers to stopping offending are experienced across both urban and rural places, these can be exacerbated by rurality and accompanied by additional, unique challenges. Rural citizens face more challenging circumstances with regards to access to housing, substance use and mental health supports and employment (see Perez, 2007). These conditions are more likely to be criminogenic than conducive to desistance.

Safe, secure housing is one of the most fundamental needs and critical to the ability to desist. Once housing is obtained, other needs can be met. However, in rural and remote locations, there can be a lack of affordable housing stock, particularly safe, long-term housing, impacting desistance prospects. Prejudices surrounding 'ex-prisoners' can influence the appraisal of tenancy applications, particularly in very small rural communities where the individuals' offending history is widely known. Where a rural citizen has a history of substance use or poor employment history, their chances of securing a rental may be reduced. If unemployed, they may be unable to afford the bond and advance payments required to secure the property. These issues, which are heightened in rural areas, make securing housing difficult, leading to homelessness, which may necessitate further offending (see Zajac et al, 2014; Bowman and Ely, 2020).

Stable employment is also linked to the ability to disengage from law breaking, especially for individuals who commit 'subsistence' offences – offending to meet their basic survival needs. A consistent, sufficient income can stem the need to steal money or goods. Beyond the provision of economic security, employment can enhance one's sense of inclusion, help to build prosocial connections, and provide a sense of fulfilment through meaningful work. However, in rural areas, opportunities for employment can be limited, and concentrated in traditionally masculine industries, impacting the ability of women to pursue desirable careers following release from prison (see Perez, 2017). As noted with the acquisition of housing, prejudicial attitudes against persons with a criminal record can impact employment prospects. In rural communities with increased acquaintance density, potential employers are likely to know about the individuals' offending history, which can impede employability.

Those returning to rural communities following incarceration often have access to fewer services to support (re)integration and desistance. In rural areas, there can be an absence of specialist services, and the distance to urban-based services may be impossible to traverse without private transportation in the face of poor public transit options. The relative intimacy of rural communities can mean that people are hesitant to reach out for support from services staffed by fellow community members. Without accessing various kinds of support, the individual may reoffend because the drivers of their offending are unaddressed.

Finally, connections within the community, particularly to prosocial peers, has been found to be conducive to desistance from crime, acting as a protective factor against recidivism and reincarceration (see Staton et al, 2019). The opposite is also true, that is, involvement with peers who are also involved in illegal behaviours can greatly reduce desistance. Those returning to small rural communities following incarceration may experience increased shame and stigmatization, which can hinder the ability to action desistance intentions. The rural community has the potential to play a critical role in supporting desistance from crime through the provision of inclusivity and support, which can enable individuals to action their intentions to desist and cease offending.

Conclusion

Desistance from crime is contingent on individual-level factors as well as broader structural conditions. In rural communities, where disadvantages are amplified, the ability to desist from crime becomes more challenging and therefore less likely to achieve. Investment by the state in alleviating these disadvantages through the provision of accessible housing options, long term-employment opportunities and increased rural support services will create conditions that are more conducive to desistance from crime, with the potential to reduce reoffending and reincarceration.

Suggested readings

Bowman, E.I. and Ely, K. (2020) 'Voices of returning citizens: A qualitative study of a supportive housing program for ex-offenders in a rural community', *The Prison Journal*, 100(4): 423–46.

Hale, R. (2020) 'Good intentions: Women's narratives of post-release anticipatory desistance in the context of historical and contemporary disadvantage and trauma', *Journal of Feminist Criminology*, 15: 519–44.

Perez, F. (2007) 'Female offenders in a rural environment: Access to community support agencies', Research paper, *The Griffins Society*. Available from: https://www.thegriffinssociety.org/system/files/papers/fullreport/research_paper_2007_03_f.perez_.pdf [Accessed 1 November 2021].

Staton, M., Dickson, M.F., Tillson, M., Webster, M. and Leukefeld, C. (2019) 'Staying out: Reentry protective factors among rural women offenders', *Women and Criminal Justice*, 29(6): 368–84.

Zajac, G., Hutchison, R. and Meyer C.A. (2014) 'An examination of rural prisoner reentry challenges', *Center for Rural Pennsylvania*. Available from: http://www.rural.palegislature.us/documents/reports/rural_prisoner_reentry_2014.pdf [Accessed 1 November 2021].

56

Informal and Decolonized Alternative Criminal Justice

Zahidul Islam

Informal justice systems and decolonized justice alternatives play significant roles for rural crime control and dispute settlement. They are two distinct types of mechanisms with different backgrounds, evolution and functions.

'Informal justice system' is an umbrella term that encompasses different types of customary, traditional, local, tribal and Indigenous justice systems. These systems are usually conceptualized as non-state justice systems as opposed to the formal state justice systems, which have written laws and procedures for decision making and enforcement mechanisms. However, each informal justice system is unique in its formalities and philosophical underpinnings. When people began living together in societies, the informal justice system evolved to maintain social order and cohesion. Hence, they are found in rural societies across the world from time immemorial.

Some of the informal systems studied in recent years include *Jirga* in Afghanistan, *Shalish* in Bangladesh, *Bashingantahe* in Burundi, *Adat* in East Timor and Indonesia, *Katarungang Pambarangay* in Philippines, *Mayan* in Guetemala, *Gacaca* in Rwanda, *Xeer* in Somalia and *Salif* in Sudan (see Wojkowska, 2006). Many of these Indigenous and informal justice systems survived, even in territories and states occupied by colonial powers for centuries, and many informal rural justice systems continue to play a significant role in dealing with rural crime (see McGuire and Palys, 2020).

When Indigenous justice approaches were replaced with state-led formal criminal justice systems in colonial states, the people did not accept the foreign systems for various reasons including the complexity of the systems and inconsistency with their distinguished cultural, religious or customary beliefs, norms, values and understanding of crimes and justice (see Agozino,

2019). From the beginning, public resistance and reluctance to resort to these formal systems was strong.

After gaining independence from colonial powers, the decolonization of these formal justice systems at different levels started in many countries. Decolonized alternatives are created in various ways including by reforming or harmonizing the formal justice system to suit the needs of the Indigenous population, by recognizing parallel Indigenous systems, by abolition of the hierarchy of formal over informal justice systems or by establishing new laws and guidelines that reformed the traditional informal systems to better suit the needs of the changing societies (see Agozino, 2019; McGuire and Palys, 2020).

Characteristics

Studies reveal that informal rural and decolonized alternative justice systems across the world share certain common characteristics (see UN Women, UNICEF and UNDP, 2012). They usually function within the community, have easy rules and procedures known by the community people and empower the community people to participate in the justice system as decision makers and observers. Their less cumbersome procedures do not require the engagement of professional lawyers in most cases, and they involve little or no cost for the system to function (see Kotter et al, 2015).

The community itself works as an enforcement mechanism where social pressure and shame associated with rejecting the decisions play key roles. The justice outcomes, however, may be restorative as well as punitive in nature, depending on various factors including the nature and gravity of the crimes and the existing norms, beliefs and philosophies about crimes and justice in the given society. Such characteristics provide empowerment, confidence and comfort, as well as feelings of obligation to use these systems.

Informal justice systems worldwide also share certain common weaknesses and vulnerabilities. Sometimes the systems can be influenced or dominated by powerful people and become vehicles for the exercise of their power and the promotion of patriarchal attitudes and prevalent gender norms. Thus, these systems are prone to abuse that further victimizes women and impoverished justice seekers, and they perpetuate harmful gender norms in rural social and political power structures. Other common allegations against many informal systems pertain to inconsistency with universal human rights principles as they may lack adequate transparency and accountability.

Informal justice systems across the world deal with a wide range of rural crimes which include almost all kinds of petty and grievous crimes, legally defined as crimes against property and crimes against the person. In rural communities, the state decides which of the crimes can be dealt with informally by the community or a parallel Indigenous informal system, by the state through its formal systems or jointly in partnership with non-state actors and state actors. These decisions are made based on aspects of the crime such as the source, type, interests and powers of the stakeholders involved and the legal and institutional capacity of the state justice systems to deal with the crimes.

International trends

Studies of informal systems and decolonized alternatives across the world show specific trends. Less-developed states approve, by law or by inaction, as many crimes as possible to be dealt with by the informal rural justice forums. It is convenient for these states, because it lessens the state's financial burden and responsibilities for the administration of justice. Many states assign petty crimes and domestic violence to be dealt with by the informal systems because it is thought that the rural community is capable of dealing with these cases, and it is also convenient for the community in terms of securing justice quickly and economically.

Many of the state systems deal with rural crimes related to organized armed groups, young criminal gangs, drug related crimes, communal riots, hate crimes, cybercrimes, religious communalism-related crimes and other serious crimes, because these crimes require different institutional capacities and coercive power that the communities may not possess.

In some countries, certain rural crimes can be dealt with by both the informal forums and formal courts. The victims, or in some cases the parties to a crime, decide which outlet they will pursue. In making such a decision, various factors including the nature and gravity of the case, the status and power of the parties and their assumptions as to the possibility of getting justice are considered.

Promoting non-state informal and state-led semi-formal or decolonized justice alternatives is now a growing trend to ensure access to justice for rural populations. However, the perception of rurality, the nature of rural crimes and the ideas of rural social control and social capital are changing. Therefore, there is much to explore regarding the suitability and effectiveness of various types and models of rural informal and decolonized alternative justice systems, as societies across the globe change at different paces.

Suggested readings

Agozino, B. (2019) 'Humanifesto of the Decolonization of Criminology and Justice', *Decolonization of Criminology and Justice*, 1(1): 5–28.

Kötter, M., Röder, T., Schuppert, F. and Wolfrum, R. (2015) *Non-state Justice Institutions and the Law: Decision-Making at the Interface of Tradition, Religion and the State*, London: Palgrave Macmillan.

McGuire, M. and Palys, T. (2020) 'Toward sovereign Indigenous justice: On removing the colonial straightjacket', *Decolonization of Criminology and Justice*, 2(1): 59–82.

UN Women, UNICEF and UNDP (2012) 'Informal justice systems: Charting a course for human rights-based engagement', United Nations. Available from: https://www.unwomen.org/-/media/headquarters/attachments/sections/library/publications/2013/1/informal-justice-systems-charting-a-course-for-human-rights-based-engagement.pdf?la=en&vs=5500 [Accessed 30 October 2021].

Wojkowska, E. (2006) 'Doing justice: How informal justice systems can contribute', UNDP. Available from: https://www.un.org/ruleoflaw/blog/document/doing-justice-how-informal-justice-systems-can-contribute/ [Accessed 30 October 2021].

57

Jails and Prisons

Rick Ruddell

Although there is some variation throughout the world, the operation of jails and prisons in the countryside has been the norm for centuries (see Dikötter et al, 2007). There are several key differences between jails and prisons in a North American context, and those distinctions are important. Jails are typically intended for the short-term detention of individuals awaiting a court appearance or trial, or persons sentenced to relatively short sentences. Prisons, by contrast, house individuals convicted of committing serious offences and are serving lengthy sentences. In some nations, however, a single type of facility holds both detained and long-term sentenced inmates.

Although jails are found in both urban and rural areas, most prisons are in the countryside. Placing correctional facilities in rural areas creates challenges for jail and prison personnel, the people living in these facilities and their families. Moreover, the impact of placing these facilities in rural areas on the people living in those communities is often overlooked.

Jails

There are two types of jail operations. The first is the stand-alone jail, which is typically operated and funded by a local government. Whilst some urban jails hold thousands of inmates, there are about 1,500 facilities with fewer than 100 beds in the United States and these small stand-alone facilities – that are not part of a larger network – are found throughout the world. Many of these small facilities are underfunded as they are located in economically depressed locations that draw from impoverished tax bases. This underfunding inhibits the ability of their personnel to deliver safe and humane care.

The second model of jail operations are facilities operated by departments of corrections or similar bodies and are funded by regional, state, provincial or federal governments. These jails often hold hundreds of residents, and they are generally able to provide better care than their smaller counterparts. Moreover, they are often part of a network of similar facilities that allows them to share expertize and resources; enabling them to deliver more professional services. The care jail residents receive is important, as they are several times more likely than members of the general population to suffer from disabilities and physical health problems, and more than one-half of United States jail residents have addiction problems and mental health disorders.

Prisons

Most prisons in the United States and Canada are in rural locations. Historically, most were self-sufficient facilities that had little contact with the outside world. Prisoner labour was used to construct these buildings and the residents worked in farms on the prison grounds and ate the produce they grew and animals they raised. Surplus agricultural production was sold and the funds used to lower operating costs. By the end of the twentieth century, however, this agricultural model was disappearing and prisons became more open, professionally staffed and their operations became almost entirely dependent on government funding.

In some Western nations, the number of rural prisons grew after local politicians successfully lobbied legislators to use these facilities as a form of economic development. Writing about the United States, King, Mauer and Huling (2003) report that 35 jobs are created for every 100 prison beds. These economic gains must be balanced against the adverse environmental impacts and the stigma of being labelled a 'prison town', which may reduce other investments in a community. Whitfield (2008) also identifies the social problems associated with prisons, including that many inmates are from cities far from the prison and this is a barrier to receiving family visits. As a result, some families move to these rural communities to maintain contact and they can possibly – along with the correctional officers and their families who also moved to these prison towns – disrupt community life in some places.

Locating prisons in rural areas can make it difficult to recruit and retain qualified personnel as there is often a shortage of residents suited for correctional work. It is also difficult to attract medical and other professionals to work in the countryside. Staff turnover can be high and this places some correctional administrators in an ongoing cycle of recruiting, training and attempting to retain those personnel, which is costly and reduces their focus on providing rehabilitative interventions. Thus, the economic benefits of locating prisons in the countryside must be weighed against these social costs (see Ruddell et al, 2020, 2021).

Summary

Placing prisons in rural locales can be disruptive, especially when these communities become dependent upon government funding for their economic wellbeing (see Hale et al, 2022). Rural jails, by contrast, are vulnerable to economic downturns and are often underfunded. This hampers the ability of jail administrators to provide safe, rehabilitative and humane care, which can contribute to higher levels of crime in their communities when these individuals are released from custody.

The impacts of incarcerating people in rural correctional facilities are often outside of our awareness and these institutions tend to operate out-of-sight and out-of-mind unless some newsworthy event is reported by the media. Although conditions of confinement are improving in most nations, many of the challenges their administrators are confronting today are persistent problems defying simple solutions. Many of these challenges are interconnected and some of their origins can be traced back to historical arrangements including placing these facilities in the countryside.

Suggested readings

Dikötter, F. and Brown, I. (2007) *Cultures of Confinement: A History of the Prison in Africa, Asia, and Latin America*, Ithaca, NY: Cornell University Press.

Hale, R., Harkness, A. and Mulrooney, K. (2022) 'Punishment, politics and the realities of rurality', in M. Bowden and A. Harkness (eds) *Rural Transformations and Rural Crime: International Critical Perspectives in Rural Criminology*, Bristol: Bristol University Press, pp. 164–82.

King, R.S., Mauer, M. and Huling, T. (2003) *Big Prisons, Small Towns: Prison Economics in Rural America*, Washington, DC: The Sentencing Project.

Ruddell, R., Mays, G.L. and Sturgeon, W. (2021) 'Rural American jails: Rising demands, tight money, and limited options', *International Journal of Regional, Rural and Remote Law and Policy*, 9(1): 1–14.

Ruddell, R., Mays, G.L. and Winfree, T. (2020) *Corrections: A Critical Thinking Approach*, London: Routledge.

Whitfield, D. (2008) *Economic Impact of Prisons in Rural Areas: A Review of the Issues*, Duagh: European Services Strategy Unit.

58

Judicial Policies and Procedures

Alyssa M. Clark

It is common for judicial policies and procedures – the rules and established steps for adjudicating criminal cases – to operate differently in a rural context compared with an urban or suburban context. Courtroom actors must tackle obstacles specific to rural communities, such as large geographical distances, fewer monetary resources due to a low tax base and deep social ties to the community, amongst others. As a result, courtroom policies and procedures may be more informal and less bureaucratic in nature.

Because of geographic barriers and slower disposition times owing to infrequent court sessions, many rural communities have altered the simple delivery of adjudication services. In the United States, in the state of New York, a justice court or a regionalized equivalent is available to hear all types of criminal and civil cases in each of the state's 1,486 towns and villages with the goal of delivering justice to each constituent's door. In Brazil, a country whose judiciary has been opposed owing to its large bureaucracy and slowness in delivering verdicts, there is a traveling riverboat that serves as a courtroom for the most remote residents. Similarly, through a grant with the United States Department of Justice, the Cheyenne River Sioux Tribe located in South Dakota was able to pilot a mobile courtroom.

In locations where mobile courts are not an option for overcoming large geographical barriers, rural courts may allow teleconferencing for court appearances. This is prevalent in rural Australian courts given the huge distances covered by many Australian jurisdictions. Using teleconferencing, courtroom actors can conduct various types of hearings, link incarcerated persons to courtrooms, obtain witness testimony or link magistrates to busier courts to assist in finalizing a court's caseload. Teleconferencing has also been a proposed method of service delivery for rural courts in the United States.

To combat the obstacle of fewer resources, and potentially the inability to attract qualified personnel, judges in rural communities tend to have varying credentials and responsibilities (see Carroll, 2016). In the United States, 31 states do not require their judges to be admitted to the Bar and in 22 states non-lawyer judges may preside over misdemeanours that carry a jail sentence.

Unlike urban courts, where judges can specialize in a particular case type, judges in rural communities may be required to be generalists who handle civil as well as criminal matters and will handle a case through all stages (for example, not just one stage of the case such as arraignments). Further, in a United Sates context, public defenders (where applicable) and prosecutors, if part-time, might oversee their own law practices in addition to their government positions and responsibilities.

In United States urban courts, there is funding for ancillary services, such as court administrators, court reporters and bailiffs. In rural communities with limited resources, these positions might not exist, or court actors take on these roles and responsibilities. Judges, or court clerks if resources allow for the position, may take on the role of the court administrator – those who assign and schedule court appearances for judges based on court rules. Although it is less bureaucratic, because one would go to the judge or clerk directly, there is more responsibility placed on the respective court actor.

In many rural courts, there is not a court reporter who records the proceedings in real time and preserves the record for the possibility of appeal. In some cases, a court might have a tape recorder that can record the proceedings, but there is not a transcription readily available. If there is not a tape recorder or stenographer, then there might be a hearing to restore the record based off a judge's informal notes, as it used to be done in New York in the United States. Finally, there might not be a designated bailiff to protect the court.

Aside from solutions to logistics, court actors must overcome obstacles in getting legal defence representatives (counsel or solicitors/barristers) assigned to cases, particularly for indigent defendants. Clark, Davies, and Curtis (2021) found that rural judges in New York recognized the importance of legal representation as a mandate and its functional role in courtroom procedures. Although there were procedures in place to apply for free legal counsel for indigent defendants, there were many shortcuts if needed, such as not requiring proof of income, automatic assignment when incarcerated and a willingness to depart from official guidelines when needed – making the process more informal or less bureaucratic. When logistical barriers prevented counsel from being present at the defendant's first court appearance, judges fell back on more informal protections such as advising defendants directly of their rights.

The need for defence counsel in the face of daunting obstacles – coupled with a need to ensure a timely disposition – is further complicated by the well-documented rural attorney shortage. This shortage can result in informal or unique workarounds. Partially in response to the rural attorney shortage that many rural communities have experienced, Sierra Leone started a programme using community-based paralegals in rural locales rather than solely working with attorneys. An estimated 40 per cent of the population in Sierra Leone are paralegals (see Sesay, 2014). In the United States, a stipend programme for new attorneys was piloted in rural South Dakota and there is a mentorship programme in rural Arkansas.

Finally, when reviewing previous research, Eisenstein, Nardulli and Flemming (1988) concluded that judges, attorneys and defendants in rural communities in the United States were often acquainted and that the personal connections amongst all parties resulted in an avoidance of adversarial conflict and informal cooperation and compromise. In rural communities, judges in the United States accept more guilty pleas at the first appearance, rather than engage in adversarial proceedings. In some instances, this cooperation or compromise can benefit convicted defendants. For example, judges in rural communities can fashion more just and relevant solutions to disputes, solely due to the community's social ties, rather than incarceration or monetary punishments.

Suggested readings

Carroll, D. (2016) 'Should non-lawyer judges be sending people to jail? SCOTUS asked to review', 12 December, *Pleading the Sixth*, Available from: https://sixthamendment.org/should-non-lawyer-judges-be-sending-people-to-jail-scotus-asked-to-review/ [Accessed 27 September 2021].

Clark, A.M., Davies, A.L.B. and Curtis, K. (2021) 'Access to counsel for defendants in lower criminal courts', *The Justice System Journal*, doi: 10.1080/0098261X.2021.1927267.

Eisenstein, J., Flemming, R.B. and Nardulli, P.F. (1988) *The Contours of Justice: Communities and their Courts*, Boston, MA: Little, Brown and Company.

Sesay, D. (2014) 'Community-based paralegals in Sierra Leone: Case studies and stories', Sierra Leone: NAMATI, Available from: https://namati.org/wp-content/uploads/2014/10/Daniel-A-STORY-FROM-THE-FIELD-final.pdf [Accessed 27 September 2021].

59

Populism and Punitiveness

Kyle Mulrooney and Jenny Wise

The shared logic of populism

Populism tends to be a vertical politics of the bottom and middle positioned against the top, often taking the form of a reaction or revolt against established structures of power and associated elites. It is not bound to ideological boundaries or party politics, with recent examples of the 'noble' people vs the 'self-serving elite' coming from both the right and left of the political spectrum. However, right-wing variants of political populism tend to also look downward upon an outgroup and thus often champion the people against an elite that they accuse of coddling a third group (for example immigrants).

Populism may also be understood by the essence of the conflict and the subject matter of policies pursued, as well as the extreme nature of the demands that populists tend to make. For instance, the conflict is often broader than a single issue but about a larger pursuit such as going back to better times. Likewise, different political decisions will cause varying levels of conflict over issues. The proposal for a more stringent vetting process of immigrants compared to an out-right ban on individuals coming from certain countries is an example. The former policy decision is less likely to open a chasm between the people and the elite the same way that a call for an out-right ban would.

Much of this shared political logic is evident in penal populism which, conceptually, describes a standing temptation for contemporary political actors to treat crime and its control in a populist or popular mode (see Pratt, 2007). Dominant criminological perspectives exploring penal populism tell us something of political motivations and pressures to get tough on crime; particularly, that penal populists are embracing democracy at work by responding to public opinion, and they are actively taking into account – for personal purposes – what they might gauge to be a public punitive stance.

Penal populism represents an attack on reason, and by proxy on the experts (see Judis, 2016), elites and 'soft-on-crime' politicians who advance penal moderation, in the name of a more 'common sense' and democratized approach to crime and punishment. Penal populism is also inherently downward looking in that penal populists accuse the elite of not only coddling criminals, but of prioritizing them over the law abiding. This is especially apparent in the central role of the victim in populist discourse and policy, whereby the needs of victims and the management of offenders are pitted against one another.

Penal populism may also be evidenced by the essence of the conflict itself, by the subject matter of policies pursued as well as the extreme nature policies that penal populists tend to make. For instance, penal populists tend to emphasize areas with emotional and sensational appeal by focusing on statistically rare but shocking crimes and offences, whether or not this matches empirical reality, and focus on escalating punishments for criminal behaviour upwards (such as mandatory minimum sentences, 'three-strikes and you're out' sentencing, the death penalty, austere prison environments).

Penal populism demonstrates that the public is highly influential in guiding crime policy with many politicians shaping their penal policies according to what they perceive as the most vocal public demands. Thus, attitudes of the public around matters of law and order remain a very important area to research and understand, however populism, punitive attitudes and their interaction have distinct geographic dimensions.

Distinctive rural features

Populist politicians appear increasingly attracted to rural communities who may feel forgotten and disenfranchised yet, together, can exact considerable political power. For example, in the 2016 American elections, 47 per cent of the votes for Donald Trump came from rural areas and small metro areas, despite these geographical areas comprising only 36 per cent of the total votes made within the election. Declining health and rising death rates, fear of cultural displacement and more generalized economic anxiety have primed such rural communities to be receptive to populist politics.

There is some indication that there are distinct differences in rural and urban residents in terms of values, voting patterns and punitive attitudes. Ideologically speaking, people located in rural areas are more likely to vote conservatively which reflects, in part, value differences within questions of moral traditionalism (see Loader and Sparks, 2016).

There is evidence that attitudes towards crime and its control differ depending on location. For example, the limited research available suggests that those who live in rural areas are more likely to strongly support punitive approaches to issues of law and order than people from metropolitan areas.

Research from 2019 focusing on Canadians found that there were significant variations dependent upon geographical location across all dimensions of punitiveness (refer to Mulrooney and Wise, 2019).

Specifically, in this Canadian research with regard to the goals of punishment, the rural favour punishing violent young offenders significantly more than urban counterparts (see Mulrooney, 2022). Similarly, whilst there exists support for limiting the rights of offenders in the name of cracking down on crime within both rural and urban areas, the rural support was significantly greater. Finally, the rural support of the death penalty was significantly greater than the urban classifications. Overall, within Canada there appeared to be a decrease in punitive attitudes; however, as the urban is driving this reduction, the gap between the rural and urban appears to be growing.

Explaining why the rural holds more punitive attitudes than the urban is multifactorial and related to the specific local characteristics of rural spaces such as, for example, crime rates, perceptions of crime, confidence in the police/the justice system, amongst others. Yet the gap between the urban–rural on punitivity aligns with the urban–rural divide as one of the greatest political fault lines in present-day politics. In the Canadian research, support for populist values, minority threat and conservative political values were significant predictors of punitive attitudes, and this was reflected in the difference in these measures between rural and urban locations. Understanding how broader values, ideology and politics relates to punitive attitudes and penal outcomes is necessary for understanding populism and punitiveness in the rural.

Suggested readings

Judis, J.B. (2016) *The Populist Explosion: How the Great Recession Transformed American and European Politics*, New York: Columbia Global Reports.

Loader, I. and Sparks, R. (2016) 'Ideologies and crime: Political ideas and the dynamics of crime control', *Global Crime*, 17(3–4): 314–30.

Mulrooney, K.J.D. (2023) *Resisting the Politics of Punishment: Political Culture and the Evolution of Canadian Criminal Justice Policy*, London: Routledge.

Mulrooney, K. and Wise, J. (2019) 'Punitive attitudes across geographical areas: Exploring the rural/urban divide in Canada', *International Journal of Rural Criminology*, 5(1): 19–46.

Pratt, J. (2007) *Penal Populism*, London: Routledge.

60

Post-release, Rural Re-entry and Recidivism

Kyle C. Ward

Upon leaving jails and prisons, justice-involved individuals face considerable obstacles in their post-release transition into the community. Research has demonstrated challenges related to obtaining employment and housing, attaining basic needs (such as identification and clothing), collateral consequences stemming from their criminal history, family and social support issues, and difficulty obtaining treatment or services related to substance use or mental or physical health. Whilst all these factors can impact recidivism rates, most research has focused on those returning to urban areas. Whilst fewer in number, individuals transitioning from incarceration *to* rural communities face many of these same challenges; however, some re-entry challenges are exacerbated or manifest differently in rural locations (see Ward, 2017).

Rural re-entry is defined as the process of leaving incarceration and returning to a rural area. The overall topic of re-entry (generally referred to as prisoner re-entry) gained traction in 2003 and 2005 by the publication of seminal works of Joan Petersilia's *When Prisoner's Come Home* and Jeremy Travis' *But They All Come Back*, respectively (see suggested readings). Research on re-entry generally examines the factors that impede an individual's successful transition to the community, often leading to recidivism (that is, re-arrest, re-conviction or re-incarceration).

Re-entry programming, that often begins whilst incarcerated (in-reach) and continues into the community, have been used as a method to combat recidivism with varying levels of success. The Counsel of State Governments (in the United States) maintains a repository of programme evaluations that demonstrate success called the 'What Works in Reentry Clearinghouse'. Out of 102 programmes listed in 2021, 60 per cent showed to either be 'effective' or 'promising' in numerous re-entry outcomes. Whilst producing mostly positive results, the vast majority of the evaluations in the Clearinghouse relate to programmes in urban areas, leaving questions about the effectiveness of rural programmes.

In 2006, Eric Wodahl (2016) called for a rural perspective for re-entry as rural communities have unique features that often make urban-based policies and programmes culturally, economically and socially ineffective. As rural areas are marked by smaller populations, a corresponding lower tax base results in minimal funding for social services compared with more urban areas. In addition, a general lack of public transportation, housing and diverse employment opportunities can further impact the re-entry process. Below is a brief articulation of each of the major rural re-entry issues identified in the extant literature.

Transportation

In rural areas, the lack of public transportation, loss of license because of the nature of an offense and a need to get to a job or programming have been found to be compounding issues rural individuals face in the re-entry process. Walking, riding a bicycle or accessing a taxi or rideshare service may not be possible in some rural areas, resulting in some driving with a suspended license, putting them at high risk of recidivating (see Zajac et al, 2014).

Employment

Employment is typically the most cited challenge for those transitioning from incarceration, regardless of where they are living. Rural areas often have fewer job opportunities, with their economy centering on limited employers. Employers often refuse to hire formerly incarcerated individuals or, if they do hire, may take advantage of these employees who often feel stuck in these positions. Furthermore, parole stipulations and treatment appointments may restrict travel, preventing parolees from traveling far for work.

Housing

Housing availability is sparce in rural areas. Shelters, public and social housing are more limited, leading individuals into the private rental market or staying with family or friends. Coupled with the financial strain relating to employment challenges, private renters often refuse to rent to those with criminal records. In addition, staying with family and friends poses an additional challenge for some owing to strained relationships or lifestyles that may clash with someone trying to abide by the law. Individuals in treatment are often told to avoid old 'people, places and things', as they may have contributed to their incarceration in the first place.

Mental health care and substance abuse treatment

Rural individuals in need of mental health care often have few options in rural areas. In the United States, inmates often lose their private health insurance upon sentencing to jail or prison. Upon release, they may struggle to re-enroll or face difficulty obtaining appointments with service providers who take government insurance. Whilst health care exists in many correctional instructions, their availability and fidelity can vary greatly between facilities. Upon release, those returning to rural areas are often given limited mental health medications and often wait weeks for appointments.

Those seeking substance abuse treatment face substantial challenges in rural areas. Whilst treatment programmes are often available, they are frequently limited in number and type of intervention offered. Recruiting and retaining skilled treatment providers is often a challenge in the United States owing to lower tax bases in rural areas.

Services/programming

Whilst re-entry services or programmes are viewed as scarce in rural areas, they often exist in some form. Whilst these programmes may not be comprehensive 're-entry programmes', many areas have decentralized services that can help individuals in their re-entry process. Often missing in rural areas are programmes geared towards correctional rehabilitation that focus directly on criminogenic needs.

Acquaintance density

Rural areas are often marked by a higher level of density of acquaintance compared with urban areas. More residents are aware of each other's circumstances and histories. This often leads to stigma and shaming for those the community views with a negative image or are associated with poor influences prior to their incarceration. This ties in with treatment or services as the few treatment providers in rural areas often interact with the same individuals. On the other hand, acquaintance density could be positive. If a returning individual is viewed as an otherwise upstanding citizen who had made a mistake, the community be more forgiving, offering help or employment.

Suggested readings
Petersilia, J. (2009) *When Prisoners Come Home: Parole and Prisoner Re-Entry*, New York: Oxford University Press.
Travis, J. (2005) *But They All Come Back: Facing the Challenges of Prisoner Re-Entry*, Washington, DC: Urban Institute Press.

Ward, K.C. (2017) *Rural Jail Reentry: Offender Needs And Challenges*, London: Routledge

Wodahl, E.J. (2006) 'The challenges of prisoner reentry from a rural perspective', *Western Criminology Review*, 7: 32–5.

Zajac, G., Hutchison, R. and Meyer, C.A. (2014) 'An examination of rural prisoner reentry challenges', *Center for Rural Pennsylvania*, Available from: http://www.rural.palegislature.us/documents/reports/rural_prisoner_reentry_2014.pdf [Accessed 30 September 2021].

61

Punishment and Rurality

Rosemary Gido

Worldwide and compared with urban population centres, state penal punishment sanctions have unique and distinct consequences for rural communities and people. The United Nations *World Social Report 2021* establishes that extreme poverty, defined as living on less than $USD1.90 a day, is primarily a rural phenomenon. Internationally, four out of five people live in this condition, characterized by increased rates of socio-economic inequality, particularly in the wake of the spread of COVID-19. Even prior to this pandemic, a pattern of global rural spatial inequality was identified, linked to urbanization, technological innovation, climate change and out-migration.

International research findings acknowledge a relationship between persistent poverty and increased rates of crime and punishment that impact the most vulnerable in these spaces – Indigenous people, racial and ethnic minorities, women, children and immigrants. Whilst the connection between socio-economic inequality and punishment inequality varies across nations, owing to differences in structural and cultural dimensions of power that shape penal practice, the specific effects of the inequality of punishment are evidenced in rural populations. These outcomes are related to international trends in the overuse of incarceration, the proliferation of drug control laws and policies and increased detention of immigrants (see Karstadt, 2021).

Globally, over 11 million people are incarcerated, with prison overcrowding rates of 110 per cent across 102 nations. Echoing the United States' mass incarceration 'binge', international rates of imprisonment grew in the first 15 years of the 2010s: Oceana – 59 per cent; Asia – 29 per cent; and Africa – 15 per cent. In England, Wales, the United States and Brazil, the percentage of Black and multi-race people in carceral facilities far exceeds their proportion in each nation's general population. Similarly, Indigenous peoples are significantly over-represented in prisons in Canada and Australia.

Whilst mass incarceration has been examined primarily through an 'urban lens', recent prison studies have identified a number of United States rural punishment inequality issues stemming from greater jail utilization, new prison and jail construction and opioids use. For example, the Vera Institute has reported that, compared with United States urban jails, rural county jails have higher rates of pretrial detention because of the lack of pretrial services and diversion programmes and the housing of inmates from overcrowded state and federal facilities.

Most significantly, the 1990s prison and jail building boom occurred mainly in the nation's most economically depressed rural areas, and yielded 350 new rural county prisons and an 11 per cent increase in jail capacity in rural counties and small towns (see Kang-Brown and Subramanian, 2017). Accompanying the opioid epidemic's concentration in the United States' rural Northeast, Midwest and Mountain West, medical and behavioural health system deficits have exacerbated the addiction-to-incarceration pipeline in these regions.

Worldwide, particularly in Asia and the Global South, the overuse of prison systems comes from decades of enhanced enforcement and harsher penalties for drug offenses. Notably, these drug policies have had the most impact on women as indicated by increased rates of imprisonment compared to men. Even as the United Nations has continued to emphasize the gender-related issues of violence, crime and punishment through human rights rules and interventions, a similar profile of imprisoned women across these countries reflects an unequal patriarchal criminal justice system and actor discrimination.

As well, there is a failure to address marginalized women's pathways to crime via extreme poverty, male violence and abuse victimization, mental health disorders and trauma (see Cyrus R. Vance Center for International Justice, 2021). For example, rural women farmers in Colombia, Mexico and Peru who engage in the growing of illicit coca and opium poppy crops to sustain their families face violence and control by criminal drug traffickers who recently have begun recruiting children into their organizations. The assignment of women to exploitative jobs in illicit drug enterprises obviates their key roles in agricultural production and natural resource sustainability.

Finally, the scope and complexity of international migration, particularly mobility fuelled by displacement events related to war and climate change crises, are also documented in unequal punishment trends that expose rural migrants to crime and punitive detention and control policies (see Bosworth, 2019). Reports on immigrant relocations to rural areas of the Global North suggest that they are more likely than the native populace to be at risk of sustained poverty and involvement in crime. United States census and other international data predict higher and more sustained population growth in urban areas, exacerbating problems of rural economic investment and resource deficits in health, education and infrastructure that preclude addressing current criminal justice system practices related to concentrated disadvantage. A growing body of research on rural immigrants in China's largest cities finds criminal activity and high rates of unemployment; when they are convicted they are more likely to receive longer fixed term prison sentences.

The emerging field of border criminology highlights today's intersections of immigration and criminal justice system processes that reduce legal due process and criminalize migrant status. With European and North American anti-immigrant political campaigns and recent surges in the numbers of refugees seeking asylum and escape from climate-threatened farming regions, overwhelmed border patrol and policing resources often appear to constitute one system of deferred justice. United States detention centres overcrowded with unaccompanied migrant children and youth reflect a mobility surge from mostly northern Central American countries, with the vast majority of émigrés under the age of 21 and from rural families in Honduras, Guatemala and El Salvador where poverty rates and childhood malnutrition have grown since the global recession of 2007. Worldwide, human rights activists and legal scholars cite the growing use of detention, increase in detention facilities and lengths of stay, reports of sub-standard conditions and abuse and barriers to legal representation as evidence of 'crimmigration' and a growing system of penal confinement.

The World Bank has estimated that the COVID-19 pandemic added 88 million people to the ranks of the extreme poor, for a total of 150 million in 2021. Given that punishment inequality is highly correlated with socio-economic inequality globally, rural marginalized people in overcrowded prisons, jails and detention centers have been severely impacted by COVID-19 infection and mortality rates. The pandemic-instigated release of 700,000 incarcerated persons internationally offers an opportunity to review penal practice and policy and to revisit prison reform and decarceration proposals, particularly for their impact on rural populations.

Suggested readings

Bosworth, M. (2019) 'Immigration, detention, and the transformation of justice', *Social and Legal Studies*, 28(1): 81–99.

Cyrus R. Vance Center for International Justice. (2021) 'Vance Center leads discussion on global trends in women's incarceration', February, Available from: https://vancecenter.org/women-in-prison [Accessed 24 October 2021].

Kang-Brown, J. and Subramanian, R. (2017) 'Out of sight: The growth of jails in rural America', June, Vera Institute, Available from: https: vera.org/downloads/publications/out-of-sight-growth-of-jails-rural-america.pdf [Accessed 24 October 2021].

Karstedt, S. (2021) 'Inequality and punishment: A global paradox?', *Journal of Criminology*, 54(1): 5–20.

World Social Report (2021) 'Reconsidering rural development', United Nations Department of Economic and Social Affairs, Available from: https:un.org/development/desa/dspd/wp-content/uploads/sites/22/2021/05World-Social-Report-2021_web_FINAL.pdf [Accessed 24 October 2021].

62

Restorative Justice and Therapeutic Jurisprudence

Ziwei Qi

'Restorative justice' is a process meant to involve those who have a stake in a specific offense and to collectively identify and address harms, needs and obligations in order to heal at the individual, family and community levels. As Braithwaite (2020) points out, restorative justice sees crime as an imbalance of social relationships and harms done to the victim, family and community.

A restorative approach fundamentally differs from a traditional criminal justice approach because achieving justice is about making amends, restoring the relationships and addressing the offender's accountability and the victim's reparations of harms. Such an approach also includes problem-solving policing or 'restorative policing', including crisis intervention teams, on-scene victim assistance units for domestic violence calls, or police-facilitated family group conferencing for juveniles.

The concept of 'therapeutic jurisprudence' originates from the function of mental health law, focusing on the therapeutic impact of legal rules and procedures, as well as the psychological competency and wellbeing of offenders involved in the court process. Therapeutic jurisprudence focuses on the reintegration of the offender into society by addressing rehabilitation through cognitive-behavioural intervention.

Origins and evolution of restorative justice and therapeutic jurisprudence

Restorative justice reflects ancient and Indigenous practices employed in cultures around the globe. For example, 'talking circles' – originating from Indigenous tradition – are a core component of the restorative process, using a structural framework to build relationships and to address conflict within a community. In the modern context, restorative justice emerged in the 1970s as mediation or reconciliation between victims and offenders. The positive response by the victims led to the first victim–offender reconciliation programme in Ontario, Canada.

The concept subsequently acquired various names, such as victim–offender mediation, as it spread through North America and Europe in the 1980s and 1990s. 'Family group conferencing' started in New Zealand in 1989, to respond to Māori people's concerns with the number of their children being removed from their homes by the courts. In Australia, a community-based group – the Aboriginal Youth Night Patrol – supports the welfare of young people by providing safety for those at risk of danger or anti-social behaviour. In rural China, judges (or 'horseback judges') travel by horseback to mediate family disputes in highly remote areas.

Restorative justice in the United States primarily involves the juvenile justice system and problem-solving courts in the criminal justice system, such as drug and drunk driving courts, family courts and domestic violence courts. Problem-solving courts gained much acceptance in major metropolitan areas for the effectiveness of offenders' treatment, victim–offender reconciliation and low recidivism rates.

Restorative justice and therapeutic jurisprudence in rural settings

In rural and remote locations, magistrates may have difficulty applying therapeutic and restorative principles owing to a lack of time, support or local resources. However, many successful examples in rural settings may shed new light on the benefits of restorative justice and therapeutic jurisprudence. For example, in rural Alaska, several restorative justice-orientated initiatives addressed the unique needs of local crime problems, such as teen drinking (see Hyslop, 2012). In rural North Carolina, teen courts have incorporated therapeutic programmes to address high-risk youths' psychological and behavioural functioning leading to decreased aggression and violence and increased pro-social lifestyles (see Evans et al, 2016). A 'traveling court' approach, where sentencing judges travel to remote rural villages to mediate disputes, has also developed in some areas to overcome issues associated with geographic isolation and insufficient resources.

Problem-solving courts in the United States have gained some momentum in rural communities. For example, Hays – a rural college town in Northwestern Kansas with a population of 20,000 – has developed a drug court in the 23rd Judicial District in response to the devastating impact of the opioid epidemic in rural America, which has been successful in providing treatment and alternative sentencing options for first-time, non-violent drug offenders. In rural Georgia, a Mental Health Court initiative attempted to address the mounting needs of mental health treatment and financial and professional shortages. In rural Minnesota, Domestic Violence Court initiatives are being tested to address victims' needs and safety and offender accountability. Other therapeutic approaches, such as trauma-informed care in policing, may reduce the incidence of many social, medical and psychological issues prevalent in rural areas.

Zehr (2002) notes that community-level buy-in is critical to the success of restorative approaches. Rural communities may hesitate to employ such an approach without sufficient staff, proper guidelines, community-level support and ongoing assessment. The legal infrastructure in rural areas is distinct from more populated communities. For a restorative justice programme to succeed, there must be intensive support from both the criminal justice system and the community at large. For instance, local police departments must participate in restorative practices; judges must be willing to adopt restorative-oriented sentencing standards; prosecutors must balance the desire for retribution and reduction in recidivism; and defence attorneys must deliberate therapeutic legal processes with their clients.

Other community support, such as from educators, religious leaders and local organizations, should be involved and supportive of the process on an ongoing basis. Once the community buy-in is established, specific protocols and guidelines should be set forth to train the personnel and staff involved in the process. Finally, continuing programme assessment and evaluation is crucial to the long-term success and funding requirements for rural jurisdictions.

Restorative justice and therapeutic jurisprudence aim to address offender accountability, victim needs and pathways to justice at a collective level. The philosophy inherent in both initiatives may be suitable in a rural setting where collective interests are high. When there is a dilemma, such as when there may be only one judge or attorney with authority to approve such a programme, each stakeholder should be fully apprized of their role in the therapeutic process and make their commitment known before the programme begins. Additionally, everyone involved in the offense should have an equal opportunity to participate in the justice procedure and outcomes without coercion or manipulation. Both restorative justice and therapeutic jurisprudence focus on the solution rather than the punishment for the crime.

Suggested readings

Braithwaite, J. (2020) 'Restorative justice and reintegrative shaming', in C. Chouhy, J.C. Cochran and C.L. Jonson (eds) *Criminal Justice Theory: Explanation and Effects*, vol. 26, New York: Routledge, pp. 281–308.

Evans, C.B.R., Smokowski, P.R., Barbee, J., Bower, M., Barefoot, S. and Werth, J.L. (2016) 'Restorative justice programming in teen court: A path to improved interpersonal relationships and psychological functioning for high-risk rural youth', *Journal of Rural Mental Health*, 40(1): 15–30.

Hyslop, P. (2012) 'Restorative justice in rural Alaska', *Alaska Journal of Dispute Resolution*, 1, Available from: https://ssrn.com/abstract=2602687 [Accessed 21 June 2021].

Wadkins, T. and Campbell, J. (2021) 'Drug court recidivism in the rural Midwest: A 3-year post-separation analysis', *Journal of Drug Issues*, 51(3): 407–19.

Zehr, H. (2002) *The Little Book of Restorative Justice*, Intercourse, PA: Good Books.

Access to Justice and Responses to Crime

63

Access to Justice

Rachel Hale

The right to access justice

Access to justice is a fundamental human right. Whilst there is no single definition, accessible justice typically refers to fair and widely understood laws, access to adequate legal supports and services, impartial and equitable justice system procedures and the right to recourse where these things are not experienced. A broader contemporary definition acknowledges 'extra-legal' factors, such as inequalities in health, housing and employment, which create and perpetaute barriers to justice.

The notion of accessible justice posits that individuals interacting with the justice system should be treated fairly and equally, regardless of class, ethnicity, indigeneity, age, gender, sexuality and ability. Accessing justice therefore demands an inclusive system which enables active participation (see Canadian Forum on Civil Justice, 2015). The justice system, and associated services, should be accessible in terms of cost, language, distance and physical space, so as not to exclude or obstruct individuals from pursuing justice. It is important to acknowledge the significance of access to informal customary justice, particularly for Indigenous persons.

Access to justice is central to the 'rule of law' – a core ideological principle of modern Western democracies – though this does not necessarily guarantee access. Contrastingly, in developing countries, particularly post-conflict authoritarian regimes, access to justice is relatively deficient and may not be an aspiration of the state. Global disparities in the prioritization of access to justice highlight the impact of *place* – a central consideration in rural criminology.

Rural barriers to accessing justice

The bearings of rurality on access to justice are vast, affecting a range of parties – the accused, offender and victim – in different ways. Persons who are already marginalized are more likely to experience barriers to accessing justice, including ethnic minority and Indigenous peoples, women, people with disabilities and those experiencing mental illness, poverty and homelessness. Rurality adds another dimension to the inaccessibility of justice for these individuals.

Though not monolithic, rural communities tend to experience food and housing insecurity, intergenerational poverty, transportation and communication barriers and low education levels (refer to Pruitt et al, 2018). These disadvantages, which themselves are unjust, create barriers to accessing justice from which further injustices can stem (see Statz, 2021). For example, a poor rural litigant who is unable to afford private legal representation, in the absence of pro bono (free) legal support, may have to represent themselves at trial. Without prior legal training, they are likely unable to execute complex legal processes, such as presenting evidence, responding to objections and cross-examining witnesses. This can affect the trial outcome, potentially leading to the loss of an otherwise winnable case.

A shortage of lawyers in rural areas is a significant issue affecting access to justice (see Pruitt et al, 2018 for more on the US 'rural attorney shortage'). Without access to legal advice, rural dwellers may not realize they have a legal need to begin with, let alone that the justice system could provide recourse. Poor incentives to practice law rurally, particularly for new graduates, contributes to this shortage in the United States. In rural Ukraine, problems with essential court infrastructure, such as heating and sewage, can make judicial appointments undesirable (see Lapkin, 2019). Globally, there is a need for legal practitioners who are motivated to practice in rural areas and familiar with the unique legal needs of rural communities.

Where rural legal services do exist, they are often under-resourced, lacking adequate space, equipment or staffing to meet the needs of clients, particularly in complex cases. Rural residents may consequently have to engage urban services, requiring considerable travel. Without private transportation, and in the absence of public transit options, accessing metropolitan services becomes unfeasible. In particularly remote areas, there may not even be viable roads on which to commute. Issues with accessing justice in rural settings can be exacerbated following disasters (see Hale et al, 2021)

Some rural citizens have no choice but to engage with urban justice services. For example, offenders under court-mandated orders may be required to attend metropolitan reporting and testing sites as a condition of their parole or probation, often on numerous occasions over an extended period. Without a means of transportation, the individual may fail to attend, thus breaching their order conditions, potentially leading to (re)incarceration.

Virtual justice services may counter the tyranny of distance. However rural citizens might not own the technology (computers, smart phones) required to access online services, and when they do, poor phone and internet coverage can act as an impediment to 'electronic justice' (see Lapkin, 2019 for more). This symbolizes a further access barrier when technological solutions are touted as the panacea to the rural access problem (see Statz et al, 2021).

Impacts on rural victims

Rural barriers to justice can place victims of crime at risk of further harm. Regarding women survivors of family violence, physical distance from support services can impede the ability to escape violence. The close-knit nature of rural communities may produce conflicts of interest, where police have a pre-existing relationship with the perpetrator and are therefore reluctant to intervene. Owing to the infrequency of rural hearings, victims can wait long periods of time until the matter is heard, facing potential harm in the interim. And in older court buildings without separate waiting areas, survivors may be forced into proximity with their abuser, placing them at risk of further harm (consider George and Harris, 2014).

In developing nations, the violation of the rights of people in remote areas can be high, yet their level of legal literacy very low, impeding the ability to seek justice for harms suffered. In these communities, there can be an absence of reliable authorities from whom rural citizens can seek protection, or even a formal system of justice through which to pursue matters. In remote developing nations, *access* is only beneficial if a strong, legitimate system of *justice* exists on the other side, which is not always the case due to government corruption, coupled with poor accountability and oversight. In these rural communities, there are sometimes no legal consequences for victimization.

Conclusion

Many unique barriers to accessing justice are experienced by rural citizens, constituting a rural access to justice crisis. Looking beyond the legal realm to address broader socio-structural inequalities, which create legal needs and access barriers in the first instance, is critical to addressing this crisis. Responses tailored to the unique needs of rural communities are vital, necessitating further rural criminological inquiry.

Suggested readings

Canadian Forum on Civil Justice (2015) 'Rural & remote access to justice: A literature review', Report prepared for the Rural and Remote Access to Justice Boldness Project, Available from: https://boldnessproject.ruralandremoteaccesstojustice.com/wp-content/uploads/2016/01/Rural-Remote-Lit-Review_newcoverpage.pdf [Accessed 24 October 2021].

George, A. and Harris, B. (2014) *Landscapes of Violence: Women Surviving Family Violence in Regional and Rural Victoria*, Geelong: Deakin University, Available from: http://www.deakin.edu.au/__data/assets/pdf_file/0003/287040/Landscapes-of-Violence-online-pdf-version.pdf [Accessed 24 October 2021].

Hale, R., Stewart-North, M. and Harkness, A. (2021) 'Post-disaster access to justice: The road ahead for Australian rural communities', in A. Harkness and R. White (eds) *Crossroads of Rural Crime: Representations and Realities of Transgression in the Australian Countryside*, Bingley: Emerald, pp. 167–79.

Lapkin, A. (2019) 'The problems of access to justice in rural areas (on the example of Ukraine)', *Proceedings of 7th International Interdisciplinary Scientific Conference Society, Health, Welfare*, SHS Web of Conferences, 68, Available from: https://doi.org/10.1051/shsconf/20196801018 [Accessed 24 October 2021].

Pruitt, L.R., Kool, A.L., Sudeall, L., Statz, M., Conway, D.M. and Haksgaard, H. (2018) 'Legal deserts: Multi-state perspective on rural access to justice', *Harvard Law and Policy Review*, 13(1): 15–156. Available from: https://readingroom.law.gsu.edu/faculty_pub/2745/ [Accessed 24 October 2021].

Statz, M., Friday, R. and Bredeson, J. (2021) 'They had access, but they didn't get justice: Why prevailing access to justice initiatives fail rural Americans', *Georgetown Journal on Poverty Law and Policy*, 28(3): 321–76.

64

Access to Legal Representation

Andrew L.B. Davies and Shelby Peck

The meaning and importance of access to legal representation

Access to legal representation refers to the ability of a defendant in a criminal case to talk privately with a lawyer. Such access can be very important for defendants because confronting a criminal charge in court is complicated. Rules of criminal procedure and the criminal codes that stipulate punishments and sentences are generally mysterious to laypeople. Criminal defence attorneys are professionals trained to understand legal systems and to provide confidential advice to people facing prosecution. As such, access to legal representation can be critical to assuring defendants receive justice.

Access to legal representation is important even before a trial formally begins (see Worden et al, 2017). Lawyers have a role in the prevention of mistreatment of their clients by the justice system through unjust detention or torture before a defendant's case is heard in court. An arrested person who is unable to access legal representation immediately may face significant pressure to plead guilty or make other important decisions under duress and without full appreciation of their consequences. Where access to legal representation is obtained only after interrogation by law enforcement agents, it may avail a defendant of precious few additional options (see both Davies and Clark, 2019 and Pruitt and Colgan, 2010).

Obstacles to legal representation in rural places

In 2013, the United Nations endorsed the notion that states should consider the provision of legal representation for criminal defendants to be their duty and responsibility (see United Nations Office on Drugs and Crime, 2013). It singled out rural areas as a special concern. States, though, frequently provide only limited funding for legal representation to criminal defendants.

This can have particularly serious effects in rural places where providing access to legal representation is often costly and complicated (see Pruitt and Colgan, 2010). Rural lawyers frequently have to travel great distances to meet their clients. Rapidly linking an attorney to a defendant may simply be impossible where terrain or weather are challenging.

These challenges mean that access to legal representation is often measurably worse in rural areas. In Nepal, for example – where the right to free counsel is enshrined in the country's constitution – attorney assistance in some rural regions is limited to a single government-appointed lawyer with the capacity to assist only around two per cent of defendants annually. In more populous areas, the presence of non-governmental organizations and other service providers assures legal representation is more widely available.

Studies of the distribution of lawyers tend to show attorneys are disproportionately rare in rural areas. In Manhattan – part of New York City in the United States – 1 in 17 people was reported to be a lawyer in 2020, whilst in New York's rural 'upstate' counties the rate was as low as one in one thousand. Evidence from Australia suggests the number of lawyers practicing in rural areas is declining relative to population (consider Rice, 2011).

When lawyers are absent, access to legal representation may be absent too. One study in the American state of Texas showed not only that fewer defendants were represented by court-appointed lawyers in rural areas, but also that representation rates fell even further in rural jurisdictions where attorney populations were low (consider the work of Davies and Clark, 2019).

Solving rural legal representation shortages

In some rural jurisdictions, programmes to make legal representation more widely available have proven successful. Following a lawsuit alleging failures to provide adequate access to counsel, rural jurisdictions across New York State in the United States were required to develop programmes to assure lawyers would always be present. The so-called 'counsel at first appearance' (or CAFA) programme used state funds to put in place systems that would guarantee access to legal representation even when people were arrested late at night in remote areas and brought to court with little notice. Research verified that the programme was successfully implemented in several rural counties (consider Worden et al, 2017).

Video conferencing is sometimes advocated as a tool for attorney–client communication with the potential to increase access to legal representation in rural regions. Remote communication tools may reduce costs and other liabilities associated with bringing arrested people and their attorneys together in person. The COVID-19 pandemic, which forced many justice systems to operate entirely remotely for much of 2020, made the matter of whether video conferencing was a suitable modality for such conversations salient.

To date, there is little clear evidence on the benefits or drawbacks of video-conferencing technology for attorney–client communication. Significant concerns have been raised, however, around problems associated with poor and unreliable technology (particularly in rural areas where needed hardware and internet access may be less widely available), reduced assurances of confidentiality between attorneys and their clients and the limited ability of attorneys to build trusting relationships with clients over video.

Conclusion

Spatial inequities in access to legal representation for criminal defendants raise questions about the overall equity of justice systems. Defendants in rural places face the same dangers as those in urban ones of unlawful detention, unjust sentencing and even wrongful conviction. The duty of a defence lawyer, in addition to rebutting the state's case, is to remain loyal to the defendant, their interests and their preferences. In their absence, defendants in rural areas risk legal peril without the advice and assistance that those prosecuted in cities enjoy.

Suggested readings

Davies, A.L.B. and Clark, A. (2019) 'Gideon in the desert: An empirical study of providing counsel to criminal defendants in rural places', *Maine Law Review*, 71(2): 245–72.

Pruitt, L. and Colgan, B. (2010) 'Justice deserts: Spatial inequality and local funding of indigent defense', *Arizona Law Review*, 52(2): 219–316.

Rice, S. (2011) 'Access to a lawyer in rural Australia: Thoughts on the evidence we need', *Deakin Law Review*, 16(1): 13–46.

United Nations Office on Drugs and Crime (2013) 'United Nations Principles and Guidelines on Access to Legal Aid in Criminal Justice systems', United Nations, Available from: https://www.unodc.org/documents/justice-and-prison-reform/UN_principles_and_guidlines_on_access_to_legal_aid.pdf [Accessed 24 October 2021].

Worden, A.P., Davies, A.L.B., Shteynberg, R.V. and Morgan, K.A. (2017) 'Court reform: Why simple solutions might not fail – A case study of implementation of counsel at first appearance', *Ohio State Journal of Criminal Law*, 14(2): 521–51.

65

Closure of Law Enforcement Stations

Christian Mouhanna

Since the turn of the twenty-first century, police organizations have been increasingly closing or reducing the opening hours for small police stations in rural areas. These restrictions are explained by the implementation of a 'new public management' agenda, which has been imposed on public services and which is characterized by a focus on profitability criteria, ratios of civil servants per inhabitant and – for the police – on the crime rate.

Less densely populated areas have, therefore, seen many of these public services disappear. Amongst these, small police units that did not cover enough inhabitants according to management criteria were withdrawn in favour of more populated, often urban, areas. Several strategies were used to achieve this result; either the police stations in question were closed or – for fear of too strong of a reaction from the residents who remained in the area – these police stations remained open but with far fewer staff, drastically reduced working hours, or pooled itinerant officers moving from one station to another. This feature has been prominent in countries such as France (see Maillard and Mouhanna, 2016).

These cuts and closures, though, are not only the outcome of managerial imperatives. Although successful in slowing or thwarting previous reforms, few police officers and few professional unions have mobilized to fight against this phenomenon. Furthermore, it is increasingly rare to find police officers with rural backgrounds who are interested in and familiar with rural communities' particularities. Although rural areas are reputed to be quieter, they experience unique crime problems with which many police officers are uncomfortable (see Mouhanna, 2016, in suggested readings). Whatever their social background, the majority of police officers, especially when they start a family, aspire to live near urban centres where services and leisure activities are more numerous and accessible.

Centralization of forces

Another reason for police station closures, linking new public management and police aspirations, is the generalization of large police stations as part of a larger movement to centralize forces (see Blesse and Diegmann, 2018). This movement is not recent. The generalization of the equipment of police officers with motorized vehicles, since the beginning of the twentieth century, then that of the telephone after the Second World War, encouraged urban police services to engage in the model of the central station and reactive policing. Formerly scattered over the territory and criss-crossing the cities, and having time outside the emergency period to interact with the citizens of their sector, police officers have been grouped together in larger and larger buildings, under the watchful eye of their superiors. More controlled, these police officers have been converted for the most part to reactive emergency policing. An emergency telephone call triggers the intervention of a patrol car which must arrive on the scene as quickly as possible, and leave just as quickly to respond to the next call.

Less affected by this movement until the middle of the twentieth century, rural police have now embarked on the same path of consolidation. The new public management model and the search for savings on personnel costs, as well as the aspirations of many police officers and the desire of chiefs to restrict the autonomy of police officers in the field, have led the rural world into centralization. This organizational structure protects officers from the pressing demands of the population and makes them feel safer when grouped together. The police officer assigned to a small town or who works in several villages often becomes an important figure in the local network. As a result, the officer is known and approachable, and is often called upon by the population to solve a variety of problems. Conversely, the anonymity of a large group – the specialization by area and no longer by territory – as well as the reactive model allows the police officer to free themself from this immersion in a demanding social environment.

Centralization, therefore, also leads to the abandonment of community-oriented policing policies through the disappearance of direct and permanent contact with citizens (see Mouhanna, 2011, in suggested readings). Owing to the lack of time for contact outside a state of emergency, police officers are at best only engaged in patrols that move around the territory and lack frequent and strong human contact. The closure of police stations or limitations on their opening hours have the advantage – for the managers of the services – of reducing recorded crime, even if this is at the expense of citizens who find it difficult to lodge complaints. The result is a denial of crime in rural areas due to a lack of knowledge. As for emergency calls, it is obvious that the closure of small stations has made travel and response times longer, at the expense of victims (see Smith and Somerville, 2013).

When questioned on these issues, those responsible for police reorganization policies point to new digital tools that would make it possible to maintain relations with the public, make the officers present in the field more effective and thus maintain a service that is as efficient as possible. However, technology has its limits. First, this does not solve the issue of emergency responses. Second, an entire section of the population does not have access to social networks, either for technical reasons of non-deployment of communication networks, or for lack of skills – illiteracy or digital illiteracy. Third, finding the time to respond to requests on social networks is challenging for police officers. Far from being a panacea, the deployment of new technologies does not solve the feeling of abandonment that is expressed in the sparsely populated countryside.

Even where solutions such as Neighborhood Watch exist and allow a certain surveillance capacity to be maintained, it would be wrong to think that they can replace police intervention. These networks are only legitimate if they are supported by police officers who are able to lead them and intervene if necessary. In both practical and symbolic terms, the closure of police stations shows a lack of public policy interest in rural areas.

Suggested readings

Blesse, S. and Diegmann, A. (2018) 'Police reorganization and crime: Evidence from police station closures, ZEW – Centre for European Economic Research', 1 October, Discussion Paper No. 18–044, Available from: http://dx.doi.org/10.2139/ssrn.3272123 [Accessed 24 October 2021].

Maillard, J. and Mouhanna, C. (2016) 'Governing the police by numbers: The French experience', in T. Delpeuch and E.J. Ross (eds) *Comparing the Democratic Governance of Police Intelligence*, Cheltenham: Edward Elgar Publishing.

Mouhanna, C. (2016) 'From myth to myth: Rural criminology in France', in J.F. Donnermeyer (ed) *The Routledge Handbook of Rural Criminology*, London: Routledge, pp. 65–73.

Mouhanna, C. (2011) 'Rural policing in France: The end of genuine community policing?', in R.I. Mawby and R. Yarwood (eds) *Rural Policing and Policing the Rural: A Constable Countryside*, Farnham: Ashgate, pp. 45–57.

Smith, R. and Somerville, P. (2013) 'The long goodbye: A note on the closure of rural police-stations and the decline of rural policing in Britain', *Policing: A Journal of Policy and Practice*, 7(4): 348–58.

66

Rural Crime Prevention

Tarah Hodgkinson

Crime prevention encompasses a number of actions and methods that attempt to address the causes of crime with the intention of reducing crime, victimization and fear and improving community safety (see United Nations Office on Drugs and Crime, 2021). Within this definition, crime is often based on consensus theories that define crime as infractions of the law. In addition, the nature of the data collected regarding the extent of the problem, and/or the effectiveness of the solution, is often normative. This positivist approach assumes that official crime and victimization data accurately reflect the true nature and extent of these experiences, whilst acknowledging the limits of data collection methods, such as under reporting.

Importantly, much of the crime prevention literature focuses heavily on urban contexts, assuming that rural areas lack real crime problems and instead reflect the *gemeinschaft*, or *rural idyll*, in which strong community cohesion acts as a protective factor against crime (refer to Barclay et al in suggested readings). This literature largely ignores the unique challenges in rural communities. For example, farming communities deal with high rates of theft of expensive stock and equipment that can contribute to significant losses to local livelihoods. Fly-in-fly-out communities, with transitional workers, often experience issues with drug and alcohol abuse. Many rural communities have large Indigenous or newcomer populations that may result in higher rates of marginalization, disadvantage and even hate crime. Victims of domestic violence are often unable to access resources or leave their abuser as there are no services in their communities. Furthermore, advances in technology have increased opportunities for online fraud and theft that stretch beyond geographical boundaries.

In the broader crime prevention literature, there are three levels of crime prevention strategies: primary, secondary and tertiary. Primary-level approaches attempt to prevent crime before it ever happens. These are often large-scale approaches addressing the predictors of crime. Secondary-level approaches focus on people or places demonstrating higher levels of risk for criminal behaviour. Tertiary-level crime prevention approaches address crime, once it has already happened, attempting to prevent further offending.

Within the crime prevention literature, there are three core approaches: Crime Prevention through Social Development (CPSD); Situational Crime Prevention (SCP); and Crime Prevention through Environmental Design (CPTED). CPSD tends to focus on biological, social and psychological predictors of crime. Examples of these approaches include pre- and post-natal health, parenting strategies and youth support programmes addressing factors that could lead to offending or victimization. SCP relies on opportunity theories of crime, suggesting to increase the effort to engage against criminal behaviour, or reducing rewards of committing crime, and reducing the likelihood of offending. SCP includes many target-hardening approaches, such as installation of locks or bars which improve security, and make it more difficult to offend.

CPTED uses an environmental and social approach, acknowledging the interplay of physical space and human behaviour to address how certain spatial and social contexts may be more prone to crime. Examples of these approaches include addressing neighbourhood territoriality and ownership by creating clear delineation of space through small fences or landscaping, improving sightlines to increase 'eyes on the street', consistent maintenance of buildings and properties and restricting access to certain areas. In recent years, CPTED strategies have also incorporated more social contextual factors such as activating space with legitimate activities (such as local sports games or community gardens) and building culture through neighbourhood festivals. The combination of these strategies is intended to indicate to others that residents care about their community and will intervene in illegitimate activity if required. These approaches build the necessary social cohesion and collective efficacy to ensure this happens.

Crime prevention strategies can be varied, but predominantly rely on urban-based theories of crime and different levels of the criminal justice system or public services of the state. Consequently, many of these strategies focus primarily on crimes committed by marginalized and poor peoples. There is less of a focus on white collar or environmental crime contributing to climate tragedies such as drought and pollution, that may have more devastating impacts, particularly in rural communities.

Attempts at prevention in rural communities are often difficult. Psychological and social support services that could assist at risk youth in rural communities are often inaccessible or non-existent. Rural crime prevention efforts are often led by police, but police frequently struggle to respond to calls because of large geographical distances and are unable to call on additional back up or other services for support. SCP approaches that have been expanded to include the tracking technologies for stock and equipment theft remain quite costly and inaccessible.

The spatial dispersion of residents and support services causes issues in terms of creating collective efficacy and accessing necessary services. This highlights the need to create unique, place-based approaches that are inclusive. Recent research highlights the need to meaningfully engage residents in addressing crime issues to ensure strategies that are integrated and contextually based and do not simply further download responsibility for crime and safety to already over-burdened services and stakeholders (see Hodgkinson et al, 2020).

Despite a relative dearth of empirical evidence on what works in rural crime prevention, this area is growing rapidly (refer to Harkness, 2020). Much of this work acknowledges the need to shift crime prevention to integrated approaches. Numerous integrated approaches exist in the urban landscape: consider, for example, the Scottish Violence Reduction Unit, Ceasefire; the Winnipeg Auto-theft Strategy in Canada; the Kirkholt (United Kingdom) Neighbourhood Watch; and more. However, there is far less evidence of this work in rural contexts.

Nonetheless, new strategies are rapidly emerging. 'Communities that Care', an Australian-based wrap-around programme for youths, has shown significant success in reducing youth-related offending in rural and urban communities (refer to Fagan et al, 2018). SafeGrowth, a methodology that incorporates first, second and third generation CPTED and capacity building, has also demonstrated early success in preventing crime in both urban and rural contexts (see Hodgkinson et al, 2020).

Residents and local stakeholders in rural communities often lack services and other supports necessary to implement urban-based crime prevention strategies. These integrated approaches work directly with local stakeholders to identify problems and develop solutions. As a result, future rural crime prevention strategies must work in collaborative and integrated ways to develop local capacity and capability in addressing the unique crime and safety challenges facing rural communities in the twenty-first century.

Suggested readings

Barclay, E., Donnermeyer, J.F. and Jobes, P.C. (2004) 'The dark side of gemeinschaft: Criminality within rural communities', *Crime Prevention and Community Safety*, 6(3): 7–22.

Fagan, A.A., Hawkins, J.D. and Catalano, R.F. (2018) *Communities That Care: Building Community Engagement and Capacity to Prevent Youth Behavior Problems*, Oxford: Oxford University Press.

Harkness, A. (ed) (2020) *Rural Crime Prevention: Theory, Tactics and Techniques*, London: Routledge.

Hodgkinson, T., Saville, G., Sutton, H. and Mackrell, R. (2020) 'No dress rehearsal, this is our life: Crime prevention in the hands of local residents', in A. Harkness (ed) *Rural Crime Prevention: Theory, Tactics and Techniques*, London: Routledge, pp. 149–60.

United Nations Office on Drugs and Crime (2021) 'Crime prevention', Available from: https://www.unodc.org/unodc/en/justice-and-prison-reform/CrimePrevention.html [Accessed 23 November 2021].

67

Technology in Rural Criminal Justice Systems

Jessica René Peterson

Technology has a significant impact – including both advantages and disadvantages – on rural criminal justice agencies and their capabilities regarding efficiency, effectiveness and supervision. Although the connectivity gap is narrowing, connectivity and communication remain limited by poor Internet access and cellular service in many rural settings. For example, the International Telecommunication Union found that 71 per cent of rural areas in the world had access to 4G mobile network coverage in 2020, compared with 95 per cent of the world's urban locations. This gap increases in underprivileged areas (such as Tribal areas in North America) and developing nations worldwide. Lack of funding in many rural jurisdictions can affect both the quantity and quality of technological services provided to and by justice-involved agencies such as law enforcement, the courts and corrections.

Technology in rural law enforcement

Technological tools in law enforcement have changed and improved enormously since the 1980s and are primarily used for identifying, locating and apprehending individuals engaged in crime. Computers and laptops are commonly used for recordkeeping, report-writing, suspect identification and apprehension via social media, communicating with the public, crime-mapping, data analysis and access to federal databases such as the FBI's Automated Fingerprint Identification System. Equipment such as body-worn cameras, stun and TASER guns, 'soft' projectile weapon systems, vehicle license plate readers, gunshot location technology, night vision or thermal imaging detectors and more, have become standard in many metropolitan agencies across the Global North, with some even deploying drones, robotic dogs and facial recognition software in their patrols. Whilst these devices and 'smart policing' practices bring with them controversy and many legal concerns regarding citizen privacy and biases, they do allow law enforcement to act swiftly and – at least from the law enforcement perspective – more efficiently.

The necessity for the most advanced equipment in rural locations is particularly debateable, but the lack of many devices that have become staples in urban policing is cause for concern. Law enforcement officers in rural areas may rely on outdated 'police mobile computers' and 'record management systems', lack high-quality recording devices such as body-worn cameras and dashboard cameras and have limited performance vehicles and equipment. In 2016, approximately 80 per cent of United States agencies with 500 or more officers had acquired body-worn cameras whilst less than 55 per cent of agencies with 99 or fewer officers had acquired them. Similarly, the use of body-worn cameras and closed-circuit television (CCTV) in policing has spread throughout the United Kingdom's countryside, but their use pales in comparison to urban settings and brings unique contextual challenges (see Johnstone, 2011; Miranda, 2021).

The United States' National Institute of Justice funded a national survey of nearly 240 small and rural law enforcement agencies in the early 2000s, which found that technology such as GPS, digital imaging for fingerprints and various less lethal technologies were highly under-utilized in these agencies. Furthermore, officers viewed many new technologies as less applicable to work in their communities. Relatedly, Canadian research on technology use and information sharing highlights the significance of organizational contexts, cultures and practices on technological functioning and effectiveness in emergency response.

The fact remains that, in more remote areas, a single officer may initiate a traffic stop without any knowledge of who is in the vehicle and only a traditional radio to communicate their location and situation to the agency. In the event of a violent or fatal altercation, the officer's vehicle location would not be GPS trackable. Poor or no video footage of the event would be available to use for identification or prosecution. The lack of such equipment and technologies presents a disadvantage to community members, already short-staffed law enforcement and any resulting cases that proceed through the court system.

Technology in rural courts and corrections

Beyond the challenges that the lack of advanced technology in rural policing can create in the formal processing of cases, rural courts lack technological tools and access that can improve case management. The courts may not have full access to digital records and deal with outdated computing resources. Availability of e-filing options and remote court appearances are often limited. Furthermore, client–lawyer communication is impeded by the connectivity gap, particularly given the lawyer shortage experienced by rural communities. Virtual opportunities for trials, especially in remote villages and settlements in countries such as Ukraine, are limited even in the wake of the COVID-19 pandemic and greatly restrict rural residents' access to justice (see Metzger et al, 2020).

Lack of funds is a pattern reflected in all three components of rural criminal justice systems. Technological advancements in the context of corrections are typically applied to assessment, supervision, identification of wrong-doing and monitoring and control of justice-involved individuals. Regardless of widespread facilities in rural communities, security and supervision in institutional or community-based corrections may lack the sophistication of their urban counterparts. When new tools and equipment become available, they can increase or improve the ability for the correctional system to provide treatment – rehabilitation or healthcare – or connect individuals to their families and legal aid.

Future directions for technology in rural criminal justice systems

It is not all bad news regarding technology in rural criminal justice systems. Although access is limited, evolving technological advancements do expand rural capabilities to help bridge the gap between geographic distances. For example, inmates in rural prisons may now have the ability to visit with family via video teleconferencing who otherwise may not be able to physically travel. Rehabilitation and treatment delivery methods and reach are enhanced through the use of technology. Technology use has streamlined pre-trial activities, case management and billing whilst increasing lawyer–client communication without the need to travel long distances. Increased access and reliance on social media have extended and improved criminal offending in rural spaces (for example, illicit market communications or militia group formation), but those same social media platforms – especially amongst dense social networks – can be utilized to help rural officers locate missing individuals, juvenile runaways or fugitives from nearby communities.

Some non-urban communities have implemented new technologies for addressing uniquely rural issues, such as the use of sensor lights to increase guardianship in Australian farms or drones to police rampant livestock theft in rural South Africa. The deployment of surveillance tools in rural communities has increased the ability for law enforcement agencies to build and analyse 'big data', which affects the ability of law enforcement to predict crime, react to crime and problem solve in their communities. Furthermore, as technology use increases in everyday rural life, such advances help or alter the criminal justice response, microchipped animals become easier to locate and the increased use of home surveillance systems aids in apprehension and prosecution (see Harkness and Larkins, 2020).

Whilst technology availability lags behind in rural areas, its development and use is slowly helping to increase efficiency, effectiveness, communication, access and other abilities of justice-related agencies and the communities being served. As the connectivity gap continues to narrow in rural locations and rural community members become more familiar with them, researchers will be better able to reach remote residents through virtual interviewing methods, access increasingly digitized records in or about justice-related agencies and more. Even when survey responses from rural residents via email are limited, such responses may have been lost completely without email. Recent innovations such as satellite imagery not only help locate illegal activity but become useful data for identifying rural communities or conducting spatial mapping analyses (see Weisheit, 2022). Technologies discussed here and throughout Part III of this encyclopedia will continue to increase access to rural residents, criminal justice system actors and data that will move the field forward.

Suggested readings

Harkness, A. and Larkins, J. (2020) 'Technological approaches to preventing property theft from farms', in A. Harkness (ed) *Rural Crime Prevention: Theory, Tactics and Techniques*, London: Routledge, pp. 226–44.

Johnstone, C. (2011) 'Big Brother goes to the countryside: CCTV surveillance in rural towns', in R. Mawby and R. Yarwood (eds) *Rural Policing and Policing the Rural: A Constable Countryside?*, London: Routledge, pp. 81–92.

Metzger, P., Meeks, K. and Pishko, J. (2020) 'Greening the desert: Strategies and innovations to recruit, train, and retain criminal law practitioners for STAR communities', Report, *Deason Criminal Justice Reform Center*. Available from: https://www.smu.edu/-/media/Site/Law/Deason-Center/Publications/STAR-Justice/Greening-the-Desert/Report-Greening-the-Desert-FINAL.pdf?la=en [Accessed 4 November 2021].

Miranda, D. (2021) 'Body-worn cameras "on the move": Exploring the contextual, technical and ethical challenges in policing practice', *Policing and Society: An International Journal of Research and Policy*, doi: 10.1080/10439463.2021.1879074.

Weisheit, R. (2022) 'Future directions for rural research methods', in R. Weisheit, J.R. Peterson and A. Pytlarz (eds) *Research Methods for Rural Criminologists*, London: Routledge, pp. 221–33.

PART IV

Rural Peoples and Groups

Introduction to Part IV: Rural Peoples and Groups

Cassie Pedersen

Crimes that occur in rural areas are unique in character and impact, posing distinct challenges for rural communities. For example, rural peoples might express disbelief that 'one of their own' would engage in criminal offending; the tight-knit nature of rural communities can make it difficult for victims to report crime to the police; and issues with resourcing can lead to inequitable access to justice for rural peoples and groups when compared to their urban counterparts.

The emergent field of rural criminology has revealed an urban-centric bias at the centre of criminological enquiry that overlooks the unique issues experienced in rural locales. Compounding this, criminological research has assumed a primary focus on people belonging to dominant groups, with considerably less attention paid to those who dwell on the peripheries. When such groups have been considered, there has been the tendency to cast them as 'deviant' and 'other'. The criminal justice experiences of people from minority groups are gaining increased attention in criminological research, but there is still a gap in terms of embracing a uniquely rural perspective.

Rural peoples and groups are diverse in composition and encompass all human actors residing in rural spaces – whether they are well-known members of the community or those who lie outside the mainstream. Whilst there is a considerable deal of diversity in rural settings, such areas are typically characterized by tight-knit communities that hold conservative values and subscribe to traditional ways of living.

This can pose various challenges for people who lie on the margins of society, with some peoples and groups (for example, Indigenous peoples, people who identify as LGBTIQA+, people with disabilities, lifestyle migrants, working tourists and youth) grappling with feelings of alienation, exclusion and isolation. Conversely, other non-dominant rural peoples and groups (for example, outlaw motorcycle gangs, rural enclaves, some Indigenous groups and youth sub-cultures) may deliberately reject conventional lifestyles and actively embrace non-conformity.

The entries in this section serve to challenge the urban hegemony within mainstream criminology and to shed light on the experiences and narratives of rural peoples and groups. Some of the entries in this section consider criminal justice experiences of dominant groups residing in rural areas, whereas others consider the experiences of people from marginalized and fringe groups. The contributors in this section draw together justice-related themes from diverse groups and pave the way for a form of criminology that moves beyond an 'add rural and stir' formulation.

68

Anti-government Groups and Militias

Joseph DeLeeuw

Although no single definition exists for anti-government groups and militias, they do share several similarities in their ideologies, operations and appearances. The ideologies of anti-government groups and militias are often related to fears of government over-reach into their members' lives, threats to constitutional rights and potential restrictions on gun ownership, concerns regarding immigration and a host of conspiracy theories. Historically, the majority of individuals associated with these movements have not engaged in violence or acts of terrorism. The most common activities associated with these groups include their regular meetings, training exercises and participation in demonstrations or rallies.

Groups within these movements can often be identified by the military or tactical style apparel they wear and equipment they carry. Some groups utilize distinct uniforms or employ patches, flags or other symbols to indicate their membership in or association with a specific group or movement. The more organized groups amongst these movements are known to utilize military style leadership structures that oversee the group's operations and tactical style field training. Groups affiliated with these movements have also been known to coordinate with other nearby groups to share resources, intelligence, planning and training opportunities (see Chermak in suggested readings).

In addition to more organized anti-government groups and militias, there are countless other small groups affiliated with these movements that actively attempt to conceal their existence. These more isolated groups pose a significant challenge for law enforcement because they are more difficult to identify, track and disrupt. The less public exposure a group has, the fewer opportunities law enforcement will have to disrupt the group or identify the potential radicalization of the group as it moves towards criminal activity.

The membership of anti-government groups and militias in the United States is largely composed of White individuals. Whilst many of these groups have made public declarations espousing their opposition to racism, diversity amongst group membership remains limited. In recent years, there has been some diversification of group membership as more groups have begun recruiting new members based on emerging connections between these movements and far-right politics.

In 2020 and 2021, images of anti-government and militia groups in the United States captured international attention. In 2020, groups across the United States attempted to demonstrate their support for law enforcement by counter-protesting during nationwide protests in response to the murder of George Floyd and other incidents involving police misuse of force. In 2021, these groups took center stage again as individuals and groups affiliated with these movements were heavily involved in the 6 January 2021 insurrection at the United States Capitol.

The origins and rising to prominence of these modern anti-government and militia groups in the United States can be traced back to the 1990s. The 1992 shootout at Ruby Ridge, Idaho, and the 1993 siege in Waco, Texas, provided fuel for anti-government groups and the militia movement, as both incidents were viewed by members as clear examples of a tyrannical government in action (see Pitcavage, 2001). The 1995 bombing of a federal building in Oklahoma City, an attack that was viewed by the perpetrator as a response to the incidents at Ruby Ridge and Waco, also increased awareness of the militia movement. At the time of the attack, the perpetrator, Timothy McVeigh, was reported to have connections with the militia movement. These events, and the subsequent media attention they drew, put the militia movement in the national spotlight and helped anti-government groups and militias recruit new members.

Law enforcement efforts to disrupt the militia movement at the end of the 1990s, and renewed American patriotism following the 9/11 terrorist attacks in 2001, contributed to a sharp decline in the number of militia members and in the number of anti-government groups and militias in the early 2000s. These groups began their resurgence in 2009 following the election of United States President Barack Obama. In the years that followed, membership in anti-government groups and militias increased, as did the overall number of groups operating in the United States.

The modern militia movement publicly displayed its strength during the 2014 armed standoff with the United States Bureau of Land Management in Nevada and the 2016 occupation of the Malheur National Wildlife Refuge in Oregon in which members of anti-government groups and militias engaged in a four-week armed standoff with law enforcement. In both cases, these incidents attracted support and participation from groups located across the country.

By the end of 2020, several anti-government and militia groups were using public comments by President Donald Trump as evidence of his support for their movements. Other comments by Trump, particularly related to accusations of a 'stolen' election, were used by these groups to engage existing and new members and to frame efforts to overturn the results of the 2020 United States presidential election as necessary to defend the constitutional rights of their members. The results of these efforts were on display during the 6 January insurrection when well-known members of these movements were seen in videos and photographs storming the United States Capitol.

Anti-government and early militia groups established their roots in rural parts of the United States (see Berlet and Sunshine, 2019). They utilized rural areas because of their available space, lower levels of law enforcement observation and access to wooded areas where they could hold training exercises. As time progressed and the movements became more connected with far-right political ideologies, the growing anti-government movement, as well as many militias, have expanded their recruitment efforts to more urban and suburban areas.

Whilst anti-government and militia groups have continued to use rural areas for training exercises, they have more recently become associated with urban areas owing to images of militia and anti-government group members protesting or counterprotesting in the streets of large cities or at state capitals. The 6 January 2021 insurrection and the continuing efforts to frame the 2020 presidential election as illegitimate will remain valuable recruitment tools for anti-government and militia groups. As conspiracy theories surrounding a stolen election remain prominent, so will their value to groups that wish to urge members and supporters to act out against the government.

Suggested readings

Berlet, C. and Sunshine, S. (2019) 'Rural rage: The roots of right-wing populism in the United States', *The Journal of Peasant Studies*, 46(3): 480–513.

Chermak, S.M. (2002) *Searching for a Demon: The Media Construction of the Militia Movement*, Boston, MA: Northeastern University Press.

Pitcavage, M. (2001) 'Camouflage and conspiracy: The militia movement from Ruby Ridge to Y2K', *American Behavioral Scientist*, 44(6): 957–81.

69

Indigenous and First Nation Peoples

Juan Tauri

One of the distinctive features of settler-colonial jurisdictions – namely New Zealand, Australia, Canada and the United States – is the significant over-representation of Indigenous peoples in all facets of the criminal justice system. Research consistently shows that Indigenous peoples are over-represented in arrest, conviction and imprisonment statistics, as well as rates of victimization, especially for crimes involving sexual and intimate partner violence.

The lived experiences of Indigenous peoples have long been associated with rurality, meaning that community structures are located in geographical spaces we understand today to be 'rural'. Appending Indigenous lived experience with rurality has become associated with socio-economic deprivation that manifests in a range of poor social outcomes, including low educational attainment, poor health outcomes, drug and alcohol dependency, high rates of child abuse and/or negative engagement with childcare and protection services, intimate partner and other forms of violence (see both Guggisburg, 2019 and McCausland and Vivian, 2010). It is no surprise, then, that connections between the concept of rurality and Indigenous peoples' experiences of offending and victimization has long been established in criminology. Furthermore, it is becoming a key focus of research and analysis of the Indigenous lived experience within the developing sub-discipline of rural criminology (see Jones et al, 2016).

However, focusing investigation and analysis of Indigenous peoples' experiences of crime and victimization within the geographical and conceptual space of 'rurality' is problematized by the fact that the demographic reality of Indigenous lived experience is not the same for all Indigenes. For example, in the Canadian context, only 26 per cent live 'on reserve', meaning that 74 per cent of Canadians who self-identify as Indigenous live 'off reserve'. In comparison, in the United States context, the rate of reserve-based residence is much higher, up to 43 per cent. However, this means over 50 per cent reside off reserve.

Finally, a significant proportion of Aboriginal Australians live in urban contexts, a situation that continues to increase, whereas in New Zealand over 80 per cent of Māori live in urban contexts and have done so since the mid-1960s. Thus, the diverse geographical location of Indigenous peoples in settler-colonial contexts means that utilizing a *rural criminological lens* to engage with their lived experiences of social harm must include an acknowledgement of the significant differences generated between Indigenous peoples within and across settler-colonial jurisdictions.

The need to be epistemologically and theoretically aware of the issue of 'difference' means the application of a rural criminological lens to the Indigenous experience of social harm must also consider the impact of the historical and contemporary colonial project on Indigenous peoples. Cunneen and Tauri (2016: chapter 2) identify the key elements of a critical analysis of the colonial project that would be beneficial to a *rural criminological* engagement with Indigenous peoples (whether they are 'urban/rural', or 'on reserve/off reserve'). To begin with, inclusion of a critical analysis of colonialism enables an Indigenous-centred analysis and understanding of the design and impact of a range of assimilative policies and interventions that played out in the rural context. These include the establishment of reservations, the forced removal of children and their indoctrination in reserve/residential schools, the banning of Indigenous language, cultural and spiritual practices and the imposition of an alien, repressive White justice system (see Ross, 1988).

If our analysis of the situation is to have meaning to Indigenous peoples, then the over-representation of Indigenous peoples in crime and victimization statistics needs to be contextualized within a much broader framework of the effects of colonialization. The key components of the colonial project, including the long-term social and economic marginalization of Indigenes, the denial of citizenship rights for Indigenous peoples and the limited recognition of Indigenous law and governance are all important components to understanding their over-representation in criminal justice systems. In other words, colonial systems of control are not merely of historical interest, they have material effects on the contemporary position of Indigenous people within settler-colonial states.

That the rural geographical space was a fundamental component of the process of colonial dispossession of Indigenous peoples everywhere is unquestionable. That it remains so is only partially recognized within contemporary criminology. As the settler-colonial context developed over time and the imposition of a capitalist mode of production and economy took hold, the increasing urbanization of the population and economic activity occurred. It is irrefutable that the process of urbanization for Indigenous peoples was comparatively much slower. Unlike New Zealand, which instituted few laws and policies prohibiting 'free movement' of Māori between the rural and expanding urban context (in fact, their movement was actively encouraged post-Second World War to provide cheap labour for the development of urbanized industries), Canada, Australia and the United States imposed legislation, policies and surveillance strategies designed to expedite the sequestration of Indigenous peoples in 'rural' contexts, such as reservations; processes that continued to be used well into the twentieth and twenty-first centuries.

The criminalization of 'sequestered Indigenous spaces', such as the reservation, was a central platform of the colonial project in those jurisdictions where it appeared. For example, in Australia, reserves and missions administered their own penal regimes outside, and parallel to, existing formal criminal justice systems. In the state of Queensland, legislation provided reserve superintendents with a range of judicial functions: they could constitute a court exercising broad powers, and legal representation for the accused was only by permission of the court (the superintendent). Furthermore, Indigenous police serving on the reserves were placed under the supervision of the superintendent, as was the local prison.

The interconnections between the colonial and neo-colonial epochs that exist in settler-colonial jurisdictions is evidenced by the continued use of geographically defined sequestration strategies, aggressive 'frontier-style' policing tactics (such as Canada's Royal Canadian Mounted Police responses to Indigenous protests against oil pipelines in 2020) and the continued marginalization of Indigenous responses to social harm. These ongoing 'colonial projects' are clearly of importance to Indigenous peoples, and provide members of the developing school of rural criminology with issues through which they can build empowering research partnerships with Indigenous scholars and communities.

Suggested readings

Cunneen, C. and Tauri, J. (2016) *Indigenous Criminology*, Bristol: Policy Press.

Guggisberg, M. (2019) 'Aboriginal women's experiences with intimate partner sexual violence and the dangerous lives they live as a result of victimisation', *Journal of Aggression, Maltreatment and Trauma*, 28(2): 186–204.

Jones, N., Lithopoulas, S. and Ruddell, R. (2016) 'Policing rural Indigenous communities: An examination of practices in Australia, Canada, New Zealand and the United States', in J.F. Donnermeyer (ed) *The Routledge International Handbook of Rural Criminology*, London: Routledge, pp. 355–64.

McCausland, R. and Vivian, A. (2010) 'Why do some Aboriginal communities have lower crime rates than others? A pilot study', *Criminology and Criminal Justice*, 43(2): 301–32.

Ross, L. (1998) *Inventing the Savage: The Social Construction of Native American Criminality*, Austin, TX: University of Texas Press.

70

LGBTIQA+ Identities

Cassie Pedersen

LGBTIQA+ is a continually evolving acronym that refers to lesbian, gay, bisexual, transgender, intersex, queer and/or questioning and asexual and/or ally. The plus sign represents diverse sex, gender and sexual identities that lie outside of LGBTIQA. It can be difficult for people who identify as LGBTIQA+ to feel accepted in rural communities owing to the dominance of conservative values, including the maintenance of traditional family structures and gender roles. This can lead LGBTIQA+ people to experience heightened levels of social isolation, exclusion, discrimination and marginalization in rural settings.

Whilst a growing body of literature considers the unique issues and challenges of LGBTIQA+ people in rural settings, further research into how rurality and LGBTIQA+ status bear on offending, victimization and criminal justice responses is needed. An intersectional approach is also required in considering how age, race, ethnicity, class, disability and so on shape the criminal justice experiences of LGBTIQA+ individuals in rural areas.

Towards a rural queer criminology

The voices and experiences of people who identify as LGBTIQA+ have been largely ignored within traditional criminological enquiry. Where mainstream criminology has examined the experiences of LGBTIQA+ people, it has assumed deviant and deficiency-centred approaches which serve to further marginalize and stigmatize sex, gender and sexuality non-conforming people (see both Fileborn, 2019 and Dwyer et al, 2015).

Queer criminology has responded to these historical oversights by examining issues including – but not limited to – the criminalization of same-sex relationships, hate crime victimization amongst people who identify as LGBTIQA+, intimate partner violence in LGBTIQA+ relationships and tensions between police and LGBTIQA+ people. However, the focus of queer criminology has been predominately urban-centric, with a paucity of literature considering the criminal justice experiences of LGBTIQA+ individuals in rural settings. In view of this, there have been recent calls for a rural queer criminology that addresses the criminal justice experiences of people who identify as LGBTIQA+ and how rurality bears on these experiences.

Victimization experiences

People who identify as LGBTIQA+ are at a heightened risk of hate crime victimization. This is true of urban settings, but the risk is amplified in rural contexts. Although harassment, verbal and physical abuse are all-too-common occurrences for people who identify as LGBTIQA+ in rural areas, there is a reluctance to report instances of victimization to police owing to a lack of trust and/or fear that police will hold prejudicial views against LGBTIQA+ communities (see Boso, 2013). Rural barriers to reporting hate crime victimization are further compounded by fears that a person's undisclosed LGBTIQA+ status will be revealed to family members and broader rural communities and that this, in turn, will lead to rejection and ostracization (see Chakraborty and Hardy, 2015).

Intimate partner violence (IPV) and family violence (FV) in rural settings are receiving increased attention, however, much of this work is focused on people in heterosexual relationships. Likewise, research examining IPV and FV amongst people who identify as LGBTIQA+ is gaining momentum; however, much of this research is urban focused.

Broadly speaking, LGBTIQA+ people experience comparable, if not higher, rates of IPV and FV as their heterosexual counterparts but further work is needed to ascertain the unique issues and challenges faced by LGBTIQA+ people residing in rural areas. People who identify as LGBTIQA+ who experience IPV and FV experience multiple barriers to justice, including heteronormative and exclusionary legislative frameworks, fears of being 'outed', a lack of appropriate LGBTIQA+-specific support services and distrust towards criminal justice personnel. These barriers traverse rural and urban areas alike but are exacerbated in rural settings.

Justice responses

The systematic exclusion, marginalization and discrimination of LGBTIQA+ people are considered risk factors for poverty and homelessness, which give rise to higher rates of victimization and offending. People who identify as LGBTIQA+ have also reported being over-policed in rural settings for presenting as visibly queer (see Woods, 2017).

Historically, police have actively contributed to the criminalization and construction of LGBTIQA+ people as deviant. Consensual same-sex relationships have been – and continue to be in some parts of the world, including countries in Africa, Oceania and the Middle East – criminalized. Since the decriminalization of same-sex relationships and subsequent legalisation of same-sex marriage in some places around the globe, policing organizations have endeavoured to build positive relationships with people who identify as LGBTIQA+. Although some LGBTIQA+ people have reported positive interactions with rural police, negative relationships between sexual minorities and police persist.

There is a small, but growing, body of literature examining the experiences of LGBTIQA+ people in courts as both victims and perpetrators of crime, with considerably less research assuming a distinctly rural focus. Anti-LGBTIQA+ biases – which tend to be more pronounced in rural places – can influence the deliberation of juries and the outcome of criminal cases. There have also been reported instances of rural judges and magistrates holding prejudicial views against LGBTIQA+ defendants, which can impact sentencing outcomes.

In both rural and urban settings, perpetrators of violence against LGBTIQA+ individuals have relied on so-called gay and trans panic defences to avoid convictions or receive lenient sentences. Gay and trans panic defences assume different guises depending on the jurisdiction in which they are invoked but they typically rely on provocation, diminished capacity or self-defence. In Australia, for example, a partial defence of provocation has historically been called upon to downgrade murder charges to manslaughter on the basis of alleged homosexual advances. In international contexts, similar defences have been utilized when men have responded violently towards transwomen after discovering their trans status.

Whilst many countries have abolished gay and trans panic defences, they continue to be utilized in some parts of the world and illuminate the entrenchment of homophobia and transphobia within international criminal justice systems. There is limited research in this space with a distinctly rural focus, but it is not difficult to imagine that such defences would be more likely to be accepted in rural contexts given the conservative values typically dominating these spaces.

Suggested readings

Boso, L. (2013) 'Urban bias, rural sexual minorities, and the courts', *UCLA Law Review*, 60(3): 562–637.

Chakraborty, N. and Hardy, S.J. (2015) 'LGB&T hate crime reporting: Identifying barriers and solutions', Equality and Human Rights Commission, Available from: https://www.equalityhumanrights.com/sites/default/files/research-lgbt-hate-crime-reporting-identifying-barriers-and-solutions.pdf [Accessed 9 November 2021].

Dwyer, A., Ball, M. and Barker, E. (2015) 'Policing LGBTIQ people in rural spaces: Emerging issues and future concerns', *Rural Society*, 24(3): 227–43.

Fileborn, B. (2019) 'Policing youth and queerness: The experiences and perceptions of young LGBTQ+ people from regional Victoria', *Current Issues in Criminal Justice*, 31(3): 433–51.

Woods, J.B. (2017) 'LGBT identity and crime', *California Law Review*, 105(3): 667–734.

71

Lifestyle and Amenity Migration

Nick Osbaldiston

Across the world, there has been a push for those within the middle-classes to seek out places that are distinct from urbanity in regional, rural and coastal townships. Defined in the social sciences as 'lifestyle and amenity migration', this transnational and internal migratory phenomenon often involves a counter-urbanization trend.

Migrants feel as though their city lives are unfulfilling, inauthentic and time-consuming. There is also a feeling that cities are risky, polluted and unhappy places to live in. In contrast, migrants feel pulled towards areas that are considered pristine, spacious, natural and slower. They are also drawn to communities that they perceive of as warm, friendly and hospitable. Such narratives of these places are built through cultural themes that have emerged throughout modernity (see Benson and O'Reilly, 2009). As such, much of the literature on this phenomenon shows that desires to move are sparked in an individual's imaginations well before the actual shift.

This migratory phenomenon is both transnational and internal. Several research projects have shown how British people leave behind what they consider to be dreary and stressful lives in the urban cities of the United Kingdom to set up new lives in rural France or coastal Spain (see Benson, 2011). Others have shown how Europeans, facilitated by the mobility allowed by the European Union, will move transnationally, seeking out new spaces in areas such as rural Sweden, Germany, Italy and Turkey. Furthermore, there is evidence of people seeking out new lifestyles from North America into Central and South America, as well as Europeans moving into East and South-East Asia, Australia and New Zealand. Significant research has shown shifts internally in places such as Canada, the United States, Australia and China as people move away from large cities into small townships (see Gosnell and Abrams, 2011).

This movement comes with certain unintended consequences. Researchers have shown that rising in-migration creates incentives for local governments to increase development, creating pressure on environments. These can include issues of water security, inappropriate development that scars landscape, increased risks of exposure to natural disasters such as wildfires and other pressures on local infrastructure including energy and sewerage. In addition, population increases place pressure on economies by inflating local housing prices, creating difficulties for existing vulnerable populations. Several researchers have shown that gentrification has a significant impact on local communities owing to this phenomenon. This can lead to extant populations leaving to find cheaper housing options elsewhere.

Researchers tend to highlight the relative privilege migrants have in their ability to shift into places of high environmental and cultural value. They emphasize the capital (social, cultural and economic) migrants hold and bring with them. For instance, North Americans benefit greatly through inequalities of national economies whereby the monetary value of the United States dollar holds greater value inside Latin American countries, such as Costa Rica. People living a comfortable middle-class lifestyle in the United States will have far greater purchasing power in a small rural village in Central America, for example. Subsequently, migration agencies have developed advertising for less expensive but more appealing lifestyles in relatively poorer regions. Migrants, especially retirees or semi-retirees, can afford significantly better housing and services in these places (see Hoey, 2014).

Similar findings appear in Australia where individuals — for instance, living in Sydney — can take advantage of the high costs of housing, sell their homes for large sums and then acquire places amongst rich natural and environmental beauty in regional towns. This has an impact on local communities, but also transforms townships through housing costs. Furthermore, this can lead to local authorities prioritizing what they see as desirable for these new migrants over the needs of extant populations.

Migrants, of course, do not experience everything with little complication in their journey. Several describe the disappointment of unmet expectations of their new places. These can include structural difficulties, such as trying to navigate the processes of local governance whilst also trying to fit into local cultures, climates and practices. Researchers have further shown that migrants, at times, experience unexpected negative emotions. They can be naïve to the isolation of regional life having come from socially enriching urban living.

Research has shown that migrants felt that the communities they moved to would be warm, friendly and positive to their arrival. Whilst sometimes this does occur, several migrants experience loneliness and a feeling that they do not fit into the local social networks and dynamics. At times, migrants are also unaware of the difficulties of acquiring services in regional areas which range from good quality internet through to the arts. As such, the experience of lifestyle and amenity migration is one that is an ongoing negotiation between the tensions of the emotions and the feelings of satisfaction being in spacious, beautiful and diverse environments free from the difficulties of urban life (see Hayes, 2018).

This issue holds importance for the study of rural crime because of the changing social and economic demographics communities are experiencing due to this phenomenon. As migrants shift, they come with expectations around issues such as policing. Rural townships tend to have limited resources associated with this and, as such, can be something that newcomers are unaware of. Furthermore, rural crime in places of disadvantage can also include exposure to risks and dangers uncommon to ex-urbanites. Higher rates of drug offences, difficulties with property theft in some areas and the growing need to manage environmental crime (such as illegal dumping) are all areas that migrants may need to negotiate in their new lifestyles.

Suggested readings

Benson, M. (2011) *The British in Rural France*, Manchester: University of Manchester Press.

Benson, M. and O'Reilly, K. (2009) 'Migration and the search for a better way of life: A critical exploration of lifestyle migration', *The Sociological Review*, 57: 608–25.

Gosnell, H. and Abrams, J. (2011) 'Amenity migration: Diverse conceptualizations of drivers, socioeconomic dimensions, and emerging challenges', *GeoJournal*, 76: 303–22.

Hayes, M. (2018) *Gringolandia: Lifestyle Migration under Late Capitalism*, Minneapolis: University of Minnesota Press.

Hoey, B. (2014) *Opting for Elsewhere: Lifestyle Migration in the American Middle Class*, Nashville, TN: Vanderbilt University Press.

72

Outlaw Motorcycle Clubs

Mark Lauchs

Outlaw motorcycle clubs (OMCs) are the elite social class of the motorcycle community. They see themselves as the most committed to the lifestyle of 'the biker'. They also see themselves as lying outside of the mainstream motorcycle community and society at large, and enjoy provoking shock and rage from the majority and consequently conflicting with them through violence and other forms of crime.

OMCs live in a parallel social world. The club itself and fellow members are the primary concern of members, whilst their job and family hold a position like a hobby; important only when there is sufficient time and focus once club business is fulfilled. OMC members' rejection of society is intentional as they have created a fantasy world of social interaction with their own rules, territory and culture. Within this world are distinct groups – the individual clubs, built off a single model but otherwise interacting with other participants in this 'game' (see Lauchs et al, 2015).

Men do not accidentally or naively become bikers. Full membership is preceded by a 'hang around' phase, in which they are allowed to socialize and ride with members, and a formal 'prospect' period of months or years in which they are effectively subordinate members. Members must follow orders of officeholders, keep club business secret, actively participate in rides and socialize with their fellow members (see Schmid, 2021).

OMC culture has proved very popular with men from around the globe with the number of OMCs growing in every continent to well over 4,000 active clubs worldwide. Alongside the growth of clubs is a competition for domination of areas by the large international clubs: Hells Angels; Bandidos; Outlaws; Rebels; Gremium; No Name; and Mongols. This interplay between the 'imperialists' and local clubs is referred to as the 'politics' of the OMC world. Political conflict can occur over territory in any part of the world.

There are two types of clubs that interact with rural communities. Clubs with between five and 20 members tend to be in smaller communities, where they can feasibly afford a clubhouse. Whilst still OMCs, they focus on the lifestyle and avoid serious criminal activity and OMC politics. Conversely, the large clubs are much more likely to be in urban environments for the convenience of local members and territorial ambition. This propensity is increasing as the younger members of these clubs reject a lifestyle centred on the clubhouse and participate in the nightclub and rave scene. Their primary interaction with rural communities is through riding on highways.

OMC crime

Joining an OMC increases the likelihood that a man will commit a crime even if they had no criminal history prior to joining the club. It is not yet clear why this occurs, but perhaps is part of the process of acquiring both membership and self-identity with an outlaw motorcycle lifestyle. Further, OMC members have a higher propensity to commit crime than the average criminal population. This crime varies significantly across clubs and chapters within clubs, with a small proportion of members committing most of the crime. However, committing crime is more likely amongst members of large urban clubs than small rural clubs.

OMCs pose three types of criminal threats: members are very misogynistic with the consequent coercive interplay with women; they are recognized around the world as criminogenic groups with involvement in organized crime and OMCs share a 'warfare mentality'. The clubs have a reactionary view of women whom they class as property. Nonetheless, there are some women attracted to the hyper-masculinity of bikers. This can lead to two types of crime associated with a club visiting a smaller community: potential sexual assault and rape between members and local women and violence driven by jealousy between local men and the visiting bikers (see Lauchs, 2017).

United States policing agencies recognized OMC criminal activity in the 1980s and today there is an international consensus that OMCs bring criminal activity (see Delaney, 2014). The main participants in serious criminal activity are the well-known international clubs such as the Hells Angels, Bandidos and Outlaws, but also include their subordinate clubs and other non-aligned clubs. OMCs combine a reputation for violence and a powerful 'wall of silence' or code of omerta that makes them ideal allies and participants in serious crime. However, crime is less frequent in rural communities as the marketplaces for organized crime are metropolitan. Any associated crime outside these regions tends to be instrumental in furthering the metropolitan criminality, such as transporting drugs or guns across jurisdictions under the guise of engagement in long distance rides or 'runs' (see Barker, 2014).

OMC culture promotes violence through its 'warfare mentality'; clubs are continually at war with one another over honour and territory. Clubs proactively seek conflict with other clubs and try to engage in war, leading to their opponents losing territory and even being closed down. These wars are expensive and involve an arms race to ensure that each club is better armed than their opponents. The income from crime buys the resources such as weapons needed to win the battles for supremacy, and escalation of conflict requires more weapons funded by more crime. Thus, the traditional OMC culture and the more recent criminal culture are complementary.

This combat increases when foreign clubs move into a nation. The Hells Angels and other large clubs have engaged in a form of imperialism, not only forming chapters around the world but fighting wars to ensure they are the dominant club in the nations. The other possible outcome is consolidation in the number of clubs as smaller and weaker clubs are either patched over, subordinated or closed by more powerful clubs. Small rural clubs are much more likely to become the victims on consolidation rather than territorial battles which focus on the cities.

The community are endangered by these wars as the violence is public and deadly. Civilians have been killed or injured as collateral damage of bombings, drive-by shootings and public brawls.

Suggested readings

Barker, T. (2014) *Outlaw Motorcycle Gangs as Organised Crime Groups*, Cham: Springer.

Dulaney, W.L. (2014) 'A brief history of "outlaw" motorcycle clubs', *Ulysses East London Newsletter*, 12(73): 1–11, Available from: https://www.ulyssessa.co.za/eastlondon/EastLondonMarch2014.pdf [Accessed 2 November 2021].

Lauchs, M. (2017) 'Are outlaw motorcycle gangs organized crime groups? An analysis of the Finks MC', *Deviant Behavior*, 40(3): 287–300.

Lauchs, M., Bain, A. and Ball, P. (2015) *Outlaw Motorcycle Gangs: A Theoretical Perspective*, Basingstoke: Palgrave Pivot.

Schmid, C.J. (2021) 'Ethnographic gameness: Theorizing extra-methodological fieldwork practices in a study of outlaw motorcycle clubs', *Journal of Contemporary Ethnography*, 50(1): 33–56.

73

People with Disabilities

Marg Camilleri

People with disabilities are not a homogenous group and impairments will affect individuals differently. As well, disability can be diversely defined, depending on jurisdiction. The *United Nations Convention on the Rights of Persons with a Disability* defines disability as ongoing impairments that are physical, mental, intellectual or sensory (see United Nations, 2016). Such impairments interact with a range of barriers that hinder one's capacity to participate fully, effectively and equally in society.

This definition, whilst not inclusive of all disabilities, makes two main points. First, the distinction between the terms 'disability' and 'impairment' is important. 'Impairment' refers to the constraints of the impairment on the individual, whilst the term 'disability' refers to the constructed physical, social and systematic barriers which are disabling within environments designed for an 'able-bodied' population. The second point acknowledges that impairments may be visible or invisible to others and may be acquired, temporary, permanent or lifelong.

Data from primary sources, and as reported in the literature of the experiences of victimization and offenders with disabilities, lack nuance. In many jurisdictions, the literature pertaining to offenders with disabilities is more prevalent compared with the experiences of victimization (see Fitzsimmons et al, 2011; Ortoleva and Lewis, 2012). Despite the increased risk of victimization, few reports are made to police; once made, reports seldom reach court.

The challenges of accessing justice are mediated by factors such as attitudinal, economic, gender, race, sexual or gender identification and indigeneity which, when combined with disability, compound and further diminish access to justice. Steeped in tradition and formality, justice systems are inherently conservative and incorporate ableist practices and assumptions.

In the justice system, deficit characterization of victims and witnesses with cognitive impairments inform generalized perceptions about their credibility and capacity, whilst people with a disability who are accused of crimes are more readily characterized as being untrustworthy. Lawyers representing accused persons with cognitive impairments may not fully understand the implications of their clients' impairments, therefore compromising effective representation.

Access to services

Other impediments specific to rurality, which may also limit participation and access to the justice system more broadly, include the distance required to access limited advocacy resources, police stations and courts; and the limited and potentially inaccessible transport options available to successfully traverse these distances. Access to legal services for the purpose of advice or court representation can also be limited. Small towns may have no or limited access to private law firms (see Law Council of Australia, 2018).

In some jurisdictions, only one government-funded legal service may be available across large geographic areas. In some jurisdictions, legal services may offer pro bono services through law schools or private lawyers offering their time in areas experiencing significant disadvantage. Few options to access legal services – irrespective of whether they are fee for service, government funded or pro bono – may mean that individuals within the community seeking assistance in civil matters are prevented from accessing legal assistance in their town, owing to a conflict of interest.

The impact of rural place adds further complexity to the experience of victims and accused (see Camilleri, 2019). Such experiences, whilst unique to rural areas, do not imply homogeneity across these settings. Such settings are mediated by a combination of interrelated factors including the diversity of people who reside within the town, the impairment of the person, if they are a witness or accused and the policy and resource decisions of government. For example, the lack of police personnel at a rural station and a lack of training to recognize cognitive impairment, or to interview the victim or accused without fully comprehending how such interviews should take place and how questions could be adapted to suit the comprehension needs, have unintended consequences which can be detrimental to case outcome, irrespective of their status in the justice system.

There is evidence that, in some jurisdictions, justice systems are improving their response to the access needs of victims and accused with disabilities. These responses include awareness raising, the use of technology, intermediaries and special measures for victims, such as remote witness facilities where victims in regional areas can provide evidence without the need to travel to major cities. Whilst these strategies offer some level of amelioration for victims with disabilities, such options are, for the most part, urban-centric in focus.

Technology can, to some extent, ameliorate challenges associated with the tyranny of distance and other access needs specific to some impairments. Assuming, however, that such ameliorations or other measures would render them universally accessible would not be accurate. At this point, it is important to acknowledge the role of traditional systems of justice practiced by Indigenous communities globally. Such systems would, to some extent, mitigate issues of accessibility for members of Indigenous communities, which result from the perspective of distance, language and cultural barriers as compared to formal state systems of justice.

The access needs of people with disabilities who interact with the formal justice systems either as accused or as victims/witnesses are varied and, as such, the response requires an inclusive approach. Access to a just response should not be contingent on a person overcoming the limitations of impairment. Rather, it is incumbent that systems of justice strive to be accessible to persons with diverse needs.

Research which explores the dimensions of access to justice for people with disabilities is growing inconsistently across the research landscape. The interaction of the accused and offenders with a disability – including interaction with police, courts and corrections – has occupied the primacy of research attention. Gradually, researchers have been drawn to the experiences of victims and witnesses with a disability, in particular, highlighting the justice system responses to victim/survivors of gendered crime. To date however, the dimension of rural spaces and the impact of rurality on access to justice for people with disability has received sparse attention.

Suggested readings

Camilleri, M. (2019) 'Disabled in rural Victoria: Exploring the intersection of victimisation, disability and rurality on access to justice', *International Journal of Rural Criminology*, 5(1): 88–112.

Fitzsimons, N.M., Hagemeister, A.K. and Braun, E.J. (2011) 'Interpersonal violence against people with disabilities: Understanding the problem from a rural context', *Journal of Social Work in Disability and Rehabilitation*, 10(3): 166–88.

Law Council of Australia (2018) 'Access to justice: The Justice Project final report – Part 1', Law Council of Australia, Available from: https://www.lawcouncil.asn.au/justice-project/final-report [Accessed 2 November 2021].

Ortoleva, S. and Lewis, H. (2012) 'Forgotten sisters: A report on violence against women with disabilities: An overview of its nature, scope, causes and consequences', Violence Against Women with Disabilities Working Group, Available from: https://womenenabled.org/pdfs/Ortoleva Stephanie Lewis Hope et al Forgotten Sisters - A Report on Violence Against Women Girls with Disabilities August 20 2012.pdf [Accessed 2 November 2021].

United Nations (2016) 'Tool kit on disability for Africa: Access to justice for persons with disabilities', United Nations, Department of Economic and Social Affairs – Social Inclusion DSPD and DESA, Available from: https://www.un.org/development/desa/dspd/2016/11/toolkit-on-disability-for-africa-2/#English [Accessed 2 November 2021].

74

Rural Enclaves

Joseph F. Donnermeyer

The definition of an enclave is multi-dimensional and can consider a mix of geographic, cultural, economic, ethnic, legal, religious and sociological features. Nonetheless, the two fundamental characteristics of enclaves are that they occupy a territory or space and, within these, the inhabitants (or, as least the vast share of them) are distinctive in some way.

Perhaps the best way to illustrate an enclave is through an example of two historically related religious groups: one in the two countries of Canada and the United States and the other in Mexico. One is not a rural enclave, and the other is. In the United States, there are now over 600 Amish communities. Clearly the Amish are distinctive with their horse-and-buggy lifestyle, plain dress and use of the Pennsylvania Dutch language (a variant of German). However, they are *not* an enclave. Non-Amish Canadian and United States citizens are neighbours to the Amish, sharing the same space and, in all but a few places, vastly outnumber the Amish. The area where the Amish live may have a distinctive flavour, such as 'eggs for sale, no Sunday sales' signs and horse droppings on the road, but it is not an enclave.

To the south in the Mexican state of Chihuahua is a related group known as Old Colony Mennonites. They, too, are distinctive from the majority population in that area, which also outnumbers them. However, what qualifies them as an enclave is that they live in segregated communities known as colonies, even though they may travel to a nearby town for supplies, medical care and other services. Similarly, other religious groups related to both Amish and Old Colony Mennonites are the Hutterites of the Great Plains states of the United States and prairie provinces of middle Canada. They also live in segregated colonies, where they communally share most of the property and are sometimes referred as the oldest socialist society in human history, having adopted this lifestyle over 400 years ago.

There are many other religiously based enclaves, such as: conservative, polygamous communities that broke away from the mainstream Mormon church and are located mostly in rural localities within the western region of the United States (see Foster and Watson, 2019); Der Bruderhof ('place of the brothers') communities found mostly in the northeastern region of the United States (as well as Australia, England and Germany); the Exclusive Brethren communities, many of whom are rural, located in Australia, New Zealand and the European continent; and the Uyghurs, a mostly Islamic group located in the Xinjiang Autonomous region of far northwestern China. Even Boko Haram, a terrorist group operating in northeastern Nigeria and spilling over the border into Cameroon, Chad and Niger, is a religiously based and mostly rural enclave that is seeking to cleanse Nigeria of Western influences through violence and kidnapping.

Rural enclaves can also be defined primarily by territory, such as Vatican City or the tiny countries of Brunei, Monaco and Andorra, amongst others. Technically, they are enclaves, but problematic for a criminological examination of enclaves because they are sovereign countries (and not very rural). However, there are some amazing rural residuals, such as the village of Lai Cho Wo and other small rural clusters in areas beyond the dense population of urbanized Hong Kong. Their populations have declined, yet some villagers prefer their rural enclave to living in the urbanized areas of Hong Kong, with its vast skyscrapers and traffic jams.

Rural enclaves can also be distinctive primarily because of their ethnic or racial character. In the United States, the descendants of former slaves working on plantations along the coast and on several coastal islands of Georgia and South Carolina came to be known as the Gullahs – with a distinctive language and customs from even other rural, African–American cultures. The synergy of strong African roots mixed with the European peoples now living in these coastal regions (often the owners of slaves before the Civil War), plus relative geographic isolation, produced a unique culture that mostly fits with the definition of a rural enclave.

The Karen people of Eastern Myanmar, like the Gullah, are a synergy brought about by the meeting of people from the Gobi Desert region of China who moved to their present location over two thousand years ago. Settler societies are today those countries with large numbers of European immigrants during colonialization who subsequently decimated and discriminated against the Indigenous populations (see Cunneen and Tauri, 2016). Indigenous tribes in the Amazon (including the Yanomamo and Kayapo) as well as those situated at the Orinoco River (such as the Warrau, Guaica and Maquiritare) can also be understood as rural enclaves. These groups are subjected to strain owing to logging and land-clearing, in addition to experiencing violence at the hands of ranchers and drug cartels. Many of these Indigenous cultures are today examples of rural enclaves.

It is also possible to consider itinerant or nomadic groups as examples of rural enclaves. For example, centuries-old nomadic livestock herders in Africa (such as the Tuareg) and the Middle East (such as Bedouins) cover vast regions, but these areas are delimited by climate and trade routes. The population of many nomadic groups have lost their rural enclave lifestyles under the economic and cultural forces of globalization, yet nomads still populate many regions of the world. It can additionally be argued that, in more recent times, some motorcycle gangs and perhaps travellers' groups primarily operate in rural enclaves if they mostly operate in rural areas, although features of both groups stretch the definition (see Griffen, 2014; Lauchs et al, 2015). The main point is that some groups carry their territory with them – that is, they live and move about in areas with similar characteristics.

Another category that represents examples of rural enclaves are intentional communities and communes. Many have a religious basis, but not necessarily. Some are anti-capitalist and anti-technology, advocating a more luddite lifestyle. A great number of these rural enclaves are agricultural and mostly advocate the consumption of self-raised organic foods, a vegan diet and a level of self-sufficiency with minimal dependence on the world around them.

The huge diversity of groups and peoples who might qualify as rural enclaves challenges any definition which is not broad and encompassing. With the idea of territory and the distinctiveness of the population that inhabits it, a more grounded consideration of the criminological dimensions of rural-located enclaves can be garnered.

Often, people living in rural enclaves are the frequent victims of crime, from theft and vandalism to violence of all varieties (see, for example, Encyclopedia entries for genocide and hate crimes; see also Karstedt et al, 2021). There are further issues related to access to justice by many of the people living in rural enclaves who are both ignored and discriminated against by the criminal justice systems of the countries where they are located. Especially, this is the situation for Indigenous groups in various settler societies who are over-represented in prisons but paid less attention to by law enforcement when they are the victims of a crime. Violence and imprisonment represent the situation of Uyghurs in China and it is the government of China that has initiated hostile actions against this group as the area became populated with more mainline groups who migrated from the east.

From a criminological perspective, many rural enclaves can also be seen as engaged in criminal lifestyles, such as outlaw motorcycle gangs and travellers' groups. As well, the insular nature of some rural enclaves, such as polygamous Mormon communities, can hide crimes that occur within, such as violence against women and forcing girls to marry at a very young age.

The criminology of rural enclaves is a vastly under-studied area in rural criminology. Yet the number and diversity of rural places around the world where distinctive groups reside calls for much greater attention from rural criminologists.

Suggested readings

Cunneen, C. and Tauri, J. (2016) *Indigenous Criminology*, Bristol: Policy Press.

Foster, C.L. and Watson, M.T. (2019) *American Polygamy: A History of Fundamentalist Mormon Faith*, Cheltenham: History Press.

Griffen, R. (ed) (2014) *Indigenous, Nomadic and Traveling Communities: Education as a Humanitarian Response*, London: Bloomsbury.

Karstedt, S., Nyseth Brehm, H. and Frizzell, L.C. (2021) 'Genocide, mass atrocity, and theories of crime: Unlocking criminology's potential', *Annual Review of Criminology*, 4: 75–97.

Lauchs, M., Bain, A. and Ball, P. (2015) *Outlaw Motorcycle Gangs: A Theoretical Perspective*, Basingstoke: Palgrave Pivot.

75

Rural Folk Crime

Rob White

The notion of 'folk crime' refers to offences that are generally perceived by perpetrators and other members of their community as not being particularly criminal, offensive, harmful or dangerous. A central idea is that 'we all do it' and so those caught doing it are not necessarily deemed 'evil' or 'unworthy' enough to warrant suffering unpleasant penalties and/or the stigma attached to ordinary criminal sanctions. Such crimes are frequently committed repeatedly by the same offenders, are well known in the offenders' community and do not impair the offenders' public identity as respectable and law-abiding citizens (see White, 2016).

Folk crimes feature significantly in rural contexts of crime, criminality and victimization. Specifically, rural folk crime has been related to hunting and gaming laws, land clearance, water use and nature harvesting of items such as mushrooms, fish, firewood and flowers.

Conservationism and environmental protection have had a major impact on the ways in which traditional users of natural resources engage with forests and lands, local rivers and coastal fringes insofar as previously acceptable practices have frequently been transformed into highly regulated and/or illegal acts. This is especially the case in regards to hunting, cutting down of trees and harvesting from traditional foraging areas, as shown historically in the United States and evident today in Africa and Scandinavia. Restrictions also generally apply to fishing practices (for example, catch sizes and limits) in relation to lakes, rivers, coastal marine areas and ocean waters.

For some, subsistence requirements demand that traditional practices of harvesting and foraging continue as before. And in some circumstances, those who resist the imposition of new laws such as hunting and fishing bans may, in effect, take on the mantle of 'folk hero', at least in their eyes and those of their supporters.

Important moral distinctions are also made regarding how to interpret activities such as hunting and the cutting down of trees. This has been described as forming part of a 'moral ecology' (see Jacoby, 2003). For example, taking wood from a state forest was not necessarily seen by local Adirondack residents as a 'crime' but rather as quite legitimate if done for the purposes of subsistence (such as for firewood, buildings materials and the like). This 'theft' of trees from protected conservation areas was therefore seen to be perfectly fine if not done for the purposes of future market gain (such as selling firewood) (see Jacoby, 2003).

Activities such as bird, turtle, abalone or lobster poaching may be a genuine folk crime in the sense that it is something that everyone knows about, and that everyone allows to happen since it is not perceived to be 'really' wrong in most respects (unless certain informal protocols and boundaries are violated, such as 'not leaving enough for other people').

In Costa Rica, for example, turtle poaching is prevalent because of a range of intersecting factors: the tradition and the history of the practice, which has been occurring for many hundreds of years; the value to local people, as food and because the shells and skins have traditionally been used for household objects and jewellery; the qualities of the object, in that turtle eggs are believed to have aphrodisiac qualities; income sources for local people based upon demand in external consumer markets; tourism and the appeal of local souvenirs based upon turtle products; lack of government regulation insofar as there is no apparent profit for the government in prosecuting cases; and the pressures of the black market which generates high illegal demand for turtle-based goods. The subsequent demise of the turtle population is thus due to multiple push and pull factors (see Toreng and Rankin, 2005).

Various rationalizations are used to justify rural folk crimes. Many of these involve comparisons between 'good' folk and 'bad' folk on the basis of particular social practices and assumptions regarding character. For instance, techniques of neutralization include 'others are worse' (such as dropping beer cans all over); 'our own code guides us' (for example, 'we don't kill in mating season'); and 'we are good folk' (for example, 'we are hard-working individuals and good family men'; 'we don't disturb the patterns of the wildlife'). As indicated, rural folk crimes can also be highly gendered.

Like folk crime itself, responses to folk crime are variable and depend on local context. For instance, the role and attitudes of police towards tree theft may demonstrate patterns of accommodation so as to preserve the social and cultural closeness of police with the local community. This accommodation, in turn, may serve to preserve the image of the forest community as a desirable place, frequented by honest people requiring minimal policing.

Criminalization in relation to rural folk crime is thus a socially constructed process.

There are, as with victims, considerable variations in offenders. For example, much wildlife poaching is committed globally by traditional peoples, many of whom are poor and economically vulnerable. The nature of wildlife crime varies depending upon the specific crime (for example, illegal fishing on the high seas; trade in lizards), the cultural context within which natural resource use occurs (for example, Indigenous people and traditional ways of life), the character of the market in relation to wildlife (for example, personal use versus profit making) and the relationship between local people and criminal syndicates (for example, chains and networks of connection). In other words, not all people are in equal circumstances, and some are more powerful than others (see Duffy, 2010).

Folk crime in rural contexts can represent a legitimate activity traditionally engaged in by local populations, it can constitute a major threat to species and ecosystems when it is inserted into global economic and trading systems and it can be a reaction to policies imposed from 'elsewhere' that do not make sense to those whose lives over many generations have celebrated the very thing that is now being criminalized.

Suggested readings

Duffy, R. (2010) *Nature Crime: How We're Getting Conservation Wrong*, New Haven, CT: Yale University Press.

Jacoby, K. (2003) *Crimes against Nature: Squatters, Poachers, Thieves, and the Hidden History of American Conservation*, Berkeley, CA: University of California Press.

Toreng, S. and Rankin, E. (2005) 'Long-term conservation efforts contribute to positive green turtle *chelonia mydas* nesting trend at tortuguerio, Costa Rica', *Biological Conservation*, 121(1): 111–16.

Von Essen, E., Hansen, H., Kallstrom, H., Peterson, M. and Peterson, T. (2014) 'Deconstructing the poaching phenomenon: A review of typologies for understanding illegal hunting', *British Journal of Criminology*, 54: 632–51.

White, R. (2016) 'Re-conceptualising folk crime in rural contexts', in J.F. Donnermeyer (ed) *The Routledge International Handbook of Rural Criminology*, London: Routledge, pp. 299–308.

76

Tropes of Rural Offenders and Victims

Belinda Morrissey and Kristen Davis

Rural offenders and victims experience the same sorts of crime as their urban neighbours, but studies have found that the context and meaning of those crimes differ dramatically. Specifically, rural victims are vastly more affected by certain crimes, just as rural offenders are vastly more enabled to commit them.

These differences in experience of crime are due, primarily, to the tropes or rhetorical devices used to depict and to understand rural crime. Drawing upon research by Moody (2002), Marshall and Johnson (2005) and Youngsen et al (2021), the following five sections are the most important responses to rural crime. These tropes underpin the very different relationship rural people have with certain crimes to that of the urban population. They serve to create the figure of the victim and offender and to make sense of crime and criminal behaviour in rural areas.

'It couldn't happen here'

This response is very common in rural areas when crime, particularly violent crime, occurs. This disbelief serves to mark that crime is a rarer experience in the country than the city. The occurrence of crimes such as murder, rape and sexual assault create a large amount of publicity in and of themselves and, when they occur in a rural setting, they create a bombshell event from which escape is impossible. Victims must work through their recovery whilst centre-stage to a mainstream news cycle and overwhelming interest from those living in the locality who know them personally.

Rural offenders, likewise, are forced into public life amid either a hostile or a disbelieving community. These offenders compel citizens in rural localities to accept that there is a dark underbelly to the rural and that, indeed, such crimes can and do 'happen here'. An alternative oppositional mentality can argue for the offender's innocence, with rural citizens offering support and denouncement of the victim's behaviour. This cycle then has enormous effect in limiting and even derailing that victim's possible recovery.

'We look after our own'

Rural communities are frequently praised for their tight-knit nature, where everyone supports each other. However, whilst this may have been the situation for some rural communities in the past, it is no longer viable. Indeed, this trope undermines that cosy myth altogether. Many rural areas are no longer populated by people who have lived there for generations. Instead, this population now incorporates a variety of groups, some of which have no background in rural life. Consequently, country people divide their communities into two groups – the 'desirable' and the 'undesirable'. The desirable may include commuters, business people and self-funded retirees. The undesirable often are people on government benefits, gays and lesbians, racial/ethnic minorities, the poor and the homeless. Support from the community, even when experiencing crime, is available to the desirable, but rarely to the undesirable, under this 'us and them' mentality.

This concept of looking after one's own grew from demographic and economic factors regarding the geographic isolation of rural communities. Rural people often live in houses that are far apart and invisible to neighbours. The inadequacy of public transport in country areas serves to make isolation even more evident. The only way to combat this tyranny of distance is through vehicle ownership, so access assumes an importance not seen in the city.

Consequently, property crime, such as the theft of a motor vehicle, disproportionately affects rural victims who are left without any transport. Farm crime, which is specific to rural areas, can result in severe damage to the management and productivity of farm businesses and their consequent failure. Even damage to a phone box in a rural area can be much more important than in the city; it may be the only one and it could well be vital in summoning help in a dangerous situation, given that broadband services are notoriously less reliable.

Conversely, a rural setting can aid offenders immeasurably. Drug production and concealing the proceeds of crime flourish very successfully in the country, where the very remoteness of farms and houses works for offenders, not against them, making it relatively easy to hide such operations.

Domestic violence is an important case in point. Domestic offenders thrive in this situation as their victims are unable to leave houses secluded on remote farms, and their neighbours are too distant to witness their behaviour. Coercive control is particularly effective in such circumstances, with offenders controlling the use of transport and telecommunications with more ease given the isolation of rural inhabitants. Further, ownership of firearms is very common in rural areas and research on rural domestic homicides has found that fatal injury was most commonly due to their use. Consequently, rural domestic violence victims have been found to experience worse psychosocial and physical damage than their urban counterparts.

Rural people are regularly described as having restricted access to support services, including those for domestic violence, drug and alcohol support, rape and sexual assault, housing, education, childcare, legal services and courts. In some cases, this access is actively resisted in rural areas, with agencies for victim support being represented as unnecessary and incompetent in their approach due to their lack of understanding of the ways rural communities function. This restriction makes leaving a domestic offender far more problematic than a similar case in the city. Rural victims often have nowhere to gain support for crimes committed against them and nor do rural offenders when they wish to change their behaviour.

'Everyone knows everyone'

Whilst many rural communities praise themselves for their tight-knit nature, where everyone knows everyone else, this factor can also impede rural victims' ability to speak out about crime. Lack of anonymity and consequent ostracism are real possibilities for victims who make public abuse by an offender who is well known in an area, where even visiting a doctor's surgery to get help for injuries sustained can be a public event.

'Put up with it'

Traditional ideas long held in some rural communities about keeping one's problems to oneself, and 'putting up' with abusive behaviour to ensure community stability, are largely responsible for the low reporting of crime in the country. This means that rural residents may not report domestic violence, racism and anti-social behaviour. Consequently, the lack of confidentiality leads victims of domestic violence, rape and drug use, in particular, to refuse to get any help at all. Ethnic minorities living in rural areas experience similar issues when faced with racist abuse.

'We can cope'

Rural communities often boast of resilience and independence in the face of adversity. Indeed, self-reliance is considered inbred in country dwellers, unlike those in the cities, who are seen as needing help constantly. This attitude is especially apparent in investigations of major crime where rural citizens tend to resent the importation of city police when they only trust their own local force. This trope of autonomy can work effectively to deter victims from seeking help and reporting crime.

Suggested readings

Marshall, B. and Johnson, S.D. (2005) *Crime in Rural Areas: A Review of the Literature for the Rural Evidence Research Centre*, London: Jill Dando Institute of Crime Science.

Moody, S.R. (2002) 'Responding to victims of crime in rural areas', in B. Williams (ed) *Reparation and Victim-Focused Social Work*, London: Jessica Kingsley Publishers, pp. 84–103.

Youngsen, N., Saxton, M., Jaffe, P.G., Dawson, M. and Straatman, A-L. (2021) 'Challenges in risk assessment with rural domestic violence victims: Implications for practice', *Journal of Family Violence*, 36: 537–50.

77

Working Tourists

Donna James

Working holiday tourists can be traced back to the seventeenth- and eighteenth-century European trend of 'tramping'; a practice whereby young lower- and working-class men travelled around Europe to undertake labour for economic necessity. In the late 1950s to early 1960s, the middle to upper classes in Great Britain adopted the practice of tramping in the form of long-term budget travelling for fun and adventure.

In 1962, the British Universities North America Club began offering gap year work and volunteer exchange programmes in North America (refer to Wilson et al, 2009). This was a pivotal moment that saw working holidays grow in popularity, starting with Great Britain and expanding beyond Europe and into other White colonial nations (namely Australia, Canada, Ireland, New Zealand and into North America). Following this period of growth, Cohen (1973, p. 91) described the working holiday as a practice whereby 'youths from one country travel into another to work for short periods, mostly during summer-school vacations'.

The nature of what it means to be a working holiday tourist has since changed drastically. Initially, working holiday programmes were championed for enabling freedom of movement between citizens from English-speaking nations with strong social ties and, more recently, for enabling a wider breadth of travel experiences and cultural exchanges amongst young people, whilst fostering closer ties between reciprocal partner countries.

However, working holiday programmes have been criticized by many scholars and social commentators. This is because governments of more privileged nations are increasingly using working holiday tourists to meet the demands of their unskilled workforces – often at the expense of prioritizing working holiday tourists' safety and welfare. The positions that working tourists are typically encouraged to fill (often through incentives such as visa extensions) usually exist in jobs that are undesirable to local citizens. These jobs are commonly found in rural or regional areas (for example, farm work and fruit and vegetable picking) and are typified by dangerous, hard, manual labour, unsafe and poor conditions, precarious and seasonal work and low pay (consider Reilly, 2018).

As working holiday tourists are pushed into rural areas of their host nations to find work, they can experience social isolation owing to racial and national hierarchies. Further, because they are perceived as temporary, cheap sources of labour, they are commonly subject to poor working and living conditions. Such conditions often go unnoticed by authorities because the rural location of most unskilled working tourist jobs makes it difficult for regulatory bodies to check the standard of employment and living conditions of working holiday tourists.

The adverse conditions of working holiday jobs are compounded by a lack of regulation of working holiday programmes. In many countries, working holiday programmes have not been aligned to meet the changing role of working holiday tourists in their host countries. Despite the changing nature of working holidays over time – from cultural exchange to unskilled labour workforce – working holiday programmes have not significantly changed in their design and governance. Accordingly, there is little to no oversight or regulation in some countries when it comes to managing working tourists' labour rights, living conditions and welfare.

The plight of working holiday tourists is further compounded by the existence, and subsequent lack of regulation or oversight, of unscrupulous secondary service providers (for example, contractors, labour hire firms, gang-masters and accommodation providers) who act as intermediaries between working tourists and employers. For example, in Australia where working holiday tourists are required to undertake 88 days of 'specified work' (work in an industry where there is demand for unskilled workers, in a rural, regional or northern area of the country) if they wish to extend their working holiday visa by a second or third year, working tourists commonly seek out 'working hostels' which provide access to both accommodation and work.

Working hostels are shared accommodations that are typically run by a contractor who liaises with local employers to assist with supplying a workforce. These hostels often handle all administration of the working holiday tourists' payslips and profit by exploiting them; for example, paying them below award wages, and then subtracting money for inflated rent, transport fees (to the workplace) and finders' fees (for providing them with work). As housing and labour hire legislation is state-based in Australia, contractors can move between states to evade regulators pursuing violations.

Worse still, many working hostels and contractors target working holiday tourists who have little to no English language skills and minimal access to social networks in Australia, which makes them difficult to detect and prosecute. Subsequently, there is widespread exploitation (including wage theft, pension theft and underpayment or non-payment of wages) amongst working holiday tourists in Australia and in other various nations and some working holiday tourists are more vulnerable to exploitation than others due to the long-standing social inequalities around nationality, race and gender. In addition to exploitation, many working holiday tourists (especially women) are commonly subject to workplace sexual harassment and sexual assault.

As most working tourists endure both a precarious work and a precarious visa status whilst working in their host nation, they can fear that employers will compromise their ability to remain employed or in the host country if they seek support from authorities when a crime has been committed. Additionally, many working tourists suffer significant language barriers in their host country which greatly compounds the barriers they face to reporting their victimization to exploitation or sexual violence, or the actions of bad actors, to authorities. Such a problem is not easily resolved because temporary labour migration has become a global issue which is inherently tied to domestic labour markets and the continuation of global dominance of White Western countries and colonialism. Hence, many governments recognize that avenues for reform would come at a significant cost to their labour chains and profits, leading to a political stalemate on the issue (see Li and Whitworth, 2016; Reilly et al, 2018).

Suggested readings

Cohen, E. (1973) 'Nomads from affluence: Notes on the phenomenon of drifter-tourism', *International Journal of Comparative Sociology*, 14(1–2): 89–103.

Li, Y.T. and Whitworth, K. (2016) 'When the state becomes part of the exploitation: Migrants' agency within the institutional constraints in Australia', *International Migration*, 54(6): 138–50.

Reilly, A. (2015) 'Low-cost labour or cultural exchange? Reforming the Working Holiday visa programme', *The Economic and Labour Relations Review*, 26(3): 474–89.

Reilly, A., Howe, J., van den Broek, D. and Wright, C.F. (2018) 'Working holiday makers in Australian horticulture: Labour market effect, exploitation and avenues for reform', *Griffith Law Review*, 27(1): 99–130.

Wilson, J., Fisher, D. and Moore, K. (2009) 'The OE goes "home": Cultural aspects of a working holiday experience', *Tourist Studies*, 9(1): 3–21.

78

Youth and Youth Sub-cultures

Matthew D. Moore

The development of criminological theory has been grounded on urban centres with urban youth as the focus. From Walter Miller's explanation of the focal concerns to the Chicago School's development of social disorganization theory, criminological theories have focused almost solely on urban youth and urban centres. The lack of theoretical explanations for crime in rural areas has hampered our understanding of crime and deviant behaviour (see Donnermeyer, 2007).

Rural areas are distinct from urban areas. Research has demonstrated that drug use, gun availability and poverty differ in rural and urban centres. Moreover, some crimes are unique to rural areas, such as livestock theft. Scholars have also pointed out that rural areas are often seen as homogenous by criminologists. However, rural areas display a wide variety of characteristics, such as poverty level, racial composition and unemployment. Therefore, there is a need for the development of criminological theory based on rural areas.

One of the areas of interest may be the examination of youth sub-cultures within rural areas. Rural areas are often believed to be devoid of gangs or any type of sub-culture that may produce crime (see Weisheit and Wells, 2001). Criminologists have argued that any gang activity in rural areas was due to migration from urban areas. For example, families may move from an urban area and bring their gang affiliations and activity to the rural area. Another line of reasoning is that rural youth may copy the gang symbols and activities they see youth in urban areas using. Yet some scholars have argued that migration and copying do not explain the activity found in rural areas. Research has shown that most gang members in rural areas are homegrown.

Rural areas have a unique culture. Research has demonstrated that gang activity in rural areas does not mimic that of urban areas (see Dukes and Stein, 2003; Howell and Egley, 2005). Urban gang activity may not have the same appeal to youth in rural areas. Instead, rural youth may create their own sub-culture and gangs based on their unique experience. For example, drug use is a problem in urban and rural communities. Researchers have found that rural youth are more likely to use different types of drugs, such as inhalants and methamphetamine, than their urban counterparts. Youths may be drawn into gang activity because of the opportunities and unique experiences found in rural communities.

The rural youth are more isolated from others and often lack the businesses and organizations found in urban areas. This boredom can lead to deviant behaviour and crime that is not found in urban centers. The rural youth may frequently engage in relatively minor forms of deviant behaviour, such as driving through cornfields, to more damaging criminal behaviour, such as homicide. Scholars have pointed out that much of our knowledge of crime has been misguided. In the 1990s, the United States experienced a decline in crime. However, the decrease was found mainly in urban areas, with rural areas experiencing an increase during this time. Moreover, the assumption that rural areas have less crime than urban areas is also incorrect. Scholars have highlighted that crime is higher in rural areas of Canada. In the United States, some rural areas have higher crime rates than some urban areas.

The smaller populations found in rural areas create a less stable form of a gang. Researchers have shown that youth gangs in rural areas are unstable. The loss of a few members can mean the end of the gang. The small number of youths in rural areas means that the gang may be vulnerable to a member being arrested, moving away or maturing out of the gang. When a member or two leave the gang, there may be no other youth available to take their place. Therefore, youth gangs in rural areas may be around for a short period and then gone in a few years.

Some misunderstandings of crime and deviant behaviour in rural areas can be attributed to the lack and quality of data found in rural areas. Scholars have suggested that one of the reasons criminologists have ignored rural areas is owing to problems with data.

First, rural areas may have a difficult time collecting data. Rural areas may not have organizations that can survey residents about their experiences with police, courts and victimization. This can leave a gap in our understanding of what crimes are prevalent in rural settings.

Second, scholars have argued that youth engaged in crime in rural areas may be dealt with informally. Researchers have pointed out that rural residents may be more distrustful of the police and other government institutions. Therefore, they may be less likely to inform the police of a crime that has taken place. Instead, rural residents may handle the crime more informally.

Third, some scholars have pointed to the idea that deviant behaviour amongst rural youth may be seen as 'kids being kids'. In urban areas, individuals are not likely to know all the youth in the area. When a deviant behaviour or crime is committed, they would be more likely to view the behaviour as deviant. In rural areas, the victim may know the youth that is involved and believe the act is simply the youth doing what kids do.

Many people idealize life in rural areas. Rural life is often viewed as picturesque with no poverty, crime or other social ills that plague urban areas. This view of rural life is wrong. Rural youth experience disrupted families, poverty and crime. Parents will often have to migrate long distances for their job, which can leave young people alone for long periods of time. Rural areas experience persistent and concentrated poverty just as urban centres do (see Weisheit, 2016).

The rural youth develop their own sub-culture based on their lived experiences. Returning to Walter Miller's focal concerns, rural youth may have different concerns than urban youth. When examining social disorganization theory, some rural areas may experience high levels of disorganization that would rival any urban centre. The unique space that the rural youth occupy demands further research and investigation.

Suggested readings

Donnermeyer, J. (2007) 'Rural crime: Roots and restoration', *International Journal of Rural Crime*, 1(1): 2–20.

Dukes, R.L. and Stein, J.A. (2003) 'Gender and gang membership: A contrast of rural and urban youth on attitudes and behavior', *Youth and Society*, 34(4): 415–40.

Howell, J.C. and Egley Jr., A. (2005) 'Gangs in small towns and rural counties', *NYGC Bulletin*, 1: 1–6.

Weisheit, R. (2016) 'Rural crime from a global perspective', *International Journal of Rural Criminology*, 3(1): 5–28.

Weisheit, R. and Wells, L. (2001) 'The perception of gangs as a problem in nonmetropolitan areas', *Criminal Justice Review*, 26(2): 170–92.

PART V

Geographic Status of Rural Criminological Research

Introduction to Part V: Geographic Status of Rural Criminological Research

Alistair Harkness and Joseph F. Donnermeyer

Despite rural criminology's origins dating back to the 1930s, the growth of rural criminology has not been even across the globe. The 'big four' academic bases of rural criminological study – the United States, the United Kingdom, Australia and to a slightly lesser extent Canada – have hitherto dominated the scholarship landscape in book chapter and journal article form.

This is, in part, attributable to the lure of wealthier, better-resourced institutions which happen to be located in these parts of the world. That is, scholars will relocate across borders to where jobs and opportunities exist, and then develop to an extent localized research interests. There are, of course, barriers which exist which make scholarship challenging in certain geographic places too, not just in terms of resourcing but prevailing research priorities.

As with many other disciplines, much of the rural criminological literature is provided in English alone. The higher education sector places much weight on citations and other so-called metrics, which serves to isolate scholars performing vital and cutting-edge locally specific research. Many voices on crime and criminology beyond the urban places of the 'big four', therefore, have largely been excluded from traditional criminology.

This section seeks to identify the geographic status of rural criminology based on the seven continents. Here we have utilized the CIA Factbook maps as the delineation between continents.

Contributors were asked to restrict observations to approximately 1500 words – no mean feat when considering the huge and diverse populations, land masses and socio-cultural differences which exist between and within continents. However, what is presented here is a snapshot of key developments and, it is hoped, will serve as a portent of further geographical specific rural criminological work in the years ahead.

79

Africa

Willie Clack and Emmanuel Bunei

Conceptualizing the energetic developing field of rural criminology is challenging and doing justice to a study field within a continental context is ambitious. Indeed, the Global North possesses more examples of scholarly work in some areas of criminology, but believing it is a European or North American discipline is a false impression. Neglecting the contributions and historical developments of criminology on the African continent impedes the advancement of criminological scholarship overall. Africa is host to two of the ten oldest universities globally; however, there is a neglect of historical contributions mainly owing to language. Therefore, understanding the African continent – with diversity centred around regions, culture, gender, ethnicity, religion, colonization and linguistics – is imperative to discussing criminology in general, and rural criminology specifically.

Five distinct regions and dominant languages are identifiable in Africa: West Africa (Francophone); Central Africa (mostly Francophone); North Africa (Arabic speaking); East Africa (Swahili with an Anglophone influence); and the Southern part of the continent (Anglophone). The division illustrates one principal distinction: linguistics, which is paramount as the words used to codify various laws regarding the same crimes are diverse within Africa and worldwide. Yet multi-lingualism is absent or rare in academia, challenging comparative epistemological questions.

For example, some easily identifiable examples of linguistic challenges in rural criminology emanate from how violent crime and livestock theft are defined. Essentially, violence is illegal criminal behaviour in rural towns and farms, commonly referenced as 'rural violence' in the Global North. However, in South Africa scholars use the unique phrases 'farm attacks' and 'farm murders' when referring to violent crimes on agricultural operations (see Clack and Minnaar, 2018). Also, livestock theft in different parts of the world and across the African continent uses different terminology: for example, stock theft (South Africa); cattle raiding (European countries and the United States); larceny (the Caribbean and certain states in the United States); cattle rustling (Eastern and Northern Africa); cattle lifting (India); or cattle duffing (Australia and New Zealand) (refer to Masiola and Tomei, 2015).

It is imperative, therefore, first to understand the linguistics used before engaging in comparative research and keyword searches. Another challenge is the hegemony so prevalent in the criminology of the Global North, not only against rural criminology but also against scholarship from Africa, Asia and South America. Hence, the exclusion of African scholars from contributing to rural criminology is more than linguistics, but the mainstream and urban-centric culture of criminology. Articles published by scholars in the Global South do not get much visibility in international scholarship as they do not typically get published in the Web of Science or Scopus. The articles published about rural crimes in Africa are mostly from only a few countries, such as South Africa, Kenya and Nigeria.

Cultural differences need to be considered when studying and defining rural crimes in Africa. Estimations are that there are over 3,000 different ethnic communities with different cultures impacting on how they define crime in Africa. This is apparent in how crimes such as domestic violence, child marriages, female genital mutilations and agricultural crimes (especially livestock theft) are defined. Also, these different cultures have an impact on how communities resist some social and cultural practices that have been criminalized.

Rural crimes can be divided into exceptional crimes, which are more violent with a low occurrence probability, and ordinary crimes, which are mostly economical and occur more frequently. Grote and Neubacher (2016) identify five broad types of rural crimes within the Africa context as violent crimes (exceptional), farm/agricultural crimes, environmental and wildlife crimes, corruption and so on (ordinary). Generally, over the years, rural crime in Africa has been largely ignored and under-researched by academics, particularly from a criminological perspective.

Violent crimes

Violent crimes involve harm caused by one person to another person and include murder, assault and so on. Across Africa, some violent crimes are specific to certain regions and countries. For example, most research attention on violent crimes in rural South Africa is towards so-called farm attacks or farm murders, which have been taken out of context and politicized more often than not.

Farmer murders are a crime quite particular to South Africa and a few other countries in the Global South, but rarely occurring in the Global North. Yet an examination of what can be found in popular search engines is generally limited to agriculture. However, gender-based violence, domestic violence, violence against children, violence against women, especially female genital mutilations, and violence against female teachers have received prominent research attention in rural Nigeria, Kenya, Uganda and South Africa. Much of this literature remains under the radar of mainstream criminology.

Agricultural/farm crimes

Farm crimes are generally economical and aimed at property, including farming-related commodities, supplies or equipment, or behaviours that otherwise influence farm production. These crimes have direct and indirect impacts on the farming and consumer communities that pay for the losses. Some of the common farm crimes in Africa include the theft of livestock (across all regions of Africa) and theft of crop produce, especially coffee (Kenya and Uganda), beans (Ethiopia), vanilla (Madagascar), cassava (Malawi), oil palm (Cameroon) and green maize (Kenya) (see Bunei et al, 2016).

The most prevalent farm crime in Africa is livestock theft, which has the most significant financial and emotional effects on farmers. Livestock theft is endemic and is regarded in some communities as a legitimate sport: stealing for restocking and stealing for retaliation has cultural and economic roots. Evidence of the organized nature of the crime is also apparent. Research on this topic has emerged in East Africa in the Karamoja region (Uganda, South Sudan, Kenya), West Africa (Nigeria), Southern Africa (Botswana, Lesotho, Namibia, South Africa and Eswatini) and central Africa (Cameroon).

Environmental crimes

Environmental crimes directly impact the environment, which can occur in both urban and rural settings. Environmental crimes are mainly concerned with five activities, namely: wildlife crimes; illegal logging; illegal fishing; illegal mining; and environmental (industrial) pollution. Africa, in some instances, is a victim of the developed world with crime such as environmental pollution and wildlife crimes having a link to developments in the Global North.

In East Africa, the most prevalent wildlife crime is the poaching of elephant and rhino tusks and sandalwood (a tree known for its scent). These wildlife crimes are highly organized criminal activities that involved both local rural criminals and international criminal actors. Unfortunately, rural Africa is the victim of global supply–demand dynamics for many types of flora and fauna.

Figure 2: Political map of Africa[1]

Warchol's book (2017), frequently cited within environmental crime publications regarding the transnational illegal wildlife trade in Southern Africa, is a developmental pillar within this field of study. Southern African academic society became a global leader on the topic. Researchers such as Warchol (United States) and Herbig (South Africa) are rated as amongst the top ten researchers in the world in terms of environmental crimes, but much more recognition for their rural crime research in Africa is needed.

Corruption

Corruption in Africa is a critical challenge and obstacle for rural communities and is endemic in society. Inequality in rural Africa is a significant contributor to this phenomenon and places emphasis. Corruption is not limited to government tenders but is also evident as public officials are involved in criminal activities in many African countries. Claiming a 10 per cent levy on tenders (such as contracts, usually with governments) has become a normality in business deals. Many officials are reported as being involved in corruption scandals in rural areas or those within the criminal justice system involved in crimes such as the illegal wildlife markets, livestock theft, copper theft and so on (see Bhengu, 2021).

Conclusion

Globally, there has been increased scholarly attention to rural criminology. Unfortunately, rural criminology in Africa, as a field of study, is still in its infancy and is dispersed across several academic fields. Whilst there are several interdisciplinary scholarly articles that have covered several topics that are in the domain of rural criminology, few have exclusively tackled them from a rural criminological perspective. Also, most of the scholarly articles are dominated by few countries with most emanating from South Africa, Kenya, Nigeria and a few from Ethiopia. Yet there is evidence that rural crime and criminality is diverse and contextual. Thus, there is a need for increased studies on rural crime from other regions, countries and communities in Africa, especially the central and northern parts. Likewise, there is a need to extend rural criminological studies of the impact of global issues on rural crimes in Africa.

Suggested readings

Bhengu, L. (2021) 'Cops bust for stock theft after Hawks act on tip-off received in wake of Brendin Horner murder', 15 July, *News24*, Available from: https://www.news24.com/news24/southafrica/news/cops-bust-for-stock-theft-after-hawks-act-on-tip-off-received-in-wake-of-brendin-horner-murder-20210714 [Accessed 29 November 2021].

Bunei, E., Auya, S. and Rono, J. (2016) 'Agricultural crime in Africa: Trends and perspectives', in J.F. Donnermeyer (ed) *The Routledge Handbook of Rural Criminology*, London: Routledge, pp. 119–26.

Clack, W. and Minnaar, A. (2018) 'Rural crime in South Africa: An exploratory review of "farm attacks" and stocktheft as the primary crimes in rural areas', *Acta Criminologica: Southern African Journal of Criminology*, 31(1): 103–35.

Grote, U. and Neubacher, F. (2016) 'Rural crime in developing countries: Theoretical framework, empirical findings, research needs', *SSRN Electronic Journal*, Availble from: https://doi.org/10.2139/ssrn.2756542

Masiola, R. and Tomei, R. (2015) 'A global crime and world hunger', in R. Masiola and R. Tomei (eds) *Law, Language and Translation*, Cham: Springer Nature, pp. 35–46.

McFann, S.C. and Pires, S.F. (2020) 'Taking stock in wildlife crime research: Trends and implications for future research', *Deviant Behavior*, 41(1): 118–35.

Warchol, G. (2017) *Exploiting the Wilderness: An Analysis of Wildlife Crime*, Philadelphia, PA: Temple University Press.

80

Antarctica

Rebecca Kaiser and Rob White

Living and working in Antarctica means that the expeditioner is living and working in both an extreme and unusual environment (EUE) and an isolated and confined environment (ICE). Environments that fall into these categories exert stressors on the people within them and research has shown that these stressors alter these people's normal social interactions. A person's presence in an extreme, unusual, confined or isolated environment also shapes the nature of transgressions committed.

Whilst it is difficult to give a singular definition that encompasses all that can classify an environment as an EUE and/or an ICE, it has been suggested that an 'extreme' environment can be defined by its level of survivability. By this definition, such an environment is one that a human would be unable to survive in without some form of special training, equipment or supplies (see Suedfield, 2012). An 'unusual' environment is more complicated still to definitively classify but the term is most frequently applied when characterizing environments that differ greatly from the common experiences of those living in a modern, technologically advanced and primarily urban society.

An EUE/ICE is characterized by features that include physical parameters (such as temperature), psychological and social parameters (such as limited, restricted or enforced social interactions) and technological parameters (such as reliance upon modern technology). Isolated and confined environments are generally environments where the person is remote from their home and separate from any people who do not also share the space, restricted to that geographical location, and incapable of easily entering or exiting the location even in the event of an emergency. Many of the aspects that define an isolated and confined environment also characterize them as an extreme and unusual environment but the two do not necessarily always overlap.

An Antarctic station qualifies as a permanent, long term, extreme and unusual, confined and isolated environment. Humans do not have the capability of surviving the Antarctic environment alone. Inhospitable weather conditions and extremely low native temperatures make it highly unlikely that a human could survive long enough to build some form of shelter, somehow melt the ice into water or turn one of the few native animal species into a suitable dinner. From a technological standpoint, a person is only safe from their environment in Antarctica if they are inside an artificial structure; as such they are completely reliant on this structure to keep them alive.

Psychosocial research from the Arctic, the Antarctic and space stations has shown that the interpersonal tension caused by being in an isolated and confined environment increases as stress increases, significantly and continuously (see Bennett, 2016). There is also mention of social monotony and increased levels of anger, irritability, depression and insomnia. As well, it is highly challenging to avoid trespassing on another's personal space in Antarctica. Research has identified that crowding and violations of territory or personal space are significant factors in environmentally triggered aggression.

Barring some 'big' crimes that have made both international news and are referenced in scientific literature, there has not been a great deal published about criminal and/or harmful behaviour involving Antarctic expeditioners. Part of the reason for this may well be the perpetuated attitude of secretiveness that has been found on Antarctic bases.

Whilst sexual harassment against women in Antarctica has dominated recent research interest (see Nash and Neilson, 2020), other forms of transgression have also featured in research and media accounts. For example, it has been found that criminal offences such as assault are routinely dealt with by a refusal to renew the expeditioners contract or research funding. Transgressive activities also include alleged cases of animal abuse and cruelty by construction workers, such as beating gulls with sticks and chasing penguins off cliff tops, alongside instances of racing motorbikes through environmentally fragile areas. Serious alcohol use and some illicit drug use has also been recounted, as has the prevalence of alcohol-fuelled misbehaviour.

Expeditioner accounts talk about aggressive behaviours such as rock throwing, pool cue beatings, threats of death and destruction of personal property via snow ploughs. Medical drug theft, marijuana growing and narcotics sales were once well-known past times. Also mentioned was the sexual culture that considered the frequent changing of bed partners as an accepted norm. There are anecdotal stories of frequent instances of sexism, racism, bullying, vandalism, corporate malfeasance, arson and animal abuse (see Kaiser, 2021).

As people who reside within an isolated and confined environment surrounded by a greater extreme and unusual environment, expeditioners are inescapably part of the community of the base. Antarctic personnel, owing to their physical and geographical isolation, cannot easily enter or leave their environment, even in the event of an emergency, and all activities (work, recreational, social, personal) must occur within this restricted area and surrounded by their community.

Generally, there is increased tolerance for behaviours of a transgressive nature, one that exceeds what the expeditioners would have tolerated at home (see Mueller and Adler, 2004). When the people of a community must rely on each other for their very survival, it is understandable that the relationships that are established form quickly and deeply. This shared experience alongside the continued presence and reliance on each other for the continued ability to survives forges a community dynamic that is uniquely suited to engendering a heightened tolerance for transgression and similarly unique punishments to deter behaviour that threatens the homeostasis needed for the community to function successfully to ensure the community's continued survival.

Those found to have breached the line of acceptable behaviour are answerable to the community as they would be in other areas of conduct. The two common punishments doled out to those who breach the established behavioural norms are to isolate the offender or to 'other' them. Othering is the process where those who are seen to be the law-abiding, trustworthy and respectable majority of a group or community differentiates some of its members as being less, different or somehow incompatible. The result of this othering process in an Antarctic base leaves the expeditioner treated as an outsider. This othering process also happens for behaviours that are seen as a breach of more benign social norms.

The second method of punishment identified is isolation of the offender. Whilst social exclusion is an aspect of othering, actual physical isolation is both an aspect of the othering as punishment and a punishment in and of itself. Physical isolation as punishment is enforced across a spectrum of severity by expeditioners. Expeditioners may be isolated *from* certain areas (for example, the bar) or isolated *to* certain areas (such as their room).

Harmful actions and behaviours can go unreported and unacknowledged if they are not viewed as exceeding the acceptable normalcy of everyday life living on an Antarctic base. Likewise, instances of transgression may be kept from official record under the prerogative of 'What happens on the ice, stays on the ice', the Antarctic equivalent of 'what happens in Vegas, stays in Vegas'.

Intrinsically linked to heightened tolerance is the silence employed to maintain the homeostatic equilibrium of the community to ensure its continued optimal functioning, without which the lives of the community living in one of the harshest environments in the world would be threatened. Whilst some events, problems or behaviours are shared with anyone and everyone, others are kept strictly between expeditioners. For example, maintaining silence in circumstances such as bickering or 'drunken shenanigans' is of a lesser concern than more serious incidents that a station leader deals with, for the sake of maintaining community harmony.

These different layers of silence are of a protective nature, frequently employed to shield an expeditioner from the potential unpleasant repercussions arising from their behaviour. The increased acceptance and tolerance of transgression amongst Antarctic expeditioners, and the layered and complex silence under which the community operates, circumscribe both definitions of and responses to transgression.

In this extreme environment, isolated to their community, the residents who inhabit Antarctic bases thus find themselves tolerating and accepting crimes and harms that they would not allow if they were not in Antarctica. The expeditioners do this because they rely on their community for survival in this extreme, unusual, isolated and confined environment. It is the tight bonds, the comradery and solidarity of the community of Antarctic bases that ensures the safety of its residents; the unravelling of these bonds compromises this safety. The maintenance of these bonds, at least partially, lays in tolerance, acceptance and silence.

Suggested readings

Bennett, J. (2016) 'How Antarctic isolation affect the mind', 15 September, blog, *Canadian Geographic*, Available from: https://www.canadiangeographic.ca/article/how-antarctic-isolation-affects-mind [Accessed 27 February 2021].

Kaiser, R. (2021) 'Social dynamics of expeditioner transgression in Antarctica'. Criminology Honours Thesis, School of Social Sciences, University of Tasmania, Australia.

Mueller, G. and Adler, F. (2004) 'No crime in no-man's land? An Antarctic exploration', *Criminal Justice Studies*, 17(4): 405–9.

Nash, M. and Neilson, H. (2020) 'Gendered power relations and sexual harassment in Antarctic science in the age of #MeToo', *Australian Feminist Studies*, 35(105): 261–76.

Suedfeld, P. (2012) 'Extreme and unusual environments: Challenges and responses', in S.D. Clayton (ed) *The Oxford Handbook of Environmental and Conservation Psychology*, New York: Oxford University Press, pp. 348–71.

Figure 3: Political map of Antarctica[2]

81

Asia

Alistair Harkness, Joseph F. Donnermeyer and Qingli Meng

Asia is both the largest continent geographically and the most populated with over 4.5 billion people (60 per cent of the world's population), dominated by the economies and populations of both China and India. The average rural population of the 48 Asian countries is 38.2 per cent, although this varies enormously: from the city-state of Singapore with no rural population, to Sri Lanka with 81 per cent of residents residing in rural locations. There is, indeed, enormous diversity across the countries which constitute Asia, as well as diversity across regions within a country such as China – socially, economically, politically, religiously, culturally and geographically.

With Asia's unique dimensions of size and diversity, it is unsurprising that there are no single texts which assess rural crime and victimization across the continent as a whole. There are, though, locational specific studies which address a variety of topics such as the spatial distribution of rural crime mapping, child labour, green crime and violence against women in rural India; juvenile crime in rural Vietnam; lethal violence in rural Cambodia; juvenile delinquency, gangs, violence against women, women trafficking, law enforcement, drugs, corruption and land use expropriation in rural China; violence against women in rural Sri Lanka; women trafficking and child abuse in rural Thailand; drugs in Golden Triangle areas; and so on.

Many of the empirical studies accessible with a Google Scholar search are rural-urban comparative works and mostly all in English, owing to a large extent to the conventions of academic publishing. Another disconnect exists between China and the outside world because of the technical inaccessibility of Google in China. A key issue, then, is the need to develop the capacity for further Asian theoretical and empirical studies specifically on rural criminological issues – across regions, across countries or offering a holistic Asian continent approach. Donnermeyer's edited *International Handbook of Rural Criminology* (2016) has only three of its 42 chapters with a focus on

Asia: the unevenness of this geographic representation is a regret he expresses in the introduction to the volume.

Though the discipline of rural criminology is thriving in some parts of the world, there are many criminal justice issues worthy of greater exploration in a rural Asian context. For instance, the abolition of capital punishment has been a trend around the world, although not so throughout Asia: only ten Asian countries have abolished the death penalty. Most executions globally occur in Asia, with China the most active user of this punishment. There exists some scholarship aimed at explaining this global disparity, but more is necessary. It is worth considering, too, that China is the only country that has capital punishment for white-collar crimes (see Braithwaite, 2014).

'Asian Criminology'

The table of contents of the *Handbook of Asian Criminology* (refer to Liu et al, 2013) gives an indication as to the diversity of types of crime, responses to crime and the position of victims and offenders across and within Asia. Whilst chapters are neither deliberately nor overtly focused on the rural, there are subtle overtones of 'rural' within much of the scholarship: for instance, cybercrime victimization is not restricted to urban areas; and drug and human traffickers can and do take advantage of remote borders to limit detection or take advantage of corruption. In China, the problem of 'left behind children' has a significant rural dimension. Rural labourers have migrated to urban locations since the mid-1980s for employment. On many occasions, children have been left in the care of grandparents or extended families in their source regions and rural parents living in urban locations only return to visit their children occasionally. These conditions facilitate the formation of delinquent behaviours and delinquent cliques.

Because of the ethnocentric Western nature of much of social science scholarship — and this includes criminology most certainly — there have been relatively recent attempts to 'decolonize' the discipline (refer to Moosavi, 2019), although there is not unanimous support for this endeavour. Nevertheless, this action has manifested itself in the emergence of the sub-fields of 'Asian Criminology' (notably by Liu) and Southern Criminology in an effort to spotlight significant and culturally different interpretations of criminology and criminal justice with continent-specific attention.

Some key developments in criminological studies in Asia — generally and not especially with a rural focus — include the creation in 2009 of the Asian Criminological Society and the launch of the *Asian Journal of Criminology*. There are also country-specific society's such as the India Society of Criminology.

Across the Asian continent, rural criminology as a specific area of focus is yet to enter an embryonic (let alone infancy) stage. In China, for example, literature on rural crime is either scattered or published mostly in Chinese and is mostly focused on a narrow scope of rural crime issues. Furthermore, there is discrepancy between the current rural-focused criminological and criminal justice literature about China and the assimilation of Chinese studies within criminology and criminal justice topics of both a comparative nature and an international interest, especially offered in English.

The combinations of disconnection, discrepancy and deficiency in Asian rural criminology leaves significant space for rural scholars to contribute to the expansion of academic scholarship. Amongst the very many universities in China that have affiliated rural research institutes, none of them are on a trajectory of rural criminological study. In some geographical regions, certain types of crime could be quite concerning, but less so in other areas: that is, there exists spatial variations and thus explanations of the same crime patterns within different provinces and regions could be different.

By way of contrast, the only Asian nation in the top ten on the Fragile (formerly 'Failed') States Index in 2021 is Afghanistan, and research has been stymied. As a consequence of a 20-year war and the re-emergence of the Taliban in power in 2021, it is unlikely that a culture of research and scientific discovery will similarly re-emerge for the foreseeable future.

Borders

Borders, by way of their very political rather than geographical nature, are oftentimes differentially interpreted. For instance, in the context of trade and Australia's role within the region and involvement with the Association of Southeast Asian Nations (ASEAN), a former Australian Prime Minister declared that Australia was a part of Asia. There were mixed views on this sentiment.

What we do know, more or less, is that Asia shares a border at its northwest with Europe (at the Ural Maintains); with Africa (the Red Sea, the Gulf of Suez and the Suez Canal); and with Oceania (in the Malay Archipelago). Internally, across such a diverse continent with 48 countries, borders both physical and political can provide opportunities for rural offending to occur. Some of these borders are incredibly contentious, and include: the Senkaku (Diaoyu) islands in the East China Sea; the Kashmir border between India and Pakistan; the Korean Peninsula and the divide between North Korea and South Korea; and the 'border' between Taiwan and the Republic of China.

An example of the intersect between borders, the environment and criminality comes from Moreh in Manipur, on the Indian side of the Myanmar border in India's remote northeast. Notwithstanding a ban imposed by the Myanmar government in 2014 on the exporting of old-growth teak logs, Moreh is a bi-directional smuggling hub for drugs, gold and firearms into India from Myanmar and for precursor chemicals for drugs, and wildlife and exotic flora into Myanmar.

State crime and harm

Many places throughout Asia are rapidly urbanizing, to a large extent because of increasing wealth and a burgeoning middle class – and this can lead to illegal behaviour and harm. Whilst the elimination of poverty should always be welcomed, it does produce a number of challenges. For example, economic growth creates construction booms with high demand for glass and concrete, both of which require certain grades of sand. With an insufficient quantity of legally obtainable sand available, supply and demand economics has led to sand being illegally extracted leading to the degradation of riverbeds, canals and beaches. Another by-product of this illegal mining is the corruption of public officials and underpayment or non-payment of royalties to governments for mineral extraction.

Figure 4: Political map of Asia[3]

In China, land use policy and land expropriation have led to 'rent-seeking' opportunities for all levels of government officials, and at the village level in particular (see Meng's chapter 22 in Donnermeyer, 2016). As well, consumer preferences by the middle class and the wealthy for exotic foods and animal by-products for making traditional medicines has increased illegal poaching and smuggling from countries in places such as Africa to various Asian localities.

In early 2021, the military in Myanmar (formally Burma) overtook the democratically elected government of Aung San Suu Kyi in a coup. Since, the economy is suffering and there are disturbing reports of extra-judicial killings and mass arrests. Circumstances are particularly grim for the Karen people who mostly reside in rural places on the Myanmar–Thailand border. Many similar examples can also be found in other parts of Asia. For example, Muslim ranchers living in India who raise cows may be attacked by Hindus vigilantes.

Suggested readings

Braithwaite, J. (2014) 'Crime in Asia: Toward a better future', *Asian Criminology*, 9: 65–75.

Donnermeyer, J.F. (2016) *The Routledge International Handbook of Rural Criminology*, London: Routledge, chapters 5, 22 and 40.

Liu, J. (2009) 'Asian Criminology: Challenges, opportunities, and directions', *Asian Journal of Criminology*, 4: 1–9.

Liu, J., Jou, S. and Hebenton, B. (eds) (2013) *Handbook of Asian Criminology*, New York: Springer.

Moosavi, L. (2019) 'A friendly critique of "Asian Criminology" and "Southern Criminology"', *British Journal of Criminology*, 59: 257–75.

82

Europe

Gorazd Meško and Matt Bowden

Perhaps it was Emile Durkheim who was the first rural criminologist in Europe when he described mechanical societies as small, homogenous, traditional people controlling each other using informal social control mechanisms. He also delineated organic societies that are big, heterogeneous and where people are alienated from each other. This is presumably the first social science work on the divide between the rural and urban.

There has been a considerable change since Durkheim's passing – mass migration from the 'old' world continued into the early twentieth century, swelling populations in cities in the 'new' worlds of the United States, of Australia and in Europe. We can only imagine how he would feel if he could witness the blurred and complex nature of the urban and rural divide in these contemporary globalized times. Rural criminology has in Europe, as elsewhere, been slow in formation given the focus of the social sciences on the problems of crime that we have associated with urbanization.

Since 2000, there have been research projects and publications on rural perspectives, discussing rural criminology, crime, victimization, fear of crime, policing and crime prevention and reflections on rural criminology. These contributions have utlized a wide variety of theoretical approaches and methodologies. The multidisciplinary backgrounds of rural criminologists working in Europe include sociology, law, geography, safety and security studies and psychology ought to be noted; and the potential exists for transdisciplinary perspectives and approaches to emerge especially in the area of security studies. This stems from considerable work in areas of the natural and computer sciences on diverse areas such as environmental sustainability, food security and critical infrastructure protection such as cyberattacks. In Europe, the European Union invests heavily in security research under its Horizon Europe programme.

The most comprehensive work on rural crime, safety and security in rural settings with a European contextualization thus far was published by Ceccato (2016). Ceccato and a co-author also presented preventative activities in the fields of youth alcohol abuse, addiction and violence in rural Sweden. Also, a reflection on the future challenges of rural criminology research was presented by Meško (2020). Amongst others, Mouhanna (see chapter 5 in Mawby and Yarwood, 2011) discussed the misperception of safety in rural environments and the false idyll of the countryside. The work of Smith and Byrne (2019) presents the most complete picture of rural crimes in England, emphasizing poaching, hare cursing, agrochemical theft, theft of solar panels, heritage crime, illegal off-roading, modern slavery, cybercrime and the use of drones in rural contexts.

Green criminology and rural criminology, metaphorically, share DNA with each other. This is because many environmental harms occur in rural areas that are remote from the regulatory institutions of governance. The wrecking of the natural environment itself is a social harm that has major consequences for present and future generations and their access to natural resources. An example of European rural criminological research here is Eman and Meško's (2021) research on the problem of water governance, water crimes and the relation between green and rural criminology in Slovenia. Water courses transect territories and borders making it an international and geo-political concern.

Mawby, in the first decade of the twenty-first century, was one of the first European authors to discuss the myths and realities of rural policing. His research continued jointly with other researchers in the next decade, studying specifics of rural policing and characteristics of a countryside constabulary (see chapter 2 of Mawby and Yarwood, 2011). As a part of a national project on local safety and security in Slovenia, Eman and Bulovec have studied rural crime and rural policing in the Slovenian region of Pomurje, and Wooff has conducted a comprehensive work on policing in the countryside in Scotland.

A conference on rural perspectives of safety, security and rural criminology in Central and Eastern Europe held online in 2021 from Ljubljana, Slovenia, opened new avenues of research and partnerships in rural criminological research. Keynote speeches considered the development of rural criminology and the importance of the development of rural criminological thought, a research project on rural safety and security in Slovenia – towards rural criminology, policing in rural environments, perception of (in)security in rural settings, case studies of crime in regions of Eastern Europe and the use of geographic information system mapping in studying reported rural crime.

Other efforts to develop rural criminology in Central and Eastern Europe have been noticed in a special issue of the journal *Criminal Investigation and Criminology* (originally *Revija za kriminalistiko in kriminologijo*), including discussions on rural criminological perspectives, emphasizing the importance of criminology of place and safety and security of rural peoples; social ties, solidarity and threat perception of rural inhabitants; right to security in local communities; perception of security; police officers and their perception of security threats; and social processes in neighbourhoods.

A number of future challenges for rural criminological scholarship in Europe have been identified by Meško (2020). The first is the need for comprehensive European studies on rural crime, delinquency, victimization and social control perspectives. These studies ought to elaborate on issues pertaining to migration, racism and hate crimes in rural areas, where there are glaring gaps in knowledge. Cybercrime and its potential risks to rural populations, given their isolation and the need for education and awareness, also warrant attention. In addition, the question of geo-politics and borders in Europe is critical given that they transect rural areas, often cutting off rural communities from one another, as in the case of the Balkans and between Ireland and Northern Ireland.

Europe is as culturally and linguistically diverse today as it ever was. The European Union, which covers only part of the land mass of Europe, officially recognizes 24 languages. Therefore, to summarize the breadth and depth of rural criminology in Europe is a challenging one. A challenge is, indeed, being restricted to scholarship written in the English language, as it excludes informed perspectives in various other European languages. It is a critical challenge for European criminology to encourage non-English speaking researchers to publish their work in international publications to contribute to an increasing opus of rural criminological research.

A concordance analysis of the texts on rural criminology in Europe shows that rural criminology in Europe is described by specific conceptual frameworks including perspectives of rural, countryside, remoteness, social harm, crime, offender, victim, fear of crime, environment, pollution, conservativeness, organized crime, drugs, violence, hate crimes, racism, migration, place, safety, security, crime prevention, rural policing, 'country bobby', countryside constabulary, social processes, ways of life, social capital, economic capital, symbolic capital, governance and so on. It looks quite similar to 'urban criminology', but it is a significant shift from it in terms of content because it takes into consideration specific social processes, relations between people, governance and social control perspectives.

Two key developments have occurred in recent years that will tackle the gaps in knowledge identified here. The first is the establishment of the European Society of Criminology Working Group on Rural Criminology. This will provide a critical focal point for collating these diverse perspectives. A second development is the formation of the Bristol University Press book series *Research in Rural Crime* and the Routledge *Studies in Rural Criminology* series, both of which serve as platforms for the publication of monographs

Figure 5: Political map of Europe[4]

and edited collections that will harness and act as a suitable repository for ongoing and new European perspectives.

Suggested readings
Ceccato, V. (2016) *Rural Crime and Community Safety*, New York: Routledge.
Eman, K. and Meško, G. (2021) 'Water crimes and governance: The Slovenian Perspective', *International Criminology*, 1: 208–19.
Mawby, R. and Yarwood, R. (2011) *Rural Policing and Policing the Rural: A Constable Countryside?*, London: Routledge.
Meško, G. (2020) 'Rural criminology – A challenge for the future', *European Journal of Crime, Criminal Law and Criminal Justice*, 28(1): 3–13.
Smith, K. and Byrne, R. (2019) 'Horizon scanning rural crime in England', *Crime Prevention and Community Safety*, 21: 231–45.

83

North America

Denisse Román-Burgos, Joseph F. Donnermeyer and Rick Ruddell

The development of the social sciences in Canada, the United States and Mexico and other countries in Central America has been heavily influenced by these countries' European counterparts. This common root can be traced back to their colonial histories, but also to the constant waves of European immigrants after they gained independence, which contributed to shaping the populations in these three countries. Intellectuals and scholars were also part of these European immigration waves, especially in the context of the two world wars.

To some extent, these countries can be considered settler societies; that is, their histories are replete with the decimation and ongoing marginalization of the Indigenous and Black populations by European immigrants. This shared past informs current responses to crime, as these countries adopted the laws and justice systems of their colonizing nations. To a considerable extent the criminological research carried out in North America today also displays a distinctively Western orientation and has focused primarily on urban crime and justice.

Canada

Canada's rural population has been decreasing for decades, but the overall rural property and violent crime rates have been increasing and are now higher than the city rates, according to a study by Perrault (2019). Despite those trends, studies of rural crime and justice have traditionally been relegated to the periphery of criminological research.

A review of the historical literature shows that issues such as access to justice for rural peoples, rural policing and delivering community correctional services outside the cities were often addressed indirectly. Grygier's review of the criminological research of that era, for example, did not cite any exclusively rural research. Grygier's review also found that most crime-related studies were carried out by law professors, sociologists and social workers, although historians such as Marquis also increased understandings of the economic, political and social arrangements that shape responses to urban and rural crime.

The focus of Canadian scholars has often been on crime and the operations of justice systems, rather than developing theoretical explanations for rural crime. Hagan's work on sentencing disparities for Indigenous peoples in the 1980s, for example, increased awareness of their over-representation in Canada's justice system. Scholars such as Griffiths, Linden, Clairmont and Murphy built on that seminal work by examining Indigenous policing and rural justice systems in government-funded studies throughout the 1990s, and they remain active researchers. Studies of officers policing Indigenous communities have made a significant contribution to understanding law enforcement in these places and their work has served as the foundation for subsequent studies conducted by many others. Since 2010, there has been an increase in the number of Canadian scholars who have published extensively on responses to rural crime.

The United States

There were a number of rural criminological studies in the United States throughout each decade of the twentieth century, even though the literature before the 1990s was scattered and mostly descriptive. Representative of this period was the work of Clinard comparing characteristics of rural and urban offenders, Crank focusing on distinctive rural policing styles and Lee examining fear of crime amongst rural residents. One notable development before the 1990s was a cluster of studies about the impact of rapid population and economic development in energy boomtowns of the rural west by Krannich, Wilkinson and other rural sociologists employed at various land-grant universities and housed within Colleges of Agriculture. The late 1980s and early 1990s also saw a second cluster arise with the publication of a number of studies related to farm crime, again by rural sociologists (see chapter 1 in Donnermeyer, 2016).

A hallmark event in rural criminology's development was the publication in 1996 of *Crime and Policing in Rural and Small Town America* by Weisheit, Falcone and Wells (2016) from the Illinois State University. The book itself was revised twice over a ten-year period and was instrumental in synthesizing the scattered rural crime literature and initiating an identity that drew together equally scattered rural scholars who were members of the American Society of Criminology and the Academy of Criminal Justice Science.

Following on from this work was the development of three criminological theories with substantial rural roots. The first, which was actually concurrent with the publication of the first edition of the Weisheit et al book, was the development of primary socialization theory by Oetting and colleagues to examine drug use and misuse amongst rural youth. The second was the work of Lee and associates on civic community theory, which has similarities to social disorganization theory but was developed specifically to explain rates of violent crime in rural settings. The third was a focus on violence against rural women based on a theory known as male peer support theory, led by DeKeseredy and associates (see chapter 1 in Donnermeyer, 2016).

Since the third edition of the Weisheit et al book, released in 2006, rural criminology has grown to the point that there is now a Division of Rural Criminology in the American Society of Criminology. This twenty-first century cadre of rural criminologists conducts research in a wide variety of topics, including farm crime, fear of crime, environmental crime, drug use and trafficking, interpersonal violence and the criminological impacts of energy development on rural boomtowns. As well, their approach to this varied subject matter is now more theoretically and critically informed.

Mexico and Central America

Unlike the influences of the English in research and theoretical work conducted in the United States and Canada, criminology in Mexico was deeply influenced in its beginnings by the Italian School. The first professional criminologist, Quiroz, defined the field as a science concerned with explaining the causes of 'anti-social behaviour'. Fourteen years later, Rodríguez published *Criminología*, a book that followed the path traced by his mentor, Quiroz, and consolidated the discipline within the fields of psychology and law. Similarly to Canada, Mexican criminologists have mostly focused on crime and how justice systems operate, rather than pursuing further theoretical specialization. *Clinical Criminology*, another publication by Rodríguez, invited criminologists to interdisciplinary collaboration and to privilege a psychological approach, whilst the work of Palacios encouraged an approach based on the criminal law.

Mexico has experienced an increase in crime and violence since the turn of the twenty-first century, which has intensified since 2006 with the militarization of public security and the use of the armed forces to fight criminal organizations, known as the 'war on drugs'. Criminological theory, however, has not followed a comparable development nor increased specialization but has remained largely an applied discipline whose practitioners work as public servants, in district attorneys' offices or prisons. Following this trend, criminologists' doctoral dissertations completed in the second decade of the twenty-first century have focused on large-scale public security, improving social reintegration and discussing crime prevention in the context of Mexican towns and cities.

Figure 6: Political map of North America[5]

The rise and diversification of crime and violence since 2006 have become regular themes for anthropologists and sociologists. The extensive work of social anthropologists (for example, see Azaola, 2018) on prisons, crime, national security policies and human rights has been at the forefront. Similarly, scholarship on drug trafficking in rural Mexico opened the field for further anthropological and sociological studies concerned with the consequences of the 'war on drugs': for instance, on violence perpetrated by criminal organizations; the formation of civilian armed groups; and Indigenous movements. Sociologists and anthropologists have focused on the violence perpetrated against Central American migrants, human rights violations and civil society responses to crime and violence. Legal anthropologists, on the other hand, have studied customary law and practices in Indigenous contexts. Crimes and violence perpetrated against Indigenous peoples in the context of the 'war on drugs' have also become a common theme for this field.

The turn of the twenty-first century in Central America was preceded by the end of the civil wars in El Salvador, Guatemala and Honduras, a considerable increase in migration and spiralling gang violence (see Moodie, 2010). Criminology in Central American countries has followed a similar path to that of Mexico and has consolidated itself as an applied field. However, violence before and after the civil wars in Central America has also been a topic on which anthropological research has focused, for example on structural and political violence, genocide in Guatemala, human rights, human remains, gang violence, securitization and law enforcement.

Summary

There is a significant variation in the magnitude and types of rural crime throughout North American scholarship related to these offenses; nonetheless, rural criminology remained on the periphery of the criminological and sociological literature until the 1990s. Since that time, an understanding of rural crime issues has been bolstered by the publication of government-funded reports and through the groundbreaking efforts of a growing number of rural scholars and the establishment of organizations – such as the International Society for the Study of Rural Crime and the American Society of Criminology's Division of Rural Crime – that are creating a supportive environment for rural scholars and the dissemination of their findings in North America.

Suggested readings
Azaola, E. (2018) 'Violent crimes committed by juveniles in Mexico', in K. Carrington, R. Hogg, J. Scott and M. Sozzo (eds) *The Palgrave Handbook on Criminology and the Global South*, London: Palgrave Macmillan, pp. 551–67.
Donnermeyer, J.F. (ed) (2016) *The Routledge International Handbook of Rural Criminology*, London: Routledge.
Moodie, E. (2010) *El Salvador in the Aftermath of Peace: Crime, Uncertainty and the Transition to Democracy*, Philadelphia, PA: The University of Pennsylvania Press.
Perrault, S. (2019) *Police-Reported Crime in Rural and Urban Areas in the Canadian Provinces, 2017*, Ottawa: Canadian Centre for Justice Statistics.
Weisheit, R.A., Falcone, D.N. and Wells, L.E. (2006) *Crime and Policing in Rural and Small-Town America* (3rd edn), Long Grove, IL: Waveland Press.

84

Oceania

Alistair Harkness, Kyle Mulrooney and Danielle Watson

Although there exists some ambiguity over the precise constitution of Oceania, given the scattering of islands across the Pacific Ocean, it is broadly accepted that the region comprises Australia and the islands to Australia's immediate north, northeast and east contained within the sub-regions of Melanesia, Micronesia and Polynesia. The region is often delineated between Near Oceania and Remote Oceania.

Colonialism and colonial legacies in Oceania

Australia (in 1788) and New Zealand (in 1840) were the first European colonies with a physical, ongoing presence in Oceania. The French established a South Pacific presence in Tahiti–Polynesia (1840) and New Caledonia (1853) as the region offered potential sea route ports of calls to Australia and New Zealand. Britain colonized Fiji in 1874, and between 1884 and 1900, with the emergence of Imperialist Germany, annexations throughout the South Pacific occurred by Britain, France and Germany.

Colonialism in Australia has brought about an ongoing struggle between Indigenous Australians and the colonizers. Contemporaneously, Indigenous Australians still struggle with issues such a lack of access to justice and other services and over-representation in the criminal justice system (see chapters by Chris Cunneen in Harkness et al, 2016; Harkness and White, 2021). In New Zealand, such impacts have similarly been felt by the Māori people. In both countries there exist a strong inter-relationship between social, economic and health inequalities and criminal justice system exposure, issues often exacerbated by remoteness and rurality.

Oceania was a strategic source of power for Western nations, geographically, during the twentieth century: notably for military purposes in the Pacific theatre of World War Two, and for atmospheric and underground nuclear testing. The effect of European colonization on Oceanic island nation states has had enormous impacts: though treatment of Indigenous peoples; culturally in terms of art, sport and language; and both the positive and negative outcomes of a tourism industry.

Various non-government organizations based in Australia and New Zealand maintain an ongoing presence and role in facilitating access to justice and delivery of justice services throughout the Oceanic region: Caratas Australia, for instance, supports a range of programmes in the Solomon Islands, Samoa and Fiji.

Rural criminological study in New Zealand and Australia

Scholarship pertaining to rurality and crime in New Zealand is yet to emerge, although there has been some work on rural policing specifically (such as by John Buttle et al, 2010). The publicly held literature on rural crime is almost entirely derived from the police themselves and insurance companies offering rural crime prevention advice, and from media reports of the incidence of rural crime. There is significant scope, therefore, for this gap in academic research to be addressed.

Along with the United States, Canada and the United Kingdom, Australia constitutes one of the 'big four' when it comes to rural criminology research theorizing and empirical research outputs. This is owing to the sheer amount of attention and work focusing on rural crime coming from these countries but is also a consequence, in part, of the prioritization of Western criminology and the traditional absence of attention to work outside this cannon.

Such studies in Australia, though, have been somewhat ad hoc, with a focus historically on localized case studies as opposed to broader bodies of research. That is not to understate the significance of some of the work, though. A very useful example is the 1989 work of O'Connor and Gray (1989) which offered a ground-breaking exploration of rural crime and victimization within a local context, and identification of particular social structures in rural places.

More recently, a series of edited collections have emerged with an Australian-centred rural criminology focus (see Barclay et al, 2007; Harkness et al, 2016; Harkness and White, 2021). Each of these volumes have adopted broader approaches to criminal offending and victimization, encompassing an array of cross-disciplinary and practitioner perspectives.

These contributions have also sought to dispel myths of a rural idyll whilst elucidating the extent of a range of matters such as violence, youth crime, Indigenous justice, drugs, sentencing, media representations of rural crime, access to justice and so on. In the twenty-first century, there has been a particular focus placed on farm crime by Australian-based researchers, notably Elaine Barclay in New South Wales and Queensland, Alistair Harkness in Victoria and Kyle Mulrooney in New South Wales. These collections have also attended to an array of criminal justice approaches: by police, the courts and corrections agencies.

The University of New England, based in Armidale in rural New South Wales, Australia, has a very long history in rural crime research and can be considered the birthplace of contemporary rural criminology owing in large part to the early pioneering work of Elaine Barclay, Pat Jobes and Joseph F. Donnermeyer. This university's leadership role in this space was solidified in November 2018 with the convening of an 'International rural crime and law conference', with national and international attendance.

This was strengthened further in September 2019 with the launch of the Centre for Rural Criminology, a rebadge and relaunch of the previous Centre for Rural Crime which was established in 2004. Australia is the home-base of the International Society for the Study of Rural Crime Incorporated: established in March 2019, the society serves as the epicentre of international rural crime networking, uniting those with research interests in rural crime and rural society.

Rural criminological study in the South Pacific

The South Pacific is comprised of small island developing states, many of which would adhere to classifications of rural spaces based on geographic location, population sizes, gross domestic product and development status. Though rurality is a prominent and common factor for all states (more so the multi-island jurisdictions) across the region, the South Pacific has neither been a primary focus for rural criminologists nor have aspects of rurality taken precedence in other criminological discourses about the region.

Focused research aimed at developing understandings about rurality and crime in the South Pacific context are not visible in existing literature. Apart from the findings of donor-funded projects on the vulnerabilities of rural livelihoods to climate change, the South Pacific remains largely absent from rural criminology scholarship. Aspects of rural criminology, however, are visible in cross/multi-disciplinary accounts of crime, criminality, issues of access to justice and responses to other social problems (see Forsyth et al, 2020).

Though not self-identified ruralists, island criminologists have acknowledged the need to extend the criminological imagination to re-imagine contextualizations of rurality in non-Western contexts. They draw attention to the inapplicability of applying Western models to understand crime in contexts far removed from those which inform ways of thinking about rurality and crime.

Figure 7: Political map of Oceania[6]

Increased occurrences of organized and transnational crime in rural spaces across the South Pacific, as well as international prioritization of improved access to justice for women and girls, particularly those in outer islands in multi-island jurisdictions, have drawn attention to the lack of scholarship on crime and victimization. Though not currently the case, international emphasis on the criticality of responding to human–social, physical, economic and environmental vulnerabilities in less developed countries, as well as the expansion of the rural criminology agenda, will likely prompt increased focus on the application of a rural criminological lens to research on the South Pacific.

Suggested readings
Barclay, E., Donnermeyer, J.F., Scott, J. and Hogg, R. (eds) (2007) *Crime in Rural Australia*, Sydney: The Federation Press.
Buttle, J., Fowler, C. and Williams, M.W. (2010) 'The impact of rural policing on the private lives of New Zealand police officers', *International Journal of Police Science & Management*, 12(4): 596–606.

Forsyth, M., Dinnen, S. and Hukula, F. (2020) 'A case for a public Pacific criminology?', in K. Henne and R. Shah (eds) *Routledge Handbook of Public Criminologies*, London: Routledge, pp. 163–78.

Harkness, A., Harris, B. and Baker, D. (eds) (2016) *Locating Crime in Context and Place: Perspectives on Regional, Rural and Remote Australia*, Sydney: The Federation Press.

Harkness, A. and White, R. (eds) (2021) *Crossroads of Rural Crime: Representations and Realities of Transgression in the Australian Countryside*, Bingley: Emerald.

O'Connor, M.E. and Gray, D.E. (1989) *Crime in a Rural Community*, Sydney: The Federation Press.

85

South America

Vania Ceccato and Monica Perez

Criminology in South America is growing but, like its North American counterpart, the discipline is highly urban-centric. From the seminal article by del Olmo (1999) to more recent works on the subject, the word 'rural' is hardly mentioned, if at all. The discipline that was once considered a European import has evolved to become multidisciplinary, yet it neglects criminogenic conditions outside the urban realm.

There are an array of criminogenic conditions and complexities that characterize the countryside of this vast region of the world, with its 14 countries and more than 430 million inhabitants, one quarter of them living in rural areas. Whilst it is important to reflect upon South America as a region and its commonalities in terms of rural crime, it is essential to recognize the risk of over-simplification when conveying the idea of a rural South American criminology. Despite these countries' shared historical paths, the region is far from being homogenous: countries differ in size, population, penal codes, policing, criminal justice systems and, last but not least, the nature of rural crime.

Criminality in rural South America is complex, not only because of very different rates of rural populations: from Guyana with more than 73 per cent to Uruguay with less than five per cent. The political, economic and social histories of the regions within these countries also differ. The scarcity of criminological research and lack of systematic data available for analysis pose additional challenges to determining the scope, magnitude and characteristics of rural criminality in South America (see Jaramillo, 2016; Instituto Para el Desarrollo Rural de Sudamérica, 2019; Instituto de Pesquisa Econômica Aplicada, 2020).

Rural areas in South America are contested places: that is, places of conflict and violence. The roots of rural crime in South America are strongly linked with unequal and excluding societies. People in rural areas have suffered from political marginalization, dispossession of land, slavery, lack of control over governmental measures of land exploitation, use of violence and the destruction of their cultural and social organizations. These have been central issues since the conquest and colonization of this territory through the establishment of non-democratic regimes in the twentieth century (in Argentina, Bolivia, Brazil, Chile, Colombia, Paraguay, Venezuela and Uruguay), to the current dominance of major foreign economic and political powers over rural territories and lives. In many of these countries, rural violence has increased over the 2010s. For example, in Brazil, the largest country in South America, homicides in rural areas increased 75 per cent between 2007 and 2017, whilst in urban areas they increased 41 per cent. Land concentration, intensive exploitation of natural resources, organized crime – linked to smuggling and trafficking of drugs, cargo theft and large-scale migratory flows – are often associated with conflicts and lethal violence in rural areas.

Another salient criminological problem of this region is crime related, namely drug production and trafficking. The cultivation of coca bush, which involves mainly Colombia, Bolivia and Peru, declined over the period 2000–13, more than doubled over the period 2013–18 and declined again in 2019, though not by much (UNODC, 2021). In addition to crimes associated with illegal coca manufacturing and trading, drug production and trafficking have brought enormous costs in violence, particularly in homicides and forced displacement of farmers, but also in terms of increased corruption and inequality.

These crimes currently threaten the security of transit countries such as Brazil and Argentina. Drugs produced in South America mainly supply external demand. Apart from the use of cocaine in Brazil, the prevalence of drug use (of cannabis, opioids, opiates, amphetamines and ecstasy) in these countries is low. In Colombia, in particular, drug production and trafficking became associated in the 1980s with an armed conflict that has lasted for five decades. This conflict has had devastating consequences for people in rural areas, including random and targeted homicides, massacres, sexual violence, torture, kidnapping, extortion and child recruitment carried out by guerrillas and paramilitary groups, as well as by the country's military forces.

Criminology has identified the extensive and mostly legal extraction of natural resources as another major threat to rural South America. In addition to the destruction of the environment, in the form of deforestation, water pollution and loss of biodiversity, these activities have resulted in the illegal occupation of land, forced displacement of peoples (Indigenous and farmers), sexual exploitation of women, annihilation of local cultures and knowledge and the murder of Indigenous and rural people and leaders (see Goyes, 2021).

Violence against women constitutes a major societal problem in rural South America. In Brazil, Indigenous women in illegal gold-digging areas are particularly vulnerable to harassment and sexual violence, besides suffering the effects of toxic mercury. In Colombia, official reports reveal high rates of violence against rural women, often associated with armed conflict, the production of illicit drugs and narcotrafficking and illegal mining. These reports have especially documented violence against women leaders who seek to return to their land that is illegally occupied by armed groups. In Ecuador, official reports show that over 60 per cent of rural women have experienced some form of gender-based violence (see Edeby and San Sebastián, 2021). Although women and girls account for a smaller share of total homicides than men, they bear by far the greatest burden of family-related and intimate partner homicide. According to the 2019 UNODC Global Study on Homicide, the world average rate of feminicide was 1.3 per 100,000 women in 2017, whilst in the Americas the rate was 1.6 per 100,000 women, lower than the African (3.1) but higher than the European (0.7) or Asian (0.9) rates.

South American countries share several of the same challenges when investigating and prosecuting crimes in rural settings, associated with the extensive isolated areas where offenders can hide and weapons can be hidden, the absence of witnesses and the lack of technological tools (such as security cameras). Furthermore, police are often at the centre of controversy. In a ranking of countries by confidence in law and order, Latin American and Caribbean states exhibit the lowest confidence in the police in the world (see McCarthy, 2018), despite the fact that in rural areas trust was higher.

Despite being fragmented and often unacknowledged, essential criminological knowledge has been and is currently produced about rural South America. More evidence is available through annual reports about the current situation and conflicts related to the access to and restitution of the land (for example IPDRS reports), and in recent decades more specific groups of Indigenous peoples, farmers, women and afro-descendants have actively demanded their right to participate in decisions about the land and denounced the crimes against their environment and communities.

A first suggestion for future criminological research in South America is to include the dimension of rurality as a criterion of analysis. Currently, many national and multinational studies on violence do not differentiate between rural and urban areas or exclude rural areas altogether (such as the 'Victimization and Perception of Safety Survey' in Ecuador). Another issue that demands attention is the fact that many problems in South America transcend country frontiers. Many criminal activities are simultaneously present in several countries or connect several countries through the flow

Figure 8: Political map of South America[7]

of goods or individuals. To identify them is key to designing strategies of prevention and control that are specific to the crimes and the places where they occur.

Suggested readings

del Olmo, R. (1999) 'The development of criminology in Latin America', *Social Justice*, 26(2): 19–45.

Edeby, A. and San Sebastián, M. (2021) 'Prevalence and sociogeographical inequalities of violence against women in Ecuador: A cross-sectional study', *International Journal of Equity in Health*, 20(130), https://doi.org/10.1186/s12939-021-01456-9.

Goyes, D.R. (2021) 'Environmental crime in Latin America and Southern green criminology', *Oxford Research Encyclopedias: Criminology and Criminal Justice*, Oxford: Oxford University Press, https://doi.org/10.1093/acrefore/9780190264079.013.588.

Instituto Para el Desarrollo Rural de Sudamérica (2019) *Informe 2018. Acceso a la tierra y territorio en Sudamérica*, La Paz, Bolivia, Available from: https://www.sudamericarural.org/images/impresos/archivos/Informe-2018-IPDRS.pdf [Accessed 5 August 2021].

Instituto de Pesquisa Econômica Aplicada (2020) *Atlas da violencia do Campo*, Available from: https://www.ipea.gov.br/atlasviolencia/download/23/info grafico-atlas-da-violencia-no-campo [Accessed 3 August 2021].

Jaramillo, A. (ed) (2016) *Atlas Histórico de América Latina y el Caribe: Aportes para la decolonización pedagógica y cultural*, Estudios de Integración Latinoamericana, Universidad Nacional de Lanús, Argentina, Available from: http://atlaslatinoamericano.unla.edu.ar/assets/pdf/tomo1.pdf [Accessed 2 August 2021].

McCarthy, N. (2018) 'Where the global confidence in law and order is highest and lowest', 7 June, *Forbes*, Available from: https://www.forbes.com/sites/niallmccarthy/2018/06/07/where-global-confidence-in-law-and-order-is-highest-and-lowest-infographic/?sh=614ff9aa6eb2 [Accessed 12 August 2021].

Rocha García, R. (2011) *Las Nuevas Dimensiones del Narcotráfico en Colombia*, Oficina de las Naciones Unidas contra la Droga y el Delito (UNODC) y Ministerio de Justicia y del Derecho, Bogotá.

UNODC (United Nations Office on Drugs and Crime) (2021) *World Drug Report*, Available from: https://www.unodc.org/unodc/en/data-and-analysis/wdr2021.html.

Notes

1. Figure 2: Orthographic map of Africa with colonial borders, except Somalia. Available from: https://commons.wikimedia.org/wiki/File:Africa_(orthographic_projection).svg. This file is licensed under the Creative Commons Attribution-Share Alike 3.0 Unported license.
2. Figure 3: Antarctica (orthographic projection). Available from https://commons.wikimedia.org/wiki/File:Antarctica_(orthographic_projection).svg. Permission is granted under the terms of the GNU Free Documentation License, Version 1.2 or any later version published by the Free Software Foundation.
3. Figure 4: Asia (orthographic projection). Available from: https://commons.wikimedia.org/wiki/File:Asia_(orthographic_projection).svg. Permission is granted under the terms of the GNU Free Documentation License, Version 1.2 or any later version published by the Free Software Foundation.
4. Figure 5: Europe (orthographic projection). Available from https://commons.wikimedia.org/wiki/File:Europe_orthographic_Caucasus_Urals_boundary_(with_borders).svg. This map is ineligible for copyright and therefore in the public domain because it consists entirely of information that is common property and contains no original authorship.
5. Figure 6: North America (orthographic projection). Available from: https://commons.wikimedia.org/wiki/File:Location_North_America.svg. This file is licensed under the Creative Commons Attribution-Share Alike 3.0 Unported license.
6. Figure 7: Orthographic map of the Australasian part of Oceania: Australia, New Guinea, Island Melanesia, and New Zealand, but excluding the Maluccas. Available from: https://commons.wikimedia.org/wiki/File:Oceania_(orthographic_projection).svg. This file is licensed under the Creative Commons Attribution-Share Alike 3.0 Unported license.
7. Figure 8: South America (orthographic projection) Available from: https://commons.wikimedia.org/wiki/File:South_America_(orthographic_projection).svg. This file is licensed under the Creative Commons Attribution 3.0 Unported license.

Index

Page numbers in *italics* refer to figures.

A

access to justice 251–3
  accessible justice, definition 251
  Australia 338, 339
  Indigenous peoples 251, 338
  New Zealand 339
  people with disabilities 290–2
  right to access justice 251
  rule of law and 251
  rural barriers 252–3, 271
  rural barriers: impacts on rural victims 253
  rural citizens engaging with urban justice services 252–3
  traditional systems of justice 292
  urban/rural areas disparity 217
  virtual justice services 253
  women and girls 341
  see also legal representation; rural courts
Adler, Freda 18
Afghanistan 142, 143, 326
  Jirga 224
Africa 29, 198, 314, *318*
  agricultural/farm crimes 316
  bushmeat problem 103, 157
  colonialism 138, 314
  corruption 317
  domestic violence 315, 316
  environmental crimes 316–17
  exceptional/ordinary rural crimes 315
  female genital mutilation 315, 316
  languages and linguistics 314
  livestock theft 138–9, 314–15, 316
  organized crime 138–9, 316
  resource extraction 100
  rural criminological research 314–17
  Sahara Desert 119
  Sahel 119
  trophy hunting 158, 159, 160
  violence against women 315, 316
  violent crimes 314, 315–16
  violent extremism 119
  wildlife crime 316–17
Agnew, Robert 17
Agozino, B. 198, 199
Akers, Ronald 18
animal rights and welfare
  animal cruelty 134, 145, 152, 171, 172, 320
  animal rights activism 130–1
  animal rights debate 129–30, 131
  animal welfarism 172
  culls 209, 211
  'endangered', 'threatened', 'extinct' species 171
  factory farms 130–1
  Five Freedoms for Animal Welfare 134–5
  Humane Farming Association 130–1
  PETA (People for the Ethical Treatment of Animals) 130
  protection of endangered species 159, 172
  rural criminology and 131
  speciesism 170
  Universal Declaration of Animal Rights 134
  Universal Declaration of Animal Welfare 134
  wildlife/domesticated animals 170–1
  see also blood sports; hunting; trophy hunting; wildlife crime
anomie/normlessness 17, 38
Antarctica 162, 319–22, *323*
  animal abuse and cruelty 320
  EUE (extreme and unusual environment) 319–21, 322
  ICE (isolated and confined environment) 319–21, 322
  illicit drug use 320
  punishment 320, 321
  silence and tolerance of transgression 321–2
  violence against women 320
  'what happens on the ice, stays on the ice' 321
Anthropocene 53
  criminological theory and 11, 53–5

anthropology 336
anti-government groups and militias 273–5
  1992 Ruby Ridge shootout, Idaho 274
  1993 Waco siege, Texas 274
  1995 bombing, Oklahoma City 274
  2014 standoff with United States Bureau of Land Management, Nevada 274
  2016 Malheur National Wildlife Refuge occupation, Oregon 274
  2021 6 January Capitol insurrection 274, 275
  conspiracy theories 273, 275
  ideologies of 273
  military style leadership 273
  United States 274–5
  White membership 274
anti-social behaviour 23, 246, 303, 335
  Australia 182, 183
  Canada 182, 183
  citizen–police interactions 182
  community participation in local governance 182
  definition 181
  'Farmwatch' 182, 183
  Netherlands 182
  police–community relationships 181–3
  policy 181
  rural/urban settings comparison 181
  United Kingdom 181
  youth 182–3
AOD (alcohol and other drug) *see* drugs
Aransiola, J.T. 47, 48
the Arctic 162, 320
Armenia 89
ASEAN (Association of Southeast Asian Nations) 326
Asia 324, *327*
  'Asian Criminology' 325–6
  Asian Journal of Criminology 325
  borders 326–7
  corruption 324, 325, 327
  criminology research 324, 325–6
  Handbook of Asian Criminology 325
  incarceration 242
  population 324
  resource extraction 100
  state crime and harm 327–8
Australia 29, 315, 326, 338
  access to justice 338, 339
  anti-social behaviour 182, 183
  Caratas Australia 339
  Centre for Rural Criminology 340
  colonialism 151, 338
  crime prevention 263
  dark tourism 79, 80
  extremism 119
  farm crime 126, 127, 182, 183, 191, 340
  fraud 67
  hunting 151, 153

incarceration 241
Indigenous peoples 277, 278, 338
legal representation 256, 278
LGBTIQA+ people 282
lifestyle and amenity migration 285
neo-Nazi group, Victoria 119
Port Arthur Heritage Site, Tasmania 79
public order policing 202
RCPT (Rural Crime Prevention Team, New South Wales Police Force) 192–3
residential burglary, Victoria 109
resource extraction 100
restorative justice 246
rural courts 231
rural criminological research 313, 339–40
rural enclaves 295
Trial Bay Gaol 79
University of New England, Armidale, New South Wales 340
violence against women 114, 115
wildfires 166, 168
wildlife crime 172
working tourists 306–7

B
Bahn, C. 205
Baker, David 201–4
Bangladesh 138
  Shalish 224
Barclay, Elaine 108, 152, 340
Bauman, Zygmunt 15, 34
Baumol, William 101, 102
Beccaria, Cesare 16
Becker, Howard 24–5
Bentham, Jeremy 16
biosocial theories 16–17
Birmingham School of Cultural Studies 23
blood sports 133–5
  animal harm and death 133–4, 135
  badger baiting 133
  bullfighting 133, 135
  cockfighting 133, 134, 135
  criminalization of 135
  dog fighting 133, 134, 135
  'field sports'/blood sports distinction 133
  fox hunting 133, 134
  gambling 134
  hare coursing 133, 134
  international perspectives 134–5
  masculinities 135
  rural communities 134, 135
  as rural and green crimes 134
  see also animal rights and welfare
Bolivia 142, 172, 344
Botswana 159, 316
Bowden, Matt 1–7, 11–12, 13–15, 33–6, 329–32
Box, Matthew 151–4
Braithwaite, J. 245

INDEX

Brantingham, P. and Brantingham, P. 48
Brazil 29, 139, 241
  drugs 142, 143, 344
  rural courts 231
  rural violence 344
  violence against women 345
  wildfires 167
Brennan, Ann 191–4
Bronfenbrenner, Urie 44
bullying 76, 104, 105, 320
Bulovec, T. 330
Bunei, Emmanuel 314–18
Burke, R.H. 16
Burundi: *Bashingantahe* 224
Butler, G. 80
Button, M. 66
Byrne, Richard 95–7, 330

C

Cambodia 89, 324
Cameroon 138, 295, 316
Camilleri, Marg 290–3
Canada 29, 40
  anti-social behaviour 182, 183
  incarceration 241
  Indigenous peoples 276–7, 278
  punitiveness 236
  restorative justice 246
  rural crime rates 309, 333
  rural criminological research 313, 333–4, 339
  rural enclaves 294
  rural population 333
  wildlife crime 172
capitalism 18, 23, 34
  corporate capitalism 72
  informational capitalism 35, 36
Carr, P.J. 182, 183
Carrington, K. 64
Ceccato, Vania 1, 21–2, 46–9, 330, 343–7
Centre for Rural Criminology, University of New England (Armidale, New South Wales) 6
Chakraborti, N. 91
Chambliss, William 18, 71
Chesney-Lind, M. 18, 32
Chicago School of Sociology 11, 17, 20–1, 308
children
  child abuse 76, 104
  child labour 145, 324
  China: 'left behind children' 325
  crime/punishment/poverty relationship 241
  human trafficking 96, 97
  migrant children 243
  organized crime and 242
China 324
  community corrections 216

crime/punishment/poverty relationship 242–3
criminology 325–6
Cultural Revolution 89
death penalty 325
'horseback judges' 246
'rent-seeking' 328
restorative justice 246
Uyghurs, Xinjiang Autonomous region 295, 296
CITES (Convention on International Trade in Endangered Species of Flora and Fauna) 159–60, 170, 171
civic community theory 11, 13–15, 20, 43, 45, 335
  compared to social disorganization theory 13–15, 335
  data and sample 14–15
  limitations 14–15
  variables 14–15
Clack, Willie 22, 137–40, 314–18
Clark, Alyssa M. 218–20, 231–3
Clarke, R. 46, 47
classical theories 16–19
Clifford, M. 162
Clinard, Marshall B. 334
Cohen, E. 305
Cohen, L.E. 47
Cohen, Stanley 24
collective efficacy theory 17, 21
Collins, Victoria E. 18, 70–3
Colombia 29, 172
  drugs 142, 143, 242, 344, 345
  livestock theft and organized crime groups 138
  violence against women 345
colonialism/colonization 54, 137, 210, 305, 307, 333
  Africa 138, 314
  Australia 151, 338
  colonial violence 78
  decolonization 225
  Global South 198, 199, 210, 211
  Indigenous peoples 201, 224, 276, 277–8, 296
  Oceania 338–9
  settler-colonial jurisdictions 276, 277–8, 296, 333
  South America 344
  see also informal and decolonized justice systems
community corrections 215–17
  challenges 217
  China 216
  community re-entry and 215, 216, 217
  corrections staff 216
  funding and resources 217
  rehabilitation of offenders 215, 216, 217, 267

rural community corrections 216–17
sanctions as alternatives to
  incarceration 215
technology 267
urban community corrections 216
conflict theory 18
consumer 34
  consumer fraud 19, 66–8, 75
  consumer-oriented economies 79
  meat consumption 146
Cornish, D. 46, 47
corporate crime 18–19, 21, 70
  corporate capitalism 72
  definition 70
  food crime 147
  white-collar crime 70–1, 262, 325
  see also state–corporate crime
corruption 173, 199, 344
  Africa 315, 317
  Asia 324, 325, 327
  police corruption 141, 184, 185
  state 119, 253, 317
  water-related corruption 163
Costa Rica 142, 285, 299
court reform challenges 218
  elected judges 219
  formalism 218
  fragmentation of courts 218, 219
  funding 218–19
  rural courts 218–19
  rural courts: recommendations for reform
    implementation 219–20
  Unified Court System 218
  United States 218–19, 220
courts
  domestic violence courts 246, 247
  drug and drunk driving courts 246
  restorative justice and problem-solving
    courts 246
  see also court reform challenges; rural courts
COVID-19 pandemic 34
  incarcerated persons, release of 243
  internet and 75
  poverty 241, 243
  service provision for rural drug-related
    harms 82
  violence against women 117
  virtual justice services 256–7
Crank, John P. 334
crime
  as culturally constructed 208, 211
  definition 162
  as endemic product of inequality 37
  'as entertainment industry' 23
  as imbalance of social relationships and
    harms 245
  as infractions of law 261
  politics and 23
  'subsistence' offence 28, 222, 299

crime control
  cultural criminology and 23
  devolving of crime control from the 'police'
    to third sector 181
  rural areas approach to 235
crime pattern theory 22, 46
crime prevention
  Australia 263
  CPSD (Crime Prevention through Social
    Development) 262
  CPTED (Crime Prevention through
    Environmental Design) 20, 46, 262, 263
  crime prevention devices 47–8, 262
  definition 261
  farm crime 127, 191
  illegal hunting 153
  livestock theft 127, 263
  primary-, secondary- and tertiary-level
    approaches 261–2
  rural crime prevention 36, 262–3
  SCP (Situational Crime Prevention) 46,
    47, 48, 209–10, 262, 263
  service provision 262, 263
  social crime prevention over policing 38–9
  technology 127, 263
criminal behaviour 16–17, 18, 177, 235, 262,
  301, 309, 314
  place-based theories 20–2
  primary socialization theory 43
  rational choice 46
  social disorganization theory 21
criminal farmers 102, 103, 156
  see also rogue farmers
criminal justice systems 18, 127, 177
  Indigenous peoples, over-representation
    in 276, 277, 296, 334, 338
  punitiveness 34
  rural crimes dealt with by state justice
    systems 226
  rural criminal justice systems 177–8
  state justice systems 224
  unequal patriarchal criminal justice
    system 242
  see also informal and decolonized
    justice systems
criminology
  'Asian Criminology' 325–6
  British 'new criminology' 23
  Global South 198
  rural/urban dichotomy 198
  as science 16
  shift from criminal, unlawful behaviours to
    harmful, immoral behaviours 54
  sociology and 11, 21, 116, 334, 336
  Southern Criminology 210–11, 325
  urban-centric bias 271, 315, 333, 343
critical criminology 18, 30
  critique of 37–8
  rural critical criminology 31, 91

INDEX

Crook, M. 54
Cross, Cassandra 66–9
cultural criminology 23–5
 'carnival of crime' 23
 media 23, 24, 25
 popular culture 23, 24
Cunneen, Chris 277
Currie, Elliot 37, 38
Curtis, K. 232
cybercrime 59, 74–6, 226, 325
 consumer fraud 66–7, 75
 cyber-bullying and cyber-stalking 76, 115
 definition 74
 as everyday crime 74–5
 examples of 75
 phishing 66–7, 75
 ransomware attacks 75, 76, 164
 Russia 76
 water-related cyberattacks 164
cybersecurity 52, 74, 106

D

Daly, Mary 18
Darwin, Charles 130
Davies, Andrew L.B. 232, 255–7
Davis, Kristen 301–4
De Villiers, J. 111
death penalty 235, 236, 325
Del Olmo, R. 343
DeKeseredy, Walter S. 1, 18, 25, 37, 40–2, 43, 63, 114–17, 335
DeLeeuw, Joseph 273–5
Descartes, René 129
desistance from crime 221–3
 factors supporting desistance 221, 223
 as process 221
 rural barriers to desistance 222–3
 see also post-release
differential association theory 18
digital technology
 digital illiteracy 260
 police engagement with rural communities 260
 policing 266, 267
 technology-facilitated violence 105, 106
 teleconferencing 231, 256–7, 267
 virtual justice services 253, 256–7
 see also cybercrime; cybersecurity; internet; technology
disabilities *see* people with disabilities
diversionary schemes 215
domestic violence 63, 199, 208, 210, 261, 303
 Africa 315, 316
 against women 99, 110
 domestic violence courts 246, 247
 drunkenness and 110
 informal justice systems 226

isolation 302–3
private space and 211
restorative justice 245
see also family violence; violence against women
Donnermeyer, Joseph F. 1–7, 13–15, 16–19, 20–2, 25, 37, 41, 43–5, 59, 74–7, 108–10, 199, 215–17, 294–7, 313, 324–8, 333–7, 340
 International Journal of Rural Criminology 2
 Routledge International Handbook of Rural Criminology 2, 102, 324–5
Doorewaard-Janse van Vuuren, Cecili 111–13
drug cultivation, manufacture and trade 35, 85, 103, 141–3, 302, 345
 cocaine 141, 142–3, 242, 344
 heroin 141
 marijuana/cannabis 38, 103, 141, 143, 157, 320
 methamphetamine 141, 143
 opiates 142, 242
 South America 142–3, 344, 345
 United Nations Office on Drugs and Crime 142, 143
 women 242
drugs (alcohol and drugs) 208, 226, 261
 community-based participatory action 86
 County Lines 85, 96
 definition 84
 desistance from crime and 222
 domestic violence and 110
 drug courts 246
 drug epidemics 24, 81, 246
 economic risks shaping rural drug-related harms 81–2, 103
 Left Realism on 38, 39
 marijuana/cannabis 24–5, 84, 86, 344
 peer cluster theory 43–4
 physical conditions shaping rural drug-related harms 82
 policies 83, 86, 242
 poverty and 38, 81
 primary socialization theory 43, 44–5
 public health responses to rural drug-related harms 83
 PWID (people who inject drugs) 82
 resource extraction, crime impacts of 98, 99
 rural drug use 81, 84–5, 308, 309
 service provision 82, 83, 303
 Shetland heroin case 85
 social conditions shaping rural drug-related harms 82–3
 stigma 82, 83
 unemployment and 81
 United Kingdom 85, 96
 United States 81, 103, 157
 urban drug use 85

353

violence against women and 116
'war on drugs' 335, 336
women 242
Durkheim, Emile 11, 14, 17, 329

E
Eck, J.E. 47
Ecuador 142, 345
Edmondson, C. 219
Edwards, T.D. 162
Eisenstein, J. 233
El Salvador 142, 243, 336
Eman, Katja 162–5, 330
employment 222, 237, 238, 239
see also unemployment
Encyclopedia of Rural Crime 59
  purpose of 2, 4–5
  structure 5–6
Engelmann, Larissa 181–3, 205–7
environment-related issues
  biodiversity 28, 54, 159, 170, 172, 344
  climate change 34, 53, 149, 164, 166, 167, 168, 211, 242
  desertification 54
  environmental protests 202
  global warming 29, 163, 166, 167
  greenhouse gas emissions 166, 168
  'moral ecology' 299
environmental criminology 26–9, 211
  Africa 316–17
  biopiracy 29
  blood sports 134
  contamination/pollution 26, 29, 163, 262, 316
  eco-justice 27, 28
  ecocentric approach to environmental harm 26–7
  ecocide 29, 54
  environmental crime, definitions 26, 27, 28, 29, 162
  environmental crimes and harms 26, 27, 28, 199, 211, 286
  environmental degradation 27, 199
  environmental laws/regulation 19, 27
  factory farms 131
  green criminology 27–8, 54, 131, 134, 158, 164, 211, 330
  hazardous waste 26, 29, 71–2
  illegal dumping 26, 286
  logging 26, 27, 199, 202, 203, 295, 316
  mining 26, 27, 29, 53–4, 195, 202, 316, 327, 345
  non-human entities 27, 28, 29
  responses to environmental crimes 28
  rights of/duties to nature 27
  state–corporate crime 27, 70, 71–2
  water and 'rural green criminology' 162–3, 164

  see also animal rights and welfare; folk crime; resource extraction; water; wildfires; wildlife crime
Ethiopia 138, 316, 317
Europe *332*
  Criminal Investigation and Criminology 330–1
  European Society of Criminology Working Group on Rural Criminology 331
  languages 331
  Research in Rural Crime series (Bristol University Press) 331–2
  resource extraction 100
  rural criminological scholarship 329–32
  Studies in Rural Criminology series (Routledge) 331–2
extremism 118–20
  addressing rural violent extremism 120
  Africa 119
  Australia 119
  civic society and 120
  definition 118
  Germany 119
  social control and 120
  Switzerland 119
  vulnerability of rural communities to violent extremism 118–19

F
Falcone, D.N. 334
family violence 63, 76, 104, 199
  financial dependency 64
  international rural context 64
  LGBTIQA+ people 281
  male peer support and 64, 65
  rural features 63, 211
  service provision 65, 211
  under-reporting of 63
  see also domestic violence; violence against women
farm crime 302
  Africa 316
  Australia 126, 127, 182, 183, 191, 340
  crime prevention 127, 191
  definition 125
  policing 125, 126, 127, 191
  reporting of 125, 126, 127, 191
  South Africa 22
  victimization 125–6, 191
  see also violence against farmers
fear of crime 23, 205, 206, 329, 331, 334, 335
  women's fear of crime 211
Feeley, M. 218, 220
Felson, M. 47
feminism/feminist theories 11, 18, 30–2, 37, 116
  critical criminology and 30
  intersectionality 30, 31, 32
  radical feminism 116
  rural policing 211

transformative critical feminist
  criminology 32
see also patriarchy
Finn, K. 99
First Nation peoples *see* Indigenous and
  First Nation peoples
Flemming, R.B. 233
Floyd, George 274
folk crime 298
  Costa Rica 299
  criminalization of rural folk crime as
    socially constructed 299
  definition 298
  fishing 298, 300
  'folk hero' 298
  illegal hunting 151, 298–9
  justifying rural folk crimes 299
  land clearance 298–9
  nature harvesting 298
  offenders 300
  poaching 172, 299, 300
  rural folk crime 298–300
food crime 145–7, 155
  blurred boundaries between offending and
    victimization 146
  definitions 145
  fertilizers 146
  illegal meat trade 209
  impact of 147
  monoculture crops 145, 146
  pesticides 145, 146, 147
  rationale for 146–7
Foucault, M. 35
France 258, 338
fraud 66
  consumer fraud 19, 66–8, 75
  cost of 67
  definition 66
  food fraud 102, 155, 156, 157
  fraud vulnerability 67, 68
  online fraud 68, 261
  phishing 66–7, 75
  in rural context 68
  rural tourism 109
  water fraud 163

G
Gaines, L.K. 185
gangs 210, 226, 296, 324
  drugs and County Lines 85, 96
  gang violence 336
  urban gangs 308
  see youth sub-cultures
Garland, D. 34–5
Garriott, W. 45
gender-related issues *see* feminism/feminist
  theories; LGBTIQA+ people; male peer
  support; masculinity theories; patriarchy;
  violence against women; women

genocide 19, 88–90
  Armenia 89
  Cambodia 89
  China, Cultural Revolution 89
  Darfur 89
  definition 88
  Guatemala 89
  Holocaust 78, 88, 89
  individual risk factors 90
  national risk factors 88–9
  Rwanda 89, 90
  sub-national risk factors 89
Germany 119, 338
Giddens, A. 34
Gido, Rosemary 241–4
Global North 48
  crime in rural Global North 198
  fraud 67
  'metropolitan criminology' 210
  rural violence 314
  technology 265–6
  trophy hunting 161
Global South
  colonialism 198, 199, 210, 211
  crime in rural Global South 198
  criminology 198
  fraud 67
  incarceration 242
  modern slavery/human trafficking 95, 96
  policing the rural Global South 198–9
  resource extraction 199
  Southern Criminology 210–11
  trophy hunting 161
globalization 34
  globalized nature of countryside 208, 210
  'glocalization' 35
  state–corporate crimes 72
Goodall, O. 102, 156
Gottfredson, Don 17
Gray, Allison 145–7
Gray, D.E. 339
green criminology *see*
  environmental criminology
Grote, U. 315
Grygier, T, 333–4
guardianship 109, 127, 267
Guatemala 89, 142, 243, 336
  Mayan 224
guns 133, 273, 308
  cross-border livestock theft 139
  gun ownership 64, 115, 273, 303
  OMCs (outlaw motorcycle clubs) 289
  trespass and illegal hunting 151

H
Hagan, J. 334
Hale, Rachel 91–4, 118–21, 221–3, 251–4
Hall-Sanchez, Amanda 30–2, 110
Hardy, S-J. 91

Harkness, Alistair 1–7, 59, 108–10, 125–8, 151–4, 203, 215–17, 313, 324–8, 338–42
Harris, Bridget 104–7
Harry, Casandra 195–7
hate crime 91–3, 226, 261
  cybercrime 76
  definition 91
  distal effects of 92
  explanations for rural hate 92–3
  intersectionality 91
  LGBTIQA+ people 92, 281
  othering 93
  police and law enforcement 92, 93
  service provision 92
  as under-reported and under-researched 92
Hawaii 86
Hayden, Karen 1, 23–5
Herbig, F.J.W. 317
heritage see rural heritage crime
Hesselink, Anni 111–13
Hirschi, Travis 17
Hobbes, Thomas 17
Hodgkinson, Tarah 261–4
Holocaust 78, 88, 89
Holocene era 53, 54
homelessness 67, 98, 222, 252, 281, 302
Honduras 142, 243, 336
Hong Kong 67, 295
housing 64, 98, 251, 285, 303, 306
  challenges faced by offenders 215
  desistance from crime and 221, 222, 223
  housing insecurity 252
  re-entry 222, 237, 238
Huling, T. 229
human trafficking 35, 208
  children 96, 97
  definition 95
  facilitation of 96
  Global South 95, 96
  Islamic State 96
  migration and 96
  organized crime 96–7
  transnational/internal trafficking 96
  women 96
  see also modern slavery
hunting 209, 211
  2020 NSW Farm Crime Survey 152
  Australia 151, 153
  badger and deer hunting, United Kingdom 102
  by First Nations people 153
  hunting culture and woman abuse 31, 115
  illegal hunting, impact of 151, 152
  illegal hunting prevention 153
  illegal poaching 151, 209, 211, 328
  poaching/illegal hunting distinction 151
  regulation and licenses 133, 135, 152, 153, 159
  Sweden 152
  United States 153
  violence against women and hunting culture 31, 115
  see also animal rights and welfare; folk crime; trophy hunting; wildlife crime

I

Iceland 85
incarceration
  alternatives to 215
  Asia 242
  Australia 241
  Canada 241
  China 296
  COVID-19 pandemic 243
  early release 215
  Global South 242
  Indigenous peoples 241, 276, 295
  mass incarceration 241–2
  minorities 241
  overuse of 241, 242
  prison reform and decarceration 243
  reincarceration 223, 253
  sanctions as alternatives to 215
  stigma and 223, 229
  United States 241, 242
  women 242
  see also jails and prisons; post-release
India 111, 138, 143, 325
  rural criminological research 315, 324, 326–7, 328
Indigenous and First Nation peoples 261, 272, 295
  access to justice 251, 338
  Australia 277, 278, 338
  Brazil 345
  Canada 276–7, 278
  colonialism 201, 224, 276, 277–8, 296
  crime/punishment/poverty relationship 241
  hunting 153
  incarceration 241, 276, 295
  Indigenous tribes, Amazon 295
  land theft 199, 344, 345
  legal representation 278
  New Zealand 277, 278, 338
  'on reserve'/'off reserve' 276–7
  over-representation in criminal justice systems 276, 277, 296, 334, 338
  policing 334
  rural criminological engagement with 277
  rurality 276
  sequestration of 277–8
  settler-colonial jurisdictions 276, 277–8, 296, 333
  traditional systems of justice 292
  United States 277, 278
  violence against women 99, 345

wildfires, impact of 167
Indonesia 86, 167, 172, 199
   Adat 224
industry/industrialization
   animal husbandry 130
   demise of heavy industrialization 33–4
   industrial modernity 33
   industry insiders 155, 156
   rural and ocean-based
      industrialization 53–4
   urban-based industrialization 53
informal and decolonized justice systems
   (alternative justice systems) 224–6
   access to informal customary justice 251
   characteristics 225–6
   decolonized justice systems 225
   examples 224
   Indigenous justice systems 224
   international trends 226
   non-state justice systems 224
   rural crimes dealt with by 226
information age 34
   informational capitalism 35, 36
   see also digital technology; internet
Innes, M. 205
insiders 157
   industry insiders 155, 156
   insider crimes 102, 103
International Journal of Rural Criminology 2, 6
International Society for the Study of Rural
   Crime 6, 336, 340
internet
   anti-social behaviour on 23
   connectivity: urban/rural gap 265, 268
   COVID-19 pandemic 75
   fraud 68, 261
   virtual justice services 253
   see also cybercrime; cybersecurity;
      digital technology
interpersonal violence *see* technology-
   facilitated violence
intersectionality 91, 210, 280
   feminist theories 30, 31, 32
   technology-facilitated violence 104–5
IPBES (Intergovernmental Science-Policy
   Platform on Biodiversity and Ecosystem
   Services) 170
Iran 142
IRE (illegal rural enterprise) 101–2, 103
Islam, Zahidul 224–7
isolation 302
   consumer fraud 67
   court reform challenges 219
   domestic violence 302–3
   drug cultivation, manufacture and trade 141
   family violence and rurality 63, 64, 65
   farm crime 126
   hate crime 92, 93
   LGBTIQA+ people 280

   physical isolation as punishment 321
   prosecution of crimes 345
   violence against farmers 112, 113
   violence against women 116
   violent extremism and 119, 120
   youth 309
Israel 111

J
jails and prisons 228–30
   funding 228, 229, 230
   jail/prison distinction 228
   jails 228–9, 230
   overcrowding 228, 241, 242
   pretrial detention 242
   prison towns 229
   prisons 229
   private health insurance 239
   rural location 228, 229, 230, 242
   service provision 228, 229, 239, 242
   stand-alone jails 228
   teleconferencing 267
   United States 228–30, 242
   urban jails 228, 242
   see also incarceration
James, Donna 305–7
Jobes, Pat 340
Jones, C. 108
Johnson, S.D. 301
judges 219, 246
   rural courts 231–2, 233

K
Kaiser, Rebecca 319–23
Kenya 112, 138, 159, 315, 316, 317
Kim, S. 80
King, R.S. 229
Klingele, C. 215
Koeze, E. 75

L
labelling theory 18, 21, 24
labour
   child labour 145, 324
   forced labour 97, 145
   labour migration 307
   mistreatment of workers 18
   see also modern slavery; working tourists
Laos 142
Latin America 29
   see also South America
Lauchs, Mark 287–9
law enforcement
   as enforcement of codes, standards and
      ideals 209
   see also police/policing; police
      station closures
law enforcement misconduct 184–6,
   345
   examples 184, 186

Henry A. Wallace Police Crime
  Database 185–6
police corruption 141, 184, 185
police misconduct trials 185
in rural jurisdictions 185, 186
United States 185–6
violence-related police crime 186
Lee, Matt 13, 14, 43, 45, 335
Left Realism 18, 37–9
  contradictions and strengths 39
  crime as endemic product of inequality 37
  key principles 38
  Left Realism/'plain left realism' 37
  'Square of Crime' 38
legal representation 232
  access to legal representation: meaning and
    importance 255
  Australia 256, 278
  barriers to 243, 255–6
  CAFA programme (counsel at first
    appearance) 256
  Indigenous people 278
  Nepal 256
  rural areas 252, 255–6
  rural attorney shortage 232–3, 252,
    256
  solving rural legal representation
    shortages 256–7
  United Nations on 255
  United States 256
  video conferencing 256–7
Lesotho 112, 139, 316
LGBTIQA+ people 271, 280, 302
  anti-LGBTIQA+ biases 282
  Australia 282
  decriminalization of same-sex
    relationships 282
  discrimination and marginalization
    of 280, 281
  gay and trans panic defences 282
  hate crime 92, 281
  intimate partner violence and family
    violence 281
  isolation 280
  justice responses to victimization 281–2
  rural queer criminology 280–1
  stigma 280
  technology-facilitated violence 104
  under-reporting of crimes 281
  violence against women 42
Liederbach, John 184–6
lifestyle and amenity migration 271, 284–6
  Australia 285
  impact on local environment, infrastructure
    and economy 285
  rural crime 286
  United States 285
Lilly, J.R. 16
Lindsey, P.A. 159

livestock theft 5, 112, 261, 308
  Africa 138–9, 314–15, 316
  borderlines enforcement 137
  Colombia 138
  cross-border livestock theft 137
  cross border livestock theft: religious
    challenges 138
  cross-border livestock theft amongst
    demographic groupings 138–9
  cross border livestock theft and organized
    crime 138–9, 316
  Lesotho 139
  Madagascar 139
  mountainous borders and 139
  prevention of 127, 263
  as 'quintessential rural crime' 125
  RCPT (Rural Crime Prevention Team,
    Australia) 193
  rivers, oceans and cross-border livestock
    theft 139
  South Africa 267, 315
  technology 263, 267, 268
  terminology for 314–15
  Uruguay–Brazil border 139
Lombroso, Cesare 16–17
Lopez, J.J. 185
Lovell, Jarret S. 129–32
Lynch, Michael J. 18

M
Madagascar 139
male peer support 40–2
  family violence and 64, 65
  separation/divorce sexual assault
    41–2
  variants of 40
  violence against women and 31, 40–2, 43,
    115, 116, 335
  see also masculinity theories
Marquis, Greg 334
Marshall, B. 301
Martin, K. 99
Marx, Karl 17, 18
Marxism 11, 30
masculinity theories 31, 37
  blood sports 135
  illegal hunting 171
  rural masculinities 31, 32, 64, 65, 135
  trophy hunting 160
  see also male peer support
Mauer, M. 229
Mawby, R. 108, 330
McElwee, G. 101, 102
McKay, Henry D. 17, 20
McVeigh, Timothy 274
media 18, 23, 24, 25, 230
  see also social media
Meng, Qingli 74–7, 324–8
Merton, Robert K. 17

INDEX

Meško, Gorazd 50–2, 162–5, 329–32
Messner, Michael 17
Mexico 29, 137, 333
  Clinical Criminology 335
  Criminología 335
  criminological research 335–6
  drugs 142, 143, 242, 335, 336
  militarization of public security 335
  Old Colony Mennonites 294
migration 329, 331, 336
  anti-government groups and militias 273
  anti-immigrant political campaigns 243
  children 243
  crime/punishment/poverty relationship 241, 242–3
  'crimmigration' 243
  detention centres 243
  gang activity and 308
  human trafficking and 96
  immigrants 25, 64, 243, 295, 333
  international migration 242
  labour migration 307
  populism and immigrants 234
  rural to urban migration 54, 72, 241, 242–3, 325
  urban to rural migration 308
  see also lifestyle and amenity migration
Miller, Walter 308, 310
minorities 91, 271, 282, 302
  crime/punishment/poverty relationship 241
  incarceration 241
  racism 76, 303
  see also Indigenous and First Nation peoples; LGBTIQA+ people; people with disabilities
modern slavery 95–7, 173, 208, 330, 344
  definition 95
  domestic servitude 97
  forced labour 97
  MSHT (Modern Slavery Human Trafficking) 95
  organ harvesting 97
  sexual exploitation 96, 97
  United Kingdom 95
  United States 95
  see also human trafficking
modernity theories 11, 33–6
  consumer society 34
  culture of control 34–5
  industrial modernity 33
  late modernity 35
  liquid modernity 15, 34
  modernity/tradition dichotomy 33
Moody, S.R. 301
Moore, Brandon 88–90
Moore, Matthew D. 308–10

moral panics 24, 30
Morash, M. 32
Morocco 143
Morrissey, Belinda 301–4
Mouhanna, Christian 258–60, 330
Mulrooney, Kyle 125–8, 151–4, 191–4, 234–6, 338–42
Mutongwizo, Tariro 198–200
Myanmar 142, 167, 295, 326–7, 328

N

Namibia 159, 316
Nardulli, P.F. 233
neo-liberalism 33, 34, 207, 209
Nepal 256
Netherlands 182
Neubacher, F. 315
New Zealand 29, 276, 315, 338
  access to justice 339
  Indigenous peoples 277, 278, 338
  restorative justice 246
  rural criminological research 339–40
  rural enclaves 295
Nicholas, Louise 148–50
Nigeria 29, 315, 316, 317
  Boko Haram 138, 295
  drugs 86, 143
Nolan, J. 93
non-human entities 11, 53, 54, 146, 158
  crimes against 211
  environmental criminology 27, 28, 29
  wildlife crimes 170, 171, 173
  see also animal rights and welfare
North America *337*
  Canada 333–4
  Mexico and Central America 335–6
  rural criminological research 333–6
  United States 334–5
Nurse, Angus 133–6, 158–61
Nyseth Nzitatira, Hollie 88–90

O

Obama, Barack 274
Oceania 338, *341*
  colonialism and colonial legacies 338–9
  rural criminological research in New Zealand and Australia 339–40
  rural criminological research in the South Pacific 340–1
O'Connor, M.E. 339
Oetting, Eugene 43, 335
offence *see* crime
offenders
  challenges faced by 215, 237
  folk crime 300
  offenders with disabilities 290, 291
  rehabilitation of 215, 217, 239, 245, 267
  supervision and management of 215
  tourists as offenders 109–10

wildlife crime: categories of
offenders 171–2
see also re-entry; rehabilitation; rural crime tropes: offenders and victims
OMCs (outlaw motorcycle clubs) 271–2, 287–9
  Bandidos 287, 288
  Hells Angels 287, 288, 289
  membership 287, 288
  misogyny 288
  OMC crime 288–9
  OMC politics 287, 288
  organized crime and 288
  Outlaws 287, 288
  'warfare mentality' 288, 289
opportunity theories of crime 262
organized crime
  Africa 138–9, 316
  children and women 242
  environmental crimes 316
  human trafficking 96–7
  insiders and outsiders 155, 156, 157
  livestock theft 138–9, 316
  mafia 155, 156, 157
  OCGs (organized crime groups) 96–7, 155
  OMCs (outlaw motorcycle clubs) 288
  organized crime–rural nexus 103
  police corruption and 185
  rural organized crime 102, 155–7, 185, 208
  South Pacific 341
  terrorism and 96
  water-related organized crime 164
Osbaldiston, Nick 284–6
othering 93, 321
outsiders 156, 157, 185, 321
  'alien conspiracy' thesis 156

P

Pakistan 138, 142, 326
parole 215, 238, 252
patriarchy 18, 30, 32, 114, 116, 189, 199
  unequal patriarchal criminal justice system 242
  violence against rural women and 25, 31, 41, 76
Peck, Shelby 255–7
Pedersen, Cassie 1–7, 271–2, 280–3
peer cluster theory 43–4
people with disabilities 64, 271, 290
  access to justice 290–2
  assistive technologies 105, 292
  disability, definition of 290
  'disability'/'impairment' distinction 290
  gendered crime 292
  offenders with disabilities 290, 291
  technology-facilitated violence 104
  victimization 290
  United Nations Convention on the Rights of Persons with a Disability 290

Perez, Monica 343–7
Perrault, S. 333
Peru 142, 172, 242, 344
Petersilia, Joan 237
Peterson, Jessica René 1–7, 177–8, 187–90, 215–17, 265–8
Philippines 111
  Katarungang Pambarangay 224
Piche, J. 78
place-based theories 17, 20–2, 104, 263
  crime mapping 20, 324
  rural criminology 21, 31, 251
  rural feminist criminology 32
  violent extremism 118–19
  see also social disorganization theory
Plato 17
police discretion 187–9
  definition 187
  effects of the rural on discretion, decision making and informal sanctions 187–9
  informal sanctions 187, 189
  restorative justice approach 187
police engagement with rural communities 191–3, 206
  digital technology 260
  farm crime 191
  lack of engagement 192, 206, 259
  RCPT (Rural Crime Prevention Team, New South Wales Police Force) 192–3
  specialized rural crime officers 191, 192
police/policing 195
  'abstract policing' 206
  acquaintanceship 125, 177, 187–8, 189
  anti-social behaviour: police–community relationships 181–3
  arrests by police 187, 188, 189, 201
  'community-condoned' policing 185, 189
  community policing 189, 196, 201, 209–10
  drug cultivation, manufacture and trade 141
  farm crime 125, 126, 127, 191
  'frontier-style' policing 278
  'hard' policing 206, 207
  hate crime 92, 93
  illegal hunting prevention 153
  Indigenous peoples 334
  informal policing 181, 206, 210
  legitimacy 201, 206
  non-state actors 195, 196, 209
  partnerships 206, 209
  plural policing 209
  reactive emergency policing 259
  'restorative policing' 245
  SIDS (small island developing states) 196–7
  'smart policing' 266
  social control 187
  social crime prevention over policing 38–9
  'soft' policing 181, 206, 207
  technology 199, 260, 266, 267

INDEX

urban policing 207
see also law enforcement misconduct; police discretion; police engagement with rural communities; police station closures; public order policing; reassurance policing; rurality and policing
police station closures 258–60
  centralization of forces 259–60
  emergency calls 260
  France 258
  'new public management' 258, 259
policy
  anti-social behaviour 181
  critical feminist criminology 30, 32
  drug-related policies 83, 86, 242
  Left Realism 37, 38
  penal populism 235
  rural areas as neglected by policy makers 208
  study of criminal justice systems 177
  trophy hunting 159
  violence against women 116–17
Popper, N. 75
popular culture 23, 24, 79, 80
populism 234–6
  penal populism 234–5
  political populism 15, 234
  punitiveness and 235
  rural areas and 235, 236
  rural features 235–6
  shared logic of 234–5
  urban/rural divide 236
pornography 25, 31, 76, 115
post-release 237–9
  challenges 215, 237
  women 222
  see also desistance from crime; re-entry; recidivism
Potter, G.W. 185
Pound, Roscoe 218, 219
poverty
  COVID-19 pandemic 241, 243
  crime/punishment/poverty relationship 241, 242–3
  drugs and 38, 81
  intergenerational poverty 252
  rural areas 241, 310
Presdee, M. 23
primary socialization theory 43–5, 335
  substance use and misuse 43, 44–5
probation 215, 252
public order policing 201–3
  Australia 202
  dialogue initiatives 202
  dissent 201, 202
  environmental protests 202
  protests 202–3
  rural/urban comparison 202–3
  specialist intervention 203

punishment
  Antarctica 320, 321
  crime/punishment/poverty relationship 241, 242–3
  physical isolation as punishment 321
  rural punishment inequality 242, 243
  see also death penalty; incarceration
punitiveness
  Canada 236
  community corrections 216
  criminal justice systems 34
  informal and decolonized justice systems 225
  populism and 235
  urban/rural gap on punitivity 235–6
Pytlarz, Artur 33–6

Q
Qi, Ziwei 245–8
Quinney, Richard 18
Quiroz Cuarón, Alfonso 335

R
race
  anti-government groups and militias: White membership 274
  feminist theories 31
  violence against women 42
  White hunters 160, 161
racism 76, 274, 303, 320
Radcliffe, Sir Cyril 138
rape and sexual assault 111, 186, 288, 301, 303
  see also violence against women
rational choice 46–8
  crime opportunities 47, 48
  critique of 47
  environmental and situational factors 47–8
  'involvement decisions'/'event decisions' 46
Ray, H. 98
re-entry (community re-entry) 237–9
  acquaintance density 239
  challenges 238–9
  community corrections and 215, 216, 217
  employment 222, 237, 238, 239
  housing 222, 237, 238
  mental health care and substance abuse treatment 237, 239
  rural re-entry 237–9
  service provision 222–3, 239
  transportation 238
  'What Works in Reentry Clearinghouse', United States 237–8
  see also post-release; recidivism
reassurance policing 205–7
  partnership working 206
  'reassurance gap' 205
  'signal crimes perspective' 205
  see also police/policing

recidivism 223, 230, 237, 246, 247
　see also desistance from crime; post-release;
　　re-entry
rehabilitation 215, 217, 239, 245, 267
Reiss, Albert John 17
religion
　drug-related harms and 142
　religious challenges in cross border livestock
　　theft 138
　religious enclaves 295, 296
Rennison, C.M. 42
reporting of crimes 271
　family violence 63
　farm crime 125, 126, 127, 191
　hate crime 92
　reducing recorded crime 259
　under-reporting 63, 92, 127, 261, 281,
　　304, 309
　working tourists 307
Republic of the Congo 29, 159
resource extraction 29, 53, 98–100, 116
　Africa 100
　Asia 100
　Australia 100
　crime impacts 99, 344–5
　Eastern Europe 100
　gaps in knowledge 100
　Global South 199
　life course of resource-based booms 98–9
　South Africa 344–5
　South America 100
　United States 99
　violence against women 99, 116
　see also environmental criminology
restorative justice 245–7
　Australia 246
　Canada 246
　China 246
　community buy-in 247
　definition 245
　domestic violence 245
　informal and decolonized justice
　　systems 225
　juvenile justice system 245, 246
　New Zealand 246
　origins and evolution of 245–6
　police discretion 187
　problem-solving courts 246
　'restorative policing' 245
　rural settings 246–7
　solution rather than punishment for the
　　crime 247
　United States 246–7
　see also therapeutic jurisprudence
right-wing politics
　far-right 119, 274, 275
　populism 234
Rodríguez Manzaneka, Luis 335
Rofe, M.W. 79

rogue farmers 101–3, 156
　definition 101–2
　IRE (illegal rural enterprise) 101–2,
　　103
Román Burgos, Denisse 333–7
Romps, D. 167
Rosenfeld, Richard 17
routine activities theory 22, 46, 47, 109
Routledge International Handbook of Rural
　Criminology 2, 102, 324–5
Ruddell, Rick 98–100, 228–30, 333–7
rule of law 251
rural area
　acquaintance density 92, 177, 187–8, 189,
　　191, 216, 222, 239, 303
　connectivity: rural/urban gap 265, 268
　definition 1–2
　globalized nature of 208, 210
　lower tax bases 219, 231, 238, 239
　population 2, 309, 343
　poverty 241, 310
　punitivity: rural/urban gap 235–6
　rural-based industrialization 53–4
　rural dystopia 79–80
　rural idyll 79, 91, 109, 119, 156, 201, 206,
　　207, 208–9, 211, 261, 310, 339
　rural peoples and groups 271–2
　rural/urban comparisons 202–3, 217,
　　232, 236
　rural/urban divide 1, 76, 156, 198, 236, 308
　as 'socio-spatiality' 35
　transition of societies from agrarian and
　　rural to urban and industrial 17
　urban to rural migration 308
rural courts 231–3
　Australia 231
　Brazil 231
　cooperation 233
　court actors 232, 233
　domestic violence courts 247
　drug courts 246
　judges 231–2, 233
　legal defence representatives 232
　mobile courts 231
　paralegals 232
　problem-solving courts 246
　public defenders and prosecutors 232
　reform challenges 218–19
　reform implementation:
　　recommendations 219–20
　restorative justice 246–7
　rural attorney shortage 232–3, 252
　Sierra Leone 233
　technology 266–7
　teleconferencing 231, 267
　'traveling court' 246
　Ukraine 252, 267
　United States 231–2, 233, 246–7
　urban/rural courts comparison 232

INDEX

women survivors of family violence 253
see also access to justice
rural crime tropes: offenders and victims 301–4
  'everyone knows everyone' 303
  'it couldn't happen here' 301–2
  'put up with it' 303
  'we can cope' 303–4
  'we look after our own' 302–3
rural criminological research 2, 6
  'big four' 313, 339
  CIA Factbook maps 313
  comparative research 315
  geographic status of 313, 314–46
  Global North 314, 315
  linguistic challenges 314–15, 326, 331
rural criminology 2, 19
  animal rights and 131
  chronology of developments in 2, *3–4*
  data problems 309
  growth of 2, 313
  meaning of rurality as base for 211
  origins 313
  rural crime theories 11–12
  rural queer criminology 280–1
  water crime and 163
rural enclaves 271–2, 294–7
  Australia 295
  Boko Haram, Nigeria 295
  Canada 294
  crime in 296
  Der Bruderhof communities 295
  enclave, definition 294, 295, 296
  Exclusive Brethren communities 295
  Gullahs 295
  Hutterites of the Great Plains 294
  Indigenous tribes, Amazon 295
  intentional communities and communes 296
  Karen people, Myanmar 295
  New Zealand 295
  nomadic groups 296
  Old Colony Mennonites, Mexico 294
  religious enclaves 295, 296
  sovereign countries as 295
  United States 294, 295
  Uyghurs, Xinjiang Autonomous region 295, 296
rural heritage crime 148–50
  definition 148
  impact of 150
  incidental rural heritage crime 149
  legality/illegality 148–9
  rural heritage, definition 148
  rural heritage harms 149, 150
  rural heritage-specific offences 149
  targeted rural heritage crime 149
  state rural heritage crime 149, 150
  study of 149–50

rurality and policing 330
  animals' role in policing 211
  challenging traditional perspectives 210–11
  cultures and 208–11
  rural Global South 198–9
  rural police 184, 195, 201, 203, 206, 262–3
  rural police as protectors and prosecutors 201
  'rural policing'/'policing the rural' distinction 208
  rural policing scholarship 195
  rurality and criminality/policing as socially constructed and contested 208, 210, 211
  technology 266
  withdrawal of state policing 208
  see also police engagement with rural communities; police/policing; police station closures
rurban 2
Russia 76
Rwanda 89, 90
  Gacaca 224

S

safety and security studies 21–2, 50–2, 330
  local safety and security in rural communities 51–2
  rural security 36
  'safety', definition 50
  'security', definition 50
  'security field' 35, 36
  security services, definition 51
  state and 35
Sampson, Robert J. 17
Schwartz, Martin 37, 40
Schwendinger, Herman and Julia 71
sentences 228, 232, 235, 243, 255, 282
  community-based sentences 217
  restorative-oriented sentencing 247
  suspended sentences 215
service provision 181, 303
  crime prevention 262, 263
  drug-related harm 82, 83, 303
  family violence 65, 211
  hate crime 92
  jails and prisons 228, 229, 239, 242
  re-entry 222–3, 239
  violence against women 116–17, 253
  youth at risk 262
Shaw, Callie 98–100
Shaw, Clifford 17, 20
Shearing, Clifford 53–5
Shukla, R.K. 45
SIDS (small island developing states) 195–6
  crimes of interpersonal violence 196–7
  policing 196–7

policing by non-state actors 196
SIDS Exclusive Economic Zones 197
Sierra Leone 233
Skaggs, S.L. 188
slavery *see* modern slavery
Slovenia 51, 330
Smith, Emiline 53–5
Smith, K. 330
Smith, Robert 101–3, 155–7
social bonding 21
social capital 89, 196, 226, 331
  rural social capital 102, 156, 209
social control 17
  arrest as formal method of 187
  cultural criminology 23, 24
  informal sanctions 187
  informal social control 47, 93, 98, 205, 329
  rural feminist criminology 31
  social disorganization theory 13, 20–1
  violent extremism and 120
social disorganization theory 15, 31, 44, 45, 310, 335
  Chicago School of Sociology 17, 20–1, 308
  compared to civic community theory 13–14, 335
  critique of 21
  importance of 21
  peer-reviewed research 21
  rural criminology 21, 31
  structural antecedent/systemic version 21
social learning theory 17–18, 43
social media 24, 75–6, 96, 106, 130, 265, 267
  police engagement 192
  rural security and 36
  rural social media 192
social support theory 40
sociology 11, 12, 17, 33, 329
  Chicago School of Sociology 11, 17, 20, 308
  criminology and 11, 21, 116, 334, 336
  rural sociology 13
  symbolic interactionist sociology 24
Somalia: *Xeer* 224
Sotlar, Andrej 50–2
Souhami, A. 206, 207
South Africa 139, 315, 317
  farm crime 22
  livestock theft 267, 315
  resource extraction 344–5
  trophy hunting 159
  violence against farmers 111, 112, 314, 315–16
South America 346
  colonialism 344
  drugs 142–3, 344, 345
  resource extraction 100
  rural areas as contested places 344
  rural criminological research 343–6
  rural violence 344

wildlife crime 172
South Sudan 112, 138, 316
Southern Criminology 210–11, 325
Sri Lanka 324
Stallwitz, Anke 84–7
Stanley, Janet 166–9
state–corporate crime 27, 71–2
  environmental crimes and harm 27, 70, 71–2
  scholarship on 72
  state–corporate violence against women 115
  wildfires 167
state crime 18–19, 21, 70
  Africa 317
  Asia 327–8
  corruption 119, 253, 317
  definition 71
  land theft 199
  state rural heritage crime 149, 150
  see also genocide; state–corporate crime
Stewart-North, Melina 91–4
stigma 63, 67, 229, 239, 298
  drug-related harm 82, 83
  incarceration 223, 229
  LGBTIQA+ people 280
Stinson, Philip Matthew 184–6
Stone, P. 78
street crime 23, 37, 38
sub-cultures 23, 38, 42, 115, 272
  criminal sub-cultures 17, 18, 21, 24
  youth sub-cultures 272, 308–10
substance use and misuse *see* drugs
Substance Use and Misuse 45
Sudan
  Darfur genocide 89
  Salif 224
surveillance 202, 208, 260, 278
  surveillance technologies 35, 48, 267–8
Sutherland, Edwin H. 18, 70
Sweden 22, 152, 284, 330
Switzerland 119
symbolic interactionism 24

T

Tanzania 159
Tauri, Juan 276–9
Taylor, Ian 18
technology
  crime prevention 127, 263
  drones 47, 131, 266, 267, 330
  future directions in rural criminal justice systems 267–8
  Global North 265–6
  illegal hunting prevention 153
  livestock theft 263, 267, 268
  people with disabilities 105, 292
  policing 199, 260, 266, 267
  in rural courts and corrections 266–7

in rural criminal justice systems 265–8
in rural law enforcement 265–6
surveillance technologies 35, 48, 267–8
United Kingdom 266
United States 265, 266
see also digital technology
technology-facilitated violence 104, 105–6
intersectionality and vulnerability 104–5
LGBTIQA+ people 104
main victims of 104
motivations for 105–6
spacelessness of technology 104, 106
terrorism 96, 118, 167, 174
Boko Haram 138, 295
Islamic State 96
water-related terrorism 164
Thailand 324, 328
theft 208, 302
Africa 316
crop produce theft 316
farm crime 125, 198, 261, 316
land theft 198–9, 344, 345
rural tourism 109
tractor and plant theft 157
water theft 28, 163
see also livestock theft
therapeutic jurisprudence 245
rural settings 246–7
solution rather than punishment for crimes 247
see also restorative justice
Thomas, Natalie 81–3
Thomas, P.M. 185
Tönnies, Ferdinand 156
tourism 108–10, 126, 299, 339
Australia 79, 80
crime and 108–9
crimes against tourists at rural locations 109
dark tourism 78–9
fraud 109
guardianship 109
leisure/tourism distinction 108
rural dark tourism 79–80
tourists as offenders 109–10
Travis, Jeremy 237
trespass 151, 152
illegal hunting and 151
Tri-Ethnic Center for Prevention Research, Colorado State University (United States) 43
American Drug and Alcohol Survey 44
trophy hunting 158–61
Africa 158, 159, 160
'Big 5' species 158
communities and 160–1
definition 158
game hunting 158, 159
masculinity and 160
South Africa 159

trophy hunting: international context 159–60
trophy hunting, rurality and recreation 158–9
United States 159
White hunters 160, 161
see also animal rights and welfare; hunting; wildlife crime
Trump, Donald 235, 275
Turvey, R. 197

U

Uganda 138, 316
Ukraine 252, 267
unemployment 64, 67, 111, 119
China 243
desistance from crime and 222
drugs and 81
rural areas 112, 308
see also employment
UNESCO (United Nations Educational, Scientific and Cultural Organization) 134
United Kingdom 338
2015 Modern Slavery Act 95
anti-social behaviour 181
drugs and County Lines 85, 96
fraud 67
hunting 102
Left Realism 37
modern slavery 95
rogue farmers 102
rural criminology 313, 330, 339
technology 266
Thatcherism 33
violence against farmers 111
working tourists 305
United Nations 242
on genocide 88
on human trafficking 95
legal representation in rural places 255
SIDS (small island developing states) 195
Universal Declaration of Animal Welfare 134
World Social Report 2021 241
United Nations Convention on Biodiversity 170
United Nations Convention on the Rights of Persons with a Disability 290
United Nations Office on Drugs and Crime 142, 143, 255
United Nations Sustainable Development Goals 51
United States
2021 6 January Capitol insurrection 274, 275
2021 Dixie fire, California 166, 168
Academy of Criminal Justice Science 334
Alaska 1, 85, 246
American Society of Criminology 334, 335, 336

Amish communities 294
anti-government groups and militias 274–5
Appalachia 31
Arkansas 233
California goldfields 98
Crime and Policing in Rural and Small Town America 334
drugs 81, 103, 157
fraud 67
hunting 153
incarceration 228–30, 241, 242
Indigenous peoples 277, 278
law enforcement misconduct 185–6
legal representation 256
lifestyle and amenity migration 285
modern slavery 95
North Carolina 246
North Dakota reservation, oil boom 99
re-entry 237–8
Reaganism 33
resource extraction 99
restorative justice 246–7
rogue farmers 102, 103
rural courts 231–2, 233, 246–7
rural crime rates 309
rural criminological research 313, 334–5, 339
rural enclaves 294, 295
South Dakota 231, 233
technology 265, 266
trophy hunting 159
violence against women 114, 115, 117
wildfires 166, 168
wildlife crime 172
urban area
  anti-social behaviour 181
  connectivity: urban/rural gap 265, 268
  criminology: urban-centric bias 271, 315, 333, 343
  deviant behaviour 309–10
  drug use 85
  policing 207
  punitivity: urban/rural gap 235–6
  rural/urban comparisons 202–3, 217, 232, 236
  rural/urban divide 1, 76, 156, 198, 236, 308
  rural to urban migration 54, 72, 241, 242–3, 325
  urban-based industrialization 53
  urban-based theories 20
  urban-centric neoliberal ideals of crime management 207
  urban community corrections 216
  urban jails 228, 242
  urban youth 308, 309–10

V
vagrancy laws 18
Van de Ven, Katinka 81–3
victimization 20, 109, 261
  cyber victimization 75, 325
  farm crime 125–6, 191
  fear of re-victimization 113
  food crimes 146, 147
  fraud victimization 67, 68
  hate crime 91, 92, 280
  Indigenous peoples 100, 276, 277
  Left Realism 38
  LGBTIQA+ people 280, 281
  people with disabilities 290
  place-based theories 22, 104
  'Victimization and Perception of Safety Survey', Ecuador 345
  violence against women 114, 242, 276
violence
  Africa: violent crimes 314, 315–16
  Brazil: rural violence 344
  colonial violence 78
  farm attacks/farm murders 314, 315–16
  gang violence 336
  gun ownership and 64, 115
  rural violence 314
  SIDS (small island developing states) 196–7
  violence-related police crime 186
  see also domestic violence; extremism; family violence; genocide; technology-facilitated violence; violence against farmers; violence against women
violence against farmers 111–13
  as axiom 111–12
  definition 111
  distinctive features 112
  impact of 112–13
  motivation for 112, 113
  South Africa 111, 112, 314, 315–16
  United Kingdom 111
violence against women 18, 25, 37, 64, 76, 114–17
  Africa 315, 316
  Antarctica 320
  Australia 114, 115
  Brazil 345
  Colombia 345
  COVID-19 pandemic 117
  crime, punishment and 242
  cyber-bullying and cyber-stalking 76, 115
  drugs and 116
  economic characteristics of rural settings 64
  feminicide 345
  hunting culture and 31, 115
  Indigenous women 99, 345
  LGBTIQA+ people 42
  male peer support and 31, 40–2, 43, 115, 116, 335
  OMCs (outlaw motorcycle clubs) 288
  patriarchy and violence against rural women 25, 31, 41, 76
  policy and practice 116–17

resource-based booms and 99, 116
risk factors 115–16
rural courts 253
rural/urban rates 114
scholarship on 115
service provision 116–117, 253
state–corporate violence 115
theoretical frameworks 116
types of violence 115
United States 114, 115, 117
working tourists 307
see also domestic violence; rape and sexual assault
Vold, George B. 18

W

Wainwright, T. 143
Walby, K. 78
Walters, Jared 53–5
Walton, Paul 18
Warchol, G. 317
Ward, Kyle C. 237–40
water 162, 285, 330
  contaminated groundwater 145, 147, 163
  folk crime 298
  human right to water 164
  'rural green criminology' and 162–3, 164
  scarcity of clean drinking water 164
  violation of water compliance and enforcement 163
  water contamination/pollution 29, 148, 163
  water crime, definition 162
  water crime, present and future 164
  water crime, types of 163–4
  water crime as minor crime 164
  water fraud 163
  water-related corruption 163
  water-related cyberattacks 164
  water-related organized crime 164
  water-related terrorism 164
  water theft 28, 163
  water use 28, 146, 298
  see also environmental criminology
Watson, Danielle 195–7, 338–42
Websdale, Neil 25
Weisheit, Ralph A. 1, 14, 141–4, 188, 334, 335
Wells, L.E. 14, 334
Wendt, Sarah 63–5
Wentzlof, Chloe Ann 184–6
White, Rob 26–9, 170–3, 298–300, 319–23
Whiteside, Cameron 191–4
Wilcox, P. 20
wildfires 166–8, 285
  2021 Dixie fire, California 166, 168
  Australia 166, 168
  Brazil 167
  causes of 166, 167–8
  climate change and 166, 167

human-caused ignition 166, 167, 168
  impact of 167
  state–corporate crime 167
  United States 166, 168
  wildfire prevention 166, 168
wildlife crime 170–3, 300
  Africa 316–17
  Australia 172
  Canada 172
  categories of offenders 171–2
  definition 170
  endangered wildlife 172
  illegal hunting 170, 171, 172
  motivations 171
  non-human animals 170, 171, 173
  poaching 151, 172, 316, 328
  South America 172
  trafficking and using of non-human animals 170, 172
  types of 172
  United States 172
  wildlife, definition 170
  see also animal rights and welfare; hunting; trophy hunting
Windle, James 37–9
Wise, Jenny 78–80, 234–6
Wodahl, Eric 238
women
  access to justice 341
  crime/punishment/poverty relationship 241, 242
  drugs 242
  fear of crime 211
  human trafficking 96
  incarceration 242
  organized crime and 242
  post-release 222
  see also feminism/feminist theories; violence against women
Wooff, Andrew 181–3, 205–7, 330
working tourists 271, 305–7
  Australia 306–7
  British Universities North America Club 305
  exploitation 306–7
  Great Britain 305
  reporting of crimes 307
  risks 306–7
  tramping 305
  as unskilled, cheap labour workforce 305, 306
  violence against women 307
  working hostels 306

Y

Yarwood, Richard 208–12
Young, Belinda 166–9
Young, Jock 18, 37, 38
Youngsen, N. 301

youth 271, 310
　anti-social behaviour 182–3
　arson 167
　'Communities that Care', Australia 263
　County Lines, United Kingdom 85, 96
　deviant behaviour 309
　isolation 309
　juvenile delinquency 20, 309
　migrant youth 243
　restorative justice and juvenile justice system 245, 246
　service provision 262
　urban youth 308, 309–10
　violent extremism 119
　see also working tourists
youth sub-cultures 272, 308–10
　copying 308
　rural drug use 309
　urban to rural migration 308
　see also gangs; youth

Z

Zehr, H. 247
Zhang, Dawei 215–17
Zimbabwe 159

www.ingramcontent.com/pod-product-compliance
Lightning Source LLC
Chambersburg PA
CBHW051523020426
42333CB00016B/1758